BLOOMING WITH THE POUIS

BLOOMING WITH THE POUIS

CRITICAL THINKING, READING AND WRITING ACROSS THE CURRICULUM

A Rhetorical Reader for Caribbean Tertiary Students

PAULETTE A. RAMSAY • VIVIENNE A. HARDING
JANICE A. COOLS • INGRID A. McLAREN

Ian Randle Publishers
Kingston • Miami

First published in Jamaica, 2009 by
Ian Randle Publishers
11 Cunningham Avenue
Box 686
Kingston 6
www.ianrandlepublishers.com

National Library of Jamaica Cataloguing in Publication Data

Blooming with the pouis: critical thinking, reading and writing across the curriculum: a Rhetorical Reader for Caribbean Tertiary Students/ Paulette A. Ramsay ... [et al]

p. ; cm.

Includes index

ISBN 978-976-637-341-2

1. Critical thinking – Study and teaching – Caribbean Area 2. English language – Rhetoric – Problems, exercises, etc. 3. Criticism – Authorship – Problems, exercises, etc. 4. Academic writing – Problems, exercises, etc. 5. Literature – History and criticism – Theory, etc.

I. Ramsay, Paulette, A.

808.0427 - dc 22

Cover and Book Design by Ian Randle Publishers
Printed and Bound in the United States of America

For Eric King, Mertel Thompson, Kathryn Brodber
and members of the ELU, Department of Language,
Linguistics and Philosophy, UWI, Mona

TABLE OF CONTENTS

SECTION 2
ARGUMENT

EDUCATION & SCIENCE

FAMILY LIFE

HISTORY & POLITICS

MUSIC & CULTURE

SECTION 3
MIXED MODES

SECTION 4
PASSAGES FOR ADDITIONAL READING & ANALYSIS

PREFACE

The idea for preparing a Rhetorical Reader for Caribbean students at the tertiary level developed as a result of teaching writing courses and guiding students for a number of years, to improve their critical and analytical skills for academic reading and writing. The absence of reading material with relevance to the Caribbean was particularly disturbing as all the major texts used in the courses had been imported from North America and dealt exclusively with North American issues and contexts. This concern grew as students frequently revealed their unfamiliarity with supplementary texts authored by Caribbean scholars, journalists, writers, musicians, folklorists among others, which were given to them in lectures and seminars. It was therefore, with the firm conviction that Caribbean students also need to read and analyse texts with Caribbean foci — in other words, texts by Caribbean authors, as well as texts authored by non-Caribbean writers, about the Caribbean, that led to the publication of this collection.

The texts which have been selected for the Reader have not only been written by some of the most influential Caribbean essayists and thinkers of modern times, but are based on real Caribbean situations and debates about issues which are important to individual Caribbean territories, as well as to the region as a whole. These texts will help students to regard reading as not just an academic exercise, but an active engagement with the society in which they will work and become responsible citizens.

Moreover, the Reader presents a journey throughout the Caribbean — the journey of the imagination — as students will be presented with texts from other Caribbean societies apart from their own and will, therefore, recognise their similarities as well as differences and develop an understanding and appreciation of the wide diversity and hybridic richness of their Caribbean culture.

The choice of reading material has been influenced by the principles of Writing Across the Curriculum which emphasizes the development of writing skills in all academic disciplines. The reading of texts from different disciplines is integral to this approach, and as a result, careful attention has been given to the selection of articles which discuss a wide variety of subjects related to Caribbean literature, culture, geography, history, economics, education, religion, and the pure and applied sciences. The texts are followed by exercises which are not only designed to help students develop an understanding of reading as a process which involves thinking, probing and learning, but are also useful in assisting them to comprehend and learn the approach taken by different disciplines to writing.

Through these texts, students in tertiary institutions in the Caribbean will be inspired to unlock the meaning of new words, expand their vocabulary as they read and write to clarify meaning for themselves, as well as for various disciplinary and even non-disciplinary audiences. The exercises, moreover, are intended to guide students to ask questions that are both important and complex, about different topics and subjects. As a consequence, their writing will be enhanced as they will do tasks which require them to analyse, synthesise, integrate their ideas with the ideas of others, and to make important decisions and stylistic choices for their own writing.

Undoubtedly, Caribbean students, who will also be reading texts from other parts of the world, will have a better appreciation of the connections and interconnections among ideas the world over, and of how Caribbean texts participate in the global conversation to which Glissant refers when he states 'the process of Diversity is persistent. Western literatures will discover the process of belonging and will become again a part of the world, symbolic of many nations — that is, a cluster of narratives.'[1]

Finally, students will enjoy the texts as they will be motivated to become critical readers, critical thinkers[2] and critical writers. As they discover the connections among reading, language and ideas, they will become empowered to produce good writing, for others to read, both within and outside of their own disciplines. The title, *Blooming with the Pouis*, was chosen in celebration of the beautiful flora of the Caribbean. Those of you who know the pouis are also familiar with its illuminating effect on any area in which it blooms. This is the wish for you that you will bloom in your writing and illuminate every idea you express and communicate to others with great brilliance!

Paulette A. Ramsay

Notes

1. Edouard Glissant, *Caribbean Discourse Selected Essays* (Charlotteville: University Press of Virginia, USA, 1992) 102.
2. Critical thinking is underpinned by two approaches to reasoning — induction and deduction. We will study these in greater depth in the section on Argument.

ACKNOWLEDGEMENTS

We are heavily indebted to a number of persons who contributed in different ways to the process of producing this Reader. Dr Mertel Thompson, retired lecturer in Rhetoric and Composition, of the Department of Language, Linguistics and Philosophy, the University of the West Indies, and Dr Curdella Forbes, Associate Professor of Caribbean Literature at Howard University in the United States, who both reviewed different aspects of the manuscript, must be thanked for their suggestions and advice regarding the exercises and the texts used. We are thankful to all the academics, literary critics, journalists and all those who willingly allowed us to include their essays, book chapters, newspaper and magazine articles in the text.

We thank Ian Randle Publishers for supporting this text and for being willing to publish it. Their independent reviewer provided invaluable assistance through the demand for changes which helped to improve the standard of the text. Althea Aikens was a tremendous source of assistance, as she typed a significant portion of the material. Gabrielle Blackwood is thanked for spending much of her time typing and scanning articles. Carlo Ramsay and his team at the Mona Information Technology Services (MITS) must be recognised and thanked for their services with scanning and reproducing some of the articles. Juliet Lawson is also thanked for her help with the typing. Stephany Blair must be thanked for the time she spent locating and contacting copyright holders and typing. Marc Ramsay, La-Raine Carpenter and Jevvor Duncan must be thanked for assisting in different ways, known well to them.

We are thankful to the students with whom we worked over the years, who participated in exercises similar to many of the ones included in this text. Finally, we thank Lileth O'Connor-Brown and Alison Altidor-Brooks for their feedback on the section of the text which was used as a pilot project in a writing course which they taught. We are grateful to everyone who supported this project in one way or another.

Finally, the text has been beautifully enhanced by the photograph of the pouis. For this we are indebted to Dr. Clinton Hutton, whose wonderful photography also enhances different sections of the University of the West Indies, Mona.

The Editors and Publisher are grateful to the authors and original publishers for permission to reproduce their work in this volume. Listed below are the original publication details.

EXPOSITION

Education

M. Kazim Bacchus, 'Utilization, Misuse and Development of Human Resources in the Early West Indian Colonies'. Ontario: Wilfrid Laurier University Press, 1990, 1–30.

Errol Miller, 'Access to Tertiary Education in the Commonwealth Caribbean in the 1990s'. In Glenford D. Howe, ed. *Higher Education in the Caribbean: Past, Present and Future Directions*. Kingston: University of the West Indies Press, 2000, 117–41.

David Barker, 'The North-East Trades and Temperature Inversions: Notes for the Classroom'. *Geography in the Caribbean Classroom* 9, no.1 (1998): 58–65.

Gender & Family Life

Maureen Samms-Vaughan, 'The Impact of Family Structure on Children'. Gleaner Online. Accessed April 16, 2006, Sept 25, 2006, from *http://www.jamaicagleaner.com/gleaner/20060416/focus/focus2.html*

Maureen Samms-Vaughan, 'Family and Family Life'. *Children Caught in the Crossfire*. Grace, Kennedy Foundation Lecture. Kingston: Grace, Kennedy Foundation, 2006.

Barry Chevannes, *What We Sow and What We Reap: Problems in the Cultivation of Male Identity in Jamaica*. Kingston: Stephenson's Litho Press, 1999.

Linda Peake and D. Alissa Trotz, *Gender, Ethnicity and Place: Women and Identities in Guyana*. London: Routledge, 1999, 174–97.

Music & Culture

Wendy-Ann Brissett, 'All Hail, Nutmeg'. *Sky Writings* Sept.–Oct. 2005. Kingston: Creative Communications Inc., Ltd. 2005, 46–47.

Barbara Gloudon, 'In Celebration of the Patty'. *The Best of Sky Writings: A Tapestry of Jamaica* Oxford: MacMillan Caribbean and Kingston: Creative Communications Inc., Ltd., 2003, 136.

Alex D. Hawkes, 'In Search of the Perfect Patty'. *The Best of Sky Writings: A Tapestry of Jamaica*. Oxford: MacMillan Caribbean and Kingston: Creative Communications Inc., Ltd., 2003, 137.

Maureen Warner-Lewis, *Guinea's Other Suns: The African Dynamic in Trinidad Culture*. Dover, Massachusetts: The Majority Press, 1990, 115–24.

Rex Nettleford, 'The Spirit of Garvey — Lessons of the Legacy'. *Jamaica Journal* 20, no. 3 (1987): 3–6.

Trevor McDonald, *Clive Lloyd: The Authorised Biography*. London: Granada Publishing, 1985, 27–31.

Louise Bennett, 'Introducing Bredda Anancy'. *The Best of Sky Writings: A Tapestry of Jamaica*. Oxford: MacMillan Caribbean and Kingston: Creative Communications Inc., Ltd., 2003. 309–10.

Rachel Sieder, 'Honduras'. In Minority Rights Group, ed. *No Longer Invisible: Afro-Latin Americans*. London: Minority Rights Publications, 1995, 235–238.

Religion, History & Politics

Michael Manley, 'Atlas: Excerpted from *A History of West Indies Cricket*'. *The Best of Sky Writings: A Tapestry of Jamaica*. Oxford: MacMillan Caribbean and Kingston:

Creative Communications Inc., Ltd., 2003, 309–10.

Bridget Brereton, 'Oil and the Twentieth Century Economy, 1900–62: The History of Oil Production in Trinidad'. In Brereton, B. ed. *A History of Modern Trinidad 1783–1962*. Kingston: Heinemann Educational Books (Caribbean) Ltd., 1981, 199–205.

Matthew Roberts, 'Small Islands, Big Media: Challenges of Foreign Media in Covering the Caribbean'. *Caribbean Quarterly* 40, no. 2 (1994): 8–22.

Kathleen Royal and Franklin Perry, 'Costa Rica'. In Minority Rights Group, eds. *No Longer Invisible: Afro-Latin Americans*. London: Minority Rights Publications, 1995, 215–18.

Science & The Environment

Ralph Robinson, 'What to look for Under the Sea'. *The Best of Sky Writings: A Tapestry of Jamaica*. Oxford: MacMillan Caribbean and Kingston: Creative Communications Inc., Ltd., 2003, 124–6.

Susan Milius, 'Flowers, Not Flirting Make Sexes Differ: Caribbean Hummingbirds.' *Science News*, July 22, 2000, http://findarticles.com/ article.cfm accessed April 18, 2007.

Sarah Simpson, 'Coral-Killing Dust'. *Scientific American*. Accessed November 6, 2000, from *http://scientificamerican.com/article.cfm>*

Woods Hole, 'Major Caribbean Earthquakes and Tsunamis A Real Risk'. *Science Daily* (February 8, 2005).

Fillian N. Dujon, 'Minimum Building Standards and Environmental Guidelines'. St. Lucia National Research and Development Foundation, 2003.

Emily Rose, 'What You Should Talk to Patients With Hypertension About: A Special Focus on Nutrition'. *Pharmacist Caribbean* 5, no. 3 (2005).

J.F. Lindo and T.S. Ferguson, 'Parasitology, the emergence of Angiostrongylus Cantonensis as a cause of Eosinophilic Meningitis in the Caribbean: What the Clinician needs to know'. *Postgraduate Doctor Caribbean* 21, no. 1 (2005): 10–1; 1–4.

ARGUMENT

Education & Science

J. Hayter and M. Egan, 'Computers in the Mathematics Classroom: Reviewing Developments, Exploring Possibilities'. *Transforming the Educational Landscape Through Curriculum Change*, eds. Monica Brown and Clement Lambert. Kingston: Institute of Education, University of the West Indies, Mona, 2004, 107–28.

Pathmanathan Umaharan, 'Biotechnology: Relevance for Caribbean Agriculture'. University of the West Indies, St. Augustine, 2006.

Elsa Leo-Rhynie, 'Inefficiency of the Educational System'. *The Jamaican Family: Continuity and Change*. Kingston: Grace Kennedy Foundation, 2003.

Paulette A. Ramsay, 'The Right to Write'. Letter to the Editor. Unpublished.

Family Life

Clinton Chisholm, 'Womb Rights'. *A Matter of Principle*. Spanish Town, Jamaica: Autos Books, 1997, 114–15.

Elsa Leo-Rhynie, 'Outlook for the Future'. *The Jamaican Family: Continuity and Change*. Grace, Kennedy Foundation

Lecture 1993. Jamaica: Grace, Kennedy Foundation, 2003, 42–46.

Oliver Mills, 'Are Caribbean Youth in Crisis?' Accessed April 26, 2006, from *http://caribbeannetnews.com*.

History & Politics

Leota Lawrence, 'Women in Caribbean Literature: The African Presence'. *Phylon: The Atlanta University Review of Race and Culture* 44, no. 1 (1983): 1–11.

Philip Sherlock, 'The Arawaks Arrived Before Columbus'. In *The Best of Skywritings: A Tapestry of Jamaica*. Oxford: MacMillan Caribbean and Kingston: Creative Communications Inc., Ltd., 2003, 328–29.

Hilary McD. Beckles, 'White Women and Slavery in the Caribbean'. In Verene Shepherd and Hilary McD. Beckles, eds. *Caribbean Slavery in the Atlantic World: A Student Reader*. Kingston: Ian Randle Publishers, 2000, 659–69.

Verene A. Shepherd, 'Livestock Farmers and Marginality in Jamaica's Sugar-Plantation Society: A Tentative Analysis.' In Verene Shepherd and Hilary McD. Beckles, eds. *Caribbean Slavery in the Atlantic World: A Student Reader*. Kingston: Ian Randle Publishers, 2000, 613–20.

Jamaica Kincaid, *A Small Place*. New York: Farrar, Straus and Giroux, 2000, 1–5.

Mark Brantley, 'The Plight of the Guyanese Migrant Worker'. Accessed October 25, 2006, from *http://caribbeannetnews.com*.

Morris Cargill, 'Putting on the Dog.' The *Gleaner*. Accessed February 25, 1999, from *http://www.jamaica-gleaner.com/gleaner/19990225/cleisure/c4.html* .

Wendell Abel, 'Shackled to the Past, Trapped in the Present.' The *Gleaner*. Accessed March 2004, from *http://www.jamaica-gleaner.com/gleaner/20040331/health/health1.html*.

Music & Culture

Curwen Best, 'Caribbean Music and the Discourses of AIDS'. *Caribbean Quarterly* 45, no. 4 (1999): 70–9.

Curdella Forbes, 'A Review of *Aunt Jen*, by Paulette Ramsay'. *Caribbean Quarterly* 50, no. 2 (2004): 81–84.

Pamela O'Gorman, 'On Reggae and Rastafarianism — and a Garvey Prophecy'. *Jamaica Journal* 20, no.3 (1987): 85–87.

Stephen Vasciannie, 'Dutty Wine'. The *Gleaner*. Accessed November 6, 2006, from *http://www.jamaica-gleaner.com/gleaner/20061106/cleisure3.html*.

Carolyn Cooper, *Sound Clash: Jamaican Dancehall Culture at Large*. Palgrave Macmillan, 2004.

Wendell Samuel, 'Migration and Remittances: A Case Study'. In D. Pantin ed. *The Caribbean Economy: A Reader*. Kingston: Ian Randle Publishers, 2005, 573–74.

Mixed Modes

Sultana Afroz, 'The Manifestation of Tawhid: The Muslim Heritage of the Maroons in Jamaica'. *Caribbean Quarterly* 45, no. 1 (1999): 27–40.

Maureen Warner-Lewis, 'Jamaica's Muslim Past: Disconcerting Theories'. The *Sunday Gleaner*. October 20, 2002.

Roberto DaMatta, 'The Meal is the Message: The Language of Brazilian

Cuisine'. *The Courier*, (Caribbean Edition, May 1987).

Gordon Rohlehr, 'Trophy and Catastrophe'. *Caribbean Quarterly* 37, no. 4 (1991): 1–8.

Kevin O'Brien-Chang and Wayne Chen, 'U-Roy the Originator'. In Kevin O'Brien-Chang and Wayne Chen, eds. *Reggae Routes: The Story of Jamaican Music*. Kingston: Ian Randle Publishers, 1998, 70–74.

Rupert Lewis, 'Emancipate Yourself From Mental Slavery'. Churches' Emancipation Lecture 2000.

George Lamming, *The Sovereignty of the Imagination*. Kingston: Arawak Publications, 2004, 3–7.

Pauline Christie, 'The Legacy of our Past'. *Language in Jamaica*. Kingston: Arawak Publications, 2003.

Beverly Bryan and Gwendolyn Shaw, 'Gender Literacy and Language Learning in Jamaica: Considerations from the Literature'. *Caribbean Journal of Education* 24, no. 1 (April 2002) Kingston: School of Education, University of the West Indies.

PASSAGES FOR ADDITIONAL READING & ANALYSIS

Kathryn Shields-Brodber, 'Hens Can Crow Too: The Female Voice of Authority'. In Pauline Christie, B. Lalla, V. Pollard and D. Lawrence, eds. *Studies in the Caribbean Language II*. St. Augustine: Multimedia Production Centre, School of Education University of the West Indies, 1998, 187–203.

Paulette A. Ramsay, 'Soy una Feminista Negra — Shirley Campbell's Feminist/Womanist Agenda'. *Latin American and Caribbean Ethnic Studies* 2, no.1 (2007): 51–68.

Veront Satchell, 'The Early Use of Steam Power in the Jamaican Sugar Industry, 1768-1810'. In Verene Shepherd and Hilary McD. Beckles, eds. *Caribbean Slavery in the Atlantic World: A Student Reader*. Kingston: Ian Randle Publishers, 2000, 518–26.

Carl Campbell, 'Trinidad's Free Coloureds in Comparative Caribbean Perspectives'. In Campbell, Carl, Cedulants and Capitulants. Port of Spain: Paria Pub. Co. 1992.

F.E. Ologe and S. Segun-Busari, 'Laryngeal Tuberculosis: Diagnosis and Prevention of Dissemination'. *Postgraduate Doctor Caribbean* 21.1 (2005): 10–11.

Dharma A. Sawh, 'Chronic Heart Failure'. *Pharmacist Caribbean* 5, no. 3 (2005).

Jorge L. Giovannetti, 'Jamaican Reggae and the Articulation of Social and Historical Consciousness in Musical Discourse'. In Franklin W. Knight and Teresita Martinez-Vergne, eds. *Contemporary Caribbean Cultures and Societies in a Global Context*. Chapel Hill: University of North Carolina Press and Kingston: University of the West Indies Press, 2005.

Every effort has been made to contact copyright holders and to obtain their permission for the use of copyright material. The Editors and Publisher apologize for any errors or omission in the above list and would be grateful if notified of any correction that should be incorporated in future reprints or editions of this book.

INTRODUCTION

Dear Students,

Reading and writing are two processes which are inextricably linked and are, moreover, central to your lives as students in a tertiary institution. Your success in different disciplines will be significantly influenced by the extent to which you master these two processes. In other words, if you learn to read and write well, the skills you acquire will prove to be important in helping you grasp the content of specific disciplines and will also help you to communicate well with audiences within and outside of these disciplines.

In order to be effective writers and communicators in different situations, you must also be critical and analytical readers. This means that you become actively involved with the text as you read, so as to be able to understand the main thesis of the text, and to analyse and interpret the writer's meaning. Active engagement with the text you read will, without doubt, also improve your ability to organise your thoughts and in general, help you to be more logical in your thinking.

Critical reading means understanding certain principles about the reading process. It is a process that brings the text and you the reader together (Kirszner, 1998, 1). The text is the medium through which a writer who has a message to communicate speaks to the reader and expresses his/her thoughts and

ideas on a topic. Reading is, therefore, a process of interaction, or a transaction between reader and text. It is, moreover, a process of **active** thinking. Graves et al. (2004) characterised this interaction between reader and text as the cognitive–constructivist approach in which the reader actively searches for meaning in what he or she reads. This search for meaning depends on readers having an existing store of knowledge, or schemata that he or she draws on to construct meaning (Graves et al., 2004, 2). Indeed, when you read, you make connections between ideas, make inferences, identify ideas and understand details. The interaction between yourselves and the text is important because it is in this way that you come to understand the writer's message not just because of how the writer expresses it, but also because you often have some knowledge of the topic as well as a particular purpose for reading.

According to Irwin, readers may utilise several approaches in order to comprehend the material they read. Irwin helped to demystify comprehension by identifying five approaches — outlined below — and readers must use all five if they are to grasp concepts effectively.

Micro Approaches. Readers categorise ideas into phrases and select what is important in each sentence for retention in their short-term memory.

Integrative Approaches. These refer to how readers handle semantic and synctactic connections and relationships among sentences within the paragraph.

Macro Approaches. In using these approaches, readers process what they read, by focussing on the big picture. They recognise, for example, the elements of a story's structure or other structural patterns and select the most important information to recall and aid comprehension of a text.

Elaborative Approaches. These allow readers to make personal connections between what they read and their prior knowledge; they also make predictions, identify with characters, and try to visualise what they are reading.

Metacognitive Approaches. These include the strategies which readers employ to monitor and evaluate their comprehension. Strategies such as predicting, visualising, organising, tapping prior knowledge and self-questioning are conscious problem-solving behaviours that students use when reading (Irwin, 359).

The use of these approaches will allow you to be not just interactive, but constructive in your reading as you will respond to the text as you read, and hold dialogue with the text in different ways which will help you to discern how the writer communicates his/her point.

To read critically, moreover, means that you will use certain strategies to understand academic as well as other written material. These strategies involve finding the information, developing your own opinions and forming conclusions based on the information provided, comparing and contrasting different ideas, analysing and synthesising ideas, and recognising relationships among words and ideas in a text.

Pre-reading

Before you attempt to do any interactive-constructive reading, it is necessary to familiarise yourself with the structure and content of the text, and stimulate your own interest in the material. It is, therefore, important to learn some pre-reading strategies to enable you to connect the material to your own experiences and remember most of what you read. The following are some useful pre-reading strategies which you may apply:

i.   Read the title, and all subtitles, as these will give you a quick idea of what the text is about.

ii. Read the introduction and first paragraph as they are likely to provide an overview of the text.

iii. Read sub-headings as they form a type of outline to the essay.

iv. Read the conclusion as this should give you a condensed view of the reading.

v.   Identify the genre and rhetorical situation or context.

vi. Take a quick decision about the writer's **purpose** for writing and his/her **intended audience**. When you know why the text was written and for whom, it becomes easier for you to decide on the type of discourse. This will help you to approach the text with certain expectations, which you can use as a guide as you read.

Context, Purpose, Audience

These three factors shape or influence the material that writers produce. It is important to establish what they are as you read and analyse the material.

Context

Context or Rhetorical Situation refers to all the factors that produce the text and influence or determine the type of text and the way in which it is written. Context includes:

i. The physical context or medium/place (the medium of delivery) in which the writer expects readers to read the text. These include journals, magazines, newspapers, brochures, books, textbooks, blogs or web pages.

ii. The historical context of the issue/subject or topic.

iii. The cultural, social or political context of the subject or topic.

iv. The beliefs, ideas, principles or theories which help to inform or shape the writing.

Each time you write about any topic it is important to carefully consider your context as you communicate with your readers about a particular subject. This is what the writers of the material you read are required to do.

Some questions writers or you as students may ask about context are:

• Where will this text be placed/published or read?

• What are the political, social, religious, or historical factors surrounding this topic?

• What important words, specialised terms or phrases do I need to include in this writing, based on where it will be read?

Purpose

The purpose of a text is generally determined by the effect a writer wants to have on an audience, regarding a subject matter. The author may write to explain a topic or issue or process, to persuade readers to take a particular position, to describe a situation, place or person, or to narrate an event or story.

Some useful questions which writers and you as students may ask regarding purpose are:

• What do I want my readers to know or learn?

• Do I want to persuade readers to accept my position about this subject matter?

• Am I communicating factual knowledge or do I want my readers to interpret or analyse this subject-matter?

Audience

A writer's audience would be those persons he/she has targeted in the writing. A writer may target different groups of persons, such as university students, mixed or diverse audiences, comprising persons of different educational levels, and specialised audiences which might have expert knowledge and training in the subject being written about. For instance, a medical doctor could write two different articles on heart disease, one for secondary school students and another for medical doctors who specialise in the treatment of this disease. The writer (medical doctor) would make a number of choices to ensure that the secondary school students understand the writing. For instance, this writing would use more simple terms and detailed explanations. Similarly, the writer would ensure that the article intended for a specialist audience is written in a manner acceptable to persons who have expertise in the subject; and as such, specialised terms used would be understood by the experts.

Some questions which writers, and you as students, may ask regarding audience are:

- What interest do readers have in this topic or subject-matter?
- What previous knowledge do my readers already have about this subject?
- Are my readers experts in this field?
- Do readers share my values?
- Do readers have the same attitude as I do toward this subject/topic?
- Will my audience/readers be bored by my style of writing?
- Will readers understand the vocabulary that I use?

Genre

Traditionally, when you think of genre, the novel, play, short story and poem come to mind. However, when we discuss rhetorical situations, genre refers to all types of writing which conform to specific conventions of style, structure and form. For instance, the report you are required to write for science classes is one genre. It is always important to consider the genre in which you will present your writing.

Some examples of genres in academic writing include: essays, book reviews, scientific reports and research papers. In professional or business writing some genres would be: memos, reports, press releases, letters of application, speeches or special addresses. Genres in everyday writing would include advertisements, book reviews, music reviews, articles in magazines, letters to the editor of a newspaper, among others.

Whether or not you are required to write a poem, letter, song, or essay, you need to bear the genre in mind as you plan your writing, and aim to communicate with your audience.

Important Stylistic Features or Rhetorical Modes

Writers have a variety of resources which they use for communicating with the reader. These are referred to as **stylistic features** or **rhetorical modes**. In order for our reading to aid our writing we need to examine these **rhetorical modes/ or stylistic features** which writers employ in keeping with context, purpose and audience.

- Diction The writer's choice of words. The diction may be technical, general, denotative or connotative.
- Tone The writer's attitude to the subject, reader and sometimes himself/herself.
- Register The level of formality or informality of the language used.
- Syntax The type of sentence structure used. Long sentences have a different effect from short ones in a passage/text.

Like you, the writer begins with a sense of purpose, context and audience — all other choices are governed by these elements, for example:

- **Tone**. The writer's tone is influenced by audience and purpose. For instance, if the writer wants readers to think negatively about a topic his/her tone may be cynical, unpleasant or harsh.
- **Organisation**. Another choice that the writer makes is how to organise the text. This too is governed by the intended audience. Given the writer's purpose and the audience being targeted, he/she has to decide how to organise the text, that is, which developmental strategy or mix of developmental strategies he/she will use

to organise the essay, overall and all paragraphs, given the subject matter and the way in which he/she is attempting to convey that information.

- **Credibility**. Given that the writer has an audience and wants to fulfill this purpose, he/she will want to appear believable to the readers and may employ a number of strategies to do so.

Levels of Reading

As students in a tertiary institution who should read effectively and understand the writers' meaning, you will not just be concerned with understanding the writer's basic messages expressed through words, sentences, and paragraphs, but will also be interested in remembering the information they contain and interpreting and evaluating these materials. All of this will help you in your efforts to understand the demands of your various disciplines.

You will, therefore, ensure that you master the following levels of reading in order to develop critical thinking skills:

1. **Literal Level**. At this level, you are concerned with understanding the writer's basic message by using your knowledge of basic vocabulary and your grasp of sentence and paragraph structure to list, define, locate, label and name.

2. **Interpretive Level**. This second level assumes you understand the basic literal content — 'Who did what, when, and where?' As you think and reason about the material you are reading, you will want to know what the writer **means.**

3. **Analytical Level**. As you identify indirect or unstated meanings, you will also establish how the writer has organised his or her ideas. Finally, you will determine **why** the writer wrote (author's purpose) and **how** the purpose was achieved.

4. **Critical or Evaluative Level**. At this level you examine the author's ideas, organisation and approach, in order to judge the worth, use, and value of the text. Here you ask critical questions such as:
   - What is the purpose of the material? Is it to explain, define, compare, contrast, illustrate, persuade or entertain?

5. **Application and Synthesis**. At these levels you determine the usefulness of the material and its appropriateness for different purposes. You make careful selections about what is or is not useful to you. You ask questions such as:
   - When was it written?
   Balance dates as far as usefulness is concerned. Something that was written years ago is not necessarily useless, but we must carefully assess it to see what is applicable to us.
   - Is the author qualified to write about the subject?
   Inaccurate information can be harmful.
   - What does the title tell you?
   - What do subheadings indicate?

6. **Creative Level**. According to Craig (1999), at this level you are required to think divergently beyond the information that has been presented, to generate new ideas related to those presented.

Become an **active reader** by applying certain strategies to aid you in understanding the material you read.

Reading Strategies

The following are some reading strategies to help you read critically and analytically. This approach to reading will help you to write more effectively, as you study the way in which other writers organise their ideas for you to construct meaning. These important reading strategies will also help you to distinguish fact from opinion, question assumptions and relate information from various texts which you will read in your different courses: annotating, outlining, paraphrasing, summarising, synthesising, contextualising, exploring the significance of figurative language, looking for patterns of opposition, evaluating the logic of an argument, recognising emotional manipulation, judging the writer's credibility.

Annotating

This involves recording your reactions to the text as you read. You may use underlines, highlights and comments.

Outlining

Use outlining to identify the main idea of a text as this is an important critical reading strategy which aids in understanding the content and structure of a text. You may do a formal outline or simply write an outline in the margin as you read. The outline should distinguish between the main ideas and supporting material such as examples, quotations, reasons, comparisons. The process of outlining aids in constructive and active reading.

Paraphrasing

This involves rewriting or restating something you have read in your own words. This critical reading strategy helps you to clarify the meaning of an ambiguous or challenging passage. Paraphrasing is also useful for incorporating other people's ideas and information into your own writing. However, you must acknowledge the people to whom the ideas orginally belong.

Summarising

This critical reading strategy is widely used to help readers' understand and retain the most important aspect of the reading. It involves restating the main ideas of the text in the reader's own words.

Synthesising

This involves reading from a wide variety of texts on a topic or subject and comparing, contrasting or integrating these ideas, questioning them or even challenging them, the one against the other. Synthesising requires the use of summaries, paraphrases, and quotations to put different ideas together.

Contextualising

This evaluative strategy requires the reader to understand the historical and cultural context of a text. This is especially important when the social and historical contexts, values and attitudes of the text are different from that of the reader. To use contextualising effectively, you should compare the historical and cultural situation in which the text was produced to your own and determine how these affect your judgement and evaluation of the text.

Exploring the Significance of Figurative Language

Figurative language — metaphor, simile, symbolism, personification, hyperbole, oxymoron, among others — all enhance literal meaning by embodying abstract ideas in vivid images and by evoking feelings and associations (Axelrod, 547). List all figures of speech in a text, group them according to what they express — ideas, feelings, attitudes. Then explore the meaning of the groups and what they communicate about the topic or subject.

Looking for Patterns of Opposition

All texts carry within themselves voices of opposition. These voices may reflect the views and values of critical readers the writer anticipates, or predecessors to whom the writer is responding; they may even reflect the writer's own conflicting values (Axelrod and Cooper, 548). Students who read critically should look for patterns of opposition, established by such pairs of opposing words or phrases, for example, 'governor/ governed', 'yes/no', 'developed/under-developed', 'dominant/subordinate' which create a dialogue of opposing voices. Sometimes, they may be implied and you, as readers, will have to supply the word or phrase. The opposing pairs of words and phrases will establish a **pattern** that will help to show the writer's attitude and contribute to an understanding of the text.

Evaluating the Logic of an Argument

An argument is a claim or thesis backed by reason and support. A reader should test an argument by examining its reason and support, appropriateness, believability and consistency.

Appropriateness

These questions may be asked to test the appropriateness of an argument.

- Do the reason and support relate to the thesis?
- Is there a clear connection between the reason and support?

Believability

To test for believability you should examine the facts, examples, statistics and authorities which are offered as support in defense of a claim or thesis. Facts should be examined for their accuracy and completeness. Examples should be representative and truly typical of what they represent. Statistics are believable when they are comparable.

Authorities are people who are cited by a writer as an expert on a given subject. They must be appropriate and believable as well, that is, you should be able to accept them as experts on the topic being discussed. For instance, a writer who uses Mervin Alleyne to support claims about Caribbean dialectology would have a high degree of credibility. Similarly, research by Joseph Pereira would be an authoritative source on Cuban literature and research by Brendan Bain on HIV and AIDS would be a very credible source.

Testing for Consistency and Completeness

Ask the following questions to test for consistency and completeness:

- Are the reasons and support in keeping the one with the other or are they contradictory?
- Does the writer acknowledge counter-arguments or refute opposing arguments?

All parts of the argument should be in keeping with each other, for it to be consistent.

Recognising Emotional Manipulation

Writers often use emotional appeals to stimulate the readers' interest. This is quite acceptable as long as writers do not manipulate the reader with exaggeration or alarming statistics, frightening anecdotes or words that are emotionally manipulative to create a negative picture of others. But the constructive reader should assess whether emotional appeals are unfairly manipulative or not. Words and phrases should not distract from reason and evidence, but, rather, should enrich meaning.

Judging the Writer's Credibility

Credibility is established through the language, arguments, systems, values and beliefs implied in the writing. Writers also demonstrate their credibility by showing their knowledge of the subject; by building common ground with readers; by being fair in their opposing arguments; by showing their ability to reason logically; by choosing words carefully to show that they care about the subject.

Knowledge of Subject

Writers demonstrate their knowledge through the facts and statistics they use and the sources they rely on. Readers may also check the writer's credentials, education and professional qualification and the respectability of their publications as well as whether or not the writer is an authority in the field.

Common Ground

Writers can establish common ground by appealing to those shared values, beliefs and attitudes germane to them as well as their readers. They also use inclusive language — such as 'we' — to show that they identify with the reader; they acknowledge opposing views and show a willingness to accommodate differences of opinion.

Fairness

The writer's tone, treatment of opposing arguments and differences serve as indicators of his/her ability to be fair. For instance a writer who seems condescending toward a subject may not be fair in his/her treatment of the subject.

Discourse Communities

Writers often belong to specific communities or fields and write as members of these communities in which they share similar ideas, values, and information. Academic discourse communities relate to your different majors/fields. For instance, historians are part of the same field or discourse community and share similar backgrounds, interests and expectations. Similarly, linguists are part of the broad academic discourse community and also belong to the specific discourse community of linguists.

As tertiary level students you need to be aware of the different discourse communities from which your reading material will be taken and have an understanding of how writers write in these communities. As you read in the various fields you may ask some of the following questions:

- What are the major issues in this field?
- What methods do writers usually follow?
- What is considered to be common knowledge in the field?

- What are the main values that guide writing in this field?

Admittedly, the academic discourse community is not the only discourse community in which you, as students, move. In your everyday life you are interacting with persons in other places outside of the academic community such as the church, community centres and clubs. For this reason, not all the texts selected for this reader are strictly written for academic audiences. An attempt has been made to include articles from newspapers and magazines which have been written for diverse audiences, and conform more to the conventions of everyday writing genres, rather than to academic ones. Indeed, an important aspect of guiding you to write for academic purposes and for different disciplinary audiences, also involves examining texts which were written for non-academic purposes. To this end, articles from newspapers, magazines and blogs will be very useful in helping you to make choices as you write for different audiences.

Discourse Types

Our purpose for reading and the author's purpose will often coincide as we read. This means we will read a particular type of material/ writing based on our purpose. This type of writing is referred to as the **discourse type.** Written texts use different discourse types, modes or combinations of discourse types, depending on the writer's purpose which often depends on the discourse community to which the writer belongs. The following are the main discourse types:

1. Exposition/Expository Writing
2. Narration
3. Description
4. Argumentation

Exposition

Exposition is derived from a Latin word which means to 'explain or expound'. Expository writing provides information for readers without focusing on the writer's feelings or views about them. Hence, it

- deals with facts, ideas, beliefs
- explains, analyses, defines, illustrates, informs, instructs, classifies

Exposition answers these questions:

- What is it?
- How does it work?
- What are its constituent parts?

Narration

Narration presents action to create a story. It can be used to report on events, present information, explain procedures, illustrate abstract ideas and support arguments.

Description

Descriptive writing appeals to the senses. It expresses what something looks like, how it feels, tastes, sounds and smells. Description creates images to help people visualise things; it provides details and comparisons, and is often used with explanation.

Argumentation

Argumentation is a reasoned method of persuading or convincing others to accept or acknowledge the soundness of a position or claim. Argumentation takes a stand or makes a claim supported by evidence and urges others to accept or support the writer's position.

Argumentation and Persuasion

Argumentation is often used interchangeably with the term persuasion, but they do not mean the same thing. Persuasion refers to the writer's use of appeals to the emotions, ethics and reason to persuade an audience to accept a particular belief or follow a course of action.

Argumentation appeals to reason through the use of logically connected statements which lead to a claim. While argumentation has a formal structure in which a claim is supported by evidence, opposing views are rejected and accommodated, the single purpose of argument is to show that some points are valid and others are not. Argumentation does not try to move people to act but persuasion does.

Developmental Strategies/ Organising Principles

Writers use certain organising principles/ patterns or developmental strategies to organise their ideas. The following are the main ones used by writers.

Exemplification

This strategy is used to explain a topic or thesis by describing situations that reveal its essential characteristics. Exemplification uses:

i. specific examples to support generalisations about groups or categories;

ii. specific and typical examples to clarify abstract terms or complex terms;

iii. carefully related examples for illustration.

Process Analysis

This method explains how something works or is done in a step-by-step manner. It provides practical information/directions for assembling equipment or instructions for operation; for example, instructions for using search engines on the world wide web. There are two types of process analysis:

i. For readers who need to perform the process.

ii. For readers who need information but do not need to perform the process.

Definition

This is a way of explaining what a term means or which meaning is intended when a word has a different meaning. It is used when a writer wants to set the parameters for what something is or is not.

Classification or Division

This strategy is used to organise things, persons, ideas, names and so on into categories — subgroups or classes — based on shared characteristics. For example, your instructors may be classified into various types such as those who are friendly, those who seem more distant, and so on. Classification may also be done by placing ideas or things on the basis of the most important to the least important or by grouping things on the basis of size — for instance, the smallest to the largest.

Analogy

A figurative comparison that helps explain a complicated or abstract idea by comparing it to a simple idea. Things compared are from different classes, for example, a river may be compared to life. Generally, the two things being compared are, on the surface, not alike.

Cause and Effect

A strategy of expository writing that examines the relationship between the why (cause) and the what (effect). It explains each cause or effect fully, or may focus on either cause or effect.

Whole-Part/Enumeration/ Listing

This technique shows how the various parts fit together to form a complete picture. It deals with units of incidents, ideas and concepts.

Generalisation

A generalisation is a statement setting out a principle, law or hypothesis found in explanatory and defining paragraphs — the principles may be scientific.

Problem–Solution

This approach is used in scientific discourse, lab activities and instruction manuals. It does not necessarily state a solution, or the solution may be hypothetical.

The essays in this collection employ a range of developmental strategies and are developed mainly as exposition and argument. You are encouraged to read widely and to learn from the various texts, discourse types and genres, as this is an indispensable method of improving your writing. As students, it will be necessary for you to write so as to learn the content of your disciplines and also to communicate to persons within and outside of your disciplines. Use every opportunity to learn not just the discourse features of writing in general, but also of your specific disciplines, and to develop an awareness of how writing differs from discipline to discipline and from one context to another.

Paulette A. Ramsay

References

Axelrod, Rise B., and Charles R.Cooper. *Axelrod and Cooper's Concise Guide to Writing*. 4th ed. Boston: Bedford/St. Martin's Press, 2006.

Craig, Dennis. *Teaching Language and Literacy: Policies and Procedures for Vernacular Situations*. Georgetown: Education and Development Services, 1999.

Graves, Michael F., Connie Juel, and Bonnie B. Graves. *Teaching Reading in the 21st Century*. Boston: Allyn and Bacon, 2004.

Irwin, J.W., and C.A. Davis. 'Assessing readability: The Checklist Approach. *Journal of Reading* 24, (1980): 124-130 cited in Vacca, Richard T. and JoAnne L Vacca. *Content Area Reading: Literacy and Learning Across the Curriculum*. Boston: Allyn and Bacon, 2002.

Kirszner L.G., and Stephen Mandell. *Patterns for Successful College Writing*. New York: St. Martin's Press, 1998.

McWhorter, Kathleen. *Successful College Writing*. Boston: Bedford/St. Martin's Press, 2000.

Miller, George. *The Prentice Hall Reader*. 8th ed. Upper Saddle River: Prentice Hall, 2007.

Reinking, J.A., Andrew Hart, and Robert Von der Osten. *Strategies for Successful Writing*. Upper Saddle River: Prentice Hall, 2002.

SECTION 1
EXPOSITION

EDUCATION

Chapter 1

Early West Indian Society and Education

Very little is known from historical sources about the early upbringing of the young Ciboney or the Arawaks, the first two groups to disappear from the Caribbean scene following the Spanish occupation. But the education of their children was likely to have been, in some essential aspects, quite similar to that of the Caribs, about whom there is some limited information. The latter were essentially concerned with developing in their young, through the mainly non-formal system of education which they provided, such skills as stalking stealthily through the forests, or using the bow, arrow, and blowpipe effectively — activities directly related to their economic survival. In other words, the 'technical' or training function of their educational process was of key concern to them. As Bryan Edwards noted:

> To draw a bow with unerring skill, to wield the club with dexterity and strength, to swim with agility and boldness, to catch fish and to build a cottage, were acquirements of indispensable necessity, and the education of the children was well suited to the attainment of them.[1]

However, the survival of a society depends not only on the adults teaching their youngsters the technical skills needed to earn a living but also on inculcating in them those attitudes, values, and beliefs which give meaning and purpose to the use of the skills and to life in the society in general. In fact, while the skills which the older Caribs passed on to the children were very important, they were even considered 'subordinate' to the values which the group attempted to develop in the young. Therefore, in teaching these very necessary skills the Caribs instructed their youth, at the same time, in lessons of patience and fortitude; they endeavoured to inspire them with courage in war and a contempt of danger and death.[2]

While their teaching techniques might not seem quite humane, they were operating within the framework of the stimulus-response theory of psychology which still forms the basis of some teaching strategies used today. As part of the skill training that was given to the young boys, food would be suspended in the branch of a tree and they would have to pierce it with their arrows before they could obtain permission to eat. Their success was immediately rewarded with the food which they hit during their target practice.

With their relatively simple social structure and in the absence of a large self-perpetuating ruling group, the same education was offered to all because, especially in times of need, everyone was expected to cooperate in performing certain common but essential tasks, including helping to defend the society against possible invaders. In other words, Carib education was mainly aimed at passing on to the younger generation those skills and the underlying values and beliefs necessary for the economic, social, and physical survival of their societies. Most of the other functions associated with education in a 'modern' society — functions such as social selection of individuals for, and their allocation into, different occupational roles, and providing them with an opportunity for social mobility — were virtually absent among these Indian tribes.

This more narrow function of education no doubt contributed to its efficiency in helping the societies to meet some of their basic economic and social needs. This was partly why, as Knight noted, by the time of the Spanish colonization of these islands,

> Antillean society appears to have been self-sufficient in its simple needs. Luxuries were few, the parasitical elite class was small and the food base was perfectly adequate to support the existing population.[3]

Karl Sauer reiterated this view when he concluded that 'in productivity the West Indian native economy cannot be rated as inferior'[4]

N. K. Bacchus

Notes

1. Bryan Edwards, *The History, Civil and Commercial, of the British West Indies* (1819; London: T. Miller, 1978) Vol. 1, 46.
2. Ibid., 46-47.
3. Franklin Knight, *The Caribbean* (New York: Oxford University Press, 1978) 15.
4. Karl Sauer, *The Early Spanish Main* (Berkley: University of California Press, 1996).

CRITICAL THINKING AND WRITING

1. State, using evidence from the passage,
   a) the audience for whom you think it is intended,
   b) what you consider to be the writer's main purpose.
2. a) With reference to the passage, identify three instances where quotations from other historians are used by the writer to support his points on education among Indians in the fifteenth century.
   b) Discuss the effectiveness of this strategy.
3. With reference to the passage, identify similarities and/or differences between the strategies used to educate the Indians and those which obtain in your society.
4. a) What point is the writer making in paragraph 4 when he compares the aims of the Indian education system to those in modern societies?
   b) Do you agree with his position? Support your response with examples from your own observations and experiences.

WRITING ACROSS THE CURRICULUM ACTIVITY

5. In paragraph 2 the writer contends that 'The survival of a society depends not only on the technical skills needed to earn a living but also on inculcating in them those attitudes, values, beliefs which give meaning and purpose....' Briefly explain how this is achieved in your society.

CHAPTER 2

BRIEF HISTORICAL SKETCH OF TERTIARY EDUCATION IN THE COMMONWEALTH CARIBBEAN

The British thrust to found colonies in the New World resulted in the establishment of colonies in North America and the Caribbean at about the same time in the first half of the seventeenth century. For very different reasons, the West Indian colonies followed very similar patterns to the North American colonies in the establishment of schools and mass schooling at the elementary level. At the tertiary level, however, the patterns in North America and the Caribbean diverge sharply.

In the North American colonies, colleges were founded very soon after schools were established. Harvard College was founded in 1636, William and Mary in 1693, Yale in 1701, Princeton in 1746, King's College in 1754, Pennsylvania in 1755, Rutgers in 1766, Brown in 1765 and Dartmouth in 1769. While nine colleges had been founded in the North American colonies before the declaration of American independence in 1776, up to the end of the eighteenth century not a single college had been established in the West Indian colonies. It was not until 1830, nearly two hundred years after the founding of Harvard, when the Codrington Grammar School was transformed into a theological college, that the first tertiary institution was established in the Commonwealth Caribbean.

In other words, schools were founded in the Commonwealth Caribbean and operated for more than 150 years before a single college was established in the region.

During the seventeenth and eighteenth centuries the pattern that had developed in the West Indian colonies was for those who could afford to send their sons to England to university.[1] Brathwaite, in his study of colonial creole society in Jamaica, showed that between 1770 and 1820, 229 Jamaicans went to Oxford and Cambridge. The Jamaican practice mirrored a common pattern throughout the West Indian colonies.

It should be noted that universities were established very early in the settlement of Spanish colonies.[2] Sherlock and Nettleford have noted that in the first half of the seventeenth century the Spanish established the universities of Santo Domingo, Mexico and Lima. In the second half of the seventeenth century, Spain established five more universities in its New World colonies and followed this with the founding of another ten universities over the course of the eighteenth century. Put another way, the pattern of founding schools and colleges in North America resembled the pattern that had previously been established by the

Spanish in Latin America. The pattern in the Commonwealth Caribbean, however, differed from both Latin and North America.

Interestingly, the British West Indian colonies always had levels of enrolment at the elementary level that were comparable to North America and Western Europe, and always had higher enrolments at the elementary level than the Spanish colonies, and later the independent countries of Latin America.[3] On the other hand, the British West Indian colonies always had much lower levels of provision for tertiary education.

The most appealing explanation of this enduring difference between the Commonwealth Caribbean on the one hand, and North and Latin America on the other, is that the former were mainly colonies of exploitation while the latter were mainly colonies of settlement.[4] The majority of the colonists in the North and in Spanish America planned to make the New World their home. They therefore brought with them the infrastructure of community and intellectual advancement. The West Indian colonies were the loci of exploitation in which the majority of the colonists planned to make a quick fortune and return to Britain to enjoy their new found wealth. Accordingly, they made no long-term provisions for either community or intellectual advancement in the West Indies.

Whatever may have been the reason, tertiary education had a late start in the Commonwealth Caribbean. It was only in the first half of the nineteenth century that colleges began to be established. Even then it was only theological and teachers colleges that made their entrance. These institutions were founded to train 'native' teachers and clergy. Codrington in Barbados was the only college to offer degrees, which they did after 1835 in conjunction with Durham University in Wales. An aborted attempt was made to establish a university college in Spanish Town, Jamaica, in the 1870s, but this attempt was short lived. The college lasted less than a decade. Yet another attempt was made at Jamaica College between 1889 and 1901 which graduated thirty persons with bachelor's degrees.[5]

Between 1830 when Codrington was transformed into a college and 1950 when transition to independence had begun, there were no more than about ten small colleges training teachers, five even smaller colleges training ministers of religion, a few schools of nursing and one college training agriculturalists in the entire Commonwealth Caribbean. This very meagre provision constituted almost the entire tertiary level enterprise in the region. The only new types of institutions that had been introduced over this period of 120 years were the Imperial College of Tropical Agriculture (ICTA) founded in 1922 in St Augustine, Trinidad, and a few schools of nursing in Barbados, Guyana, Jamaica and Trinidad.

Heuman[6] explained the lethargy in building an indigenous capacity for tertiary education in Jamaica on the grounds that by restricting its size and structure, the colonial administrators justified the recruitment of British officials, technocrats and professionals. In addition, the recruitment of Europeans was seen by the local elite as one means of bolstering the declining numbers of whites in the colonies. Following emancipation and the decline in the fortunes of sugar and the plantations, there was a noticeable decline in the European segment of Commonwealth Caribbean populations. Colonial control and race seem to have been two of the factors contributing to the neglect of tertiary education provision in the region.

Following the post-emancipation period, the pattern of going abroad for tertiary education was institutionalized in the secondary school system that developed in the region in the latter half of the nineteenth century. Island scholarships were granted, for study in universities abroad, to those students who performed best in their island each year in the Cambridge examinations. By this measure, not only those who could afford it went abroad, but the brilliant offspring of those who could not otherwise have accessed this level and type of education.

Errol Miller

Notes

1. Edward Brathwaite, *The Development of Creole Society in Jamaica,: 1770–1820* (Oxford: Clarendon Press, 1971).
2. Phillip Sherlock and Rex Nettleford, *The University of the West Indies: A Caribbean Response to the Challenge of Change* (London: MacMillan Caribbean, 1990).
3. Aaron Benavot and Phyllis Riddle, 'The Expansion of Primary Education, 1870–1940: Trends and Issues,' in *Sociology of Education* 61 (1988):191–210.
4. Lloyd Best, 'Outline of a Model of Pure Plantation Economy', in *Social and Economic Studies* 17 (1968): 283–326.
5. Hopeton Gordon, 'University and Nation-Building in the Commonwealth Caribbean: Early Commitments', *Caribbean Journal of Education* 11 (1984): 184–201.
6. Gad J. Heuman, *Between Black and White: Race, Politics and the Free Coloureds in Jamaica, 1792–1865* (Westport, Connecticut: Greenwood Press 1981).

CRITICAL THINKING AND WRITING

1. State, using evidence from the passage,
   a) the audience for whom you think this is intended,
   b) what you consider to be the writer's main purpose.
2. Explain the context in which you would expect to find this article.
3. a) Identify two developmental strategies/ organizational principles used by the author to present the text.
   b) Discuss the effectiveness of any ONE of these strategies in the development of the text.

CLASS DISCUSSION

4. The final paragraph of the passage discusses the 'pattern of going abroad for tertiary education' following the post-emancipation period. To what extent is this true of the present educational system in your territory?

WRITING ACTIVITY

5. Write a two- page essay in which you compare and contrast access to tertiary level education in the post-emancipation period to present day access in your country.

Chapter 3

Geography in the Caribbean Classroom

This article focuses on the north-east trade winds which are a key influence on the Caribbean region's climate and weather. Whilst CXC textbooks cover the basics, there seems to be a lack of resource material on Caribbean climate and weather for students and teachers at A Level. The temperature inversion within the lower portion of the trade winds plays an important role in influencing the seasonal pattern of precipitation. Discussion of temperature inversion in the north-east trades is rarely emphasised in geography teaching, and is largely absent from the resource material available in schools.

The North-East Trades and Temperature Inversions: Notes for the Classroom

Caribbean weather and climate are important aspects of the region's physical geography and are integral to geography courses in Caribbean schools and colleges. An understanding of the characteristics and causal factors which determine the region's climate and weather is also essential in other science and social science subjects taught across the region. Whilst basic aspects of the region's tropical maritime climate and the north-east trades are described for CXC level, less resource material is available for the more detailed picture required at A Level. The purpose of this article is to help fill this gap, and to present concepts, facts and figures, and ideas which can be used in the classroom for a more in-depth understanding of our climate and weather. The article focuses on the structure and dynamics of the north-east trades. The hitherto neglected importance of the temperature inversion in the lower portion of the trades is highlighted.

The main streamlines of the north-east trades emanate from an ENE direction. Their constant speed, reliability and regularity fashioned their name in colonial times because they were considered ideal winds for merchant sailing ships conducting commercial trade. Their constancy of direction led to many of the region's capitals being located around sheltered harbours on the leeward coastlines of Caribbean islands, of which there are good examples throughout the Windward Islands. The directional component of the north-east trades is important for modern communications and transport too, because aircraft need to takeoff and land into a head wind. Thus, runways tend to be aligned along the same axis as the principal wind direction throughout the year. It is not surprising, therefore, that most of the region's international airports have a single runway aligned in an ENE direction. However, the geometrical shape of the larger Caribbean islands can modify the local directional component of the streamlines of the north-east trades. For example, the main runway at the Norman Manley International Airport, Kingston, is aligned ESE (rather than ENE) because the prevailing wind direction of the trade winds along that part of Jamaica's south coast is from the south-east.

The Hadley Cell: The Trade Winds and the Anti-trades

The principal features of global circulation that affect the Caribbean climate are the north-east trades, the Azores-Bermuda subtropical high pressure anticyclone and the Inter-Tropical Convergence Zone (ITCZ). The model of Hadley cell tropical circulation ties these three features together. At the ITCZ the atmospheric pressure is 1,000 to 1,010mb and the equatorial air masses rise to the tropopause whose height is about 12km. Ascending air reaches the tropopause then diverges, and moves towards either of the poles. These poleward-moving, upper tropospheric outflows of air are called the anti-trades or counter trades and travel eastwards, gradually descending, slowing down, losing heat (from long wave radiation) and increasing in density during their journey. At approximately latitudes 20 to 30 degrees north and south the anti-trades begin a very precipitous and rapid descent to the earth's surface. As the air masses descend, they are warmed adiabatically, so that they reach the

earth's surface as dry air. Under such conditions it is almost impossible for clouds to form.

The subtropical anticyclones are regions of permanent high pressure and have an elliptical shape when depicted on maps. They can occur across land or ocean. The great deserts of the world, such as the Sahara and the Arabian Desert, are found where subtropical anticyclones coincide with continental land masses. In the north Atlantic, the subtropical anticyclone is called the Azores-Bermuda high, and it has a considerable influence on the Caribbean's weather and climate. In the central cores of these oceanic anti-cyclones there is little wind and, in the days of sailing ships, they were feared by sailors who called them the horse latitudes.

Once the descending air at the subtropical anticyclone reaches the earth's surface, it diverges again, part moving towards the poles as wind systems called the prevailing westerlies. However, most of the descending air travels back to the equator as the trade winds, being deflected by the Coriolis force during the journey. Easterly trade winds blow across about one third of the earth's surface, and since 75 to 80 per cent of tropical regions are ocean, for most of their journey they blow across a water surface. Initially, over the eastern parts of oceans, trade winds are dry, but they become increasingly moist as they approach the equator. The northern and southern hemisphere trade wind systems converge near the equator at the Inter-Tropical Convergence Zone. The Hadley cell circulation system is closed because the air masses are heated once again at the ITCZ and ascend. In effect, the low pressure of the ITCZ draws the trade wind air masses in from the higher pressure, subtropical anticyclones; an endless circulatory process.

Thus, the Caribbean region is characterised by easterly winds at the earth's surface (the north-east trades) whilst above them in the upper troposphere are the anti-trades, which blow in a westerly direction. However, this model of Hadley cell circulation is greatly simplified. For example, there are important seasonal variations in the entire circulation system because the ITCZ follows the movement of the overhead sun (though lagging by a couple of months). These seasonal rhythms also affect Caribbean climate and weather. Modern meteorology has recognised, too, that upper tropospheric wind systems are highly complex. At any given locality, they may be affected by disturbances and/or air masses from more northerly latitudes, so that the anti-trades may shift or be absent for an extended period.

Hadley Cell Circulation: An Idea for Classroom Discussion

One way of introducing a discussion of Hadley cell circulation is by reference to air travel. The cruising altitude of aircraft over the Atlantic ocean places them in the upper tropospheric winds, which normally will be blowing in a westerly direction, even in the region of the Hadley cell. Some modern aircraft, such as the Airbus and Boeing 777, display wind speed, wind direction and aircraft position with respect to latitude and longitude, on a screen inside the main passenger cabin.

As an exercise, it is possible to record such data when travelling to, say, the United Kingdom, Canada or the north-eastern USA. For example, an observer could record wind direction, wind speed and position at ten-minute intervals over a two-hour period as the aircraft ascends from, or descends into, a Caribbean airport. During this period several changes in wind direction might be expected (based on the Hadley cell model), including a complete reversal of wind direction as the aircraft travels to or from its cruising altitude. The reversal in wind direction may occur as the aircraft moves between the anti-trades and upper trades, and there may be another shift in wind direction as the aircraft moves between the geostrophic upper trades and the lower trades. Students can be asked to discuss why this might happen, based on their understanding of the Hadley cell model.

It is important to recognise that the particular weather conditions and wind directions in the troposphere on any given day might be quite different from those predicted by the model of Hadley cell circulation, especially during the summer. Generally speaking, more typical and stable conditions and wind directions are to be expected from December through to June. But whether or not such observations conform to the model, or deviate according to local weather conditions on a particular day, such empirical observations can help students form an impression of the complexity, structure and inter-relationship of surface winds and the winds aloft, and act as a starting point for a discussion of the mechanism of the Hadley cell tropical circulation in relation to Caribbean climate and weather.

The Vertical Structure of the North-East trades

We noted above that in vertical profile the trade winds lie below the anti-trades. The trade winds are composed of two vertical components, the upper trades and below them the lower trades.

Figure 3.1
Vertical cross-section through the north-east trades

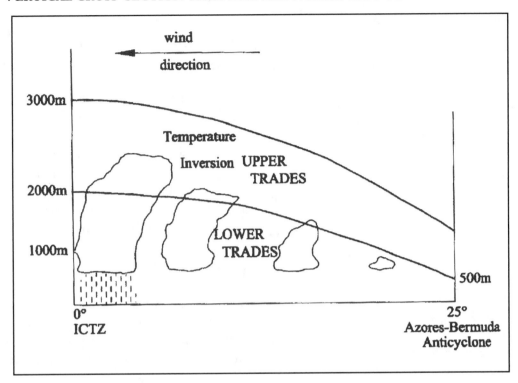

The Lower Trades

The lower trades are the portion of the trade wind air mass nearest the earth's surface. In the Caribbean Basin they blow from an ENE direction all year round. By the time they reach the Caribbean Sea they have travelled 4,000 miles over the southern part of the north Atlantic, and are therefore warm and humid. Under undisturbed conditions, the lower trades hardly ever produce precipitation, the reason being the existence of an inversion layer (figure 3.1). A temperature inversion in an air mass is a vertical layer in which temperature increases with increasing elevation, contrary to the normal condition of declining temperature with increasing elevation.

The temperature increase within the inversion layer in the north-east trades can be as much as 10 degrees Celsius near the geographical centre of the subtropical anticyclone. The inversion is created within the subtropical high pressure zone because the upper tropospheric anti-trades are warmed adiabatically as they descend to the ocean surface. However, the ocean surface cools the lowest portion of this descending air, so that the base-level of the temperature inversion is not immediately above the ocean surface. At the core of the Azores-Bermuda anticyclone, for example, the base-level of the inversion layer is at an elevation of around 450 to 600 metres (1,500 to 2,000ft) (Barry & Chorley, 1992, p. 230).

The inversion layer is created at the subtropical anticyclone in the eastern part of the north Atlantic, and is preserved as the trade winds air masses travel to westwards into the Caribbean Sea (at a height of between 1km and 2km). Thus the lower trades have two distinct layers; the inversion layer acts as a lid on top of a lower layer at the ocean surface, and its presence prevents the formation of rainbearing cumuliform clouds. For the greater part of their journey across the tropical north Atlantic the north-east trades are dry winds. Both layers become thicker as they approach the equator, so that near the equator, base-level of the inversion is much higher, around 2,500 metres (see figure 3.1). In effect, as the air masses move downstream towards the equator, the subsidence effect from aloft (that is, from the descending anti-trades) is reduced. By the time the air masses reach the Caribbean Basin, the temperature difference between the bottom and top of the inversion layer has decreased to just a few degrees.

The Upper Trades

The upper trades are the air masses above the inversion layer (but below the anti-trades). Air temperature begins to get colder again with increasing altitude. The upper trades are much thicker air masses than the lower trades, being some 6km in thickness at the subtropical anticyclone and about 10km thick near the ITCZ. They are dry stable winds with generally slower speeds than the lower trades below them and, in effect, are geostrophic easterlies (they blow from due east rather than north-east, freed from surface friction). Whereas the summits of the highest mountains in the Caribbean (in the Dominican Republic and Jamaica) experience wet conditions throughout the year, in the eastern parts of the Atlantic Ocean where the trade winds originate, the tops of high mountains poke right through the trade wind inversion into the drier upper trades. Thus the summits of the mountains in the Azores and the Canaries, which are at a similar elevation to the highest Caribbean mountains, are dry and arid whilst their lower slopes are wet and forested.

The Trade Winds and the Seasons

Most of the Caribbean region has a summer rainfall maximum, although the month in which it occurs varies from place to place. During the summer, the ITCZ moves further north, crossing Guyana, and for a time hovers south of Trinidad. The Azores-Bermuda anticyclone also has a seasonal rhythm. In summer it is located further north and covers a larger area, so that the northern limit of trades also shifts further north.

In winter there is accentuated subsidence caused by the descent of the anti-trades, and this strengthens the inversion layer in the north-east trades and lowers its base level. The strong winter temperature inversion inhibits the formation of rainbearing clouds at that time of the year and is the main reason why our winters tend to be drier than the summers. On the other hand, the trade wind inversion is weaker in the summer and its base level is higher. In the eastern Caribbean, for example, the inversion base level is about 1,000 to 1,500m metres in height in winter and 2,000m or higher in summer (Granger, 1985). It is precisely because the inversion in the trades is weaker in the summer and its base level is higher that conditions are more conducive to the development of rainbearing cloud formations during the summer rather than the winter. During the winter months the trade wind inversion is present on about 80 percent of days but only on 30 to 40 percent of days during the summer months. Further, the inversion is frequently absent during the passage of a tropical disturbance, and since tropical disturbances are more likely to form in the summer months (see below), other things being equal, summer precipitation is more likely than winter rainfall.

Much of the Caribbean region's precipitation is caused by the passage of synoptic systems such as tropical disturbances, tropical waves and tropical cyclones. A tropical disturbance is an organised but temporary synoptic system of low pressure which disrupts the normally stable weather conditions associated with the trade winds. There are several types, of different size, duration and intensity, ranging from relatively small features such as convection cells associated with thunderstorms, to tropical waves, tropical depressions and hurricanes (tropical cyclones). The major types of tropical disturbances (waves, depressions and hurricanes) are seasonal and occur mainly in the summer months, when the temperature inversion in the north-east trades is weakest. Collectively, they are the principal cause of summer rainfall maxima through most of the Caribbean Basin. They form in warm, humid air masses where the trade wind temperature inversion is weak or absent. Under such conditions, the air mass is potentially unstable and conducive to the development of towering rain-bearing clouds. Upward air movement releases large amounts of the latent heat of condensation, and the rising movement creates a lower pressure at the earth's surface.

A good illustration of how the presence or absence of a temperature inversion influences levels of precipitation is to be found in the dynamics of a tropical wave, formerly called an 'easterly wave' in older textbooks. A tropical wave is a linear trough of low pressure which can bring unsettled conditions and rain over a period of several days. Tropical waves occur most frequently in the Caribbean

between July and September, and either form in the north Atlantic (south of the Azores-Bermuda high between 5 and 20 degrees north) then move into the Caribbean Basin, or form over the Caribbean Sea itself. Similar types of weather systems also occur in the western Pacific.

Tropical waves can have a frequency of more than one per week from the point of view of a fixed location in the Caribbean. To an observer on the ground, the passage of a tropical wave is preceded by fine hazy weather with high scattered cumulus clouds. As a wave approaches, cloud levels gradually increase, well developed cumulus clouds become evident, there are occasional showers and visibility improves. As the trough passes, heavy cumulus and cumulonimbus clouds often bring torrential rain and thundery showers. Wind direction veers and temperatures fall a few degrees. Over the next couple of days weather conditions gradually improve as the trough moves further away.

Tropical waves move forward in a westerly direction at a speed of about 20 km/hour. The axis of the tropical wave is at right angles to the main direction of the north-east trades. The system may be 50km in width and several hundred kilometres in length. The trough is fairly weak at the ocean surface, with atmospheric pressure only about three millibars lower than adjacent areas, but it is much more strongly developed at elevations of about 4km. A cross section through a tropical wave is shown in figure 3.2. Ahead (west) of the trough is an area of diverging air at the surface. The area of diverging air is a fair-weather zone, where descending dry air temporarily strengthens and lowers the height at which the temperature inversion begins. There is no precipitation in front of the approaching wave because the temperature

FIGURE 3.2
VERTICALCROSS-SECTION THROUGH A TYPICAL TROPICAL WAVE

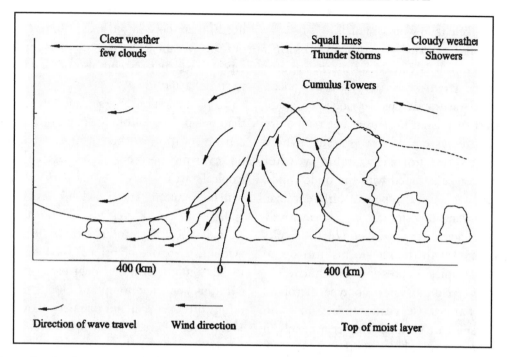

inversion has been strengthened and lowered (see figure 3.2). The strongest and lowest point of the inversion may be as much as 300km ahead of the wave.

Just behind the trough is an area of converging air, where air is ascending, so the temperature inversion is destroyed and temporarily disappears. The absence of the temperature inversion permits huge cumulonimbus rain clouds to develop, often extending as high as 600, and they bring heavy precipitation. Parallel rows of thunderstorms, called squall lines, typically characterise the area east of the main axis of the trough. As the wave passes and moves further away, the temperature inversion is re-established at a higher level, and the cumulonimbus cloud and thunderstorm activity gradually diminishes.

The pattern of summer maxima in precipitation is, of course, a simplified version of a reality whose complexity becomes more apparent as one delves deeper into the subject. Thus, for example, the islands of Curaçao, Bonaire and Aruba have winter rather than summer rainfall maxima. Superimposed over annual seasonal precipitation patterns are secular variations and trends (such as the recent El Niño–La Niña cycle) which also have an impact in the seasonal distribution of rainfall. Thus, wet and dry seasons in the Caribbean region tend to be uncertain in their timing and duration, and in the amount of rainfall expected in any given year.

To summarise briefly, in vertical profile the lower trades can be considered to be composed of two portions throughout their journey to the equator: a layer nearest to the ocean surface; and an inversion layer above. This inversion is strongest where its base-level is lowest (the eastern oceans) and weakest where its base-level is highest (the western parts of oceans like the Caribbean Sea). The inversion is weaker in the summer months and this condition is important in ensuring that most of the Caribbean Basin has summer rainfall maxima. The general picture is that lower trades form the lower tropospheric winds near the earth's surface, and the upper trades constitute the middle tropospheric winds. The westerly anti-trades are the principal upper tropospheric winds. It is important to note that the upper tropospheric wind systems in the tropics were once thought to be very simple and constant, but modern meteorology reveals them to be complex, and susceptible to disturbances and incursions from air masses from other latitudes, the results of which have important consequences for surface weather, especially in our region.

David Barker

References

Barry, R.G. and R.J. Chorley, 1992. *Atmosphere, Weather & Climate*. 6th ed. London: Routledge.
Granger, O.E. 1985. 'Caribbean Climates'. *Progress in Physical Geography* 9, no.1:16-43.

CRITICAL THINKING AND WRITING

1. Identify the dominant discourse mode, and state, using evidence from the text, the writer's main purpose and the audience for whom the text is intended.
2. The writer of this text employs several developmental strategies or organizing principles. Identify the strategy used in paragraphs 3, 4 and 5, and say how it is suited to the purpose and audience, in each case.
3. Comment on the writer's use of diction:
   a) Examine the use of specialized terms/ technical terms.
   b) Show how the diction creates the tone of the text.
   c) Examine the suitability of the tone to the content being communicated.
4. Examine, using evidence from the text, two ways in which the writer's credibility is established.
5. What do you consider to be the strengths of this article?

COLLABORATIVE ACTIVITY

6. Writing across the Curriculum Figure 2. Discuss your paragraph in small groups.

WEB ACTIVITY

7. Do an Internet search to locate an article which discusses the same topic.
   a) State how this article is similar to the one you have read, and how it is different.
   b) State which article you prefer and why.

GENDER &
FAMILY LIFE

CHAPTER 4

THE IMPACT OF FAMILY STRUCTURE ON CHILDREN

The changes in family structure that children experience during their lives are not without consequences. Western societies have found that children from father-absent homes manifest a number of internalising and externalising problem behaviours, including sadness and depression, delinquency, aggression, sex role difficulties, early initiation of sexual activity and teen pregnancy, as well as poor social and adaptive functioning and low self-esteem, as reported by Princeton sociologist, Sara McLanahan.

Behavioural Problems

School functioning is also affected, with poorer performance on academic and cognitive tests, school disciplinary problems, higher school absenteeism and dropout rates, and lower occupational attainment.

Similar problem behaviours have been identified in children from single-parent and otherwise disrupted households.

Jamaican children who live in the less stable common-law and visiting unions, and those in single-parent homes or homes with a biological and surrogate parent are more withdrawn in their interactions with others.

Additionally, children who frequently move from one residence to another, in the process of child shifting, also exhibit problem behaviour.

Child shifting, a common sequel to parental absence in Jamaica, requires children to adjust physically to their new environment but also, and of greater consequence, to adjust emotionally.

The children of incarcerated women, though relatively few in number, require special consideration because of the effects of this unique type of parental separation.

A recent report by sociologist Dr. Aldrie Henry-Lee found that women worried about their children's well-being but thought their relationships with the children were not affected.

The children, however, were depressed, cried frequently and expressed silent resentment and anger. They were frequent victims of child shifting and experienced physical and emotional abuse as well as discrimination.

The presence of these children often worsened already impoverished homes, and their schooling was often affected.

Father-Child Relationship

Sociologist Marina Ramkissoon, in her research on the interaction between Jamaican fathers and their children, investigated two aspects of the father-child relationship: physical absence and psychological absence.

Psychological absence refers to the father's absence in the minds of their children, based on emotional inaccessibility, lack of responsibility and indifference to the welfare of their children.

Taken separately, the psychological presence of the father is more important to the emotional well-being of the child.

Physical presence necessarily promotes psychological presence, but physical presence and psychological absence can lead to expressive rejection and greater psychological damage.

It is suggested that concerns about the effects of fathering on children should consider both physical and psychological presence.

Family Functioning

As shown in Ramkissoon's research and that of others, while the composition of the family is important to children, how the family functions to support children is more important to children's development.

Family functioning aimed at supporting children's development is commonly called parenting.

In the Western family structure, this is largely the role of biological parents.

However, in the varying family structures present in Jamaica, and indeed in the Caribbean, the terms 'family' and 'parenting' have much broader contexts.

Psychologist Diana Baumrind's seminal work on parenting, along with others that extended her work, identified two main characteristics of parenting: responsiveness and demandingness.

The responsive parent is accepting of the child, is warm, patient, attentive and sensitive to the child's needs. The non-responsive parent is cold, emotionally rejecting, and frequently degrades the child.

The demanding parent establishes high standards for the child and insists that the child meet these standards. The non-demanding parent makes little demands on the child and rarely tries to influence the child's behaviour.

Parenting Styles

Four parenting styles based on these characteristics can be identified: authoritative, permissive, authoritarian and uninvolved.

Authoritative parenting, where responsiveness is matched with reasonable demands, though identified before the concept of child rights became well known, is essentially parenting that recognises the rights and responsibilities of parents and children.

It is, therefore, no surprise that the children of authoritative parents have the best outcomes; these children are happy, independent, self-confident, self-controlled and achieve high levels of social and moral maturity and academic achievement.

Permissive child-rearing results in defiant, rebellious, dependent children, while uninvolved child rearing results in children with poor emotional control, low self-esteem, poor school performance and antisocial behaviour.

Jamaican parenting style has been described as authoritarian, with high demandingness, unmatched by responsiveness, where the commonest words the child probably hears are, 'Do it because I say so.' Harsh punishments accompany the authoritarian style.

Pre-school children reared in this manner are withdrawn and unhappy. Older boys show high rates of hostility, anger and defiance, while girls lack initiative and retreat from challenges.

The children perform better at school and have less anti-social behaviour than children of the permissive and uninvolved types of parenting, but are less well-adjusted and less successful than children reared in the authoritative style.

Parenting Stress

Jamaican parenting style was further investigated by administering a questionnaire, the Parent Stress Index (PSI), to the parents of six-year-olds (Samms-Vaughan, 2005).

The PSI measures parenting stress in two domains: the child domain and parent child. Total parenting stress is obtained by summing child and parent domain scores, and life stress is measured separately.

The findings show that Jamaican parents have high levels of total parental stress — much higher, for example, than those experienced by parents in the United States.

Parents living in poorer circumstances have higher parenting and life stress levels with regard to the child, parenting and stress.

With regard to the child, parents had high levels of stress because they had difficulty finding their child acceptable to them and thought their child was too demanding.

From the parent perspective, parenting was most stressful because parents lacked competence in parenting, did not feel a strong attachment to their child, had their own activities restricted by parenting and did not have the support of their spouse in parenting.

Parental depression has been shown in many studies in developed countries to reduce parenting effectiveness.

The children of depressed mothers have more behaviour problems and have lower school achievement.

However, in Jamaica, parental depression was less important as a contributor to parenting stress than competence, attachment, role restriction and spousal support.

Recent further research on parenting by sociologists Heather Ricketts and Pat Anderson supported the association between poverty and parental stress, but also found that parents who were never married, parents with large numbers of children to care for, and parents who had both younger and older children in the home, had high levels of parental stress.

Family Functioning

The impact of parenting stress on Jamaican children is not to be ignored. Parenting stress is one of four factors identified in Jamaica that affects all aspects of children's outcomes: cognitive development, school performance, behaviour problems and behaviour strengths (Samms-Vaughan, 2005).

One way that parenting stress may exert its impact is through interaction with children.

Ricketts and Anderson found that highly-stressed Jamaican parents do not spend as much time as others do interacting with their child and much of their interaction is inappropriate, with high levels of harsh discipline.

Importantly, Ricketts and Anderson showed that parental stress was reduced by access to parenting information but relatively few parents had such access.

The implication is that parenting information and support should be made more widely available, to improve parent-child interaction.

Maureen Samms-Vaughan

Source: *Sunday Gleaner*, April 16, 2006. *This article was adapted by the author for a newspaper audience. The original, an excerpt from the 2006 Grace, Kennedy Foundation Lecture entitled 'Children Caught in the Crossfire', appears in Chapter 5. Go on to Chapter 5 where you will find the original version of this article as well as questions.*

CHAPTER 5

CHILDREN CAUGHT IN THE CROSSFIRE

The changes in family structure that children experience during their lives are not without consequences. Western societies have found that children from father-absent homes manifest a number of internalising and externalising problem behaviours, including sadness and depression, delinquency, aggression, sex role difficulties, early initiation into sexual activity and teen pregnancy, as well as poor social and adaptive functioning and low self-esteem (McLanahan, et al: 1999). School functioning is also affected, with poorer performance on academic and cognitive tests, school disciplinary problems, higher school absenteeism and dropout rates, and lower occupational attainment. Similar problem behaviours have been identified in children from single-parent and otherwise disrupted households.

The absence of the typical Western family and social structure and its replacement by the mix of nuclear, patrifocal and matrifocal and quasi-matrifocal family have suggested to some that Jamaican children may not manifest similar behaviours. However, Jamaican children who live in the less stable common-law and visiting unions, and those in single-parent homes, or homes with a biological and a surrogate parent, are more withdrawn in their interactions with others (Samms-Vaughan, 2005; Samms-Vaughan, 2000). Additionally,

children who frequently move from one residence to another, in the process of child shifting, also exhibit problem behaviour. Child shifting, a common sequel to parental absence in Jamaica, requires children to adjust physically to their new environment but also, and of greater consequence, to adjust emotionally.

The children of incarcerated women, though relatively few in number, require special consideration because of the effects of this unique type of parental separation. A recent report (Henry-Lee, 2005) found that women worried about their children's well-being but thought their relationships with the children were not affected. The children, however, were depressed, cried frequently, and expressed silent resentment and anger. They were frequent victims of child shifting and experienced physical and emotional abuse as well as discrimination. The presence of these children often worsened already impoverished homes and their schooling was often affected.

Ramkissoon (2005), in her research on the interaction between Jamaican fathers and their children, investigated two aspects of the father-child relationship: physical absence and psychological absence. Psychological absence refers to the father's absence in the minds of their children based, on emotional inaccessibility, lack of responsibility, and indifference to the welfare of their children. Taken separately, the psychological presence of the father is more important to the emotional well-being of the child. Physical presence necessarily promotes psychological presence, but physical presence and psychological absence can lead to expressive rejection and greater psychological damage. It is suggested that concerns about the effects of fathering on children should consider both physical and psychological presence.

Family Functioning

As shown in Ramkissoon's research and that of others, while the composition of the family is important to children, how the family functions to support children is more important to children's development. Family functioning aimed at supporting children's development is commonly called parenting. In the Western family structure, this is largely the role of biological parents. However, in the varying family structures present in Jamaica, and indeed in the Caribbean, the terms 'family' and 'parenting' have much broader contexts.

Baumrind's (1971) seminal work on parenting, along with others that extended her work, identified two main characteristics of parenting: responsiveness and demandingness. The responsive parent is accepting of the child, is warm, patient, attentive and sensitive to the child's needs. The non-responsive parent is cold, emotionally rejecting, and frequently degrades the child. The demanding parent establishes high standards for the child and insists that the child meet these standards. The non-demanding parent makes few demands on the child and rarely tries to influence the child's behaviour. Four parenting styles based on these characteristics can be identified:

authoritative, permissive, authoritarian and uninvolved.

Authoritative parenting, where responsiveness is matched with reasonable demands, though identified before the concept of child rights became well known, is essentially parenting that recognises the rights and responsibilities of parents and children. It is, therefore, no surprise that the children of authoritative parents have the best outcomes; these children are happy, independent, self-confident, self-controlled, and attain high levels of social and moral maturity and academic achievement. Permissive child rearing results in defiant, rebellious, dependent children, while uninvolved child rearing results in children with poor emotional control, low self-esteem, poor school performance and antisocial behaviour.

Jamaican parenting style has been described as authoritarian, with high demandingness, unmatched by responsiveness, where the commonest words the child probably hears are 'Do it because I say so.' Harsh punishments accompany the authoritarian style. Pre-school children reared in this manner are withdrawn and unhappy. Older boys show high rates of hostility, anger and defiance, while girls lack initiative and retreat from challenges. The children perform better at school and have less anti-social behaviour than children of the permissive and uninvolved types, but are less well-adjusted and less successful than children reared in the authoritative style.

Jamaican parenting style was further investigated by administering a questionnaire, the Parent Stress Index (PSI), to the parents of six-year-olds (Samms-Vaughan, 2005). The PSI measures parenting stress in two domains:- the child domain and the parent domain. The child domain identifies characteristics within the child that impair a parent's ability to function, and the parent domain identifies those areas in which parental dysfunction impairs the parent-child relationship. Total parenting stress is obtained by summing child and parent domain scores, and Life Stress is measured separately.

The findings show that Jamaican parents have high levels of total parental stress — much higher, for example, than those experienced by parents in the United States. Parents living in poorer circumstances have higher parenting and life stress levels with regard to the child, parenting and stress. With regard to the child, parents had high levels of stress because they had difficulty finding their child acceptable to them and thought their child was too demanding. From the parent perspective, parenting was most stressful because parents lacked competence in parenting, did not feel a strong attachment to their child, had their own activities restricted by parenting and did not have the support of their spouse in parenting.

Parental depression has been shown in many studies in developed countries to reduce parenting effectiveness. The children of depressed mothers have more behaviour problems and have lower school achievement. However, in Jamaica, parental depression was less important as a contributor to parenting stress than competence, attachment, role restriction and spousal support. Recent further research on parenting by sociologists Ricketts and Anderson (2005) supported the association between poverty and parental stress but also found that parents who were never married, parents with large numbers of children to care for, and parents who had both younger and older children in the home, had high levels of parental stress.

The Impact of Family Functioning

The impact of parenting stress on Jamaican children is not to be ignored. Parenting stress is one of four factors identified in Jamaica that affect all aspects of children's outcomes: cognitive development, school performance, behaviour problems and behaviour strengths (Samms-Vaughan, 2005). One way that parenting stress may exert its impact is through interaction with children. Ricketts and Anderson found that highly-stressed Jamaican parents do not spend as much time as others do interacting with their child and much of their interaction is inappropriate, with high levels of harsh discipline.

Importantly, parental stress was reduced by access to parenting information, but relatively few parents had such access (Ricketts et al., 2005). The implication is that parenting information and support should be made more widely available, to improve parent-child interaction.

Maureen Samms-Vaughan

References

Baumrind, D. 1971. 'Current Patterns of Parental Authority'. *Developmental Psychology* Monograph 4, no.1 (Part 2).

Henry-Lee, A. 2005. 'The Impact of the Incarceration of Jamaican Women on themselves and their Families'. Kingston, Jamaica: Planning Institute of Jamaica.

McLanahan, S. and J. Teitler. 1999. 'The Consequences of Father Absence'. In *Parenting and Child Development in Non-traditional Families*, ed. M.E. Lamb, 83–102. Mahwah, NJ: Lawrence Erlbaum Associates.

Ramkissoon, M. 2005. 'An investigation of the physical and psychological presence of the Jamaican father'. *Caribbean Childhoods: From Research to Action. Journal of the Children's Issues Coalition* 2: 17–37.

Ricketts, H. and P. Anderson. 2005. 'Parenting in Jamaica'. A study conducted on behalf of the Planning Institute of Jamaica'.

Samms-Vaughan, M.E. 2000. 'Cognition, Educational Attainment and Behaviour in a Cohort of Jamaican Children'. Working paper No. 5. Planning Insititue of Jamaica.

———. 2005. 'The Jamaican Pre–School Child. The Status of Early Childhood Development in Jamaica'. Planning Institute of Jamaica.

CRITICAL THINKING AND WRITING

1. What is the discourse mode?
2. For what audience was this article intended? Are the two versions aimed at different audiences? Explain how you arrive at your decision.
3. Evaluate the credibility of the writer. Explain how she establishes credibility.
4. Examine the writer's choice of diction and explain how it is suited to the context and audience.
5. Comment on the tone of the text, and explain (using evidence from the text) how the tone is used by the writer to achieve her overall objective.
6. What are the differences in the way in which sources are acknowledged in the two versions of this article? Suggest reasons for these differences.
7. What other changes were made to the article to make it more suitable for a newspaper audience? Why were these changes necessary?

WRITING ACROSS THE CURRICULUM ACTIVITIES

8. Using cause and effect as the developmental strategy, write one paragraph in which you explain how parental influences affect our behaviour as adults.
9. Online research: The research findings presented by Samms-Vaughan were based on Jamaican families. Choose TWO of the issues highlighted by the research and
    a) conduct research, via the Internet, in which you gather current information on these issues in another Caribbean country;
    b) write two unified, coherent paragraphs in which you summarise your findings.

CHAPTER 6

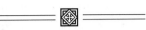

GENDER DIVISION –
THE SOWING

Common to virtually every known society is a division of labour along gender lines. The division takes as its defining axis the family, however constituted, since this is the basic unit of social organization. At its most general, work aimed at creating and maintaining a nurturing environment for the young and vulnerable members of the species is the responsibility of the female; work aimed at providing support for the unit is the responsibility of the male. In Jamaica and the rest of the Caribbean, males and females are socialized to identify domestic work as female, and work outside the domestic sphere, but supportive of it, as male. Thus, cooking, washing, bathing, grooming, dressing and nursing children, tidying up the house, and the like, are chores seen as the responsibility of the females, while chores relative to the household economy, such as animal husbandry, artisan skills, farming, wage labour, and other outdoor forms of income earning, are the responsibility of the male. The fact that many boys are required to perform some 'female' tasks, as happens in a family of all or mostly boys, or that many girls are required to undertake 'male' tasks, in a family of all girls, is of little consequence as far as the behavioural norms are concerned. What matters is the gender significance of what is done. Even as they perform such cross-gender tasks, children are made aware of their gender significance, which is usually rationalized as preparation for an independent and self-reliant life. Boys, as soon as they are able to, will resist performing such simple tasks as washing up dishes and tidying the house. Among those they find most repulsive is any chore which brings them into contact with female underwear, washed or unwashed. Also high on the list of male taboos is disposal of night soil, in families without water closets.

The gender divisions in the household are often contrasted as light work or work requiring little physical exertion as against heavy work demanding great physical strength; hence the ideas that tough work is male work and that a boy should be trained to be capable, by endurance, of tough work. The socialization of the boy child is often aimed at making him tough. His punishment is, generally speaking, much more severe than that meted out to the girl child. Believing in corporal punishment as a means of control and a means of 'bending the tree while it is young', Jamaicans further believe that from the time a boy approaches adolescence, only a man is strong enough to bend a wayward sapling. Up to that age, corporal punishment is generally exercised by mothers, thereafter by fathers, uncles or older siblings who are able to 'drop man lick'. To the provider role which a father is expected to perform is added the role of ultimate disciplinarian, the one to whom a mother appeals if the punishment she gives is ineffectual. 'Wait till yu faada come home!' often gets quicker results than the cajoling or flogging of a mother. Incidentally, this role of the father is hardly compatible with that of a warm and nurturing parent. The society cannot have it both ways. In those situations where the mother is the sole parent, her punishment of a habitually wayward son can be downright cruel.

A boy is also the first to suffer deprivation where the children are exposed. If resources do not allow for the children to attend school all at the same time, girls are given the advantage over boys. One would have thought that parents who are not able to afford 'lunch money' would make sure that the children attend school where they are able to get food supplied by the School Feeding programme. But, interestingly, the people think otherwise. No lunch money, no school. Lunch money for only one, the girl goes, the boy stays back. Necessity is made into a virtue, as suffering becomes a means of producing a hardened man who knows how to survive.

'School is girl stuff.' This declaration by an eight-year-old inner-city boy to my research assistant reveals the association of meaning built up in the minds of many boys. He was actually quite proud of the fact that it was his absence from school that allowed his sister to be present. But training in survival through deprivation and harsh treatment, and constructing male identity through provider roles, are not the only factors that give girls a school advantage. Parents will push through school any child, girl or boy, who shows exceptional intellectual endowment, but

because of their naturally earlier development, girls tend to be more favoured.

The nurture-provider gender axis forms one of the bases of gender identity among children. Whereas girls are preoccupied with acquiring nurturing skills, boys are learning from quite an early age the need to acquire money. In rural communities, their farming initiatives are encouraged; in urban communities, their initiatives are developed on the streets and in the markets. Many boys cannot guarantee their own attendance at school unless they work. In the scale of priorities, school and education rank lower than making money, although an education is also valued. By the time he was thirteen years old, Bully tells us, he owned six head of cattle in his village in Portland, his twelve-year-old brother had three, and his ten-year-old brother two. His father, he said, was proud of them. By contrast, their only sister became the only sibling to sit the Common Entrance Examination, which she passed, and she went on to Happy Grove High School. Now a forty-five-year-old JAMAL student, he refers to their early morning routine of animal husbandry as 'animal school', the real school coming several hours after and three miles away. In an inner-city community where we recently conducted fieldwork, a fourteen-year-old boy who had dropped out of school to become an armed peddler of cocaine was hoping that, when he had earned enough to be able to get himself and his mother out of the ghetto and into the United States, he would then go back to school. But for now, making money was far more important.

What does a young boy expect to do with money? He learns that this is how he begins to 'make life' and earn the respect of his family, his peers and the wider community. Making life is active, not passive. It governs gender relations as well as economic activities. By the time a boy reaches eight or nine years old, he would have already known that, in his present relationship with girls and his future relationship with women, the active role is his. 'Is man look uman, not uman look man!' By contrast, a woman who assumes the active role in inter-gender relations is considered loose. These ideas are common to females as well, and determine their expectations of males. In research carried out by Claudia Chambers and me, women reported that one of their reasons for engaging in multiple partnerships was economic. And in a study for the National Family Planning Board, more men approved of multiple partnerships than actually engaged in them, the difference being that they could not afford the outside relationship. Only in recent years have we observed successful informal commercial importers using their economic power to keep younger men, whom they do not expect to work. But, generally speaking, the construction of male identity has as a principal building block the ideal of control over economic resources. We can therefore imagine the crisis of identity suffered by a man who is failing in the imperative to 'make life', but who must relate to women. The turn to illegal activities must be understood in this context. In Herbert Gayle's study of coping strategies in an inner-city community, men are expected to 'make life' by fair means, juggling, or by foul means, hustling. Juggle, if you can, but hustle if you must. But you must do something. To do nothing is to be judged and branded 'worthless'.

As a second line of defence in the struggle to become and remain a man, hustling, raises an issue of morality. For many men, meeting the demands of a male identity is a far greater moral imperative than the virtues of honesty, and respect for property and even life. We do well to remember that Anansi is male, and in one of the tales about him, he survives at the expense of his wife and children. Survival, as a virtue, has been a part of the social and cultural life of the African-Jamaicans from the earliest times and remains a fundamental part of the ethos of the people, particularly in these hard times. And although it applies to females also — as when some women enter into relationships with men for economic reasons (no romance without finance) or when domestic helpers pilfer without remorse from employers they believe to be better off — the main thrust in the socialization for survival is directed towards the male. Apart from their exposure to deprivation, boys learn survival skills through their unsupervised exposure to the world outside the yard, to the street or the road — in effect, to the peer group.

A girl's life, for as long as she remains dependent, is surrounded by a protective ring, which starts at home, encompasses the school and ends at home. Her whereabouts are known — home, school or on an errand. Even the time it takes to get home from school is sometimes known and monitored by parents, or must be accounted for. By contrast, as soon as a boy approaches pre-pubescent years and the peer group begins to exercise its magnetic pull, he is allowed to socialize outside the home, that is 'out a' street', or 'out a' road' — out of the direct control and supervision of parents. Once his chores and errands are done, there is no demand for a boy to remain in the yard. Indeed, too great an attachment to the confines of the yard is regarded as problematic, the symptom of a maladjusted, effeminate male — a *maamaman*. Left to his own devices, a boy learns, from and with his peers, the tricks and trade of the street culture, how to navigate the dangers, how to exploit them.

As a socializing site, the street or the road or the village square is a male domain, in contrast to the yard, which is a female domain. There, males of all ages have the licence to move about and socialize without censure. Running free in this unsupervised setting, boys gather experience in risk-taking. They play their own games of chance (including gambling), model their behaviour after young male adults, hang out on the corner or in the square, fish in the river, swim in the sea, go bird-shooting, hop trucks, test and perfect their bicycle-riding skills, follow a sound system, invent or learn their own speech pattern, learn how to talk to girls, experience the art of heterosexual intercourse and homophobic discourse, and *run boat* (organize communal cooking). It is the peer group that will put the final touches, so to speak, to the construction of his male identity — his anti-homosexual heterosexuality, his power and control over women through control over financial and other resources, paternity, and the importance of respect.

The peer group virtually replaces mother and father as the controlling agents or, if not entirely a substitute, a countervailing force. An adolescent boy's friends — his 'spaar', 'staar', 'my yout', 'posse', 'crew'— exact an affinity and a loyalty as sacred as the bond of kinship, as strong as the sentiment of religion. They socialize one another, the older members of the group acting as the transmitters of what passes as knowledge, and invent new values and meanings. This is what parents mean when they speak of 'bad company'. 'Bad company' simply means, my son's friends *whom I do not know*, or *whom I do not approve of*. Its bonding power and its potential for deviance scare parents. When 'bad company' turns out to be everywhere the same, sharing the same departure from the norms of the yard and acquiring the same symbols and the same meaning, then we have a generation gap. That is all right if the

departure is not great. When, however, it results in the kinds of divergences that produce one of the highest murder rates in the world, we have not a generation gap but a generation of strangers, people we ourselves have produced but no longer recognize.

We do not, for example, know how or why it is that the gun has become such a symbol of young male identity at this turn of century, but it has. The proliferation of guns is not simply a function of the drug trade but the ultimate representation of what it means to be a man, the object of the fear and respect of others and the fearless defender of one's own self-respect. Not every youth who owns a gun is a gunman. In inner-city Jamaica and many other parts of the country, the illegal possession of the gun by many male youths functions in exactly the same way as legal possession does — as the ultimate defence. In an era in which the greatest social sin among young males today is to *dis*, that is, to show disrespect, the gun is the ultimate guarantor of respect. That, also, is why the gun salute has been appropriated from the state. The gun has become a sort of language among the young people. The most common gesture of a young male in an angry exchange is a hand tensed in the shape of a pistol and an arm pivoting in symbolic intent. And who can forget Dionne Hemmings's gesture after capturing the Olympic gold for Jamaica — her right arm and hand extended in symbolic gun salute? The so-called inner-city don is a role model not only because of his ability to command and dispense largesse, but also because he is a living source of power — the power over life and over death, the ultimate *man*. Among the youth, a common name for the penis was *rifle*, according to the study by Chambers and Chevannes. In inner-city communities, the dream of many a young boy is to be able to own a gun, preferably for himself, but jointly with the crew, if necessary.

No one willed or intended all this to be so. No political boss or don would admit that his or her drive for five-year power was intended to produce *press button* (pre-pubescent assassins) and *shata*. No television station or cable company would concede that it has any responsibility for violence and coarse behaviour becoming a way of life, nor would any franchise holder in Kingston. The parents who afford the Nike track shoes but will not afford the school fees, or who abuse teachers for attempting to discipline children, the teachers who neither teach nor mentor, the women who transport the guns, the mothers who shield the community 'protectors', the officers and agents of the law who shoot when 'attacked with a knife'— none see themselves as sharing responsibility for this generation of strangers. The failure of the system of justice to dispense justice with dispatch and equity, even the 'global' twenty-first century American society, in which one can literally walk into a store with dollars and walk out with guns, load them into a barrel and ship them to Jamaica — all have to be seen as contributing parts of the problem. And therein lies a great difficulty, for where blame is so diffuse, no one can accept responsibility. But in a way we all are responsible. We provide the building blocks, the young people design and construct their own edifice. We are reapers of our own sowing.

Barry Chevannes

CRITICAL THINKING AND WRITING

1. What is the writer's purpose? Provide support for your answer.
2. Examine some of the differences between the ways boys and girls are socialized, according to Chevannes.
3. List some of the transitional words and phrases which Chevannes utilizes in his writing.
4. How would you describe Chevannes' tone? Provide evidence from the passage.
5. What elements in the passage establish that it is not based merely on the writer's opinions or beliefs?
6. Examine the last paragraph. Note how the writer uses both simple and complex sentences. How does the sentence variation help to make the writing effective?
7. What is the main discourse mode which the writer utilizes?
8. Does the writer use a point-by-point or block-by-block method when comparing the manner in which girls and boys are socialized?
9. The main organizing principle is comparison/contrast. What other organizing principles does the writer use and how effective are these?
10. Comment on the writer's diction and register, stating how this helps the reader to identify his intended audience.

WRITING ACTIVITY

11. Note the paragraph which begins 'We do not, for example, know how or why it is that the gun has become such a symbol of young male identity at this turn of the century, but it has.' In this paragraph the three elements necessary for an effective paragraph are present. It is unified, has adequate development and is coherent. Review a paragraph which you have already written, focusing on these elements.
12. Based on your observations and experiences write a short response in your journal, indicating your reaction to the writer's

assertions about the socialization of boys and girls.

13. Write an outline for an essay in which you compare the lives of Caribbean people before and after the introduction of the world wide web and affordable cell phones. (Indicate whether you will use a point-by-point or block-by-block method).

CHAPTER 7

==== ◈ ====

RED THREAD'S FEMINISM

Red Thread emerged partially out of what Paravisini-Gebert (1997: 13) refers to as 'transisland cross-pollination'. She stresses the role interregional migration has played in the Caribbean in developing a feminist consciousness, political militancy and networks of communication (see also Yudelman 1989) on Caribbean women's organization. In the case of Red Thread members, this 'cross-pollination' was provided by the tragic aftermath of the Grenadian revolution (Lewis, 1987; Meeks, 1993), and specifically by the virtual and abrupt demise of the women's arm of the People's Revolutionary Government (PRG). These events, coupled with similar strands of experience in the Guyanese context, led to a series of questions being raised about forms of organizations around political parties and 'the national', and convinced them of the need for an independent organization for women that would set and define its own agenda and priorities. This was reinforced by experiences in the community; in one incident during the 1980s, working-class women had been detained after demonstrating against food shortages. WPA women offered help, but were emphatically told by the women, 'We don't want your (form of) politics, we want food and money' (Andaiye 1998).

Red Thread's founders were a small, middle-class, highly educated, ethnically diverse and vocal group of women who had the political commitment and long experience of organization necessary for its establishment. All were active members or supporters of the WPA who were increasingly questioning whether the party could focus specifically on the needs of women.[1] Although they had already engaged in various activities with women, such as protesting at food shortages, they disbanded the newly fledged Women's Section of the WPA and formed the autonomous organization Red Thread, thereby creating the space to raise gender issues without their being relegated to the back burner of party politics (Radzik 1992).

In the late 1980s, with the PNC's acceptance of SAPs, and especially in the early 1990s, with a return to power of the PPP and democratically held elections, an increased flow of external funds helped to foster the emergence of community action groups, NGOs and women's groups within the country, leading to a variety of positions that '…often clash with each other as women of different classes and races strive to achieve sometimes contradictory goals' (Paravisini-Gebert 1997: 7). In addition to government-based initiatives such as a National

Commission of Women and a National Policy Statement on Women, there has been a recent (1997) attempt to organize broad-based women's group, Women Across Difference (WAD). But a number of women's organizations are still not addressing issues of poverty and their implications for women. There is also a plethora of women's projects that have arisen as a result of the external funding flowing out of the Women's Decade. Established or funded by multilateral agencies, these projects target women for the distribution of aid but tend to be plagued with problems.[2] Most demands by long established women's political organizations have been aimed at equal rights such as equal opportunities in employment (usually through engagement, micro-enterprises), rather than questioning the basis of social inequalities or the ongoing organizations of women's place as being in the family. These developments have led to the reinforcing of the ideological public-private divide, with male-dominated political parties acquiescing to limited demands while making virtually 'no commitment to gender democracy in the home' (Charles and Hintjens 1998: 19).

Within this context, developments by the WRSM and the WPO have been uneven. The WPO have retained their organization intact and appear to remain committed to a party political mode of organizing women, thus restricting their contact with Afro-Guyanese women. They provide (largely unquestioning) support for the male leadership of the party, although their most prominent members now hold senior government positions and have made efforts to address questions of gender equity, pushing through legislation previously developed by women lawyers on domestic violence and the legislation of abortion, creating a Women's Leadership Institute, and mainstreaming gender into the National Development Plan.[3] Despite the progressive nature of such legislative changes, the lives of the vast majority of women remain unchanged, the high level of poverty, combined with little dissemination of information, militating against their ability to know of or access legal resources. Meanwhile, the WRSM, no longer in a position to control resources, have eschewed the patriarchal model of the women's auxiliary to form a semi-independent caucus. Symbolising this move, in 1994, they adopted the new name of the National Congress of Women (NCW).[4] However, neither the WPO nor the NCW has linked the social and economic disruptions in women's lives to the development policies and practices of the 1970s or the growth-oriented development models from the late 1980s onwards. In another important respect the NCW and the WPO are similar, in that both make little effort to work with women outside the racialised groups they have come to represent. Taking the racial polarization of the country as a given, their practices continue to perpetuate it.

Kabeer's (1994: 227) point that [p]ower relations [can] appear so secure and well-established that both subordinate and dominant groups are unaware of their oppressive implications or incapable of imagining alternative ways of 'being and doing' encapsulates the context in which these organizations work and from which Red Thread emerged. Red Thread's recognition of the way in which the economic crisis of the 1980s continues to impinge on women's lives allowed it to make a critical association between the household and the economy, the local and the global, and to critique discourses of WID and GAD for their legitimization of mainstream definitions of modernization, and development based on notions of economic rationality (Andaiye 1995; see also Udayagiri

1995). Central to their concept of development (and similar to the position of a number of Caribbean and Latin American women's organizations) is the understanding that, to many women, democracy in the home is more meaningful, and at any rate is inextricably related to democracy in the nation (see Charles and Hintjens 1998).

The Development Practices of Red Thread

Red Thread took the political vacuum of the early 1980s as its point of departure, denying the essentialist privileging of the party and its (male) intellectuals and crossing the classed and racialised ethnic divides to create gendered political subjects outside the logic of a fixed identity. Its task was one of establishing a viable cultural politics of difference, helping in small ways to reconstruct the fragmented civil society that had been turned against itself by the dictatorship of the PNC. Given the increasing level of poverty throughout the 1980s, the initial needs Red Thread identified were economic ones. Adopting what appeared to be traditional WID initiatives and focusing on income generation, it organized short-term projects in four communities, both Afro-Guyanese and Indo-Guyanese (Peacocke 1995). Red Thread chose embroidery, a skill that many women possessed even if only in a rudimentary form, as an organizing tool. The following extract from one of its founding members, Bonita Harris (1995: 38), outlines the early ethos of the group.

> The organization's name, chosen at a time when the economic stringencies of the country left the essential threads for our [embroidery] work in short supply (especially the vital colour, red), was consciously chosen, because we realized

that while there would come a time when embroidery would no longer be our main activity, our name should always remind us of where we started.

But its work went far beyond WID objectives of establishing projects to generate income.

> As women, we understood that the absence of democracy at the household level was a more pressing matter for the majority of women than the absence of democracy in national politics....Our decision was therefore to...begin the process of getting them to understand the value of their labour; to facilitate contact, work and exchange with women in other communities; to develop modes of communication and education which would allow women without formal education to learn, as well as to teach others; and to facilitate working and learning experiences which were not subservient. (Harris 1995: 38–9)

In its efforts to democratize development practices, Red Thread was also creating a new discourse, one in which politicizing cultural practices, reclaiming forms of representation and bringing them within its own control, was critical.

> It was something new for rural women, embroidery being traditionally, the skill of the genteel urban, middle-class ladies, not the rural poor, in Guyana. The lilacs, the forget-me-nots, ladies with parasols and ringlets, the pussy-cats and puppy-dogs of the *Women and Home* magazine patterns would be finally dislodged; local flora and fauna, Indian and Amerindian, Hindu and Muslim images would provide the basis and ideas for new designs. Embroidery could be a cultural and educational tool.... Embroidery was not just about 'income generation'; it was even

more, or at least equally, about consciousness raising and about valuing women's work. (Harris, quoted in Peacocke 1995: 10)

Within a few years, Red Thread had established embroidery groups in a number of communities, with a small retail outlet in Georgetown for its sales. Following the initial success of the embroidery groups, it proceeded to diversify its income-generating projects. Recognising the short supply and exorbitantly high prices of school exercise books it embarked on a project to produce these itself,[5] moving on to community-based production and sale of low-cost primary education textbooks, which led to the acquisition, in 1990, of a printing press. Throughout the 1990s the press and a desktop publishing house have provided the bulk of Red Thread's income; while operating on a commercial basis they also publish educational and cultural material on a non-profit basis. Working through an internationally funded micro-credit scheme, Red Thread has also been involved in providing credit to women who wish to establish their own businesses, as well as (since 1991) running a laundry in Linden. Although all these projects (bar the laundry) have been successful in generating (various amounts of) income, Red Thread measures its degree of success not in terms of the amount of income generated but in the women participants' commitment to taking over and running these projects themselves (Karen de Souza 1996).

In the early 1990s, Red Thread began to focus less on income generation than on efforts to change social consciousness through community education. While still engaged in embroidery, a Group Building Team was formed, which included an appointed woman from each of the communities in which Red Thread was working. Meetings of the team focused on skill development in chairing meetings, sorting out methods for organizing their work and breaking down barriers between women from the different communities (D. Radzik 1992). These meetings led to the recognition of the need to take women out of their racially segregated communities, and an Education Team was formed which brought together, on an almost daily basis, Indo-Guyanese and Afro-Guyanese women from communities outside Georgetown.

The team has received in-house training in popular education methods, as well as training from the Jamaican Sistren Theatre Collective. It has conducted hundreds of community workshops based on issues such as women's work, child abuse, family survival, community development, women's legal rights, sexual harassment, literacy, and violence against women. It has also organized workshops promoting leadership formation and skill transfer. It has been contracted to do similar work for multilateral agencies, as well as being employed to conduct the community education components of water-delivery and construction projects in the interior. Its latest project focused on the production of a series of short television videos on child abuse. The most recent addition to Red Thread in the field of education is the Research Team. Started in 1993, the team's aim was to equip women with the skills necessary to participate in conducting the research reported in this book.[6] It was after this experience that the women decided to form a permanent research team; it remains the only grass-roots women's group in the country to conduct research.

Through their work in the Education Team, members came to speak out about needs they were initially reluctant to voice. As a consequence, Red Thread started a

Health Team in 1991 and after an initial focus on women's health expanded into community health issues.[7] Domestic violence was another issue with which all of the women were familiar, but which was not initially raised. As in other Caribbean and Latin American countries, and in other world regions in the early 1990s, domestic violence emerged as probably the most important item on the agenda of many women's organizations (Moser with Peake 1996; Nelson 1996). Recognising the need to challenge the culture of silence around women's bodies, and along with a group of concerned women, Red Thread members have participated in the recently established Help and Shelter, a counselling service for battered women, transforming an issue primarily defined as private into one having a public and political status. In 1993 it produced a popular radio series on domestic violence, from which it developed the script for a play called 'Everybody's Business'. It secured funding to perform the play in various communities along the coast and in 1996 it produced a sequel for another radio series. One result has been a flood of enquiries from parents and individual women whom it has helped to file petitions in court over sexual harassment, rape and domestic violence. It has also been at the forefront of advocating, designing and producing for popular dissemination legislative information pertaining to the laws of Guyana and women's legal rights, most recently in relation to the Domestic Violence Act.

Linda Peake, and D. Alissa Trotz.

* WPO – Women's Progressive Organization
* WPA – Working People's Alliance
* WRSM – Women's Revolutionary Socialist Movement

Notes

1. They are Andaiye, Jocelyn Dow, Bonita Harris, Vanda Radzik, Danuta Radzik, Karen de Souza and Dianne Matthews. All but the last are still resident in Guyana and active to varying degrees in Red Thread. Within the context of a society in which women political organizations are attached to political parties, it has been extremely difficult for other groups not to perceive Red Thread as a WPA-based organization, despite the fact that they draw their membership from women who support the PPP and PNC as well as the WPA.

2. See Sen and Grown (1987: 91) for a general discussion of such types of organizations. In Guyana, Bonita Harris's (1995) report for CIDA on women's groups supported by the Canada Fund provides a good overview of such projects. The survey was of 14 women's groups, in at least 12 of which the initiative had come from a local man, or men, or from a parent organization although women carried out the day-to-day work of the projects. The women participants listed what they considered to be the most important issues facing them in their villages: battering of women, withdrawal and shyness, lack of money, getting parents to send their children to classes, a drop in moral standards, discrimination, and the inability to participate in community activity. These responses indicate that women do have a sense of what is important in their daily lives, yet not one of the groups' projects concerned itself with

    '… leadership training, consciousness raising, child and adolescent development, female poverty, domestic violence, rape, suicide, incest or sex education, alcohol and other drug abuse, economic education or information on the status of women in other countries' (1995: 9).

    All addressed only small-scale income-generating projects in cooking (but not nutrition), sewing, embroidery, shorthand and typing, cake decoration and crochet, English and math classes. The projects were riddled with a variety of problems. The participants were often referred to as 'he children' by the volunteer teachers, reinforcing the relations of deference and obedience that organize both male-female and child-adult relationships. Four of the organizations cited political interference with their projects. It was not documented how many women had gained employment from participating in these projects, though all training provided would have led to employment in low-paid jobs. Most problematically, all the projects relied on voluntary female labour for organization and teaching. Not only did this sustain the notion of women's work as something they did in their spare time, but it also led to only a short period of time every week being devoted to project activities. Sustainability was obviously an issue. Although these projects have not led to any difference in women's position in their communities they were making possible, albeit unintentionally, the development of Indo-Guyanese women leaders by putting them in a position to acquire the organizational and intellectual tools necessary to exercise leadership in their own affairs. But, usually uncoordinated and under-financed, peripheral to planning programmes, focusing only on traditional skills, and with little capacity to expand or promote replicability, these projects focus on what can be counted, and have only a rhetoric of participatory development. Most importantly, they tend to have no vision, having no history of organization outside of the project being implemented.

3. These prominent members are Janet Jagan, widow of Cheddi Jagan, and the current President; the Minister of Youth and Culture, Gail Teixera; and Indra Chandrapaul, Minister of Women's Affairs in the Ministry of Housing.

4. In an attempt to reassess their relationship to the PNC they no longer seek approval from the party for their projects (although these are now largely restricted to helping groups of women prepare funding requests, and organizing occasional symposia on leadership skills) and their members are not automatically expected to campaign at election times. They are also willing to work with groups that do not support the PNC, although technically the PNC still speaks for them (Johnson 1996).

5. Red Thread successfully produced 37,000 exercise books before the project was taken out of its hands, after the Ministry of Education applied to CIDA for a grant to produce exercise books, and the project was transferred to them, including funds to produce 10 million books (Peacocke 1995).

6. Initially the women spent three weeks learning about research methodologies, social survey design, questionnaire construction and interviewing techniques. In the following ten-week period they successfully completed the survey as well as in-depth interviews which they then transcribed. Since then, they have received five more training sessions on research methodologies, for which they secured funding from Linda Peake and the Canadian High Commission in Guyana. They have also been employed on five separate projects as survey interviewers for independent researchers, the University of Guyana, Region Four Democratic Council Youth Section, a Caribbean-wide research project on sex workers, and a national survey on domestic violence.

7. The Health Team has received training from Dr. Nesha Haniff, a non-resident Red Thread member.

CRITICAL THINKING AND WRITING

1. Why do you think the writers chose to write this piece? Provide support for your answer.
2. List some of the ways in which Red Thread transformed the lives of women in Guyana.
3. What is the dominant tone in the passage? Support your answer with evidence.
4. How are the rhetorical modes that are utilized here (register, syntax, diction, etc.) suited to the context?
5. How do the writers establish credibility?
6. What type of reader do you think would be interested in this passage? Provide evidence to support your answer.

WRITING ACROSS THE CURRICULUM ACTIVITY

7. Using the information provided in the passage, write a paragraph on any aspect of Red Thread which you found particularly interesting. Before writing, identify
   a) your rhetorical context : your audience, purpose, persona;
   b) the organizing principle which you will utilize.

GROUP ACTIVITY

8. In this passage, the writers make extensive use of authoritative sources. Notice how they integrate those sources with the points they are making. Choose a paragraph from one of your research essays and examine some of the ways in which you have integrated your sources.

MUSIC &
CULTURE

CHAPTER 8

━━━ ◈ ━━━

ALL HAIL, NUTMEG

Five hundred years ago nutmeg was coveted for its potent medicinal and reportedly magical properties. People used it for protection against various diseases and afflictions — from arthritis to boils to broken bones to plagues. Young men used the oil to improve virility; and tucking a nutmeg under the left armpit before attending a social event was thought to attract admirers. Others only knew of its traditional use as a spice, sprinkled on dishes to add flavour. Nonetheless, the demand for nutmeg was great and the nut became the source of the famous 'spice wars' in the late sixteenth century when the English, Dutch and Portuguese all sent out expeditions to the Far East to find the source of this elusive fruit.

Their journeys brought them to a set of tiny islands called The Bandas – to Run, the smallest and least accessible island, but the richest, thickly forested with nutmeg trees. They all came with the goal being to trade, but that quickly changed to conquest and the victorious Dutch conquerors jealously guarded their monopoly of nutmeg for years. Despite this, nutmeg was quietly brought to the West Indies in the early 1800's and around 1840, the first seeds were planted in estate gardens in the Caribbean island of Grenada where they subsequently thrived.

Nutmeg is now considered the essence of Grenada. When you visit, it is hard to miss — literally. There are actual forests of the fragrant trees and you can find at least one tree in every backyard. The bright green, yellow and red-brown of the fruit are the colours of the national flag and the picture of the fruit in the left top hand corner leaves no doubt that in the 'Isle of Spice,' nutmeg is king.

As the leading agricultural export of Grenada, nutmeg is also the island's second largest foreign exchange earner, after tourism. Grenada is, in fact, the second leading world producer of nutmeg behind Indonesia, and the island's 344 square metres of land produces a third of the world's supply. As is to be expected, the range of nutmeg products in Grenada is considerable and Grenadian cuisine is a true representation of the versatility of nutmeg.

From jams and ice-cream to cakes and sauces, the entire fruit is utilized in the food manufacturing industry. The fruit actually has three parts that are used — a yellow/brown mottled fleshy fruit; the mace — a net-like, reddish-brown covering over a brittle brown shell holding the seed; and the nutmeg seed itself. The fleshy fruit, which is called the pod by Grenadians, used to be discarded in the processing of the nut, but it is now used to produce jams, syrups and candy. Some persons also preserve the unripe fruit in sugar, then dry and salt it to make condiments and jellies. Others prefer to use the ripe fruit because it is sweeter. Local manufacturer, De La Grenade Industries, uses the ripe fruit in the production of their Morne Délice nutmeg jam, jelly and pancake syrup as well as their unique La Grenade Liqueur.

Although not used as often as the nutmeg in the kitchen, the outer covering, the mace is nevertheless a popular spice, and is one of the main ingredients in ketchup. The flavour of the mace is similar to the nutmeg, but the fragrance is softer and the flavour not as overriding. And so in the Grenadian home a small amount often lends the appropriate flavour to a tropical fruit punch.

Although some Grenadians have vacillated through the years over the desirability of mace versus nutmeg, the nutmeg flavour is considered well-matched to certain foods. They use it in meals from start to finish; the whole seed is grated in small amounts and either added just before cooking or after the meal is prepared. It is infused into many dishes including vegetables, meats, cheese and baked products. The exotic flavour is even used to manufacture a nutmeg ice- cream, a product unique to Sugar and Spice, a small family-owned Grenadian company. Started in 1987, the company was the first to offer hard, multi-flavoured ice-cream and now produces 270 gallons of traditional and local fruit-flavoured ice-cream per day, supplying restaurants, ice-cream parlours and shops around the island.

Besides using it extensively as a culinary product, Grenadians also process nutmeg and its oils to make body-care products, pain relievers and even craft items. Local manufacturer, Arawak Islands, features nutmeg in its body-care product line including soaps,

body oils and candles in coconut shells. Meanwhile, other manufacturers bottle the nutmeg oil as an ingredient in antiseptic preparations, pain relievers, chest rubs and syrups (like, for instance, Vick's Cough Syrup). Whether as a therapeutic, medicinal or culinary applicant, Grenadians have capitalised on the many characteristics of nutmeg and their success in the commercial production of nutmeg is admirable. Even after Hurricane Ivan last September, which wiped out ninety per cent of its crop, the authorities report that the island's present stock can keep Grenada on the map as world suppliers of nutmeg for the next three years.

In Grenada, it goes without saying that nutmeg is truly more than just a spice.

Wendy-Ann Brissett

CRITICAL THINKING AND WRITING

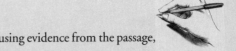

1. Identify the dominant discourse mode and state, using evidence from the passage, the writer's main purpose.
2. For whom is the text intended? Explain your answer.
   a) high school students
   b) the general public
   c) educated persons
   d) botanists
3. In what context would you expect to find this article? Justify your response
   a) a text book
   b) a journal
   c) a magazine
   d) a novel
4. Comment on the sentence structure used in this passage. Explain how the sentence structure assists the reader in identifying the audience.
5. How does the writer organise this article?
6. Identify the figure of speech in the statement 'Nutmeg is now considered the essence of Grenada.'
7. Comment on the writer's use of transitions in this article.
8. Identify the organising principle used in the paragraph beginning 'Although not used as often as the nutmeg…' (paragraph 6).
9. Comment on the writer's use of **diction,** and show how this creates the **tone** of the text and aids in communicating meaning.
10. Suggest a reason for the writer's choice of title.

WRITING ACROSS THE CURRICULUM ACTIVITIES

11. The nutmeg is an important product in Grenada and helps to define the island. Choose a crop or food item that is important to your country's culture or economic development and explain (to a non-Caribbean audience) its significance.
12. The writer makes reference to the damage done by Hurricane Ivan. Choose one developmental strategy and write a paragraph in which you explain how your country's agricultural sector has been affected by any natural disaster.

CHAPTER 9

IN CELEBRATION OF THE PATTY

There is a story going around somewhere that the Jamaican patty owes its origins to the Cornish pasty, a kind of meat and vegetable pie, which would've been introduced to the island by English settlers or travellers way back in the time when Britannia ruled the waves and cane fields. Whatever the origin, all I know is that a Jamaican patty is ours, a distinctive feature of our culinary heritage, often imitated but never duplicated.

I believe that we erred as a nation when we did not include the patty (along with ackee and saltfish, rice and peas, and jerk) on our national Coat of Arms. After all, the Arawaks and the pineapple no longer run tings, and as to the crocodile, whenever we see him (usually in a canal at Portmore) we certainly don't invite him to dinner. The patty would be far more reassuring, trust me.

For better, but never worse, it has become a national symbol, a touchstone, especially for Jamaicans exiled, for whatever reason, on distant shores. Even those who have shaken the dust off their feet from our Island of Challenges are never happy until they have located the nearest patty shop in their new homeland. But no matter what patty shops are abroad, savvy travellers will return from a visit to the Rock with a couple dozen patties destined for the microwave.

What, then, is the secret of the patty? What is the power which it exerts over us? Some people take it very seriously indeed. A gentleman of unabashed Victorian upbringing was heard denouncing an upstart, a 'hurry come up' who was 'exhibiting himself' as a man of substance in a certain corner of Foreign. He also happened to be the proprietor of a baking establishment. Faced with one of the man's displays of self-importance, our Jamaican gentleman gave him short shrift. 'He should be tried for treason. The man makes the worst patties in the world.'

Real men might not eat quiche but any red-blooded Jamaican man recognizes the virtue of a hot patty alongside a cold Red Stripe. Some people feel impelled to add the adjective 'beef.' This is quite unnecessary. With a real patty, you shouldn't have to ask 'Where's the beef?' I know that in an age of beta-carotene and free radicals, red meat is high on the list of undesirables, but patties filled with substances other than beef should not lay claim to the name.

If you insist, you may partake of envelopes of pastry filled with red peas, split peas, chick peas or some other form of legumes ... calaloo, cabbage or other vegetable matter. While these may be nutritionally correct they are not patties. Pastries yes, but patties, no. And what of the bona fides of chicken and lobster patties? These are not to be admitted into the inner circle as legitimate members of the patty family either.

Okay, okay, but please understand that they're so treated only because their contents have some weight, some substance. But let's get down to the meat of the matter…the qualities of a real patty.

ONE — The crust must not weigh heavily upon the digestive system. Light and flaky are attributes to be encouraged.

TWO — In the contents, the gravamen, the real beef, must reflect the virtues of a seasoning hand, an understanding that skellion and thyme, onion and good country pepper, in appropriate quantities, enhance the flavour of ground beef.

THREE — The temperature: a real patty is served hot, not lukewarm, certainly not cold. The steam must rise from the very core of its being when teeth make the breakthrough from crust to filling. It is not only hot by name, but hot by nature. A cold patty is an insult to sense and sensibilities. Cocktail patties tend to fall into this category. They're often served anything but hot.

FOUR — How to eat a patty.

I know this girl who always splits the patty open at the seam, exposing the rich, steaming, meaty filling. She knows the precise moment when the meat is cool enough (not cold) to close up the crust and enjoy. She defends this method by reminding us that there is no greater pain than having the roof of one's mouth seared by a really hot patty. Others find their enjoyment in modest-sized bites, blowing in between each one, alternating with sips of some appropriately cold brew.

It has come to my attention that some reckless persons have taken to 'invading' the patty by opening the crust and inserting slices of cheese, bacon or some other 'foreign substance' upon the beef. It makes for 'good eating', or so they say. I have no urge to prove them right, although I will admit to the knowledge that patties can claim legitimate relationships with other edibles.

There was, for instance, the patty and cruss of another era. 'Cruss' (or crust, if you must) was a crisp fold of pastry shaped to nestle the patty in its warm embrace, sold from a 'patty pan' a two-tiered tin box equipped with hot coals to heat the precious contents. There is also that old standby, patty and coco bread, still known today (thank heaven). For my money though, a good patty should stand on its own merits. No need 'to gild the anthurium,' as a philosopher friend of mine would say.

One final word of advice….Whatever you do, never be seen eating a patty with a knife and fork … not even at a black tie affair. (You would be so lucky!).

Barbara Gloudon

CRITICAL THINKING AND WRITING

1. Explain the context in which you would expect to find this article.
2. Identify the figurative devices used in the following excerpts:
   a) 'But let's get down to the meat of the matter';
   b) 'For better, but never worse, it has become … a touchstone, especially for Jamaicans exiled, for whatever reason, on distant shores';
   c) '"Cruss" … was a crisp fold of pastry shaped to nestle the patty in its warm embrace'.
3. In this article, Gloudon graphically and humorously conveys her great love for the Jamaican patty. Examine the features of the article that help to convey her attitude.
4. Examine the use of colloquialisms and state how these are suited to the audience and the context.
5. Identify examples of
   a) denotative diction;
   b) connotative diction.

WRITING ACROSS THE CURRICULUM ACTIVITIES

6. Gloudon has obviously had a pleasant experience with the Jamaican patty. Write a poem or a song in which you reflect on your own sentiments toward the 'patty'.
7. Choose one paragraph from the article and re-write it to reflect a different tone. State the tone that you are attempting to create.

CHAPTER 10

IN SEARCH OF
THE PERFECT PATTY

Its marvellous filling typically consists of cubes of meat, diced white potatoes (called 'Irish', or 'Irish potatoes' in Jamaican marketplaces), onions, and sometimes turnips, all with suitable seasonings. But no one is really sure about the name anymore than anyone is really quite certain about just what goes into an authentic Jamaican patty.

The pastry crust must, for the connoisseur, be flaky and lightly browned, either with yellow food colouring or, if you are a purist, with a dash of the liquid made by steeping some of the scarlet seeds of the annatto, an elegant small bushy tree with pretty big pink blossoms and prickly pods which turn red when mature. The filling for the customary patty contains finely-minced beef, perhaps with a chunk of fully-ground lean pork for added flavour. Some onions or escallions are sometimes put into the mix, along with a bit of filler, in the form of leftover bread.

Then comes the vital addition of the 'seasonings', which usually include a grand series of often-secret spices, but more publicly-acknowledged garlic, salt, ground black pepper, Jamaican pimento (allspice) and, perhaps, sweet green peppers. The final addition during the mixing and blending of the filling for the Jamaican patty is a lesser, or greater, involvement with one of the hottest of all volcanic bush capsicum peppers in the world, of which there are many varieties used in authentic Jamaican cuisine.

The Scotch Bonnet comes in several colours, from waxy yellow to green or splendid scarlet. Country pepper can be any one of a formidable series of capsicums; and some people opt for the slender little bird pepper, the green ones usually being hotter than the vivid Christmas-red ripe ones, these so fiery that care must be taken to remove all of their seeds and inner ribs with care, for in preparation, some people even get a rash on their fingers through absorption of the juices. But an addition of these hot peppers, usually prepared and minced after seeding and de-veining, is essential for culinary success.

The filling, generally prepared by professional 'patty-makers' in our best known establishments throughout the island, is put into the pastry circles, then folded over, and the edges crimped with a moist fork. These are then baked 'just until done', as one of the Kingston experts in this delicacy informed me. He would never use such a modern culinary apparatus as an oven timer, for he has been baking and making his sought-after patties for more than twenty-five years. He knows precisely what should go into both the pastry and the 'special filling'; and he knows exactly how hot this big oven should be, by testing the heat with his fingers before the big trays of patties are put in. And, of course, he knows just when to remove the baking trays, after the filling has settled a bit and when they can safely be taken out to be kept hot in the patty warmer, a glass-fronted case which is kept in many Jamaican shops and bakeries.

Alex D. Hawkes

1. Explain, using evidence from the passage,
   a) what you consider to be the writer's main purpose;
   b) the context in which you would expect to find this article.
2. What do you think Hawkes hopes to achieve by beginning his article in the way that he does?
3. Identify the dominant organizing principle and evaluate its effectiveness.
4. In spite of the similarity in the topic of Gloudon's and Hawkes's articles, the two articles are very different. Compare and contrast them in terms of the tone, purpose, register, language, and organisational structure.
5. To what extent does the title prepare you for the content of this article?
6. How does Hawkes's use of adjectives contribute to the overall effect of the passage?

COLLABORATIVE ACTIVITIES

7. Small group discussion: Identify popular foods that are indigenous to various West Indian countries (for example, roti in Trinidad). Explore the importance of each to the culture of the particular country.
8. Using process analysis as a developmental strategy, explain to someone how you would prepare a dish of your choice.

CHAPTER 11

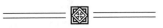

AFRICAN FEASTS IN TRINIDAD

This essay surveys African festive occasions which are known to have been celebrated in Trinidad. Some have fallen into disuse since about the 1930s, but a few are still observed. These descriptions, written in 1969, are not the author's eye-witness reports, but derive from the attestations of persons who participated in these ceremonies.

Yearly Religious Feasts

Saraka — This is derived from the Hausa **sadaka**, referring to a ceremony in which alms are given to the needy. The ceremony was, and still is, observed by Hausa and Yoruba descendants and others who imitate their practice. The **saraka** is often in response to a dream in which a dead ancestor indicates the time has come for the performance of these yearly rites. It is felt that failure to carry out this yearly obligation results in misfortune, and it is performed out of a religious conviction that sacrifice — that is, the shedding of blood and charity — will ensure prosperity for the coming year. The **saraka** is an act of ancestor reverence, and often, neglected ancestors — those whose descendants have failed to offer **saraka** — will visit a series of misfortunes upon the living offenders, or will appear in a dream to chide the descendants. **Saraka** are also given as thanksgiving ceremonies after recovery from illness or after job promotion.

A lady of central Trinidad, born in the 1890s, described her Hausa father's **saraka** in the following way: It was a daytime affair. At sunrise, her father said prayers and sacrificed an animal. Before offering the animal, he dug a hole in the ground into which blood was allowed to run. The hole was afterwards covered over. Before a fowl was sacrificed, he fed it a piece of dirt, a corn grain and a little water. The fowl's neck was then plucked and afterwards cut, all the while prayers being said. In the case of a goat, prayers were offered before the goat's neck was severed in one blow. Later, food was distributed to the children present first.[1]

Another informant, this time in south Trinidad, in a brief reference to her Hausa father's **saraka,** mentioned that he *bisimilah* [2] (blessed) the food before it was distributed. Food consisted of goat, sheep and fowl meat. Salt was not used in the cooking. The first course was always a glass of sweetened milk and an **akara** — flour and water made into balls and fried. Apart from this, there were rice meals: white rice was soaked overnight. Half of this was pounded, water mixed into it, and sweetened with milk and sugar. This was called **gumba.** The other half was used to make **waina**. It was made by mixing the soaked rice with white sugar and keeping the mixture damp. It was then served on top of the **akara.**

Yoruba **saraka** were held in Tunapuna, among other places, up to the first two decades of the century. Some say that the **saraka** gave away to the greater popularity of **shango** feasts, which came in from Grenada.[3] One ceremony in the **saraka** was the sprinkling of plain and 'sweet' water[4] and rum by the leader of a family procession which went three times around the house. This, and the plate of unsalted food each member of the procession carried, represented offerings to the ancestral spirits. These plates were later placed in special order (probably of seniority of the ancestors) on a table. The pipe and tobacco, or any item much identified with a particular ancestor, were also carried in the procession.

One informant remembered that musical accompaniment to dances on the occasion was provided by three drums, but did not name them. Food consisted of goat meat, sweetbread,[5] chilibibi,[6] ground black-eyed peas *(vigna sinensis)* unsalted and fried in balls to make **akara**, black-eyed peas boiled soft with oil and pepper, cornmeal and cassava **kuku**,[7] breadfruit and banana **fufu**.[8] Drink included sorrel *(hibiscus sabdariffa)* and ginger beer.

Shango — This is a religious ceremony involving animal sacrifice, the anti-clockwise circling of dancers, the singing of Yoruba chants to deities, and the possession of some of the dancers by these deities or 'powers' or 'saints'.[9] The Yoruba generic name for 'deities' is **orisha**, a term also used by **shango** members. Indeed, **orisha** has recently been extended to refer to the religion itself. On the other hand, the word **ebo** (sacrifice) appears to have been used at one time by some

Yoruba descendants to designate **orisha** ritual. As for the term **Shango,** this derives from the name of one of the pantheon of Yoruba deities. In situations of exile — in Sierra Leone and the New World — the name **shango** came to epitomize **orisha** worship because Shango was originally a king of the Oyo people. The Oyo were prominently represented among the enslaved Yoruba, and the cult of **shango** was an institutionalized state religion throughout the Empire. Thus, the incorporation of the cults of various deities into a single ritual is a New World peculiarity. In original Yoruba practice, separate **ebo** for individual deities would be held at varying times, in varying shrines, and by differing priests.

Shango feasts usually begin around 8 p.m. and go on till well into dawn. Devotees either spend the days at the shango tent[10] or 'palais' or go home on mornings to return in the night. The daytime is devoted to the preparation of food.

On the first morning of the **ebo**, the **amungwo**[11] (priest) faces east, prays and makes an offering of food. An animal sacrifice is also given. The animal head is placed on the **perogun**[12] (earth mound) near the entrance to the yard where flags on poles are flown and a sword or cutlass is stuck into the ground. Here water jars are kept and candles burnt.

Men and women devotees wear white clothes, though colored cummerbunds in the case of the men and copious colored headties for the women are distinguishing symbols of the **orisha** which generally manifest on the devotees during possession. The gods are said to 'ride' the devotee possessed. He dances to steps characteristic of the deity and may obtain the gift of prophecy at this time. Music is provided by three drums and by an accompanying **shac-shac** at times. The drums are called the mother drum, the kongo[13] and the umele.[14]

Over time, many **shango** ceremonies have come to assimilate aspects of Christian liturgy: Catholic rosary recitation at the start, followed by Protestant hymns in long meter,[15] but to drum accompaniment. The Yoruba chants and dance-movements, however, occupy the major portion of the services, including communal feasting. In recent decades, this syncretic form of African/Christian worship has come to be called 'Shango Baptist.' In such services, food is put on a table centrally placed in the ceremonial area and is served at various intervals during the night, the children before adults.

Vudunu — This is a Rada[16] ceremony held around September each year in Belmont, where a family descended from a late nineteenth century Dahomean immigrant still lives. The feast appears to resemble **shango** in several respects, as it involves possession and extends over a number of days.[17] Some of the deities, or **vodun**, are the same as those invoked in the Haitian **vodun** and correspond with several in the Shango, for the historical reason that the Aja-Fon people of Dahomey trace their origins to Ife, the spiritual home of the Yoruba. Not only do the Yoruba and Aja-Fon share old cultural links, but Dahomey was at one time a tributary state of the Yoruba empire.

Vudunu are held in the day, and sacrifices of morocoys, goats and fowl are made. Sheep are taboo. Cocks are killed in a different spot from hens. Women at these ceremonies dress in white with plain headties. I do not know the men's wear.

When there used to be distinct Yoruba communities, the Rada and Yoruba would give mutual invitations to their feasts.

Secular Feasts

This heading is a trifle misleading, in that there appears to be a religious element present in nearly all the following feasts, even though one is justified in referring to them as secular either because of the predominance of 'pleasure songs'[18] in some of them, or because they do not involve animal sacrifice.

Birth — It appears that the Yoruba held a consultation at the birth of an infant to ascertain through divination the spiritual agent responsible for sponsoring the child's appearance in the world. This deity was hence the child's patron. Unfortunately, it was also possible for **were**,[19] spirits, to sponsor a child. As a result, it was enjoined that sexual intercourse should not be approached in drunkenness or in dissension. A whole night of drumming accompanied a child's Christian christening ceremony.

Initiation — Two women in south Trinidad spoke of Yoruba feasts held for girls around fourteen and fifteen. At this, elders discussed the future of the young ladies, recommending that they should not marry outside the Yoruba ethnic group. They were anointed with oil and sometimes given facial markings and Yoruba names.

Marriage — The Yoruba wedding in central Trinidad was characterized by a long procession from the church to the wedding house led by a drummer. **Shac-shac**-shaking women brought up the rear, their busts stuffed to exaggeration as fertility symbols. The songs they sang were rich with sexual references. The procession comprised both witnesses to the church marriage and those who assembled at the churchyard or along the way after hearing the gunshot that signalled the end of the church ceremony. The Congos in south Trinidad held two-day wedding feasts during which drums and shac-shacs made music.

Often a drumming competition was entered into between drummers employed by the girl's family and those supporting the groom.[20]

African Dances — The following is a description of the Yoruba dances held earlier in this century at Tunapuna. Such dances are still held by Yoruba and Congo descendants in some rural areas of the island.

Some years ago in Tunapuna various sections of the Yoruba community threw an African dance, or 'bele'[21] once a year. One of the main annual dances was that put on by the Societies of St. Peter and St. John, probably Church-sponsored, as most of these Yoruba seem to have been Catholics. These societies celebrated their annual anniversaries by attending Mass and then inviting in the priest to bless the food for the feast. The occasion continued with drumming and dancing.

Belmont Yoruba nine miles away were invited and so were those from St. Joseph, two and a half miles distant. As a matter of fact, prior to the start of the dance, the societies would go in procession back to Tunapuna after having collected their St. Joseph guests. A gunshot set off within earshot of St. Joseph would notify the people there of the procession's impending arrival.

Dancing took place in a bamboo-framed tent roofed by carat[22] leaves. There was also a married ladies' tent from which undesirable females were excluded for immoral behavior such as 'dealing'[23] or marital infidelity. Judgement was based upon divination using a calabash. By this means the diviner would be able to describe the dress worn by the wrong-doer. At some of the dances (I do not know if the Society dances are to be included here) a fowl was sacrificed at the start of the feast. If it stood up and 'danced' headless, it was interpreted as a sign of victory and success for the proceedings.

Female celebrants dressed in *douilette*[24] and carried large handkerchiefs. For the Society dances people wore rich clothes. The ladies regaled themselves with jewelry and bought *damasin*[25] kalande (headties) for five shillings each. Men carried red handkerchiefs. It was with these handkerchiefs and fula and even towels that the best dancers were garlanded at the neck. At times they were presented with a bouquet. Music was provided by drums, as many as six, among them, said one informant, the **akaramun**, the **jakaron** and the **jigoron**. Sometimes three calabashes were used for percussion, two of which were decorated outside with string and shells or beads and passed from one person to another as they swayed to the rhythm. The third calabash was plain.

Both hosts and guests contributed foodstuff for the feast, and big pots of food were prepared with as many as eleven women sometimes stirring one pot with long sticks. There was **akasan** — fermented corn ground several times and strained, the pap being then put into a leaf and steamed.[26] Chataigne (*artocarpus atilis*) was made into a **kuku**. The slimy **oyoyo** (*corchorus olitorius*) leaf was used to make kalalu.[27] Musala bean[28] was steamed in a leaf with bits of seasoned pre-cooked meat. Corn was half-boiled then fried. **Bene** (*sesamum orientale*) was made into balls and sugar-cake. Rice, black-eyed peas, potato, cassava and farine (cassava grated and dried into a flour) also formed part of the menu. A lot of olive oil was used in the preparations. Some of the food was cooked with salt, but the '**jumbi** food' was unsalted. This was food for the ancestral spirits and consisted of a small part of whatever item was prepared for general use. It was put on a leaf and laid out on a table where no one could interfere with it. A lighted candle was also placed on that table.

Next day, this food was shared among all members of the host family. Sometimes the offering table was the same that constituted a household altar, on which normally was kept a small black thunderstone over which olive oil was regularly poured. Drink was supplied by tea, local coffee and cocoa, and these were taken with biscuit or bread.[29]

This religious element suggests that, on some occasions at least, the **bele** functioned as a syncretic development of the **saraka**.

The Rada held similar dances. The main difference upon which Yoruba descendants remark is that the Rada beat steel[30] and shook the **shekbe** [31] or boli, a large netted calabash. Sometimes they used a number of **shekbe** alone as accompaniment for their singing. But at times the Yoruba, and perhaps the Rada too, used three drums — a cutter[32] and two smaller drums. The **kongo** started off dictating the rhythm, the umele took up a counter rhythm. To beat the smallest drum was to **bule**, to play the middle-sized drum was to **fula**, while to beat the largest was to 'cut.' 'Cutter' was therefore another name for the **bembem**.[33]

Congos also speak of their dances, some taking place around a fire, but information about the form these occasions took is lacking, though interpretations of their songs indicate that some carry a satiric flavor. The **shac-shac** and drums accompanied these usually very spirited melodies. Three drums were used, one of which was called a 'keg.' The 'king' or 'queen' of each dance, that is, the best dancer, was crowned with hats. Rum, pork, and chicken cooked with salt were among the items served as refreshment.

Funerals and Wakes — Rada wake-keepers are said to drum on an inverted wash-tub, whereas Congos are noted for 'hauling kumbi' for wake-song accompaniment. The kumbi is a stick, one end of which is scraped heavily and repeatedly along the ground or floor to create a mournful friction rhythmically accompanying the song. One report spoke of the funeral rites for a Congo descendant who had been a champion drummer in a south Trinidad village, having been known to drum at Carnival time stick-fights till his fingertips bled. When he died, it had therefore been necessary to hold a drumming ceremony to drum his spirit out of his house, though this researcher is uncertain whether it was at the burial or the wake.

The Yoruba offered a sacrifice on the burial night, but no drums were beaten, either then or at the post-funerary feast nine nights later. Burial services were held in Christian churches.

Today's Scenario

These random descriptions of African feasts will, I hope, indicate something of the vigour and richness of one aspect of the culture of Trinidad in the latter half of the nineteenth century and up to the first quarter of the present one. This is not to say that all these feasts have been discontinued. African dances were held sporadically in the 1960s in some parts of south Trinidad and in Valencia, drumming was still done at some rural weddings. **Vudunu** and **shango** worship still persist. **Shango** has in fact experienced a revival, following on the 1970 Black Power impact on the consciousness of Trinidadians, and it is now attracting young people not previously associated with these rites. Among these are members of the academic and artistic communities. Furthermore, its practitioners now include not only persons of African descent, but several of Spanish and Indian origin.

Since the 1970s, too, efforts to regain procedural orthodoxy have resulted in significant reverses in the process of the liturgical approximation of **shango** to Christian orders of service: some groups have eliminated Christian elements in the liturgy and have introduced instead formal Yoruba prayers. Additionally, the term **orisha** is now applied to the religion as a replacement for the term **shango**, partly, no doubt, to distance the religion from its erstwhile negative associations, and partly to reconnect consciously with Africa — the term **shango** having been absorbed so securely into the Trinidad language that it has lost that sense of 'otherness.' Attempts are being made to unify the **orisha** movement into one organization, and links with **orisha** groups in Brazil, the United States, and Nigeria are being promoted. The highlight of this international activity and recognition was the visit to Trinidad in July/August 1988 of the Ooni of Ife, head of the **orisha** religion, and a public **orisha** service at the National Stadium in Port of Spain on Emancipation Day, August 1, with the Ooni, his priests, and Trinidad government officials in attendance. This 'service' in itself, however, revealed syncretism in its form and conception, with Christian analogues.

Cultural integration is taking place on other fronts as well. One such change involves the amalgamation of cultural forms belonging to the same ethnic group. For example, the function of the **saraka** has now contracted into the **shango**. The feast given in response to a dreamed request from an ancestor now takes the form of an **orisha** ceremony rather than a **saraka** — a **saraka**-motivated Shango, so to speak. The honouring of the dead thus becomes secondary to the worship of the gods. Correspondingly, it is the gods, and not the ancestors, who 'ride the heads' of devotees during **shango.** In fact, ancestors do not possess relatives either at **shango** or **saraka** ceremonies.[34]

Maintenance of these traditional customs has to date been most marked among the working and lower middle classes. This is so for those political, social, and cultural reasons which have made African ways of life fall into disregard among educated African descendants in the Western world. As explained earlier, however, the status of **orisha** worship is on the rise and its open appeal to the middle class on the increase. Apart from these recent developments, however, social flexibility and inter-class contact are such in Trinidad, and the religious and psychological needs of people so deep, that information reveals a covert retention of African religious practices among some members of the Black middle class.

Even apart from the consultation of **shango** diviners by persons across the class and color spectrum, the ethnic and cultural background of some middle-class females suggests an African-derived religious motive behind their entry into social welfare work. Both Miss Jean-Pierre, of Tunapuna/Curepe, and Miss Marie Humphrey, of San Fernando/ Tunapuna, came out of **saraka**-steeped *milieux.* An important part of their social work was the feeding of poor children, the sick, and the elderly. When one recalls that a cornerstone of **saraka** ritual was the distribution of food to neighbors and to the needy, one begins to see that the concept of spiritual benefit for charity dispensed may have been a private motive for entry into this sphere of public life. Ironically and syncretistically, membership in social welfare organizations was an acceptable public activity for bourgeois womenfolk and led upwardly mobile Black women into European-dominated social organizations.

So the old practices have lingered, in subterranean or syncretic forms. They give evidence of cultures based on a strong sense of communal identity and cohesion. They speak of deeply religious cultures, where ceremonies served as channels of communication between humankind and another world of gods and ancestral presences.

Maureen Warner-Lewis

Notes

1. This seems standard practice in all African feasts in Trinidad.
2. Arabic.
3. The same shift also occurred in Carriacou, an island off Grenada. See 'Clues from Oral History' in this collection for my deduction regarding this change. On the other hand, some people pointed to the greater attraction of possession rites in **shango** in contrast to the absence of possession in **saraka**. Present-day Nigerian Yoruba contracts **saraka** to **saaraa**.
4. Water sweetened with sugar. Also used in the Kumina religion of Jamaica.
5. A sugared bread containing grated coconut.
6. Corn parched, ground and mixed with sugar. In Jamaica, **asham**.
7. A term used in the West Indies (probably of African origin) to denote a gluey paste obtained by stirring any type of flour in hot water.
8. **Fufu** is a Twi word used in the West Indies for any starchy food which is pounded and served in balls.
9. The Yoruba deities are not only referred to as 'saints' but also equated with specific Catholic saints.
10. So called because the ceremonial enclosure is traditionally palm-roofed and open-sided. Many *palais* are now covered over with corrugated-iron sheets.
11. Derived from Yoruba **mongba** (the priest of Shango).
12. Yoruba **peregun** (*dracaena terminalis*), the shrub marking Ogun's shrine.
13. Cognate with the Yoruba drum name **konongo**.
14. Yoruba name for a type of small drum.
15. A type of hymn-singing popular in non-conformist churches in the West Indies and the United States. Each note is held for a longer period than is done in the established churches. The note at the end of each line is also noticeably prolonged. Such singing is usually done in falsetto.
16. Derived from **Allada**, the capital (before Abomey) of the kingdom of Dahomey.
17. These correspondences are recorded in Carr (1953).
18. Songs of a secular nature.
19. Yoruba for 'mad,' and carrying connotations of 'evil.' See Simpson (1970: 30-31).
20. This sort of rivalry is still found in Indian weddings in Trinidad. In the days when different drumming groups were hired by the bride's and the groom's families, lively competitions would take place when the two groups met at the bride's home on the last afternoon of the wedding. Today, when sound systems have replaced drums, the same rivalry persists. I understand, too, that in Jamaican country weddings there is a competition during the post-church festivities to see which side will present the larger quantity as well as the more expensive gifts — the friends invited by the bride's people or those invited by the groom's. This practice is retained among Jamaican immigrants in England.
21. Generally believed to derive from French *bel air* (beautiful melody), but Baker (1988) posits derivation from Kikongo **Belele** (a dance with hip movements).
22. Type of palm.
23. Necromancy, **obeah**.
24. Typical female dress of the last century and of the earlier part of this. Influenced by African and French styles, it featured a full long white lace underskirt over which was draped a vivid plaid cotton skirt caught up here and there to reveal the lacework below. The long-sleeved plaid blouse was overlaid at the neck by a **fula** or neck-kerchief, which was tucked in at the waist in front to form a V shape. Beads, heavy gold earrings and a starched plaid headtie completed the ensemble.
25. Probably French Creole for 'damask.'
26. Apparently equivalent to Yoruba **abari**. **Akasan** is the term used in south-western Yoruba dialects such as Egbado, Gun ~ /Ajase/Nago.
27. The derivation of this word is problematic. Whatever the case, it refers to a thick mush made of slimy leaves and ochro (okra) and seasoned.

28. Unidentified. But the preparation seems to resemble that of the Yoruba **moin-moin** made of black-eyed peas soaked, skinned, ground, mixed with oil and onion and steamed in balls with pieces of meat inside.

29. An informant whose mother was Grenadian but who now lives in Trinidad described the menu at such feasts as consisting of *farine* made into large dumplings called **kanu,** and **kalalu** made out of dasheen leaves as is done in Trinidad today. There was **fufu** of pounded yam, and pounded plantain eaten with gravy seasoned and colored red by *ruku (bixa orellana).*

30. In the manner of the African gong-gong.

31. See 'shagby' in Simpson (1970: 40).

32. Also spelt 'cotter' or 'cotta.' Cf. Brathwaite (1970: 12).

33. Yoruba **bembe** (a type of drum). As in the case of the Congo dances, one of the drums involved was also called a 'keg,' applied as an English generic term to replace specific names for African drums.

34. On the other hand, at least at one *palais* in recent times, that of Isaac Lindsay in Oropuche, there have been 'ancestor nights' when ancestor possession takes place. To date, however, evidence of ancestor possession in Trinidad is slim. Elder's article, by its title, suggests that he found evidence of this, but the data in the article apparently concern **orisha** worship.

References

Baker, Philip. (1988). 'Assessing the African Contribution to French Creoles'. International Round-Table on Africanisms in Afro-American Language Varieties. Athens: University of Georgia, 199-244.

Brathwaite, Edward. (1970). *Folk Culture of Slaves in Jamaica.* Kingston: New Beacon.

Carr, Andrew. (1953). 'A Rada Community in Trinidad'. *Caribbean Quarterly* 3, no. 1: 36-54.

Simpson, George. (1970). 'The Shango Cult in Trinidad'. In *Religious Cults of the Caribbean: Trinidad, Jamaica and Haiti.* San Juan: Institute of Caribbean Studies.

CRITICAL THINKING AND WRITING

1. In the introduction the writer explains, 'These descriptions, written in 1969, are not the author's eye-witness reports, but derive from the attestations of persons who participated in these ceremonies.' How does this affect your approach to the text?

2. a) Why, according to Warner-Lewis, does she write about African feasts?
   b) What is the main point that Warner-Lewis is making?

3. What do the diction, the definitions of various terms, and the overall treatment of the content suggest about the intended audience? Provide support for your answer.

4. Which organizing principle does the writer use to develop the section on 'Secular Feasts'? Comment on its effectiveness.

5. Describe Warner-Lewis's tone in this passage. Provide evidence from the passage.

6. Provide examples to show how Warner-Lewis establishes her credibility throughout the passage.

7. In what way(s) does the last paragraph function as an effective conclusion?

CLASS DISCUSSION

8. Describe a ritual that is a part of your culture. Do you see any similarities to any of the African religious feasts described by Warner-Lewis?

CHAPTER 12

THE SPIRIT OF GARVEY – LESSONS OF THE LEGACY

A hundred years after his birth, and nearly fifty years after his death, the spirit of Marcus Mosiah Garvey, visionary, freedom fighter and one of Jamaica's greatest thinkers, lives on. It is significant that of all the heroes iconised by a politically insecure people, grateful for their independence out of some three centuries of struggle, Marcus Garvey remains the most popular among the mass of the population. No surprise, really, since the issues he addressed persist with a vengeance, calling a dispossessed and groping people, if not to armed struggle, to exercise of imagination and intellect as the route to freedom and self-determination.

Among the heirs of Garvey are the popular poets of utterance — the Bob Marleys, Jimmy Cliffs, Peter Toshes and Mutabarukas — thrown up by a generation of Jamaicans who find in the tangible emblems of political sovereignty no real solution to their people's continuing degradation, which is the result of Western civilisation's unrelenting efforts to humiliate Africa and all that spring therefrom.

Garvey's redemptive vision of a tolerable future, where people of African ancestry will enjoy full recognition, status, and self-direction, remains one of the sturdiest challenges to a world that would keep large hordes of humanity in some kind of Babylonian captivity, with poverty, self-negation, and powerlessness as their daily medicine.

If the mental grasp of such disabilities is the first step towards liberation, then the ongoing and inescapable trek to final freedom must be through *action*. Garvey did not himself rule out armed struggle if, as in the Irish situation, such was necessary. But with the fullest understanding of the arenas of combat — Central America, the United States and his own little Jamaica — he turned to methods of self-reliance rooted in confraternity, mass mobilisation and unity, as well as efforts at self-improvement by embarking on economic ventures that would generate resources for further development.

Nothing that we now invoke — from Bob Marley's call to emancipate oneself from mental slavery to the PNP's call for self-reliance and the JLP's stress on private initiative in economic development — escaped Garvey's insightful gaze on the realities of a poor, depressed state of existence which is the legacy of slavery and colonialism. He is a genuine founder of modern Jamaica, a true anti-colonial advocate for all of black Africa, where he was well known among those who eventually fought for Independence, and a creative intellect who offered to the entire process of liberation-struggle some of the tersest arguments and a way of looking at a world that would celebrate man's inhumanity to man, over and above one man's obligation to another, on the basis of mutual respect and mutual understanding.

The Rastafarians, on their own admission, owe a lasting debt to the man. Their repeated invocation of his wisdom and foresight is among their greatest assets, giving them a kind of credibility and relevance to an ongoing quest for universal brotherhood, democracy and freedom, though not at the expense of the black man.

This search for space by people of African ancestry on the planet Earth is so fundamental in their day-to-day battle for survival, that its elemental nature is likely to be dismissed as metaphysical nonsense by the 'scientific' scholars, as imponderable by the economists, or as unimportant by the technocratic planners. Happily, the ordinary folk understand the force and vigour of the hope-in-despair it engenders in the breast of all who feel (and know). Sylvia Wynter, the Jamaican woman of letters, has long understood the meaning of Garvey in these terms as part of a cultural process that has sustained the African in exile, variously designated 'proletarian', 'sufferer', 'member of the masses' or any other name that the going ideology will satisfy. She wrote in *Jamaica Journal* back in 1970 (4:2):

> What Césaire was in the intellectual and cultural field, Marcus Garvey of Jamaica was in the political agitational field. His great organisation based in the United States and the massive plan for a physical return to Africa comprised the corollary of the spiritual and intellectual return of the Negritude movement. While the movement failed, it has shaken up the fantasy and stirred the imagination of millions of black 'folk' in the United States

and the Caribbean. His movement. awakened an awareness of Africa, a revaluation of Africa, and a sense of pride in the past, whose myth had been used to keep black people in servitude and self-contempt. This started the process which has led in a direct line to the present Black Power movement. . . .

The above correctly places Garvey as part of a process to which he gave much original impetus, a process that is now global in its application and universal in what it sets out to do. For the revaluation and renaissance of black culture (which is central to Negritude and the later Black Power movement) become a vain object without the consciousness of racial pride and the application of energy in practical schemes of self-improvement which Garvey and Garveyism espoused.

The scholarly contributions to a fuller understanding of the life and work of Garvey, following on the efforts by the late Amy Jacques Garvey to preserve her husband's work, are in their own way responding to the reality of a world which the mass of the population have long understood, if only because they continue to be the woof and warp of that weave.

Robert Hill's extensive and impressive documentation, John Henrik Clarke's history and textual analyses of the man's work, Tony Martin's driving pursuit of Garveyite caverns yet to be explored, Rupert Lewis's long-awaited examination of Garvey as anti-colonial champion, and Rupert Lewis and Maureen Warner-Lewis's recent collection of essays on Garvey, all attempt to bring up to date the voluminous store of information left to posterity by Garvey and those who helped to give the Universal Negro Improvement Association (UNIA) the tremendous significance it was to have for millions all over the Western world in the decades of the twenties and thirties.

These scholars are beginning to confront us with the full significance of the giant of a thinker-cum-activist that Garvey was. The substance of his philosophy and opinions as well as his dreams and programmes of action, his errors and achievements, his successes and failures, retain an awesome relevance to us almost eighty years after his entry into public life — that is, if we are to date that 'life' from the fateful and historic printers' strike of 1908 in which he was involved.

For the realities with which Garvey wrestled, and which are alive with us today, are indeed those elements of human interaction which many a social scientist would conveniently relegate to the dustbin of 'imponderables', but which real-life experience knows are often the deep social forces on which may depend the production, distribution, and exchange of a bushel of corn, a truckload of yams, a bunch of bananas, so many crate-loads of ganja, a tonne of bauxite-alumina, or even a latter-day container of high-tech winter vegetables. No doubt there are those who share with Garvey the view that internalised notions of racial (or class) inferiority are self-limiting and do not a producer of goods and services make! This is not to turn Marx on his head, though either way it would still be Karl Marx. The balkanisation of consciousness, is after all, the greatest enemy of social change in any ideological dispensation.

No one knew better than the self-educated but exceptionally discerning Garvey that the organic and dynamic interplay between material conditions and ideas emerging from those conditions, between material base and ideational superstructure, is the stuff of human existence *in praxis*. And what he in turn has

bequeathed to us, as a result of his long and sustained engagement with such phenomena, has proven to be quite capable of Explanation and Theory (the dream of the 'scientific' investigator) even while providing mythic inspiration for Black Power activists and race-conscious visionaries.

There remains a rich storehouse of knowledge yet to be tapped and organised into palatable shape. And the quest continues for some conceptual order in the current confusion of shifting paradigms beckoning us all to appropriate structural frameworks, not only to support our public policies but also to hone our methodological explorations in dealing with the unruly and chaotic phenomena that are the reality of contemporary Jamaican and Caribbean life. There is room for everyone — empiricists, humanists, positivists, and even mystics — in this quest.

Marcus Garvey understood the *problématique* very well. The 'earthly existence' he grappled with was not a simple, uncluttered, and 'one-way-street' affair. Garvey, in fact, responded directly to the contradictions, diversity and chaos of his colonial, plantation-American, economically lopsided and racially bigoted world with the vigour and the sensitivity demanded by the criss-cross complexity of human life anywhere. In fact, it is precisely because a group of imperial overlords refused to accord to a subjugated majority that fact of texture, diversity and complexity that he was forced not merely to interpret the world into which he was born, but to change it.

He sought to establish in practical terms institutional frameworks on the basis of a philosophy of life, power and human organisation that was rooted in the realities of his native Jamaica and the rest of the black diaspora. It was a worldview which was, however, no less 'universal' than those claimed by other men (of whatever race, class or cultural background) fighting for social justice, freedom and human rights. The inward stretch to race-consciousness as the basis for that mandatory inner psychological liberation and his outward reach into territorial borders beyond Jamaica and to minds beyond the 'black race', gave to his efforts the force and power it was to develop and maintain in his lifetime and after.

The 'universality' is based not only on the geographical spread of the Garvey Movement. The universality is based as much on the man's firm grasp of what up to now is demonstrably a fundamental human concern among peoples, wherever there is injustice, calculated efforts to dominate subject peoples, exploitation of the labouring masses, racial discrimination and the denial of human dignity perceived in terms of what have been severally called 'inalienable', 'natural', or just plain 'human' rights. The persistence of Garveyism remains a source of energy in liberation struggles, and strikes a responsive chord among the mass of the population in contemporary Jamaica, as it did in large parts of Africa, the United States and the rest of the Caribbean throughout the twenties and thirties. Garvey's popularity today tells us more about contemporary Jamaica which still needs to be structurally adjusted out of its congenitally unjust state, and much as well about South Africa and wherever else people are treated as less than human.

The internationalism, in the sense of territorial reach as well as the universality of the Garveyite ideas, should not be played down. But neither should Garveyism be bled of its 'blackness' in order to make it respectable and parade as part of somebody else's mainstream. Happily, the books referred to earlier and the contributions to this issue of *Jamaica Journal* to do nothing of the sort. They successfully document the activities of UNIA branches as far away as California, throughout what was then the British West Indies, in Africa (West and South), and through the international encounters with the League of Nations in the decade between 1921 and 1931. These accounts speak, as well, to the universality of Garveyism in terms of its ideational thrust as a worldwide liberation creed, but filtered through the specific and real-life experiences of black people in the world, just as Plato addressed the specific problems of the Greek city-states he knew. Garveyism was to help *determine* Western mainstream idea-systems, whether liberal capitalist, imperialist, or revolutionary socialist, and not merely to *enter* them. Out of the specificity of the experience of the Jamaican peasantry and artisan class in the context of colonial Jamaica, reinforced by the fact of Harlem (the capital of black America) and the existence of similar denigration of black people he came upon in his travels in Central America, Garvey was able to formulate a view of the world no less valid because of the source(s) of its origin.

What an excellent lesson for those of us who still believe that if Marx, Keynes or Friedman did not say it, it wasn't said; or if it is not on CNN or MTV it does not exist! The lessons that Garvey has to teach us are legion.

Rex Nettleford

References

Nettleford, Rex. 1979. *Caribbean Cultural Identity, The Case of Jamaica*. Kingston Institute of Jamaica.

Smith, M.G., Roy Augier and Rex Nettleford. 1960. *The Rastafari Movement in Kingston, Jamaica*. Mona: University of the West Indies.

Vincent, Theodore. 1986. 'Evolution of the Split between the Garvey Movement and the Organized Left in the United States 1917-1933'. In *Garvey, Arica, Europe and the Americas*, eds., Rupert Lewis and Maureen Warner-Lewis. Mona Institute of Social and Economic Research, University of the West Indies.

CRITICAL THINKING AND WRITING

1. Identify the discourse mode and state, using evidence from the passage, the audience for whom you think this passage is intended.

2. What do you consider to be the writer's main purpose? Cite statements from the text to support your answer.

3. Comment on the sentence structure and say how you think the writer's overall use of language is suited to the subject, audience and purpose.

4. Using context clues, suggest the meaning of the following words. Verify your responses by consulting a dictionary.
   a) Ideational (paragraph 18)
   b) Iconised (paragraph 1)
   c) Self-negation (paragraph 3)
   d) Confraternity (paragraph 4)

5. Identify examples of
   a) denotative diction
   b) connotative diction

6. How does the writer establish credibility?

7. Explain why Nettleford places the word 'scientific' (paragraph 7) in inverted commas.

8. Characterize the writer's tone. How does the tone contribute to the overall effectiveness of the writer in achieving his purpose?

WRITING ACROSS THE CURRICULUM ACTIVITIES

9. Out of class assignment: Based on your research on the teachings of Marcus Garvey, write a short piece of no more than 200 words in which you reflect on the extent to which Garvey's philosophy is reflected in Caribbean societies.

10. This article was written approximately twenty years ago. To what extent is it still relevant today? How relevant is it to the wider Caribbean?

CHAPTER 13

HOW THE CAPTAINCY EVOLVED

All experience is an arch wherethro' gleams that untravelled world…
Tennyson
This Lloyd is going to be a power to come in the West Indies batting when he matures.
Brian Close

A convenient point of departure is 1950, generally acknowledged as the birth of modern West Indian cricket. Of that period, none other than the great Constantine has written: 'I have always held the view that until 1950 the West Indies rarely played the cricket of which they were capable.'

Since Constantine had himself ceased playing by then it was a particularly generous view, but the evidence for his conclusion is strong enough. In 1950 the West Indies beat England for the first time in a series. The significant aspect of their victory was that it had occurred in England.

Two years earlier, England — believing that the West Indies were a pushover — had sent a weakened team on tour to the Caribbean. It was most unsuccessful, losing the last two of the four Test matches played. But in the view of many commentators the West Indian victory had not counted for much, having been achieved against an MCC side from which many of the better England players had been missing. In nothing was this more reflected than in the fact that the man chosen to lead the MCC, Gubby Allen, was *45* years of age.

There was no Compton, Edrich, Washbrook, Alec Bedser or Yardley. The West Indies duly won at Bourda by seven wickets and, three weeks later, beat England by ten wickets.

Two years later in England, Ramadhin and Valentine wrecked a bemused England team with their baffling and unreadable spin and ushered in a new age of West Indian cricket. The two players, unknown at the start of the tour, took multiple Test wickets between them and were immortalised in calypso for helping their side to a victory by 326 runs at Lord's.

Neither the England team nor English cricket writers could quite believe what was happening, and some commentators formed the view that the West Indian victory at Lord's was a flash in the pan. In a particularly ungracious comment, *The Times* of London was moved to observe before the Oval Test match that 'the West Indies would sink into a slumber of insolent security'. But the West Indies batsmen proved wide awake and pugnaciously secure. Worrell led the way with a stylish 138, Rae scored 109 and the West Indies posted a first-innings total of 503. Only the great Len Hutton, with a magnificent double century, had any answer to the West Indies' attack, and England were made to follow on. This time Valentine took six wickets for 39 runs, England were bundled out for a miserly 103, and the West Indies crushed England by an innings and 56 runs.

The sounds of the impromptu celebration calypsos which were first heard at Lord's, and which reverberated around a crowded Oval ground at the end of the series, sent an echo of pure joy far across the Atlantic to the Caribbean. Ramadhin and Valentine, 'those two little pals of mine' as the calypsos called them, and the three W's, Worrell, Weekes and Walcott, had put a new face of success on West Indies cricket by defeating England at home by three Test matches to one.

It is not always appreciated that the West Indies victory in 1950 could not have come at a more politically significant time in Caribbean terms. A few years before, West Indian patriots had begun the drive for political self-determination in the colonies. The first studies on the feasibility of West Indian self-government had just been published. In Grenada and Barbados, in Trinidad and Jamaica, talk of political progress for the islands filled the air. It was the spirit of the times.

A few years later it was to lead to an irreversible loosening of the control of the West Indies colonies by the metropolitan power through an attempt at a broad-based, self-administering West Indies Federation. The fact that the Federation was destined to fail is not terribly relevant here. The die had been cast. Times had changed. The ineluctable flow was towards political independence from Britain. Never again would it be possible to put back the clock.

This was the climate in which West Indian politicians were seeking some kind of international justification to bolster their case for a greater say in the way their islands were run. They found it in the success of the West Indies cricket team in England in 1950. This is no exaggeration. Addressing a mass political meeting in Port of Spain, in what his party had called 'the university of Woodford Square', Eric Williams, just before he became the first Prime Minister of an independent Trinidad and Tobago, drew heavily on the West Indies success on cricket fields in England to make his case for political independence from the 'mother country'. 'In 1950,' he said one evening, 'we went to learn. Now we go to teach. The West Indies have arrived. We are no longer second-class.' In the words of C. L. R. James: 'The connection between cricket and West Indian social and political life was established so that all except the wilfully perverse could see.'

Having provided a suitable metaphor for the commencement of the drive to West Indian political self-determination, West Indian cricket failed to keep pace with the changing times. Nothing illustrates this better than the return visit to England by the West Indies in 1957. Two years earlier, the West Indies had played hosts to Australia. Although the West Indian team of the time had been virtually built around the feats of Worrell, Weekes and Walcott, the West Indies Cricket Board decided in its wisdom to make Denis Atkinson, a white Barbadian insurance salesman and comparatively inexperienced Test player, Jeffrey Stollmeyer's vice-captain. It had been such an incredible decision that the view was formed very strongly that it was simply an attempt by the West Indian cricket authorities to make sure that the West Indies team was always led by a white man. Many years before, Learie Constantine had related with dignified scorn how the rumour had spread among the islands that it was the wish of the West Indies players themselves that they be captained always by a white man and that many had said that they would never play under a black captain.

Atkinson's appointment against Australia, though, was a bomb shell, and when Stollmeyer missed three of the five Test matches through injury, the inexperienced and totally unsuited Atkinson found himself leading a team in which there were far better players and far better captains than he was ever destined to be. To complicate matters, Atkinson was not only asked to lead the team but also to ignore, while attempting to do so, vociferous calls that he be sent back to sell insurance in Bridgetown. It would have been a test of character even for a much better player. Atkinson, it must be said, was not a personal failure during the series. In the Barbados Test match he scored a double century and took five Australian wickets, but he was never capable of leading the West Indies team and should never have even been considered for the task ahead of the more illustrious names in the team. Despite the consistent batting of Walcott and Weekes, the Australians won the first Test by nine wickets, the third by eight wickets and the fifth at Sabina Park, in Kingston, Jamaica, by an innings and 82 runs. Clyde Walcott distinguished himself by getting a century in both innings of that ill-fated Test match, 155 in the first and 110 in the second, but coming in response to Australia's massive first-innings total of 758 (Harvey 204, Archer 128, McDonald 127, Benaud 121 and Miller 109) the West Indies suffered one of the most crushing defeats they have ever endured against a visiting side.

It would be naïve to imagine that players like Walcott were unaware, at the time, of the extraordinary policy of the West Indies Board towards the appointment of West Indian captains. Writing after his playing days were over, Walcott makes it clear that the 'Atkinson affair' was spotted in its making, long before the Australians arrived in the West Indies. In his book *Island Cricketers*, Walcott writes:

> Before the Australians arrived in the West Indies the Board did something which at first seemed strange, in announcing the names of the captain and vice-captain for our tour of New Zealand which was to take place almost a year later. The names were Denis Atkinson and Bruce Pairaudeau. Only after this announcement had sunk in, and had caused a good deal of controversy, did the board announce that Jeff Stollmeyer and Denis Atkinson would be captain and vice-captain respectively for the Australian series about to start. Although it was hard to see why the announcement of the officials for New Zealand had to be made so far in advance, the apparent discrepancy in selection was more easily explained.

West Indies had no delusions, nor false politeness about the strength of New Zealand cricket and they had decided to send a young side, omitting all but a few of our established Test players. The choice of Atkinson as captain and — to gain experience — as vice-captain against Australia was in line with this policy. The public were not slow to ask why the 'three W's' had been left out of the reckoning, particularly after Frank Worrell had been vice-captain against MCC during the 1953–54 series. The public feeling seemed to be that the West Indies Board did not relish the prospect of having a coloured captain.

Shortly before the first Test, Jeff Stollmeyer hurt a finger in practice so [he] had to withdraw from the side. Automatically, his vice-captain, Denis Atkinson, succeeded him, but the press and the public took this as an excellent opportunity to renew their plea that Worrell should be given the captaincy. They rightly made the point that he was the more experienced player and captain, but they overlooked the fact that the thing had been decided in the selection room some time before and was unlikely to be changed now.

Atkinson's experience was, in fact, very slight. Until his selection to captain the side to visit New Zealand he had not normally led his colony, Barbados. But after the announcement, John Goddard, the usual Barbados captain, handed over to Atkinson, presumably to help the younger man gain experience. And so, lacking experience and the full confidence of West Indies cricket followers, Denis had a difficult task which was not eased when he had the misfortune to lose the toss ....

It should be said that Clyde Walcott firmly stated his belief at the time that one of the reasons for the curious conduct of the West Indies Board probably had something to do with their reluctance to appoint a professional captain, a precedent which, he pointed out, 'despite Len Hutton's reign as captain, still has its roots deeply laid in England'. But only a few years later his guard slipped and his usual generosity vanished when he predicted that the white Barbadian player, Robin Bynoe, would only have to make 'fifty in one innings and he'll be captain'.

Suffice it to say that by 1957, when the West Indies team went to England, their first visit after their great triumph seven years before, dissension and internal wrangling had bitten deeply into the body corporate of their side. John Goddard, who had stepped aside from the leadership of the Barbados team to give Denis Atkinson the required experience, was brought back to captain the West Indies at the age of 38. It is true that by 1957 the England batsmen had worked out a method of neutralising the spin of Ramadhin and Valentine. Their rule had been a simple one. If you cannot read what the bowler is doing, play him off the front foot as an offspinner, thrusting the pad forward as second line of defence if the ball still beats the bat. At Edgbaston, May and Cowdrey used the tactic effectively. Never in danger of being adjudged leg-before, since the ball was making contact with the pad such a long way from the stumps, they padded merrily on as the West Indians spinners grew hoarse with their unavailing appeals.

Trevor McDonald

CRITICAL THINKING AND WRITING

1. What is the writer's purpose in writing this piece?
2. What is the writer's attitude to West Indian cricket and to his audience? Support your answer with evidence from the passage.
3. How does the writer establish common ground with his audience?
4. The writer speaks about Clyde Walcott, using Walcott's words to support his (the writer's) points.
    a) How does this enhance the writer's credibility?
    b) What does this suggest about the use of and necessity for authoritative sources when engaging in academic writing?
5. Provide some illustrations of the writer's attempt to appeal to your senses. How does this help you to engage with the piece?
6. What does the writer's diction suggest about his intended audience?

WRITING ACTIVITIES

7. What are some of the new words that you encountered? List them, then try to understand them in the context in which they are used. Finally, look up the meanings in a dictionary.
8. Write a 250-word essay responding to any aspect of the essay that you found particularly interesting or that you reacted strongly to, whether in a positive or a negative way. Identify your intended audience and ensure that your writing displays an awareness of this audience.

CLASS DISCUSSION

9. It has often been stated that cricket is one of the forces that unite the Caribbean. Discuss some of the ways in which you believe cricket helps to unify the Caribbean.

Chapter 14

Introducing Bredda Anancy

Our Jamaican folk-stories are called Anancy stories. Anancy is an Ashanti (West African) spider god, but most Jamaicans know and love him as the 'trickify' little spider-man who speaks with a lisp and lives by his wits, who is both comic and sinister, the hero and villain of Jamaican folk-stories.

Some people feel that Anancy points up human weaknesses and shows how easily we can be destroyed by our greed, or stupidity or by putting our trust and confidence in the wrong people and things. Some people feel that Anancy shows in his stories the survival tactics employed by the weak in society in order to combat the strong. Some others feel that Anancy is just a lazy, lying, deceitful, envious and down right wicked, good-for-nothing creature. But all agree that he is a lovable rascal.

Most Anancy stories have songs and these have been the true lullabies to many Jamaican children for generations. Each Anancy story ends with the phrase 'Jack Mandora me no choose none' which means, 'Jack Mandora'— doorman, keeper of heaven's door; 'me no choose none'— it is not of my choosing, or, I take no responsibility for the tales I have told!

We call Anancy 'Bra Nancy' or 'Bredda Nancy' (Brother Anancy), or just plain 'Anancy', and when I was a little girl, there were no stories in the world I loved as much as Anancy stores. All the stories that were in the pretty foreign books with the pretty coloured pictures didn't 'sweet me' (appeal to me) like the Anancy stories which my grandmother and my great-uncle, and my friends at school told me.

We used to swap Anancy stories with each other during recess time and lunch time and those of us who knew plenty Anancy stories and could tell Bredda Nancy stories 'sweet', were very popular with our schoolmates. We were always certain of a big audience during the story-telling sessions and all the listeners became part of the story-telling too, because we all knew the little spider-man so well, with 'his cunny look' (cunning eyes) and 'him tie-tongue talk' (his lisp) and 'him trickify laugh' — 'kya, kya, kya'.

Bredda Nancy's laugh was infectious, and whenever he laughed, we would laugh too. In fact, there was a great deal of laughter during the telling of Bra Nancy stories, for Anancy never really cries, he only 'form cry' (pretends to cry) and he never really gets angry, he only 'form vex' (pretends to be angry).

The strongest and most endearing feature of Bredda Nancy is his sense of humour. Bra Nancy injects humour into everything. Even when Anancy is doing wicked things, like the time when he was beating poor Billy Goat, who was wrongfully accused of stealing a bunch of bananas — which we know was stolen by Anancy himself — Anancy's tactics were so comical, as he shouted 'yuh shteefin' shteef yuh!' (you thiefing thief), that we found ourselves laughing with Anancy instead of sympathizing with Bredda Billy Goat.

We were fascinated by the little spider-man with his many arms and legs and his magical powers. Oh yes, Anancy is a magic man! We know that we could never be like him, and we had better not try any of Anancy's tricks, for he is magic, and we are human. Before telling Anancy stories during the daytime, we had to 'mash ants' (kill an ant) or our mothers could turn into 'bankra-baskets' and never become human-beings again!

Anancy is greater than all the other heroes in the other stories. Every existing custom is said to have been started by Anancy ('is Bra Nancy mek it'). He could get himself and other people in and out of trouble like magic. He could become anybody he wanted to be, anytime he wanted — well not quite anybody: there are just one or two little times when Anancy could only be a man. Like the time when he was trying to steal away a pretty young girl by pretending to be her mother and singing the secret song which her mother used to sing for her daughter to open a secret door. But when Anancy started to sing the secret song, his voice was a man's voice and the girl was not fooled at all! So Anancy had to run to a blacksmith whom he begged to drop some hot lead down his throat to make his voice sound fine like a woman's. That was one time when Anancy could only be a man. But most of the time Anancy could change himself into what he wanted — a young girl sometimes, an old woman sometimes, or even a little baby!

Like the time when Anancy's wife was working for a rich and wicked old man who wouldn't pay her any money until she could guess his secret name. So one day Anancy told his wife to dress him up like a baby, sling him on her back and take him to work with her. Mrs. Anancy did as she was told. When they got to the rich man's house, he was sitting on his verandah rocking and fanning himself, and Mrs. Anancy begged him to allow her to leave her baby on the step of the house until she was finished working. The rich man agreed and Mrs. Anancy went about her business.

Anancy started to cry like a baby, first quietly and then louder and louder. His screams became so shrill that the old man bent over to look at the baby, and Anancy screamed and bared his teeth in the old man's face. The old man was so frightened that he shouted, 'Poor me Seckery! Look wat me live to see. Young baby with big mouth full up with long yellow teeth! Poor me ole Seckery!' He called for Mrs. Anancy to come and take up her baby. When she came and bent over the baby, Anancy whispered, 'Him name Seckery.'

So, of course, that evening Anancy's wife was able to guess the rich man's name. When mean old Seckery reluctantly gave her a big bag of money with all the back pay in it, the baby-Anancy jumped off her back and the man-Anancy picked up the bag of money, put it on his head and laughed — kya, kya, kya, kya!

Jack Mandora me nuh choose none.

Louise Bennett

CRITICAL THINKING AND WRITING

1. What is the effect of the writer's references to different perceptions of Anancy in the introduction?
2. Extrapolate a sentence which presents the writer's main point.
3. The writer utilizes a combination of discourse modes to present Anancy's attributes to the reader.
   a) Identify the different discourse types used in the text.
   b) Examine clearly how the author uses each one to highlight the attributes of Anancy.
   c) Justify the use of each discourse type.
4. Characterize the tone of the article.
5. How do you think Bennett wants the reader to respond to Anancy?
6. Comment on Bennett's use of language.
7. On what authority does Bennett write about Anancy?

WRITING ACTIVITY

8. Imagine that you have invited the writer to be the guest speaker at a function. Write the paragraph which you would use to introduce her to the audience.

EXPLORING THE WEB

9. Search the web for information on Anancy. Compare and contrast this information with what you have read in this essay.
10. Write about the folk hero in your country. Explain the ways in which this figure is viewed in your culture.

CHAPTER 15

HONDURAS

Nearly all black Hondurans belong to the Garífuna Afro-Carib population group, which currently numbers some 98,000 people. In Honduras, the experience of the Garífuna has been largely one of marginalization and disadvantage. Issues of communal land rights, and access to and protection of natural resources, have been a particular concern for the Garífuna community. While there are significant Garífuna populations in the country's capital, Tegucigalpa, and in the northern cities of San Pedro Sula, La Ceiba, Puerto Cortés and El Progreso, most Garífuna are located on the Atlantic Coast, distributed among some forty-three towns and villages from Masca in the Department of Cortés to Playaplaya in the eastern most Department of Gracias a Dios. Garífuna populations also live on the Belizean coast, in the coastal town of Livingstone in Guatemala and in the Atlantic region of Nicaragua. Beyond Central America, there are sizeable Garífuna populations in the United States, in particular in New Orleans, Miami and Los Angeles.

Origins and History

The origins of the Garífuna remain the subject of considerable controversy, but it is now generally agreed that they are the descendants of African and Carib populations from the Antillean islands of St Vincent and Dominica. Following the shipwreck of two Spanish slave ships in the mid-seventeenth century, the surviving slaves are said to have taken refuge on St Vincent, where they mixed with the local Carib population, forming maroon (free slave) communities in the north-east. The indigenous origin of much of the Garífunas' economic and cultural universe is observable today in the manner in which Garífuna women cultivate and prepare yucca, used to make casabe (cassava), and also in certain linguistic traits.

In 1775 the British conquered St Vincent and evicted the Garífuna in order to take over their fertile lands. War between the colonial forces and the Garífuna ensued, and in 1797 the surviving Garífuna, some 3,000 to 5,000, were expelled and taken to the Island of Roatán, off the Caribbean coast of Honduras. With this forced deportation of the Garífuna, the English aimed to rid themselves of a rebellious population and cause problems for their imperial rival, Spain, which controlled the territory of Honduras. Many of the Garífuna died of disease en route. The survivors subsequently populated the sparsely inhabited coastal region of mainland Honduras.

The Garífuna were often recruited as local militia by the Spanish during English incursions on the coast. However, the friendly relations between the Miskitu (allies of the British) and the Garífuna periodically aroused Spanish suspicions against the latter. It was only the heroic defence in 1820 of the port of Trujillo by Garífuna soldiers, against a British attack, that secured a series of privileges for the Garífuna, ratified in the first postindependence constitution in 1825.

During the first half of the nineteenth century, in common with many indigenous populations in Central America, the Garífuna allied themselves with Conservative forces against the Liberal reformers. The eventual defeat of the Conservatives in the mid-nineteenth century occasioned an exodus of Garífuna from Honduras to the Atlantic Coast of Nicaragua. This pattern of war and expulsion has dominated the historical memory of the Garífuna:

> If you look closely you will see that we have always had a history of danger. We were always persecuted, the powerful always wanted to humiliate us, they always wanted to take away the land of our ancestors. Fighting with our weapons, we have always escaped to the mountains and we have always defended ourselves from the bad spirits.

Religion as Resistance

During the late nineteenth century the evangelizing work of the Catholic Church began to have an impact on the Garífuna, and since the Second World War the influence of evangelical Protestant sects has increased significantly. Most Garífuna would describe themselves as Catholic, yet their religious rituals represent a syncretism between Catholicism and prior belief systems. As one

Garífuna elder stated: 'We Garífuna believe in God and in the spirits of our dead, and we will continue to be Catholics. This is our Garífuna tradition.'

Garífuna conceptions of the world combine indigenous and African elements and are centred on ancestor cults. The Garífunas' philosophical-religious system is known as *dugu* or *walagagallo* and in some respects compares with the voodoo system practised in Haiti. The idea of *gubida*, or ancestral spirit possession, continues to have a central role in Garífuna religious practices; possession of an individual is considered an illness, and *gubida* is used to explain periods of illness or abnormal behaviour. The condition is officially diagnosed by a shaman (male or female) who enters a trance to consult with the spirits of the dead. The dead are believed to be able to communicate their wishes through the dreams of their living family members experiencing *gubida*. Ritual offerings to appease the ancestral spirits include food and drink, together with animal sacrifice, and (in the case of the more elaborate *dugu* ceremony) trances and spirit possession are common. In the case of death, the Catholic mass and wake are observed, together with Garífuna rituals which include songs, dance and traditional drum music. Many African influences can be seen in dance styles — including the *punta*, now popular throughout Honduras, oral traditions, forms of drum-playing, and animal sacrifice. According to Honduran anthropologist Ramón Rivas, out-migration, together with remittances of dollars from family members living in the United States, appear to have increased the frequency and elegance of traditional religious ceremonies among the Garífuna.

Garífuna religious practices, conceived of as a collective struggle against death and illness, constitute a focus of resistance against ethnic and class oppression. José Idiáquez notes that the role of ancestors in the collective historical struggles of the Garífuna is of central importance, and it is this, he argues, together with their ability to absorb new cultural aspects into religious practices, which lends particular stability to the Garífunas' ethnic identity.

Languages

Most Garífuna speak Spanish and Garífuna. The linguistic origins of Garífuna may remain in dispute — researchers claiming it to be a mixture of other languages, including Arawak, French, Yoruba, Swahili and Bantu — but it is a central part of Garífuna ethnic identity:

> For us Garifuna, the defence of our language has always been very important. Many people have made fun of our language and the same thing happened to our ancestors. But they were never shamed by this. We speak our Garifuna language, we pray and sing in Garifuna. This is why it's important that the teachers who educate our children should be Garifuna, so that the children can learn Garifuna and our religious beliefs. Our religious beliefs and language are an important part of our culture and our Garifuna tradition and we have to defend them in the same way that our ancestors did.

The establishment, during the past two years, of a National Council for Bilingual Education, financed by the international community, has considerably strengthened Garífuna demands for the use of their language in local schools.

Rachel Sieder

Select Bibliography

Beaucage, P. 'Economic anthropology of the Black Carib of Honduras'. PhD diss., University of London, 1970.

González, N.L. *Sojourners of the Caribbean: Enthogenesis and Ethnohistory of the Garífuna*. Chicago, IL: University of Illinois, 1988.

Idiáquez, J. Sj. *El culto a los ancestros en la cosmovisión religiosa de los Garífunas de Nicaragua*. Managua, UCA, 1994.

Rivas, R. *Pueblos indígenas y Garífuna de Honduras*. Tegucigalpa: Guaymuras, 1993.

CRITICAL THINKING AND WRITING

1. What is the writer's intention?
2. Identify the writer's thesis.
3. List the main points of the article on the origins and history of the Garífuna, for a high school student.
4. Are there specific aspects of the article that are particularly effective in engaging the reader's interest? Explain your answer, using evidence from the text.

WRITING ACTIVITY

5. Conduct research on Garífuna populations in the United States. Compare information about their origins and history with the information provided about Central American Garífuna in this article.

RELIGION, HISTORY & POLITICS

CHAPTER 16

===== ◈ =====

ATLAS: EXCERPTED FROM *A HISTORY OF WEST INDIES CRICKET*

The West Indies have become a major cricketing power. But as with most other success stories, it had a beginning that was in marked contrast to the triumphs that were ahead.

The earliest West Indies Test teams were hardly equal to the challenge of the two giants of Test cricket — England and Australia.

Indeed, the West Indies had first played England in an official Test series in 1928 in England. They were not beaten so much as overwhelmed, losing all three games disastrously.

In 1929–1930, England made their first visit to the Caribbean to play the West Indies in four Test matches. The following excerpt describes the encounter and the first appearance of the young player who was to become one of the giants of the sport.

He was a compact man of barely medium height. He had the sloping shoulders often associated with boxers who can punch. He was neat, almost dapper, a somehow self-contained human being. On the cricket field his movements were precise and economical. Like many great performers, he had one feature that tended to set him apart. It was not so much an eccentricity as an idiosyncrasy. Whether batting, bowling or fielding, he always wore his sleeves buttoned at the wrist. Together with his cap, at just enough of an angle to suggest a confident nature fully conscious of itself and its environment, the long sleeves completed a picture that invited attention without the slightest departure from good taste. He was black and four months short of his twenty-first birthday. His name was George Alphonse Headley.

The 1929–30 series, the second between the West Indies and England, was a close affair. The first Test was played at Kensington Oval, Bridgetown, Barbados, between January 11 and 17. The West Indies won the toss and were off to a good start with 369, C.A. Roach making the first ever century for the West Indies in a Test match, 122. England replied strongly with 467. In the West Indies second innings, the hosts hit back with 384, including a superb 176 by George Headley, then the youngest player ever to score a Test century in his maiden appearance. In their second innings England were 167 for 3 at the close of play. This was the West Indies' first Test draw.

The second Test was played between February 1 and 6, at Queen's Park Oval, Port-of-Spain, Trinidad. England made 208 in their first innings with Hendren contributing

77. The West Indies replied with 254. In the second innings England made 485 for 8 declared. Thereupon, the West Indies struggled to 212, losing by 167 runs.

The third Test was played at Bourda, Georgetown, British Guiana, between February 21 and 26. The West Indies made 471 in their first innings, including a fine double century by Roach and 114 run out by young Headley in their first innings, with Constantine and Francis bowling magnificently to take four wickets each.

In the second innings, the West Indies made 290, with a second century by Headley of 112. With this century Headley became the youngest player to both score a century in each innings of a Test and to score three centuries in Test cricket. England fought back in their second innings but were eventually all out for 327, to lose by 259 runs. Constantine brought his total for the match to 9 wickets when he took 5 for 87 and was largely responsible for bowling the West Indies to their first-ever Test victory.

The fourth and final Test was played at Sabina Park, Kingston, Jamaica, on April 3 and 10. This match was filled with improbabilities. England began with 849 runs in their first innings, including 325 by Andy Sandham and 149 by Leslie Ames. The West Indies' cause seemed hopeless when they replied with 286. Incredibly, England batted a second time, making 272 for 9 declared. Hendren completed a fantastic series for him, with 61 in the first innings and 55 in the second. The West Indies' second innings had reached 438 for 5 when the match was abandoned because the English side had to catch the boat home. The architect of this great recovery was George Headley with 223. The series had been drawn.

The 1929–30 encounter was significant for more than the even outcome. Its place in history is assured by the deeds of George Headley. Not more than half of the Test side which had been so soundly beaten in England a few months earlier were in the team which won the toss and elected to bat at the Kensington Oval. It was the first Test match to be played in the West Indies. By lunchtime on the first day, young Headley was back in the pavilion, bowled for 21 by Jack O'Connor of Essex, not always a regular bowler. He had not been at the wicket long enough to confirm the promise that had made the selectors bring him a thousand miles from Jamaica for this game. This promise had included a double century, early in 1928, at the age of nineteen, against a strong touring side of English players led by Lionel, Lord Tennyson. But he had given a hint of things to come. At the end of the first day of the Test, it was C.A. Roach who was the toast of Bridgetown. A Trinidadian, he had delighted everyone with his brilliant 122. In the process he laid the foundation for the first solid innings put together in a Test match by the West Indies. They were all out for 369.

Not to be outdone, the English hit back with 467, 152 of which came from the Surrey opening bat, Andy Sandham, and so the West Indies prepared to bat again. In the very first over, the West Indies' E.L.G. Hoad was out, as the record shows, caught Astill, bowled Calthorpe. Headley, for not the last time in his career, was promptly required to play the part of an opening bat. When he was finally out halfway through the fifth day of the match, he had ignited the imagination of the entire island of Barbados, not so much because he compiled a massive score, not only because he was the youngest batsman to score a Test century, but more by the manner of his doing it.

Those who saw that innings will tell you that it was a joy to behold. The lightning quick footwork provided the foundation for square-cutting and hooking of the utmost authority; the deft late cut revealed the sense of timing which sets the masters apart. The drives, particularly on the off side of the wicket, which penetrated by placement rather than power, served notice that here was no mere 'basher' of the ball.

Barbadians know their cricket. They were witnessing the first major statement of a genius and they responded in kind.

Headley went on to Trinidad where his scores were modest. Then at the Bourda ground in British Guiana, he became the youngest player to score a century in each innings of a Test. Those who perform this feat are usually dubbed 'immortal', a title which reflects the difficulty of the task and the likelihood that it will be remembered. Roach had made a double century in the first innings at Bourda. It was the first of its kind for the West Indies. But Headley's feat made the greater impact. Roach's runs were accumulated in dashing style. The flashing strokes outside the off-stump made him both attractive and typical. They also suggested to the knowledgeable that he benefited not a little from luck. By contrast Headley's runs seemed inevitable.

George Headley returned home at the beginning of April already a star. By April 10 he had become a hero. His 223 in the second innings saved the match for the West Indies who, by drawing the match, saved the series and earned their first draw with England, one victory each with two matches drawn. And again Headley's innings was the innings of a master.

Thus it was that before his twenty-first birthday, George Headley, born in Panama of West Indian parents away from home, became a Caribbean hero. It is true, he entered the international arena against an England side below full strength. Harold Larwood had not made the tour. Neither had Maurice Tate, his partner and foil, who was both fast and a master of swerve; nor Wally Hammond, who could be disconcertingly quick for an over or two. Despite these absent giants and the problems they might have posed, Headley scored his runs in a manner that set him apart. He became a symbol and was to be both the cause of hope and, at least in part, its answer.

Michael Manley

CRITICAL THINKING AND WRITING

CLASS DISCUSSION

1. Discuss the appropriateness of the title to the content.
2. Explain why the writer's use of sequencing as the dominant organizing principle is appropriate for this text.
3. Examine the writer's attitude to the following:
   a) Cricket
   b) George Headley
   c) The English teams
4. What Caribbean values are highlighted in this article?
5. What do you know about the author?

WRITING ACTIVITY

6. Use sequencing to write briefly about the author's career.

COLLABORATIVE WRITING

7. Divide into small groups. Each group should choose one of the following, on which to write two or three paragraphs.
   a) The greatest cricketer in your country.
   b) The most recent World Cup Cricket competition.
   c) How cricket links the Caribbean to the rest of the world.

CHAPTER 17

OIL AND THE TWENTIETH CENTURY ECONOMY, 1900-62

The History of Oil Production in Trinidad

In the nineteenth century, Trinidad's economy was overwhelmingly agricultural, with the major export crops of sugar and cocoa accounting for the bulk of the colony's revenues and employing most of its labour force. But in the present century, oil has increasingly dominated the economy. More than any other factor, it is the development of an oil industry that made twentieth-century Trinidad relatively prosperous.

The existence of oil in Trinidad had long been known or suspected by geologists and scientists, but the oil-bearing districts in the southern part of the island were virtually unopened before 1900, still mostly covered with thick tropical forest, inhospitable and fever-ridden; and the oil industry was in its infancy before the development of the internal combustion engine in the 1890s. The first oil well in Trinidad — perhaps the first successful oil well in the world — was drilled by the Merrimac Oil Company of the USA at La Brea in 1857. Oil was struck at a depth of 280 feet, but difficulties in getting capital, as well as the limited demand for oil in the 1850s, brought the venture to an end with the

liquidation of the company around 1859. In the following decade, Walter Darwent floated the Paria Oil Company in 1865, and drilled wells at Aripero and San Fernando in 1866–7. At least three struck oil, and by 1867 production was about 60 gallons a week. Another company, the Trinidad Petroleum Company, drilled at La Brea in 1867 and struck oil at 250 feet. By 1868 a few wells were in operation around the Pitch Lake, and crude oil had been shipped to the USA and Britain. But a combination of primitive equipment, shortages of capital, heavy soils and transport difficulties forced Darwent to suspend his activities in 1868; he died at La Brea in that year, 'the first martyr to the oil industry in Trinidad', and his death marked the end of the early explorations. Drilling did not resume until the opening years of the twentieth century.

It was the development of the internal combustion engine and the car in the 1890s and 1900s that gave a decisive impetus to the oil industry worldwide. In Trinidad, the true pioneer of oil began his activities in these decades. Randolph Rust was an Englishman who arrived in Trinidad in 1881 as a young man and lived on the island for the rest of his life. Rust acquired an estate at Guayaguare in 1883; this area was virgin forest in the late nineteenth century. Teaming up with Edward Lee Lum, a Trinidadian-Chinese businessman who also owned land in the district, Rust sought to interest local entrepreneurs in floating a company for drilling in the Guayaguare area. When he failed to get support from local capitalists, partly because of the cocoa boom, he sought and obtained Canadian capital, and the Oil Exploration Syndicate of Canada was established. Rust was given a 50-square mile lease in the area, and the first well was drilled in May 1902; oil was struck at between 40 and 1,015 feet, and chemical analysis revealed it to be of excellent quality. Eight more wells were drilled between 1902 and 1907; most yielded oil, and Well No. 3 was the first to be drilled by a rotary drilling rig. In these pioneer days, the major problems encountered by Rust and his colleagues were shortage of capital, appalling transport difficulties in an area still largely covered by tropical forest, the lack of trained staff, and dangerous health conditions: malaria and yellow fever were both endemic. Rust was a tireless publicist for the Trinidad oil industry in these years. He persuaded the governor to visit the Guayaguare works less than a month after the first strike, and he lobbied both in Trinidad and in London for support from British entrepreneurs and from the government, which, he believed, would have to provide the necessary infrastructure, such as roads, railways and port facilities to serve the oil districts.

After 1904 the British government began to take an interest in developing the Trinidad oil industry because of plans to convert the navy to oil-powered ships. A British engineer, A. Beeby-Thompson, was sent to Trinidad in 1905 to prospect for a British company around Guapo, and between 1907 and 1909 he drilled several successful wells in the Guapo–Point Fortin area. His successes led to a conference in 1909 at Downing Street, attended by Beeby-Thompson, the Governor of Trinidad, and representatives of the Admiralty and the Colonial Office. As a result, British capital was invested in increasing amounts after 1909, and a British company, Trinidad Oilfields Ltd, was established in 1910. By 1911–13 the La Brea–Guapo–Point Fortin area was a modest but growing exporter and producer of oil: a small refinery and wooden pier had been built at Point Fortin, and in 1911 a second refinery at Brighton began operations. By then southern Trinidad was becoming a port of call for ships needing bunker, for these were the years when most ships, including the British navy in 1910, were converting to oil. The industry moved inland to Palo Seco, Roussilac, Siparia, Erin and Tabaquite between 1911 and 1919, as areas farther removed from the sea were opened up. Six wells were drilled at Barrackpore in 1913–14 and twelve were opened at Tabaquite during the same years.

In 1913 two major companies entered the oil industry: United British Oilfields of Trinidad (UBOT), a subsidiary of Shell, and Trinidad Leaseholds Ltd (TLL), which took over six smaller companies. UBOT was based at Point Fortin, and it was from its small refinery here that a tanker took a first shipment of 6,000 tons, in 1914, to the British navy. TLL began drilling at Forest Reserve in 1913, struck oil the next year, and by 1914 this company had a refinery at Pointe-à-Pierre, with a connecting pipeline from Forest Reserve. These two companies were to dominate the industry, but several others flourished, and by 1919 there were five refineries, and production had reached 1.9 million barrels annually; about 66 per cent of crude production was being locally refined. In fact, the oil industry was well established in Trinidad by the end of the First World War.

The first three decades of the twentieth century belonged to the hardy pioneers of the oil industry. Technology and equipment were primitive by today's standards, and blow-outs, gushers and even oilfield fires were frequent occurrences. Until the late 1920s spectacular gushers were common. Accidents were frequent: the log for Rust's Well No. 3 at Guayaguare reads 'March 23, 1903: work stopped. Boiler exploded'. Fires were a constant danger. In 1929 a spectacular fire at a runaway well at Dome Field near Fyzabad killed several people including the Trinidadian in charge of the well and the Indian family who owned the land. Labourers were usually barefooted, there were no safety hats, and in general, safety was given low priority by the rugged pioneers who opened up the oilfields. These districts were extremely inaccessible, and heavy machinery and equipment had to be manhandled through dense forest. Rust wrote, in 1910, 'the Lack of roads and railways was something marvelous … it was one terrible fight against nature'. Heavy equipment was heaved into place by human muscle, the forest was cleared by axemen, well sites and roads were graded by a 'Tattoo Gang' — men and women who dug and moved tons of earth using forks, shovels and wooden trays carried on the women's heads. Miles of forest roads were dug and hundreds of well sites were levelled by these forgotten Trinidadians, who deserve to be remembered as pioneers of the oil industry just as much as Rust and the other entrepreneurs involved.

By about 1930, however, the oil industry was changing: the day of the self-taught pioneer was passing and the industry was increasingly dominated by the technicians and the scientists. New methods of rotary drilling — first used by Rust as early as 1902–3 — were introduced by UBOT in particular, and the new techniques of using heavy drilling fluids and the 'Blow-Out Preventer' helped to control blow-outs and gushers, and to make possible much deeper wells. Between 1924 and 1930 the average depth of an oil-well in Trinidad increased from 1,386 feet to 2,284 feet, and depths of over 4000 feet became common. Exploration became more scientific: up to 1930 or thereabouts, most wells were 'wildcats', drilled without a complete geological exploration of a locality on or near surface seeps or gas vents. Geophysical methods of probing underground structures began in 1931, and were increasingly elaborated in the following years, making the location of new, high-yielding fields much more precise.

As the industry expanded, roads, buildings and settlements were constructed in previously inaccessible areas of southern Trinidad. Point Fortin became the first centre of oilfield operations as a port and a developing township: in 1907 Trinidad Oilfields Ltd set up base at La Fortunée estate, Point Fortin, in what is now Trintoc's industrial area, and buildings and clay roads were built in a region that had been wild bush and abandoned estates. After UBOT took over in 1913, a refinery, a jetty, houses, railways and pipelines were constructed, and a crude but flourishing town sprung up. Point Fortin was, in fact, 'the town that oil built', growing up in the space of fifty years from a forest clearing with a few rough huts to a modern town of about 30,000 people (1907–57). In the other oilfield areas, houses, roads, railways and pipelines were built, and gradually the southern half of the island was opened up and made accessible.

The oil industry enjoyed a boom period between 1914 and 1924. The considerable increase in production in these years was largely the result of the successful exploitation of Forest Reserve by TLL, which built a 26-mile pipeline to connect the field to its refinery at Pointe-à-Pierre, which had a capacity of 3,500 barrels per day as early as 1916. Another important company was Apex Trinidad Oilfields, which began drilling near Fyzabad in 1920, with conspicuous success, while Kern Trinidad Oilfields exploited fields at Guapo. The old Guayaguare fields were reopened by TLL in 1925, and many south-western fields — Palo Seco, Siparia, Fyzabad, San Francique — were developed in this period.

At this time the administrative and technical staff was mostly British and European, the drillers tended to be Americans, and the semi-skilled or unskilled labour Trinidadian or 'small-islander'. P.E.T. O'Connor, from a local French Creole family, was the first Trinidadian university graduate to enter the oil industry when he joined Kern in 1923. At Kern the staff in the 1920s was British and American, and O'Connor tells us that the social life of the oilfield staff camps was organized on a strictly 'whites only' basis, for the oil industry had accepted the racial segregation that was typical of Trinidad society until after the Second World War. By the 1920s the oil companies had begun to train local blacks as technicians, but many of them, resenting salary discrimination in favour of US drillers and technicians, left Trinidad to take part in the Venezuelan oil boom of these years, for in Venezuela they were treated on an equal basis with other expatriates. O'Connor notes that it was not until the 1950s that significant numbers of Trinidadians entered supervisory positions in the oil industry.

At the end of the postwar boom years, a period of consolidation and steady technical development took place. Many of the smaller, weaker companies failed, and a few large concerns, notably UBOT, TLL and Apex, dominated the industry in the period between 1924 and 1937. By 1929, with the growing demand for gasoline for motor cars, new processes for producing gas were added to the Pointe-à-Pierre refinery. But oil prices slumped in 1930–31 as a result of overproduction. Drilling was suspended on some fields and men were laid off, but crude oil production increased steadily, from a total 5.4 million barrels in 1927 to 20 million in 1939. In fact the major companies made good profits throughout the depression years of the 1930s, and the two major companies declared dividends of 35 per cent and 25 per cent in 1935–6. Low wages and a number of objectionable labour policies by the major oil companies led directly to the strikes of 1937, but 'normality' was soon restored, and the Second World War ushered in a second boom period. Trinidad's oil was vitally important to Britain's war effort; in 1938 the island accounted for 44.2 per cent of British Empire production, and the figure had risen to 65 per cent by 1946. In comparison with Middle Eastern sources, Trinidad's oil was far less vulnerable to enemy action, so long as the British and US fleets dominated the Caribbean and the Atlantic, and British war planners placed considerable emphasis on the need to expand and defend the local oil industry. To meet the growing demand for aviation fuel, the world's first iso-octane fuel plant was built at Pointe-à-Pierre in 1938, producing 10,000 barrels per day for the Royal Air Force, and in 1940–41 a virtually new refinery was built at Pointe-à-Pierre for the British Ministry of Aircraft Production, which TLL bought at the end of the war. With a greatly increased refining capacity, crude was first imported for refining in 1940; the importation of crude oil and the extension of refining proceeded rapidly during and after the war.

When the war began, in fact, the oil industry had come to dominate the economy of Trinidad and Tobago. Oil accounted for only 10 per cent of exports in 1919, but by 1932 the proportion was 50 per cent and by 1943 (in the middle of the war) the figure had reached a staggering 80 per cent. The narrowly based, primary agricultural economy of the nineteenth century had been transformed, and by 1940 Trinidad was virtually a one-export economy. Yet the numbers employed in oil, while they increased steadily, remained small in comparison with those absorbed by the traditional agricultural sector. Oil employed 801 in 1921, 3,280 in 1925, 8,000 in 1939 and 15,000 in 1944, at the height of the wartime boom. The oil workers comprised a very small percentage of the labour force during this period, and agriculture continued to employ the great majority of Trinidadians in the first 40 years of the century. The Olivier Commission of 1929-30, for instance, estimated that at least 40,000 people were then directly employed by the Trinidad sugar industry as labourers and cane farmers.

Bridget Bereton

CRITICAL THINKING AND WRITING

1. Explain the **context** in which you would expect to find this article.
2. State, using evidence from the text:
   a) what you consider to be the writer's main intention.
   b) who you consider to be the author's target audience.
   c) how the text has been shaped by context, audience and purpose.
3. Identify the sentence which presents the writer's thesis. Is this thesis adequately developed in the text? Explain your answer.
4. Cite different features of the text which suggest that Brereton is a careful writer and researcher, who has a keen interest in the subject.
5. Identify the dominant organizing pattern(s) or principle(s) used in the last three paragraphs. Comment on the effectiveness of **one**.
6. Examine three different purposes for which the writer uses dates in the text.

COLLABORATIVE ACTIVITY

7. Discuss the tasks below using the following headings:
   PURPOSE, DISCOURSE TYPE, FUNCTION OF LANGUAGE, ORGANISING PRINCIPLE, REGISTER.
   a) Write an essay for a University science class explaining the processing of a particular product.
   b) Prepare an article for submission to an academic journal on the development of bauxite mining in Jamaica and Guyana.
   c) Prepare a speech for delivery to a group of historians about the growth of a particular industry in your territory.
   d) Tell a story to a group of kindergarten students about the importance of a particular commodity — such as a precious stone — in your country.

=== ◈ ===

CHAPTER 18

SMALL ISLANDS, BIG MEDIA: CHALLENGES OF FOREIGN MEDIA IN COVERING THE CARIBBEAN

The Cost Factor

The Caribbean is by no means the easiest region to cover, in terms of its geography. Not only are the Caribbean states spread out over a very large area, but also each state has its own peculiarities which must be taken into account in any serious coverage of the region. Hugh O'Shaughnessy and R. Whitaker found out something about the complexities of the Caribbean region in May, 1980, when together they reported on US economic initiatives in the region for the *Financial Times*. Both O'Shaughnessy and Whitaker observed that the islands of the Caribbean are difficult to lump together, although most have fragile economies.[1]

The *Economist* was more explicit. Looking at the problems that arose in aviation as a result of the scattered nature of Caribbean states, Michael Elliot writing in a special survey on the Caribbean said as follows:

Air travel throughout the Caribbean acts as a metaphor for a larger truth. From Europe, New York or Miami flights descend on the islands in clustered curves; the long-distance traveller is well served by the international airlines [But] try to fly from one island to another, and you are at the mercy of strange schedules and unconscious symbolism. The easiest route from Jamaica to the Dominican Republic is through Miami. A St Lucian needs a visa to take the short flight to Martinique....Even for travel between countries of the Commonwealth Caribbean, passport controls and customs checks are required for all.[2]

Even without such difficult flight schedules, distances among the different Caribbean islands can be great. True, it is a short run from St Lucia to Martinique, St Vincent, Barbados or Dominica, for example, but it can take up to four hours to fly from St Lucia to Jamaica and much more time to fly from Jamaica to Trinidad and Tobago or Guyana.

In these circumstances, where to base foreign correspondents has always been a critical question for British newspapers. A correspondent may be based in Jamaica, but a combination of poor flight schedules and long distances will prevent him from being on top of developments taking place in, say, Trinidad or Guyana.

When the *Guardian* newspaper implemented its experiment a few years ago, by basing Nick Worrall (who later went to the BBC) in one of the islands and having him travel to the other islands to provide coverage, the paper discovered how difficult and costly it was to do so. The *Guardian* found that the cost in terms of air fares and hotel accommodation for what was, most of the time, feature material, was too high. The *Guardian* could not afford the cost, Worrall could not afford it either, and after about eighteen months the arrangement came to an end. The *Guardian* simply could not pay Worrall enough to cover his expenses and at the same time give him a reasonable income.

The alternative to having one's own correspondent in the area and having him or her travel throughout the islands, is to employ a wide array of island correspondents. The problem here, however, is that although there are some outstanding journalists in the Caribbean, these journalists tend to be very busy people. They often do well in the profession rather quickly and so the availability of young, bright journalists from the region who are interested in making 'a little bit of money' out of British newspapers is not very high, even in the larger islands of the region. Thus, you find that putting one's own correspondent in the region turns out to be too expensive and trying to depend on *stringers* does not work, because the kind of people the newspapers are looking for to perform this role are often drawn into government services or move into diplomacy.

There is a third alternative which the Americans pursue and that is to base a correspondent in Florida and use him or her to cover both Central America and the Spanish, French and English-speaking Caribbean. Not many British newspapers have tried this method, since it has been regarded as pretty much an American solution to the problem of coverage of Central America and the Caribbean. But from all accounts coming out of the American experience, this method, too, has many drawbacks particularly those related to basing costs in Miami. There is also the problem of flights out of Miami and also a certain dichotomy in covering both Central America and the Caribbean. The difficulty here arises from the fact that although Central America and the Caribbean are geographically contiguous, there is vast difference in terms of the kind of politics that is going on in these two regions.

This political dichotomy means that foreign correspondents have to deal with two very different sets of stories occurring at very different paces and tending therefore to get in the way of each other. The American way, therefore, does not appear to be an ideal solution. The Caribbean has often been referred to in political and economic terms as a shatter zone. Indeed it is a shatter zone in the context of journalism as well.

To take coverage of the Caribbean seriously, then, British national newspapers must balance the high costs involved with the relatively limited number of hard news stories the region generates. The decision by these newspapers to locate their own correspondents in the region must take account of which island is the best on which to base the correspondents, both in terms of the ability of these correspondents to access the news in as wide a number of islands as possible and the costs involved. During the 1980s an ideal solution was not found and to date the situation generally has remained the same.

Finding the Right Correspondent

It has not always been easy for British national newspapers to find 'the right man' within the Caribbean willing to 'string' for the UK press. In general, *stringers* and correspondents must be able to fit into the overall style of the particular newspapers for which they are working. Some newspapers, like the *Financial Times* for example, have been successful in identifying and employing persons who are capable of turning out copy that fits neatly into the news structure of the papers for which they are correspondents. Others find it more difficult to do so.

It is nevertheless desirable for British papers to have journalists from the Caribbean countries reporting for these papers from various Caribbean localities. For many years, British newspapers have recognised what they regard as the 'good and honourable tradition' of excellent journalism in the Caribbean, but these newspapers recognise, too, that much of this excellence is internally directed. Undoubtedly, there are good Caribbean journalists who write good Caribbean stories, but only for a Caribbean market.

The challenge for any British national newspaper wishing to cover the Caribbean therefore, would be to find a good 'local' journalist who is able to write with the right perspective for an audience which would not necessarily know much about the details of a particular story from a particular country or region. It is giving that sense of perspective that is so important. Employing such an indigenous journalist is crucial, but should not be at the expense of lowering the standards of the particular newspaper concerned. What must be borne in mind is that writing for a British national newspaper is, essentially, writing for a vast foreign market.

One British national newspaper that thinks it has managed to overcome the difficulty, in terms of recruitment of a suitable Caribbean national as its correspondent in the region, is the *Financial Times*. The *Financial Times* has employed Canute James, who is based in Jamaica and has the latitude to cover the region as he thinks necessary for the *Financial Times*. By all accounts, James is an ideal candidate for the job because, not only has he lived in England and therefore been familiar with the British way of life, but he has been quite familiar with the *Financial Times*' 'house style' and is able to fit easily into the *Financial Times*' news structure. From the point of view of the smaller islands of the Caribbean, however, Canute James's appointment as the principal *stringer* for the region has not satisfied the expectations of 'small island' people. The reason for this will be made clearer in the next section.

A Caribbean Dilemma?

The *Financial Times* may have been lucky to find a Caribbean national like Canute James to correspond for it from the Caribbean, but there are some general considerations that tend to reduce the effectiveness of 'local' journalists as British newspaper correspondents. In the first place, Caribbean journalists seldom travel around the region to get some sense of what is happening in neighbouring states. There is, therefore, a fair amount of ignorance of the region on the part of these journalists. Simple, but significant, qualitative elements of news — like accuracy, to give one example — are continually undermined by this general ignorance.

The celebrated Canute James, for instance, wrote a piece for the *Financial Times* of May 19, 1980, on an overseas trip made by OECS leaders from St. Lucia, St. Vincent and

Antigua to secure aid for their island states. In that article, James referred to St Lucia's Prime Minister as "Mr. Jack Compton".[3] The Prime Minister's first name is John, and it seems clear that had James been totally familiar with St. Lucia's politics, he would have known that. After all, Mr Compton has been head of the St Lucia Government since 1964, with only a brief two-and-a-half year break between 1979 and 1982. Canute James's error, therefore, must not be regarded as 'a slip of the pen', since James would never slip in referring to Britain's Prime Minister or the President of the United States.

From a Caribbean standpoint, errors of this kind and other signs of ignorance in foreign coverage are more forgivable when they appear in stories on the region written by foreign journalists. The situation is less pardonable where Caribbean journalists are concerned. Yet this attitude has persisted for reasons that only Caribbean journalists perhaps may understand. Within the Caribbean a 'big island–small island' syndrome has been perpetuated by Caribbean journalists, and even Canute James himself would be more inclined to focus his coverage on the region's more developed states of Jamaica, his home country base, Trinidad & Tobago, Guyana and Barbados. It may be that James is taking his cue from the paper for which he works, but there is nothing preventing him from making the *Financial Times* interested in the smaller states. This is an initiative that he must exercise and generally is free to exercise; but he chooses his area of focus selectively.

Within the smaller states of the region, there is a measure of anger and resentment over the attitude of big island correspondents, because the 'small islanders' are convinced that, notwithstanding their physical size and large populations, the more developed states have done much worse than the smaller states,

economically and socially, and therefore are not in any position to boast about their status as big islands. It is an empty boast so far as the small states are concerned. The currencies of these more developed states, with the exception of that of Barbados, have not only been seriously devalued but are not accepted anywhere in the Caribbean. These states are facing serious economic declines. Yet foreign correspondents based in these big islands continue to file reports that give readers outside the region the impression that life really exists only in these big islands.

Foreign journalists covering the Caribbean can face many frustrations when preparing their reports, because of the often large amount of background material they must provide before they can get into the actual story. In the context of hard news, this reduces the effectiveness of the story, because background information, especially that of a geographical, social or political nature, can take away from the 'urgency' of the report. To minimise the incidence of having a great amount of background information in their stories, foreign correspondents could work in collaboration with a 'man on the spot' who would provide them with only the salient points that, from a Caribbean perspective, are considered to be important. The problem arises, however, when this 'man on the spot' is himself unfamiliar with the background information.

In the years following the establishment of CANA Radio[4] in the mid 1980s, Caribbean journalists had started to travel around the islands a little more in order to undertake assignments of one kind or another for CANA. Most of them experienced 'culture shocks' when they visited neighbouring states for the first time, because before then, they had no real idea of how people lived in these states. Perhaps after these 'shocks' these journalists will truly be able to earn their title as Caribbean journalists.

Another difficulty stemming from within the Caribbean relates to the perspectives of Caribbean journalists, especially those considered to be senior journalists, in terms of the politics of the region. What is in question here is, again, the basic values which should generally be upheld by journalists with regard to the elements of news quality. Balance and fairness constitute one such element and, in general, journalists strive to ensure that their stories reflect all sides of the situation in question. The experience in the Caribbean, however, is that most of the senior journalists support the governments of the day and, to a large extent have been cultured in the art of government propaganda. Stories written by these journalists, therefore, invariably support particular government lines and can give a rather distorted picture of life in the region to readers overseas.

In St Lucia, where the OECS headquarters are based, for example, Radio St Lucia's news editor, Ernie Seon, who also strings for CANA and a number of international agencies, at one time became known among his colleagues as the personal 'mouthpiece' of Prime Minister John Compton. At the time it seemed to have been Mr Compton's personal policy not to talk to any media representative but Seon. And whereas the Prime Minister hardly met the press in the last decade, he regularly contacted Seon whenever he wished to make a statement, or report on some overseas trip. This has been the reality in St Lucia, but similar experiences can be found throughout the OECS region. In these circumstances, one would question Ernie Seon's legitimacy to correspond for overseas media, if balance and fairness in reporting is to be observed and maintained.

The level of support that Caribbean journalists have for their governments results largely from the structure of ownership and control of the mass media in the islands. To a large extent the media, especially the electronic media in the islands, are owned and controlled by the governments of the islands. Radio St Lucia, for example, is government owned and is controlled by a board handpicked by the Minister responsible for Broadcasting. It is from this base that Ernie Seon operates. The print media are generally more independent than the electronic media because many newspapers are privately owned. But even here, government influence cannot be dismissed, since most of the private newspaper owners are aligned to the ruling political party.

The state of affairs in the Caribbean, so far as ownership and control of the media are concerned, has been outlined by Aggrey Brown and Roderick Sanatan as follows:

> There is a lot of governmental power in the media. In Barbados there are state and conglomerate private interests. There is a strong private sector backing the government in Dominica. Antigua is government owned. St Kitts/Nevis has its newspapers allied to political parties — one being the party in power — and government ownership of both television and radio. In the case of Belize, it is the government and private sector. Jamaica is similar to Belize, [and] the government and private sector have ownership in St Lucia, Trinidad and Tobago, and Grenada.[5]

Given that situation Brown and Sanatan rightly point out that 'the notion of ownership of the media raises issues of access and participation outside of the corridors of either private economic power or governmental control [or both].' The question is not only one of representing the popular views of Caribbean people in the media but also one of providing consumers outside the region with an accurate picture of life in the islands.

Matthew Roberts

Notes

1. See 'Washington Hawks Eye the Caribbean' in *Financial Times* of May 9, 1980, p. 5.
2. See Michael Elliott's survey of the Caribbean entitled 'Columbus Islands' in The *Economist* of August 6, 1988, p.4.
3. St Lucia was the focus of that article entitled 'Caribbean Leaders head for Tobago', because that island's Prime Minister was the main spokesman for the touring party.
4. CANA is the Caribbean News Agency which started off as a wire service that fed the international press with news from a Caribbean perspective. Its radio unit, based in Barbados, was part of the agency's expansion programme.
5. See Brown and Sanatan's *Talking With Whom – A Report on the State of the Media in the Caribbean*, the section entitled 'Ownership and Control', p. 23.

CRITICAL THINKING AND WRITING

1. List some of the problems that the writer believes are involved in the British and American media's coverage of the Caribbean.
2. What appears to be the writer's primary reason for writing this piece? Provide support for your answer.
3. What is the writer's attitude to his audience and to the subject matter? Provide evidence from the passage.
4. Is this writer credible? Explain your answer.
5. Comment specifically on the writer's use of syntax and register, and what they suggest about his intended audience.
6. Identify the dominant tone in the passage and examine how it allows Roberts to achieve his purpose.
7. Choose any paragraph and identify the organizational pattern which the writer uses. How does the use of this organizing principle help to communicate his meaning more effectively?

WRITING TASK

8. The writer states that Hugh O'Shaughnessy and R. Whitaker observed that 'the islands of the Caribbean are difficult to lump together although most have fragile economies.' Write a paragraph, utilizing exemplification as an organizing principle, to show the extent to which this statement reflects the reality of the Caribbean.

GROUP WORK

9. In groups, do some free writing for the topic 'The Representation of the Caribbean in the American and British Media.'
   a) Discuss your ideas with other members of your group.
   b) Write an opening statement (hook) and a thesis statement on the topic.
   c) State the organizational structure which you would like to use in your essay and explain why you would like to use it.

CHAPTER 19

COSTA RICA

Most Afro-Costa Ricans live on the Atlantic Coast of the country and are ethnically and culturally closer to the English-speaking Caribbean than to Afro-Hispanic communities of much of Latin America. Mainly descended from West Indian migrant workers, they traditionally kept themselves apart from the majority population. In recent decades this separateness has begun to dissolve, along with their strong sense of cultural identity. While there have been some improvements in their socio-economic status, the community still faces significant problems of poverty and disadvantage.

First Arrivals

Official accounts of Costa Rican history do not record it, but Africans first entered Costa Rica at the very start of the European conquest in 1502. A few accompanied Columbus when he arrived on the east coast in September of that year. By 1707 the Spaniards had begun to ship Africans into Costa Rica as a substitute for indigenous labour. Many slaves were put to work on the cacao plantations that supported the colony's economy. Costa Rica also supplied slaves to other Spanish American countries. Records from the period show that the slaves included women.

Over the next 250 years it is thought that sizeable numbers of people of African origin came from the Caribbean islands to settle on the eastern, Atlantic Coast. Elsewhere, growing numbers of maroons (escaped slaves) lived in the more isolated areas.

Black Workers of Limón

To facilitate the growing trade in coffee with Europe, an eastern seaport and a railway connecting it to the rest of the country were needed in the Atlantic coastal region, soon to be officially designated as Limón Province. In 1870 Tomás Guardia, the country's President, obtained a loan from the British government to build a railway, and the construction of the first warehouse at Port Limón began on November 15, 1871.

Due to the perceived urgency of the construction work, foreign labourers were brought in. A report from December 20, 1872 reads: 'Today, at 2 p.m., the schooner Lizzie of 117 tons arrived … carrying 7 men and 123 workers for the railroad. Included are 3 women.' Most of the new migrant workers were Afro-Caribbeans. While many came directly from the islands, especially Jamaica, others travelled up the coast from what was then part of Colombia and would become Panama, where they had been working for the French canal project. Thus began a pattern of migration between the Caribbean, Panama and Limón that would persist for decades.

Caribbean workers were recruited through a subcontracting system using overseers, which meant that proper employment contracts were not drawn up. Pay was low, and the climate and conditions were harsh, with swamps, mosquitoes and prolonged rains. Many of the early migrant labourers died, despite the widely held belief that they had adjusted to the tropics.

The Keith brothers, who were contracted to build the railway, introduced the commercial cultivation of bananas beside the railway tracks. Jamaicans rather than Hispanic Costa Ricans were preferred for this work, because they had previous experience of banana cultivation and because they spoke English and were therefore considered loyal to the British Crown and the US-run company. When the French canal project collapsed in 1887, more Afro-Caribbeans came to Costa Rica in search of employment.

With the introduction of banana growing, the black workforce once more demonstrated its versatility. Canal builders turned railway builders and operators now also became farmers. The Keiths' company grew not only bananas but also cacao, sugar-cane and, further inland, coffee.

The primary concern of the migrant workers was to make some money and then return to their home islands. But although their labour on the railway and plantations sustained much of the national economy, their wages remained meagre. Few, if any, earned enough to re-establish family ties, and the threat of unemployment and poverty was ever present. Return to the islands was little more than a dream.

In 1899 the Keiths merged their plantation enterprise with the Boston Fruit Company to form the United Fruit Company. Between them, the United Fruit Company and the Keiths' Northern Railway Company ran Limón for their own advantage, controlling the province's railways, docks, steamships and land. United Fruit continued to rent hundreds of acres of national land, tax free. The company built and ran housing, supply stores, medical facilities, churches and schools, determining the distribution of settlements along the railway route.

Ethnic Relations and Racism

By the early twentieth century, Limón Province had a resident Caribbean population of many thousands, most of whom were single men, living as temporary residents. Despite their homesickness, the Afro-Limonenses came to form a permanent colony. They remained closer to the Caribbean, especially Jamaica, than to the host country, in their speech, dress, food and way of doing business among themselves.

In any case, Limón and its population remained largely isolated from the rest of the country, despite the railway. Few Afro-Costa Ricans ever travelled to San José, the capital — a distance of 103 miles, under each one of which, it was said, lay the body of an immigrant worker.

Tension existed between labourers and overseers, between black workers and native Costa Ricans, and even between the older Jamaicans and subsequent arrivals of younger Caribbean men. In general, the native Costa Ricans did not like having the Afro-Caribbeans in their midst; they spoke a different language, were Protestant rather than

Catholic and had a different way of life. The immigrants did not trust the host population either. Seeing themselves as temporary inhabitants only, the Afro-Caribbeans kept apart. Most could not speak Spanish and had no wish to learn it, regarding Spanish culture as inferior to that of Britain. Those who had children did not want them educated among the Spanish-speakers, whom they despised, preferring private schools instead.

During the 1920s and 1930s disaster struck Limón in the shape of various diseases attacking the banana plants. The United Fruit Company gradually abandoned its operations there, leaving behind its workforce. The company signed new agreements with the Costa Rican authorities and switched to the Pacific coast instead.

A ban was soon issued by Congress on any person of colour dwelling or seeking a job in the new company enclave to the west — on the grounds that jobs were needed for the Pacific coastal dwellers. (Racist legislation such as this has often been passed in Latin America. El Salvador did not, until recently, grant permanent residence to black people. Ironically, the few Afro-Americans in El Salvador are usually US diplomats.)

Many of the formerly subcontracted black labour force set up as small-scale independent growers of bananas, cacao and hemp, on land vacated by the company. Others migrated to the larger towns, initiating a gradual process of cultural adaptation.

Yet for numerous others unemployment, hunger, and despair took hold. Significant numbers of the second generation of black Costa Ricans, ironically calling themselves 'Nowhereans', saw themselves as neither British, Jamaican nor Costa Rican. Although born in the country, none of them were legally its citizens. The United Fruit Company, the railway company, the Costa Rican government, the British consulate in Limón and the Jamaican government appeared to have washed their hands of them.

It was not until 1949, when a new constitution was drawn up after the civil war — in which many Afro-Costa Ricans fought with honour — that the former Caribbean islanders obtained full Costa Rican citizenship. The indigenous peoples of Costa Rica living in the same province would have to wait even longer.

Kathleen Royal and Franklin Perry

Select Bibliography

Herzfeld, A. 'The Creoles of Costa Rica and Panama.' In *Central American English*, ed. J. Holm, 131–49. Heidelberg: Groos, 1983.

Meléndez, C. and Duncan, Q. *El negro en Costa Rica*. San José: Editorial Costa Rica, 1977.

Purcell, T.W. *Banana Fallout: Class, Color and Culture among West Indians in Costa Rica*. Los Angeles: Center for Afro-American Studies, University of California, 1993.

Stewart, W. *Keith y Costa Rica*. Sari José: Editorial Costa Rica, 1976.

CRITICAL THINKING AND WRITING

1. Do you consider the discourse mode used by the writer appropriate for this essay?

2. In what context would you expect to find this article? Explain your response in relation to what you consider to be the writer's purpose and audience.

3. In paragraphs three, four and five, *cause and effect* is used to explain two different aspects of the subject. How does this use of the strategy help the reader to understand the subject?

4. What is the writer's attitude to the subject? Explain, using examples from the text.

For further Research

5. Find additional information, using both Internet and library searches, about Afro-Costa Ricans, to share with your class.

SCIENCE &
THE ENVIRONMENT

CHAPTER 20

WHAT TO LOOK FOR UNDER THE SEA

Living within the coral itself, minute plant cells called zooxanthellae contribute to the reef-building process, and are the main source of colour in the coral communities. Since these micro-organisms require light in order to live, hermatypic, or reef-building, corals are found generally at water depths of less than one hundred feet. In this bluish zone only the diver, freed from the terrestrial world above by a self-contained air supply, can truly experience the wonders and intricate beauty of the reef environment.

Down to around thirty feet, Elkhorn coral forms extensive beds that stretch unbroken for miles, its palmate branches conforming to the direction and intensity of the water currents that bathe it and bear its food. Staghorn coral, a close relative, possesses easily broken tips, and is more susceptible to wave action. Hence, it is found in slightly deeper water, and does not extend to the surface. Reaching a height of ten to twelve feet, star coral boulders provide a haven for a multiplicity of marine organisms, such as encrusting algae and sponges, and fastened sea fans and feather stars. Marine crustacea — such as shrimps and spiney lobsters — shelter beneath the overhangs, while precariously perched coral crabs delicately glean surface

algae with their massive pincers. Sergeant majors and trunk fish nibble the algal mats, and pugnacious little damselfish dart about valiantly defending their territory against all intruders.

Another name for the majestic pillar coral is cathedral coral. Encountering them usually as a solitary colony, well away from the main reef mass, divers pay homage as they approach the gothic spires. Tiny fish, with rainbow colours, frolic at hide and seek among the sturdy, though slow-growing, branches, and octopuses retreat by squeezing their boneless bodies through very small openings in the algal-draped limestone.

Brain coral, as its name suggests, resembles the exterior of the human brain. Coral cups fuse to form sculptured rows and channels which, by nightfall, will support a myriad of hungry, plankton-feeding polyps. Set among the larger coral masses may be found a variety of smaller species, such as finger and flower coral, as well as a host of others, forming colourful moulds a foot or more across.

Distantly related to the hard corals, stinging corals are of similar appearance. They are widespread in shallow waters, and occur in abundance on eroded reef tops, wrecks and pilings. The polyps are small, and there are no visible coral cups, which accounts for the smooth appearance of the colony. Jamaican 'fire corals' are armed with special protective polyps which, if brushed against by unprotected skin, may inflict quite a painful sting that can itch for several days. Light gloves are recommended if you intend to handle rocks and coral.

Located among the reef building corals are what may appear to be elaborate flattened or feathered plants. These are, in fact, living animals called soft corals, and include the gorgonian sea fans, sea whips and sea feathers. Gorgonian corals inherited their name from the mythical Gorgons who had snakes for hair, and all who looked upon them were turned to stone! Unlike the hard corals, the skeletal core is flexible in these organisms, and the whole colony bends and undulates with the movement of water around it. Gorgonians occur in shades of purple, blue, green and orange, and may be found at all diving depths. Precious 'black coral', is well known to sub-aqua enthusiasts in Jamaica.

Whenever there are rocks, shells, submerged timbers or corals to provide suitable attachment, sponges abound. These come in a variety of sizes, shapes and colours, depending on the local conditions. In fact, it was not until the mid-eighteenth century, when internal water currents were observed, that the true animal nature of sponges was clearly established. Large barrel varieties, measuring five feet or more, are quite common on the walls of Jamaican reefs, and are capable of filtering several hundred gallons of water each day in order to obtain food and oxygen. In contrast, encrusting sponges such as 'chicken liver' form only shallow moulds, and exploit the space of crevices and other confined areas.

Often found crawling on the surface of sponges is the elegant bristle worm, or 'sea forty legs' as it is colloquially referred to in many Jamaican coastal communities, presumably after its land-based cousin. Admire, but don't touch since the lateral white bristles of this worm is its protective armament against would be predators. Among the most beautiful of the sedentary worms to be found on our reefs is the plume, or Christmas tree worm. It extends its elaborate, twin-spiralled crown into the water in order to trap plankton. Any threat of disturbance and the crown is retracted instantly. Tube-dwelling worms are also found in the sandy flats that separate the coral buttresses, as well as in the soft, white sands that extend from the shoreline to the reef. Turtle grass affords stability and support within the substratum, while also providing food and refuge for a great variety of marine organisms.

Starfish, brittle stars, sea urchins, conchs, helmets, even sea turtles, are all to be found associated with this particular habitat. Green turtles, although actually brownish in colour, are not uncommon among Jamaica's reefs, and average one hundred to two hundred pounds in weight. Happily these beautiful animals are now protected from hunters by Jamaican law.

Related to the sea urchins and brittle stars are the sea cucumbers. Milky white, and brown specimens graze the bottom sand using their tentacles, apparently oblivious to anything that is going on around them. Although there are no sea snakes in the West Indies, the spotted snake eel, often gliding across the flats or through coral rubble, may be confused with such. Reaching a length of two to three feet, Jamaican snake eels are not aggressive and may be gently handled with safety.

There are close to seven hundred species of fish associated with the coral reefs in our area, but some of them are small and may live in the sand, or take refuge by day in coral recesses. An occasional glance by the enthusiast under rocks and ledges is often rewarded through sighting of nocturnal species such as squirrel-fish and iridescent cardinal fish. Further investigation of the many coral tunnels and caves that penetrate the reef will usually reveal other nocturnal fish, such as glasseye snappers, bigeyes and glassy sweepers. These provide colour and lustre against the pale backdrop of coral limestone.

Ralph Robinson

CRITICAL THINKING AND WRITING

1. State, using evidence from the passage:
   a) what you consider to be the writer's main reason for writing this article;
   b) the assumptions he made about his intended audience in terms of
   i. level of interest in the subject
   ii. previous knowledge about the subject
   iii. general educational background/level of specialization.

2. In which subject area/discipline would this article be most appropriately placed?

3. Identify the figurative/literary devices used in the following excerpts:
   a) 'Gorgonian corals inherited their name from mythical Gorgons…'
   b) 'Tiny fish with rainbow colours frolic at hide and seek among the sturdy, though slow-growing branches…'
   c) 'Admire but don't touch, since the lateral white bristles of this worm are its protective armament against would-be predators.'

4. Describe the diction used in the passage in terms of:
   a) level of detail
   b) level of formality and technicality

5. a) Explain what the use of language/ diction reveals about the attitude of the writer to the subject.
   b) Identify the type of response that the use of language/diction would evoke in the target audience.

WRITING ACROSS THE CURRICULUM ACTIVITY

6. Write a paragraph in which you present any other feature of the environment to a similar audience. Attempt to write in a style similar to the one used in this article, using as many figurative devices as possible.

CHAPTER 21

FLOWERS, NOT FLIRTING, MAKE SEXES DIFFER – CARIBBEAN HUMMINGBIRDS

Let's not get so obsessed with attracting the opposite sex, cautions a hummingbird research team.

Sex appeal may seem like all that makes the world go round, especially to anyone reading recent scientific studies about why males look different from females, remarks Ethan J. Temeles of Amherst (Mass.) College.

Evolutionary pressure to charm and fight for a mate, or sexual selection, is usually easier to test for than natural selection, or the bottom-line pressure for survival, says Temeles. Yet he and his colleagues have found a Caribbean island where they say they can distinguish between the two.

Among purple-throated caribs, *Eulampis jugularis*, the largest hummingbird on St. Lucia, it's food and not flirtation that's driven males and females to develop bills in his-and-hers models, the researchers argue. 'This is the first really unambiguous example of ecology playing a role in the morphological differences between the sexes,' Temeles says.

To be fair, he points out, biologists never claimed sexual selection explained all gender differences. Darwin himself proposed that specialized diets led to bill differences in a New Zealand bird, the huia. Males' stubby bills allowed them to drill into trees for insects,

while the females' long, curved bills pried insects out of crevices. Verifying Darwin's theory has been difficult, since the bird went extinct more than a century ago.

Evidence has been thin to verify any claim of ecological causes for sex differences. Some studies have suggested that food preferences may foster gender-related size differences in snakes, weasels, and predatory birds. Based on anatomical studies, scientists have argued that in certain mosquitoes, male mouth parts look ideal for sipping nectar while the females' counterparts look better for sucking blood.

On St. Lucia, 'you couldn't design a better system' for studying food contributions to sex differences, Temeles crows. During breeding season, male hummingbirds sip nectar almost exclusively from *Heliconia caribaea*, whereas females eschew that flower for *Heliconia bihai*, the researchers report in the July 21 *Science*.

Measuring each gender's bills revealed that their curvature and length best fit the preferred flower. Indeed, females fed in just three-quarters the time when sipping from their preferred bloom instead of the males, Temeles reports.

Hummingbird expert Larry L. Wolf of Syracuse (N.Y.) University considers Temeles'

98

explanation for the sex differences 'quite reasonable'. Elsewhere, he notes, hummers have developed species-specific bills to fit their bloomin' diet. Caribs are just extending that bill-specialization to gender, he observes.

Their preferred flowers are also exciting, says heliconia specialist W. John Kress of the Smithsonian Institution's National Museum of Natural History in Washington, D.C. He marvels that Carib females prefer nectar from green flowers when many hummingbird-pollinated flowers blaze red or orange. In fact, the heliconia genus — related to the bird of paradise — can get downright gaudy. Kress can think of only a few other green-flowered Heliconias, all pollinated by bats.

The two species on St. Lucia appear on other islands bearing more colourful blooms, he notes. Why such differences evolved is far from clear, but, Kress enthuses, 'it's a great system.'

Susan Milius

CRITICAL THINKING AND WRITING

1. Identify and evaluate the effectiveness of the strategies used at the beginning of the article to engage the audience.
2. Name the figurative/literary devices used in the following excerpts:
    a) … it's food and not flirtation that's driven males to develop bills in his-and-hers- models… [paragraph 4, lines 3-4]
    b) …. hummers have developed species-specific bills to fit their bloomin' diet… [paragraph 9, lines 4-6]
    c) 'In fact, the Heliconia genus … can get downright gaudy.' [paragraph 10, lines 7-9]
3. Using evidence from the passage, comment on the following:
    a) register
    b) descriptiveness
    c) attention to detail
    d) level of technicality
4. Based on your response to question 3, identify the writer's target audience.
5. Explain what the use of language/diction reveals about the attitude of the writer to the subject and her audience.
6. Comment on the title of this passage.

WRITING ACROSS THE CURRICULUM ACTIVITIES

7. Undertake a web search to locate additional information on Caribbean hummingbirds.
8. Highlight what you consider to be the most interesting features of any of these species.
9. Share this information with your classmates.

CHAPTER 22

CORAL-KILLING DUST

Caribbean corals are dying. That much is certain. In the past two decades seaweed and other algae have overrun most of the delicate reefs that took stony corals (animals that secrete hard, calcium carbonate homes) thousands of years to build. Human activities, such as running boats aground, dumping sewage and over-fishing, lead to some of the destruction, but scientists are now beginning to consider a more elusive threat — soil from Africa.

Peer into the skies of Miami or San Juan on a late summer day, and you'll see that threat lurking as a reddish haze that virtually blots out the sun. Researchers have long known that strong winds periodically sweep clay-rich red soil off the dry surface of the Sahel — the region just south of the Saharan desert in North Africa — and send it across the Atlantic Ocean in giant plumes easily visible from space. The airborne dirt then rains down on south Florida and the Caribbean Sea as it has done every summer for hundreds of thousands of years. (In fact, the topsoil of Barbados is almost entirely African dust.) Only recently have researchers realized that the dust is loaded with potential coral killers — including disease spores, radioactive elements and overabundant nutrients.

Marine geologist Eugene A. Shinn of the U.S. Geological Survey in St Petersburg, Fla., became suspicious of the African dust after nearly 30 years of studying the Caribbean's reef-building corals and their perplexing demise.

When Shinn began his work — and for at least 6,000 years before that time — branching elkhorn and staghorn corals (*Acropora palmata* and *Acropora cervicornis*) dominated Caribbean reefs. To Shinn's dismay, a type of tissue-killing bacterial slime called black band disease appeared at some of his research locations in the early 1970s and has proliferated ever since. In the summer of 1983 a common species of plant-eating spiny sea urchin (*Diadema antillarum*) began dying mysteriously. Within a year, 90 per cent of them were gone. Without these urchins to graze on them, the algae quickly overran the stony corals, many of which were already sick. In a mere two decades, most Caribbean reefs went from coral- to algae-dominated.

For many years Shinn explored how water pollution might be damaging reefs in the Florida Keys. But nothing he found could explain why the same diseases were killing corals in areas far from human activity. Then in the late 1990s he noticed that the proliferation of coral disease happened to coincide with the onset of severe drought in North Africa and more dust traveling across the Atlantic, a phenomenon studied in depth by Joseph M. Prospero of the University of Miami. What's more, Shinn and Prospero realized, the greatest African dust fallout on record was 1983 — the same year as the *Diadema* die-out.

Hitching a Ride

'It was the simple correlation between the death of these corals and sea urchins and the increase in dust that first got me interested,' Shinn says. He and his colleagues suspected that the dust could be carrying spores or bacteria that were causing the diseases, but they had no evidence until recently.

In 1996, Garriet W. Smith and other researchers at the University of South Carolina identified soil fungus (*Aspergillus sydowii*) that has been killing soft corals called sea fans (specifically, *Gorgonia ventalina* and Gorgonia flabellum), which were at one time widespread in the Caribbean. The mysterious fact is that Aspergillus cannot reproduce in seawater, and yet the sea fans have been locked in an ongoing battle against the disease for a decade. Something must be providing the Caribbean waters with a continuous supply of ammunition for the disease. African dust, perhaps?

Smith and his colleagues recently isolated Aspergillus spores from African dust samples collected in the skies over the U.S. Virgin Islands, and they reported their findings in the October 1 issue of *Geophysical Research Letters*. This report is the first non-circumstantial evidence that the African dust is dangerous to corals, but some researchers are still reluctant to place too much blame. 'I'm not ready to jump on the bandwagon, but I don't want to discount it either,' says William F. Precht, a marine geologist who has studied coral reefs near Belize since the early 1980s. 'My personal feeling is that it's plausible, because these nasties do live in the dust, and we do know that the dust has been increasing over the past two decades.'

Diameda Die-Out

A single species of algae-eating sea urchin, *Diadema anitllarum*, kept Caribbean corals clean and healthy until 1983, when a mysterious, Caribbean-wide disease nearly wiped them out. With ninety percent of the urchins gone, nothing could hold the algae at bay, and they soon engulfed the corals.

Unfortunately for the corals — and perhaps for people as well — soil fungi aren't the only nasties hitching a ride with the dust. In African dust collected from the bottom of water cisterns in the Caribbean, Shinn and his colleagues discovered alarmingly high concentrations of poisonous mercury and radioactive beryllium–7. These findings were reinforced last February when scientists at the University of the Azores captured dust samples from an exceptionally large African dust plume as it drifted over their Atlantic island community some 1,500 kilometers west of Lisbon. The dust emitted gamma radiation up to 45,000 dpm per gram, roughly three times the radiation allowed in the workplace, Shinn says.

As for mercury, two particles of the dangerous metal turned up per million particles of dust. That may not sound like much, but mercury usually occurs in the atmosphere in concentrations of a few particles per billion particles of dust. Open-pit mercury mines in Algeria could be the source, Shinn speculates.

More Than a Cargo Van

Particles hitching a ride with the dust may not be the only coral killers. The dust itself could pose a threat. The dust is made up of small grains of iron, aluminum, phosphorus and other elements – all important nutrients known to support microscopic life, but an excess of nutrients can have negative consequences. Marshall L. Hayes of Duke University is investigating whether iron in the dust might encourage the growth of coral-killing bacteria. 'You don't have to bring exotic pathogens into an area,' Hayes says. 'You can have an organism that is potentially pathogenic and give it more nutrients and enhance its ability to be virulent.'

Sarah Simpson

CRITICAL THINKING AND WRITING

1. What is the writer's primary reason for writing this article?

2. With reference to the content and diction of the article, state what assumptions the writer is making about her audience in terms of their level of specialization and prior knowledge of the subject.

3. a) Identify the dominant organizational pattern used by the writer in explaining how the effect of the African dust on the Caribbean coral reef was uncovered.

   b) How does this organizational strategy contribute to the effectiveness of the article?

4. What are two strategies which the writer uses to establish credibility?

5. In which of the following subject areas/disciplines would this article be most appropriately placed?
   a) Geology
   b) Environmental Science
   c) Marine Biology
   d) Microbiology

6. a) Describe the tone and register of the article, using examples.

   b) Discuss their appropriateness for the audience which was previously identified.

   c) Evaluate the effectiveness of these stylistic features.

7. Identify the figurative devices used in the following phrases:
   a) '... and yet the seas fans have been locked in an ongoing battle...'

   b) 'Something must be providing the Caribbean waters with a continuous supply of ammunition for the disease.'

   c) 'I'm not ready to jump on the bandwagon.'

WRITING ACROSS THE CURRICULUM ACTIVITY

8. Using a more formal style than that used in this article, write two paragraphs in which you inform your audience about a non human-natural threat to any element of your environment — land, water, air.

CHAPTER 23

MAJOR CARIBBEAN EARTHQUAKES AND TSUNAMIS A REAL RISK

A dozen major earthquakes of magnitude 7.0 or greater have occurred in the Caribbean near Puerto Rico, the U.S. Virgin Islands and the island of Hispaniola, shared by Haiti and the Dominican Republic, in the past 500 years, and several have generated tsunamis. The most recent major earthquake, a magnitude 8.1 in 1946, resulted in a tsunami that killed a reported 1,600 people.

With nearly twenty million people now living in this tourist region and a major earthquake occurring on average every 50 years, scientists say it is not a question of if it will happen but when. They are calling for the establishment of tsunami early warning systems in the Caribbean Sea, the Gulf of Mexico and the Atlantic Ocean, and better public education about the real tsunami threats in these regions.

In a new study published December 24, 2004, in the *Journal of Geophysical Research* from the American Geophysical Union, geologists Uri ten Brink of the U.S. Geological Survey in Woods Hole and Jian Lin of the Woods Hole Oceanographic Institution (WHOI) report a heightened earthquake risk of the Septentrional fault zone, which cuts through the highly populated region of the Cibao valley in the Dominican Republic. In addition, they caution, the geologically active offshore Puerto Rico and Hispaniola trenches are capable of producing earthquakes of magnitude 7.5 and higher. The Indonesian earthquake on December 26, which generated a tsunami that killed (to date) an estimated 150,000 people, came from a fault of similar structure, but was a magnitude 9.0, much larger than the recorded quakes near the Puerto Rico Trench.

The Puerto Rico Trench, roughly parallel to and about 75 miles off the northern coast of Puerto Rico, is about 900 kilometers (560 miles) long and 100 kilometers (60 miles) wide. The deepest point in the Atlantic Ocean, the trench is 8,340 meters (27,362 feet) below the sea surface. The Hispaniola Trench parallels the north coast of the Dominican Republic and Haiti, and is 550 kilometers (344 miles) long and only 4,500 meters (14,764 feet) deep.

Earthquakes typically occur near faults or fractures in the Earth's crust where rock formations, driven by the movements of the crustal or tectonic plates that make up the Earth's surface, grind slowly past each other or collide, building up stress. At some point, stress overcomes friction and the rocks slip suddenly, releasing seismic energy in the form of an earthquake, which drops the stress in one area but raises the stress elsewhere along the fault line. Eighty percent of earthquakes on Earth occur on the sea floor and most of them along the plate boundaries.

Hispaniola, Puerto Rico and the U.S. Virgin Islands sit on top of small crustal blocks that are sandwiched between the North American and Caribbean plates. The island of Hispaniola faces a double risk: an earthquake from the Septentrional fault on the island itself as the plates move past each other, and an earthquake deep in the earth in the subduction zone on which the island sits. Both could cause severe damage and loss of life, although the researchers say an earthquake in the subduction zone could be more devastating and has the potential to cause a tsunami.

The two scientists studied the geology of the northern Caribbean plate boundary, looked at historical earthquake data in the region, and used three-dimensional models to calculate the stress changes in and near the trenches after each earthquake. Ten Brink, who is also an adjunct scientist at WHOI, and Lin say stress has increased for the Hispaniola area, and that the potential threat of earthquakes and resulting possible tsunamis from the Puerto Rico and Hispaniola trenches is real and should be taken seriously. In addition to establishing warning systems and informing the public about the risk, they call for improved documentation of prior earthquake and tsunami events and better estimates of future threats from the Puerto Rico and Hispaniola trenches through underwater studies.

'Every earthquake has its own character,' says Lin, who has studied mid-ocean ridges, hotspots and undersea volcanoes as well as earthquakes in Southern California, China and the Pacific. 'And not all earthquakes generate tsunamis, which form when large areas of the seafloor rise or drop suddenly, causing the ocean above to move. Many factors come into play in tsunami formation, including the size and type of an earthquake and how much the quake has ruptured the seafloor.'

Lin, a senior scientist and a marine geophysicist in the WHO Geology and Geophysics Department, says that each time an earthquake occurs on the offshore Puerto Rico and Hispaniola trenches, it adds stress to the Septentrional fault zone on Hispaniola. Since the fault is in a highly populated region and is capable of generating magnitude 7.7– 7.9 earthquakes, the public should be educated about the risk of this earthquake prone area.

The region has a long history of destructive earthquakes. Historical records show that major earthquakes have struck the Puerto Rico–Virgin Islands region many times during the past 500 years, although the locations and sizes of events that occurred more than a few decades ago are poorly known. Major earthquakes, greater than magnitude 7.0, damaged Puerto Rico in 1670, 1787, 1831, 1844, 1846, 1865, 1867, 1875, 1890, 1906, 1918, 1943 and 1946. The 1867, 1918 and 1946 earthquakes were accompanied by destructive tsunamis.

'Our results indicate that great subduction zone earthquakes, which often occur in the deep trenches off shore have the potential to add stress or trigger earthquakes on other types of faults on the nearby islands,' Lin says. 'We don't want people to overreact, just make them aware of the potential risk of such rare and yet deadly events so they are prepared. It is similar to knowing about hurricanes or tornadoes and being prepared to react when one is coming.'

Ten Brink, who studies earthquakes, tsunamis and geology in the Caribbean and Puerto Rico region, and has studied earthquake hazards in the Dead Sea in the Middle East, says there are a number of possible sources for tsunamis in the Caribbean. 'The threat of major earthquakes in the Caribbean, and the possibility of a resulting tsunami, are real even though the risks are small in the bigger picture,' ten Brink said. 'Local earthquakes such as from the fault on Hispaniola, or effects from distant earthquakes, can be severe. Landslides and volcanic eruptions can also cause major earthquakes and potential tsunamis in this region. It has happened before, and it will happen again.' He cautions that the threat of submarine landslides near Puerto Rico is real, and residents and tourists, including those on cruise ships, would have very little warning given the close proximity to shore. However, the risk is small and should be put into perspective.

The Puerto Rico Trench, which is capable of producing earthquakes of magnitude 7 to 8 or greater, faces north and east into the Atlantic Ocean. There are few land areas or islands to block a tsunami generated near the Puerto Rico Trench from entering the Atlantic Ocean. The direction of the waves would depend on many factors, including where in the trench the earthquake occurred.

Long-term ocean observatories, new generations of seismic and oceanographic sensors, and information technologies, offer great promise to earthquake and tsunami research, Lin says. He and colleague Dezhang Chu of the WHOI Applied Ocean Physics and Engineering Department received WHOI seed funding in 2004 to develop a new technology to measure seafloor change, which could be a step forwards in understanding the processes that trigger underwater earthquakes and tsunamis.

Woods Hole Oceanographic Institution (WHOI) is a private, independent marine research and engineering and higher education organization, located in Falmouth, MA. Its primary mission is to understand the oceans and their interaction with the Earth as a whole, and to communicate a basic understanding of the ocean's role in the changing global environment. Established in 1930 on a recommendation from the National Academy of Sciences, the Institution operates the US National Deep Submergence Facility that includes the deep-diving submersible Alvin, a fleet of global ranging ships and smaller coastal vessels, and a variety of other tethered and autonomous underwater vehicles. WHOI is organized into five departments, interdisciplinary institutes and a marine policy center, and conducts a joint graduate education program with the Massachusetts Institute of Technology.

Woods Hole

CRITICAL THINKING AND WRITING

1. State, using evidence from the passage:
   a) what you consider to be the writer's main reason for writing this article;
   b) the assumptions he has made about his audience, in terms of
      i.   level of interest in the subject
      ii. prior knowledge of the subject
      iii. need for knowledge on the subject.
2. a) Identify two instances where direct quotations from experts are used to support the points being made by the writer.
   b) Discuss the effectiveness of this strategy in helping the writer to achieve his purpose.
3. Describe the diction used in the passage in terms of
   a) level of detail
   b) level of formality and technicality.
4. a) With reference to the passage, identify the main organizing strategy being used in the passage.
   b) Evaluate the effectiveness of this strategy in aiding the writer's purpose.

WRITING ACROSS THE CURRICULUM ACTIVITY

5. Do further research on EITHER tsunamis OR earthquakes.
6. In a proposal of about 300 words, outline the information which you would include in a brochure to educate the general public on the threat/danger of EITHER of these disasters.

CHAPTER 24

ENVIRONMENTAL GUIDELINES FOR HOUSING IN ST LUCIA

Background

This section of the Manual outlines the main environmental management issues relating to the establishment and construction of low-cost housing units, and presents guidelines to minimize the negative environmental impacts of decisions and activities related to the establishment and construction of low-cost housing units. These guidelines are presented in a user-friendly format, for use by housing programme managers and homeowners.

In attempting to obtain documentation on the subject of environmental management in relation to low-income housing, it was found that such documentation was sparse. Further, few local regulations and technical guidelines relating to environmental management exist, and those which do exist are of little relevance to low-income housing. Consequently, this material is based primarily on the knowledge and experience of the author.

Introduction

Funding provided under the housing programme by the NRDF largely relates to the construction or expansion of wooden houses and the expansion of masonry houses. The houses are, for the most part, located outside of the larger urban areas, usually on family lands, or on rented 'house spots', and not within planned residential developments. The houses are usually located on relatively flat or moderately sloping lands, away from public paved roads and they are often serviced by footpaths or narrow unpaved roads. In the majority of cases, formal planning approval is not sought for the construction or location of the houses. It should be noted, however, that formal planning approval is not required, in St. Lucia, for expansion of residential developments when the area of the expansion amounts to less than one-third of the area of the original development.

It is commonly thought that, because of the relatively small scale of the activities involved in low-income housing, particularly when undertaken on one house at a time, the environmental problems associated with an individual low-income housing venture are generally insignificant and of limited impact. However, within any given area, a series of minor environmental problems can combine to produce significant negative impacts. For example, the indiscriminate disposal of waste into a ravine or river course by several households will cumulatively lead to the pollution of that watercourse. Also, an improper practice associated with one household can, over time, lead to a major environmental problem with impacts on an entire community. For example, the improper construction of drains on one house lot on a hillside may, over time, lead to the formation of a gully, which can cause the loss of large amounts of soil, or, inundation of properties located downhill. Therefore, as simple or insignificant as activities related to low-income housing may appear to be, they may contribute to significant environmental problems unless certain measures are adhered to. Some of these measures may be quite simple and relatively cheap. However, some low-income homeowners may be unable to afford to implement some of these measures, at least not at the same time as they are seeking to address expenses directly related to the main housing unit.

The typical environmental problems associated with low-income housing ventures in St. Lucia, are for the most part, related to the Location and Placement of Houses, Site Preparation, Drainage and Waste Disposal. Descriptions of these problems, and the guidelines on the measures which should be implemented to address these problems, are provided in the following sections.

The Location and Placement of Houses

Problems Associated with the Location and Placement of Houses

Indiscriminate and uninformed placement of houses creates both environmental hazards and danger to the occupants of these houses. A large number of the houses established through low-income housing programmes are located within unplanned developments. The houses funded through the NRDF housing programme are, in most cases, located on family lands which have not been

formally partitioned, or on rented 'house spots' which have not been surveyed. In such cases, the houses are often located away from public roads and the houses are not directly serviced by paved roads, although tracks and pathways may be found, and infrastructure such as water supply pipelines and electricity poles are not laid out in an organized manner. In such instances, there are no rules to govern the placement or location of houses, and homeowners and builders often determine the placement and location of houses based on their own judgement and preferences. Very often, no consideration is given to the future development of the surrounding lands, and, as such, the orderly future development of the area may be compromised. Invariably, after some time, the landowners would seek to rationalise and formalize the development and this process may become quite complicated because of the absence of any kind of planning during the time when houses were being located or placed. Houses are often placed so close together that it may be difficult to establish a proper road network. Plot sizes may be so small that it may be impossible for individual houses to be attached to septic tanks, even if they are upgraded and the homeowners are able to afford septic tanks.

In considering the placement and location of houses, attention should also be paid to flood risk. Houses may be located in watercourses or gullies, causing flooding of the house or nearby areas. Whereas flooding may not be a consequence of any activities undertaken by the builder or homeowner, the improper placement and location of houses in flood prone areas may result in considerable discomfort, loss of property, injury and even loss of life.

Since St. Lucia is a small island, issues related to the establishment of developments within or near coastal areas are often encountered. Among the most significant of these issues, in relation to housing developments, are the risks associated with property damage and injury to residents, as a result of storm surges. Storm surges are essentially walls of water created by a tropical cyclone (tropical wave, tropical storm or hurricane) out at sea. They can reach the shore at destructive heights, well above normal sea levels. When storm surges hit the shoreline and coastal areas, they can cause significant damage to property located within these areas, and of course they can result in the injury of residents, and even death.

There are a number of other important environmental management issues associated with housing developments in St. Lucia's coastal areas. These relate to public access to beaches, the natural erosion and accretion of beaches, pollution of nearshore waters as a result of land-based activities, and aesthetics. Public access is a sensitive issue, and several public statements have been made about the commitment of Government to ensuring that the public has free access to St. Lucia's beaches. In addition, beaches undergo natural processes of erosion and accretion, and it is desirable that these processes be allowed to take place as freely as possible, in order to maintain the natural balance of coastal ecosystems. Further, whenever waste is generated through land-based activities close to the shore, there are pollution risks associated with the disposal of such waste into the nearshore waters, and particular measures need to be put in place to minimize or eliminate these risks. The visual impact of developments in coastal areas is also important, as the attractive coastal views are important to St. Lucia's overall image as a tourist destination.

Guidelines on the Placement and Location of Houses
Placement and Location of Houses in Unplanned Developments

In deciding upon the location of houses, particularly within large parcels of land for which subdivision plans have not been prepared or implemented, consideration must be given to the future development of the area. The main issues to be considered are:

Lot sizes: lots should not be less than 3,000 square feet in area. Control of lot sizes and proper layout (subdivision) is paramount. This is the minimum lot size approved by the Development Control Authority in residential developments. It should also be borne in mind that the Ministry of Health does not normally approve septic tanks on lots below 3,000 square feet. Even if septic tanks are not an immediate priority of the homeowner, consideration should be given to the possible future upgrading of the house to include a septic tank. This not only allows proper disposal of sewage on sites using septic tanks, but also proper access to individual sites by cesspool trucks for removal of sewage.

Roads or footpaths: provision should be made for the future construction of roads. The minimum road width normally required in residential developments is 20 feet. At any rate, whenever plans are made to construct roads, a provision of 10 feet should be made for footpaths. Apart from the provision of adequate width for future roads and footpaths, consideration should be given to the appropriate alignment of these in a manner that will optimize the use of the available land area, as well as ensuring the provision of adequate linkages to established public roadways. In addition, any established rights-of-way through the property to adjacent parcels of land must be recognized and maintained.

Soil Stability and Land Slippage

In areas with unstable soils or steep slopes, the improper placement of houses can add to soil instability and contribute to land slippage. In instances where sections of a hillside are to be levelled off to accommodate a house, placement of the house too close to a slope break can cause land slippage, if the increased load on the soil exceeds its capacity. This would most likely occur during rainfall events when the weight of water in the soil would be added to the loading created by the house, to cause land slippage. It should be borne in mind, also, that slope failure or land slippage caused by placement or location of a house too close to the slope break may lead to loss of the house, and even the loss of life. The house should therefore be placed well away from the slope break so as not to contribute to slope failure. The required distance between the house and the slope break may vary according to the soil types, slope, size and type of house. However, as a general rule, the foundation of the house should not be located less than 20 feet from the top or bottom of a slope break.

In instances where houses are to be constructed at the foot of a slope, there is a risk that the slope may fail and move towards the house to partially or completely cover it. Such a scenario has been experienced on several occasions, in certain cases resulting in damage to or the complete loss of the house, and even loss of life of the occupants of the house. Slope failure and land slippage in such cases often occur during or after heavy rainfall. In order to avoid or minimize the risks associated with the location or placement of houses at the foot of a slope, efforts should be made to stabilize the slope by applying the techniques and methods described in Section 4.2. In addition, the house should be placed well away from the foot of the slope. The distance from the slope would vary depending on the height of the slope, the soil type, the types of activities undertaken on or above the slope, the level of protection given to the slope (vegetation, retaining wall) and the height of the house. However as a general rule, a minimum clearance of 30 feet from the foot of the slope should be maintained in situations where the slope height exceeds the height of the house. This distance can be reduced according to the height of the slope relative to the height of the house.

Fillian N. Dujon

CRITICAL THINKING AND WRITING

1. The author of this text has clearly identified his target audience.
   a) How effectively do you think he has communicated with his stated target audience?
   b) Why do you think the writer identifies his target audience?
   c) Briefly explain what you consider to be the reason(s) the writer decided to target a specific sector in St. Lucia.
2. Evaluate the writer's use of subheadings and comment on their effectiveness as signposts.
3. Characterize the tone of the article and justify its appropriateness to
   a) the discourse type
   b) the writer's purpose.
4. The writer employs a number of developmental strategies. Identify two dominant ones and:
   a) state where in the text they are used,
   b) examine their usefulness and suitability to the content.
5. Why do you think this article was written?
6. Do you consider the information provided to be adequate? Justify your answer.

WRITING ACTIVITY

7. What are some of the problems with housing construction which your country faces? Do research to find out the measures needed to avoid these problems. Write two paragraphs using cause and effect and illustration, to present the information you gather.

CHAPTER 25

WHAT YOU SHOULD TALK TO PATIENTS WITH HYPERTENSION ABOUT: A SPECIAL FOCUS ON NUTRITION

Hypertension may be defined as blood pressure that remains elevated over time. The topics that should be discussed with patients suffering from hypertension include: an explanation of the risks of the disease and the benefits of management, suggestions concerning regular health examinations, supporting self-care behaviours and promoting a healthy lifestyle. The promotion of a healthy lifestyle incorporates recommending a reduction in dietary sodium intake to no more than 2.4 g/day, the adoption of the Dietary Approaches to Stop Hypertension eating plan (which is high in low-fat diary products and fruit and vegetables), weight loss and increased activity as the initial treatment of hypertension.

Introduction

Blood pressure is the force of the blood against the artery walls. It is measured in millimetres of mercury (mmHg) and recorded as two numbers: the systolic pressure (the pressure as the heart beats) over the diastolic pressure (the pressure as the heart relaxes). Hypertension is blood pressure that remains elevated over time.[1]

Classification of Hypertension

There are two types of hypertension: essential and secondary. Essential hypertension is defined as high blood pressure with no identifiable cause[2] and accounts for more than 90 per cent of patients with hypertension.[3] Secondary hypertension has an identifiable cause; these include renal disease, pregnancy, or endocrine or neurological disorders. Secondary hypertension may also be induced by drugs such as estrogens, glucocorticoids, nonsteroidal anti-inflammatory agents, oral contraceptives, tricyclic antidepressants and oral decongestants.[2]

Diagnosis of Hypertension

Hypertension is defined as a systolic blood pressure of 140 mmHg or higher, or a diastolic blood pressure 90 mmHg or higher. Table 25.1 shows the blood pressure ranges used in the diagnosis and management of hypertension. An average of two or more readings, taken at two or more visits after the initial screening, is used to diagnose hypertension. If the systolic and diastolic pressures fall into different categories, the patient is classified as being in the higher category.[4]

Typically, patients with essential hypertension are asymptomatic; usually the only sign of primary hypertension is an elevated blood pressure. Patients with secondary hypertension may have symptoms suggestive of the underlying condition.

Treatment Goals

Lowering the blood pressure to <140/90 mmHg has been shown to decrease cardiovascular complications. However, in patients who have diabetes or renal disease in addition to hypertension, the target should be <130/80 mmHg. [5, 6] Most individuals, especially those over 50 years of age, will reach the diastolic goal once the systolic goal is achieved; therefore the primary focus should be control of systolic pressure.

TABLE 25.1
CLASSIFICATION AND MANAGEMENT OF BLOOD PRESSURE IN ADULTS

Blood Pressure	SBP	DBP	Lifestyle Modification	Without Compelling Indications	With Compelling Indications
Normal	<120	and >80	Encourage		
Pre-hypertension	120-139	or 80-99	Yes	No antihypertensive drug indicated	Drug(s) for compelling indications
Stage1 hypertension	140-159	or 90-99	Yes	Thiazide – type diuretics for most patients. Consider ACEI, ARB, BB, CCB or combination	Drug (s) for compelling indications. Other antihypertensive drugs (diuretics, ACEI, ARB, BB, CCB) as needed.
Stage 2 hypertension	≥ 160	≥ 100	Yes	Two-drug combination for most patients (usually thiazide-type diuretic and ACEI, ARB, BB or CCB)	

Adapted from Chobanian et al.
ACEI - angiotensin-converting enzyme inibitor; ARB - angiotensin receptor blocker; BB - â-blocker; CCB - calcium-channel blocker; DBP- diastolic blood pressure; SBP - systolic blood pressure.

What to Discuss with Patients with Hypertension

Topics that should be discussed with patients with hypertension can be summarized as follows:

- explain the risks of the disease and the benefits of management
- suggest regular health examinations and support self-care behaviours
- promote a healthy lifestyle

Explain the Risks of the Disease and the Benefits of Management

Hypertension is largely asymptomatic and may go undiagnosed for many years.[7] This increases the importance of emphasizing the management of blood pressure, as many individuals do not feel the illness is significant due to the lack of symptoms. If hypertension is uncontrolled, there is an increased risk of heart attack, heart failure, stroke, and kidney disease. For individuals aged 40–70 years of age, each increment of 20 mmHg in systolic pressure, or 10 mmHg in diastolic blood pressure doubles the risk of cardiovascular disease, regardless of whether the blood pressure was initially in the normal or the hypertensive range.[8] Management of hypertension is associated with reductions in stroke incidence of 35–30 per cent, in myocardial infarction incidence of 20–5 per cent and in heart failure incidence of > 50 per cent.

Suggest Regular Health Examinations and Support Self-care Behaviours

Data suggest that adherence to antihypertensive therapies is generally less than 50 per cent after the first year.[9] A patient's non-adherence to therapy is increased by misunderstanding the condition or treatment, denial of illness due to lack of symptoms, the perception of drugs as symbols of ill health, or unexpected adverse effects of medications. It is important to discuss with the patient the likelihood of side effects of medications in combination with the risks of not managing the illness. The main medications used in hypertension and their possible adverse effects are given in table 25.2.

Home Self-measurement of Blood Pressure

The use of home self-measurement of blood pressure should be encouraged. Home blood pressure values of approximately 135/83 mmHg or greater should be considered to be elevated. It is important to stress the appropriate procedures required for accurate measurements to be taken:[10]

- Caffeine, exercise and smoking should be avoided for at least 30 minutes prior to measurement.
- Substances containing stimulants such as phenylephrine or pseudoephedrine (which may be present in nasal decongestants or ophthalmic drops) should not be used.
- Clothing on the arm or forearm should be loose.
- An appropriately sized cuff (with a cuff bladder encircling at least 80% of the arm) should be used.
- The patient should be seated for 5 minutes prior to measurement.
- The patient should be positioned so that his/her back is supported and his/her feet touch the ground; legs should not be crossed.

TABLE 25.2
BLOOD PRESSURE MEDICATIONS

Drug category	How they work	Common names	Adverse effects
Diuretics	Act on the kidney to flush excess water and sodium from the body in the urine: sometimes called 'water pills'.	Bendrofluazide (Bezide) Indapamide (Natrilix, Frumeron) Spironolactone (Aldactone)	Dizziness Frequent urination Dry mouth
β-Blockers	Reduce nerve impulses to the heart and blood vessels, causing a reduction in heart beat frequency and force. Blood pressure drops and the demands on the heart are reduced.	Altenol (Tenormin) Propranolol hydrochloride (Inderal)	Low blood pressure Slow heart rate Fatigue
Angiotensin-converting enzyme inhibitors	These prevent the formation of a hormone called angiotensin II, which normally causes blood vessels to narrow. The blood vessels relax and pressure goes down.	Benazepril hydrochloride (Lotensin) Captopril (Capoten) Enalapril maleate (Vasolac) Lisiopril (Zestril)	Headache Dizziness Cough
Angiotensin antagonists	Shield blood vessels from effects of angiotensin II, resulting in wider blood vessels and reduced blood pressure.	Irbesartan (Avapro) Losartan potassium (Cozaar) Valsartan (Diovan) Candesartan (Atacand) Telmisartan (Micardis)	Diarrhea Heartburn
Calcium-channel blockers	Prevent calcium from entering the muscle cells of the heart and blood vessels. This relaxes the blood vessels and lowers blood pressure.	Verapamil hydrochloride (Calan SR, Caveril) Diltiazem hydrochloride (Cardizem, Denazox) Amlodipine (Norvasc) Felodipine (Plendil) Nifedipine (Nifelat, Apo-nifedipine)	Dizziness Constipation Swelling in the legs
α -Blockers	Reduce nerve impulses to blood vessels, allowing blood to pass more easily.	Prazosin (Minipress) Terazosin (Hytrin) Doxazosin	Dizziness Headache
α/β -Blockers	Slow the heart rate and decrease the force of contraction, thus decreasing the work load of the heart and lowering the blood pressure.	Labetalol Carvediol	Dizziness Postural hypotension
Nervous system inhibitors	Relax blood vessels by controlling nerve impulses.	Clonidine (Catapres) Methyldopa (Aldomet)	Dry mouth Drowsiness Dizziness Redness, itching and skin irritation if administered by skin patch
Vasodilators	Directly open blood vessels by relaxing the muscle in the vessel walls.	Hydralazine hydrochloride (Apresoline)	Fluid retention Rapid heart rate

Adapted from *Your Guide to Lowering Blood Pressure*.

- The arm should be supported at approximately the height of the heart.
- The patient should stay silent prior to and during the procedure.

Drug Interactions

Supplements such as ginseng, yohimbe, licorice, ephedra (Ma Hung), cayenne and goldenseal should be avoided as they can increase blood pressure or interact with anti-hypertensive drugs.[11] Potassium supplements and even salt substitutes should be avoided when taking angiotensin-converting enzyme inhibitors or potassium-sparing diuretics. Calcium supplements can antagonize calcium blockers, such as verapamil and should be used with caution. Decongestants, such as those found in many over-the-counter cold remedies, can cause an increase in blood pressure, which could be dangerous for people who already have high blood pressure.

Promote a Healthy Lifestyle

Recent reports from the US Joint National Committee (JNC) on Prevention, Detection, Evaluation, and Treatment of High Blood Pressure recommended the reduction of dietary sodium intake, adoption of the Dietary Approaches to Stop Hypertension (DASH) eating plan, weight loss and increased physical activity as initial effective methods of reducing blood pressure and proposed them as the first steps in the treatment of hypertension. Pharmacologic therapy would be initiated only if the goal blood pressure level is not obtained with medical nutrition therapy and lifestyle changes alone.

A Focus on Nutrition

Weight reduction

Body mass index (BMI) and waist circumference provide useful information in evaluating body weight. Both measurements can identify obesity and those at high risk of health problems. The BMI incorporates weight and height to give an indication of total body fat; a BMI of < 24.9 kg/m² indicates a healthy weight, 25-29.9 kg/m² is considered overweight, and >30 kg/m² is obese. According to the Third Report of the Expert Panel on Detection, Evaluation, and Treatment of High Blood Cholesterol in Adults (Adult Treatment Panel III),[12] abdominal obesity is indicated by a waist circumference of e" 100 cm (40 inches) in men and e" 89 cm (35 inches) in women. Weight loss of approximately 4.5 kg (10 lb) was shown to reduce blood pressure or avert hypertension in overweight patients.

Patients who need to lose weight should be encouraged to lose no more than 0.2–0.9 kg (0.5–2lb) each week, and to begin with a goal of losing ten per cent of their current weight. In order to lose 0.45 (1 lb) a week, 500 calories/day should be deducted from the diet or expended during exercise.

Adoption of the DASH Eating Plan

The DASH diet includes low-fat dairy products, with a reduction of saturated fat, total fat and cholesterol, combined with a higher content of fruits and vegetables. The diet is rich in potassium, magnesium and calcium. The breakdown of the DASH diet is shown in table 25.3. The DASH dietary pattern lowers blood pressure and, with widespread use, could reduce the number of cardiovascular events attributed to hypertension.[13]

TABLE 25.3
GUIDELINES FOR FOOD SELECTION FOR THE DIETARY APPROACHES TO STOP HYPERTENSION (DASH) DIET

Food Group	Daily servings (except as noted)	Serving Sizes	Examples and notes	Significance of each food group to the DASH eating plan
Grains and grain products	7-8	1 slice bread 1 oz dry cereal ½ cup cooked rice, pasta or cereal	Whole wheat bread, English muffin, pita bread, bagel, cereals, grits, oatmeal, crackers, unsalted pretzels and popcorn	Carbohydrates, major sources of energy and fibre
Vegetables	4-5	1 cup raw leafy vegetables ½ cup cooked vegetables ½ cup vegetable juice	Tomatoes, potatoes, carrots, green peas, squash, broccoli, spinach, lima beans, sweet potatoes	Potassium, magnesium and fibre
Fruits	4-5	6 oz fruit juice 1 medium fruit ½ cup dried fruit ½ cup fresh, frozen or canned fruit	Apricots, bananas, dates, grapes, oranges, prunes, raisins, strawberries, mangoes, melons, grapefruits	Potassium, magnesium and fibre
Low-fat or fat-free dairy products	2-3	8 oz milk 1 cup yogurt 1 ½ oz cheese	Fat-free or low-fat milk, fat-free or low-fat regular or frozen yogurt, low-fat or fat-free cheese	Calcium, potassium, magnesium and protein
Meat, poultry and fish	2 or less	3 oz cooked meats, poultry or fish	Select only lean; trim away visible fats, broil, roast or boil instead of frying; remove skin from poultry	Protein and magnesium
Nuts, seeds and beans	4-5 per week	½ cup or 1 ½ oz nuts 2 tbsp or ½ oz seeds ½ cup cooked dry beans or peas	Almonds, mixed nuts, peanuts, kidney beans, pigeon peas, sunflower seeds	Magnesium, potassium, protein and fibre

TABLE 25.3 CONT'D

Food Group	Daily servings (except as noted)	Serving Sizes	Examples and notes	Significance of each food group to the DASH eating plan
Fats and oils	2-3	1 tsp soft margarine 1 tbsp low-fat mayonnaise 2 tbsp light salad dressing 1 tsp vegetable oil	Soft margarine, low-fat mayonnaise, light salad dressing, vegetable oil (olive, corn, canola, sunflower)	This applies to added fat; all other food choices should be low fat, DASH has 27 per cent of calories as fat including fat added to foods
Sweets	5 per week	1 tbsp sugar 1 tbsp jelly or jam ½ oz jelly beans 8 oz lemonade	Maple syrup, sugar, jelly, jam, fruit-flavoured gelatin, jelly beans, hard candy, fruit punch, sorbets, ices	Make these treats low-fat whenever possible

Adapted from *Facts about the DASH Eating Plan.*

1 oz is approximately equivalent to 28 g

tbsp, tablespoon (1 tbsp = 15ml); tsp, teaspoon (1tsp =5 ml).

Dietary Sodium Restriction

Nearly all individuals consume substantially more salt (sodium chloride) than they need. As people age, sodium intake plays a more important role in the development of high blood pressure.[14] Blood pressure normally increases with age, and age-related increases in blood pressure can cause renal impairment and subsequent heightened sensitivity of blood pressure to salt ingestion. In individuals with normal blood pressure, salt restriction will result in only a small (approximately 2 mmHg) blood pressure reduction, whereas in hypertensive individuals, salt restriction can result in reductions in systolic pressure as large as 11 mmHg, such as those observed in the DASH study.[15] Dietary sodium should be restricted to no more than 2.4 g/day, which is equivalent to approximately one teaspoonful of salt. Patients who adhere to the recommended amounts of sodium intake should expect systolic blood pressure reductions of 2–8 mmHg.

Tips to Reduce Salt Intake

On average, the natural salt content of food accounts for only about ten per cent of the total intake, while discretionary salt use (i.e. salt added at the table or while cooking) provides another 5–10 per cent. Approximately 75 per cent is derived from salt added by manufacturers.[16] Patients should therefore be encouraged to be wary of processed foods.

Food labels tend to list sodium rather than salt content. Patients should be encouraged to look for the sodium content on the nutrition facts panel of food products, as even similar foods can vary significantly in the amount of sodium they contain. Foods that are low in sodium (less than 140 mg or 5% of the daily value) are low in salt.[17]

Patients who express concern over the lack of flavour of low-salt foods should be reassured that a person's preference for salt is not fixed. After consuming foods that are lower in salt for a period of time, the taste for salt tends to decrease. Use of other flavorings, such as herbs and spices, may help. Advice on how to choose and prepare foods that are low in salt/sodium is given in Table 25.4.

Physical Activity

Regular physical activity reduces systolic blood pressure by approximately 4–9 mmHg. Generally, patients are encouraged to engage in at least 30 minutes of exercise 5–6 days a week. An exercise programme may include activities such as walking, running, cycling and aerobics.

Limiting Alcohol Consumption, Cessation of Smoking and Moderating Caffeine Intake

Other approaches to lowering blood pressure include limiting alcohol consumption, reducing caffeine intake and avoiding tobacco. Moderate to heavy alcohol intake increases the incidence of hypertension.[18] The JNC 7 report recommends no more than two drinks per day for most men and no more than one drink per day for women and men of lighter weight. High levels of caffeine consumption may elevate blood pressure and increase the possible risk of stroke; patients should be advised to limit intake.[19] Cigarette smoking causes an acute elevation in blood pressure, thus increasing the incidence of stroke; patients should be advised to stop smoking to help lower the blood pressure and minimize this risk.[20]

TABLE 25.4
TIPS TO REDUCE SALT AND SODIUM

• Buy fresh, plain frozen or canned 'with no salt added' vegetables.
• Use fresh poultry, fish and lean meat rather than canned or processed types.
• Use herbs, spices and salt-free seasoning blend in cooking and at the table. If salt must be added do so sparingly at the table as opposed to in cooking, as it has a more intense flavour.
• Cook rice, pasta and hot cereal without salt. Cut back on instant or flavoured rice, pasta and cereal mixes, which usually have added salt.
• Choose 'convenience' foods that are low in sodium. Cut back on frozen dinners, pizza, packaged mixes, canned soups or broths (unless low sodium) and salad dressing — these often have a lot of sodium.
• Rinse canned foods, such as tuna, to remove some of the sodium
• When available, buy low- or reduced-sodium or no-salt-added versions of foods.
• Choose ready-to-eat cereals that are low in sodium.

TABLE 25.5
THE EFFECTS OF LIFESTYLE MODIFICATIONS TO MANAGE HYPERTENSION

Modification	Recommendation	Approximate SBP reduction
Weight reduction	Maintain normal body weight (body mass index 18.5-24.0 kg/m²).	5-20 mmHg/10 kg weight loss
Adopt DASH eating plan	Consume diet rich in fruits, vegetables and low-fat dairy products with a reduced content of saturated and total fat.	8-14 mmHg
Dietary Sodium restriction	Reduce dietary sodium intake to no more than 100 mmol/day (2.4 g sodium or 6 g sodium chloride).	2-8 mmHg
Increase physical activity	Engage in regular aerobic physical activity such as brisk walking (at least 30 minutes/day, most days of the week).	4-9 mmHg
Moderation of alcohol consumption	Limit consumption to no more than two drinks per day in most men and no more than one drink per day in women and lighter weight men.	2-4 mmHg

Effects of Lifestyle Modification

Ample evidence supports the beneficial effects of a healthy lifestyle in the prevention and management of hypertension. Lifestyle modifications can help decrease blood pressure and enhance the overall efficacy of antihypertensive therapy. Table 25.5 shows the approximate pressure that can be achieved by following the recommended lifestyle modifications.

Emily Rose

Notes

1. National Heart, Lung and Blood Institute, 'Your Guide to Lowering Blood Pressure', http://www.nhlbi.nih.gov/heatlth/public/heart/hbp/hbp_low/index.htm.

2. J.D. Jones, K.D. King, F.S. Emanuel, 'Hypertension: a clinical pharmacist's synopsis of JNC 7', *Am J Pharm Educ* 68, no. 3 (2004): article 71.

3. T. Pickering, 'Recommendations for the use of home (self) and ambulatory blood pressure monitoring', American Society of Hypertension Ad Hoc Panel, *Am J Hypertens* 9 (1996): 1–11.

4. A.V. Chobanian, G.L. Bakris, H.R. Black, et al., 'Seventh Report of the Joint National Committee on Prevention, Detection, Evaluation, and Treatment of High Blood Pressure', *Hypertension* 42 (2003): 1206–52.

5. C. Arauz-Pacheco, M.A. Parrott, P. Raskin, for the American Diabetes Association, 'Treatment of Hypertension in adults with diabetes', *Diabetes Care* 26, Suppl. 1 (2003): S80–2.

6. National Kidney Foundation. K/DOQI clinical practice guidelines for chronic kidney disease: evaluation, classification, and stratification, *Am J Kidney Dis* 39, 2 Suppl. 1 (2002): S1–266.

7. Dietitians of Canada and American Dietetic Association, *Manual of Clinical Dietetics*, 6th ed. (Chicago, IL: American Dietetic Association, 2000).

8. S. Lewington, R. Clarke, N. Qizilibash, R. Peto, R. Collin for the Prospective Studies Collaboration, 'Age-specific relevance of usual

blood pressure to vascular mortality: a meta-analysis of individual data for one million adults in 61 prospective studies', *Lancet* 360 (2002): 1903–13.

9. J.J. Caro, J.L. Speckman, 'Existing treatment strategies: does noncompliance make a difference?' *J Hypertens Suppl* 16 (1998): S31–41.

10. Canadian Hypertension Society. Blood Pressure Assessment, Hypertension Diagnosis and Follow up. 2005 Canadian Hypertension Education Program Recommendations, http://www.hypertension.ca/recommendations_2005/CHEP_2005_BP_Measure.ppt.

11. American Botanical Council: Herb Reference Guide, http://www.herbalgram.org/default.asp?c=reference_guide.

12. Expert Panel on Detection, Evaluation, and Treatment of High Blood Cholesterol in Adults. Executive Summary of the Third Report of the National Cholesterol Education Program (NCEP) Expert Panel on Detection, Evaluation, and Treatment of High Blood Cholesterol in Adults (Adult Treatment Panel III), *JAMA* 285 (2001): 2486–97.

13. F.M. Sacks, L.P. Svetkey, W.M. Vollmer, et al., for the DASH-Sodium Collaborative Research Group. 'Effects on blood pressure of reduced dietary sodium and the Dietary Approaches to Stop Hypertension (DASH) DIET', *N Engel j Med* 343 (2001):3–10.

14. National Heart, Lung and Blood Institute, 'Facts about the DASH Eating Plan', http://www.nhlbl.nih.gov/health/public/heart/hbp/dash/new_dash.pdf.

15. P. Sager, 'Dietary Approaches to Treating and Preventing Hypertension – Are They Useful?' (Presented at the 18th Scientific Meeting of the International Society of Hypertension, 20–4 August 2000, Chicago, IL, USA.)

16. R. D Mattes, D. Donnelly, 'Relative contributions of dietary sodium cources', *J Am Coll Nutr* 10, no. 4 (1991):383–93.

17. United States Department of Agriculture, 'Dietary Guidelines for Americans 2005, Chapter 8, Sodium and Potassium', http://www.health.gov/dietaryguidelines/dga2005/document/html/chapter8.htm.

18. D.G. Beevers, R. Maheswaran, J.F. Potter, 'Alcohol, blood pressure and antihypertensive drugs', *J Clin Pharm Ther* 15 (1990): 395–97.

19. A.A. Hakim, G.W. Ross, J.D. Curb, et al., 'Coffee consumption in hypertensive men in older middle-age and the risk of stroke: the Honolulu Heart Program', *J Clin Epidemiol* 51 (1998): 487–94.

20. R. Forgari, A. Zoppi, P. Lusardi, G. Marasi, G. Villa, A. Vanasia, 'Cigarette smoking and blood pressure in a worker population: a cross-sectional study', *J Cardiovasc Risk* 3, no.1 (1996): 55–9.

CRITICAL THINKING AND WRITING

1. Who is the primary audience for this article?
2. i. Explain how this article could prove useful to the following persons:
   a) medical students
   b) educated persons with hypertension
   ii. What aspects, if any, would present challenges to persons identified in 2 (b)?
3. What organizing principle/pattern is used in the second paragraph and why?
4. Write a paragraph of approximately 150 words, in which you explain any two of the recommendations which have been made to an audience of specialists.
5. Cite two factors which contribute to the writer's credibility.

COLLABORATIVE WRITING

6. Write an email to your friend who is hypertensive. Be sure to include:
   i. What causes the disease.
   ii. What measures your friend should take to control it.
   iii. Recommendations about lifestyle changes that will improve your friend's health.
7. Write a reflective essay (two pages) in which you discuss the aspects of this article that you found challenging.

CHAPTER 26

PARASITOLOGY

Angiostrongylus cantonensis, the rat lungworm, is the most common cause of eosinophilic meningitis (EM) worldwide, and is endemic in Jamaica, Cuba, the Dominican Republic and Haiti. The rat is the definitive host of *A. cantonensis*, but it also passes through a molluscan host as part of its life cycle. Humans are infected by ingesting larvae from a number of sources, and are accidental hosts. The spectrum of clinical manifestations in EM due to *A. cantonensis* ranges from a self-limiting illness with fever and headache to a severe and sometimes fatal meningoencephalitis. The majority of cases are self-limiting and resolve in about four weeks. Treatment is not optimal, but serial lumbar punctures have been used to relieve headaches. Reduction of the inflammatory response using steroids also appears to be beneficial in relieving symptoms.

Introduction

Angiostrongylus cantonensis, the rat lungworm, is the most common cause of eosinophilic meningitis (EM) worldwide. Other helminths that are associated with EM include *Gnathostoma spinigerum, Baylisascaris procyonis, Taenia solium, Paragonimus westermani, Schistosoma japonicum, Fasciola hepatica* and myiasis. There are also several non-parasitic infectious causes, including coccidioidomycosis, cryptococcosis and leptospirosis. EM is also associated with idiopathic hypereosinophilic syndrome, ventriculoperitoneal shunts, leukaemia or central nervous system lymphoma, non-steroidal anti-inflammatory drugs, antibiotics and radiological contrast agents.[1]

A. Cantonensis is epidemic in Cuba, Jamaica, Haiti and the Dominican Republic. *A. cantonensis* has been confirmed as the causative agent in all cases of EM (including fatalities) that have been reported from the Caribbean. Recent reports from Jamaica suggest that EM caused by *A. cantonensis* is an emerging threat to public health in that country. This article will examine EM in the context of the Caribbean in order to inform clinicians of its increasing importance.

Historical Introduction

The nematode *A. cantonensis* was first reported in rats in Canton province, China, in 1935; the first human infection was reported in a patient from Taiwan 10 years later.[2] Twenty species of *Angiostrongylus* have been described in rodents, carnivores and insectivores worldwide. However, only *A. cantonensis*, which affects the brain and spinal cord and sometimes the lungs, and *A. costaricensis*, which inhabits the mesenteric arteries causing abdominal angiostrongyloidiasis, are reported to cause disease in humans. The latter is restricted to tropical America, but *A. cantonensis* has been reported in Australia, South-West Pacific, South-East Asia, Samoa and Fiji, India, Ivory Coast, Madagascar, the south-eastern United States and the Caribbean.

Life Cycle and Epidemiology

The rat is the definitive host of *A. cantonensis*. The adult worms reside in the pulmonary arteries. Following fertilization, female worms lay eggs in the terminal branches of the pulmonary vessels, which subsequently hatch to release first-stage larvae. These larvae will embolise to the lungs, ascend the trachea and are swallowed and passed out in the rat faeces. They are then ingested by a molluscan host (usually land or fresh-water snails or slugs), in which they moult twice to become the infective third stage. New infections are acquired by rats when they feed on infected molluscs. Third-stage larvae will migrate to the brain of rats, where they develop into young adults in the subarachnoid space before returning to the venous system and then to the pulmonary arteries, where they develop into sexually mature adults.[2] Humans can be infected by ingesting larvae from a number of sources and are dead-end, accidental hosts.

The principal mode of infection in some endemic regions is the consumption of undercooked snails. For example, consumption of *Achatina fulica* (giant African land snail) and *Ampularium canaliculatus* is responsible for transmission in Taiwan and mainland China, while consumption of the *Pila* species of snail appears to be an important source of infection in Thailand.[2]

In addition to the molluscan intermediate host, the parasite also has a number of paratenic or transport hosts, including crabs and freshwater shrimps, that play a role in transmission to humans. For example, consumption of raw toad liver in Japan was an important mode of infection in that country.[3] In Tahiti and other Pacific islands, the consumption of freshwater prawns and terrestrial crabs appears to be an important route of infection.[3]

It is also thought that snails can contaminate vegetables with infective larvae left in slime trails, and that humans can become infected by eating such unwashed vegetables. This remains controversial since there are conflicting reports on the finding of larvae in the slime of snails.[2] An outbreak of EM among vacationers in Jamaica was linked to the consumption of a fresh salad, and this was also the likely route among the autochthonous cases in the northern Caribbean, since snails, slugs, raw shrimps and prawns are not consumed intentionally in these territories.[4,5] It is difficult to discern modes of infection in the sporadic cases in the Caribbean and this warrants further investigation. Larvae can be ingested in contaminated food and drink; good personal hygiene practices will reduce the likelihood of transmission.[3]

The Parasite in the Caribbean

Human infections have been reported from Cuba and Jamaica, while infections in rats have been reported from Cuba, the Dominican Republic, Haiti and Jamaica.[6] *A. cantonensis* infection was the cause of death in a white-handed gibbon in a zoo in Nassau, Bahamas.[3] There have been no reports of infections from Guyana or Barbados.[6,7] The occurrence of these sporadic cases confirms the endemicity of the parasite in the Greater

Antilles, but further studies are required to determine the extent to which the parasite is endemic in other Caribbean territories.

In Jamaica, the first report of EM was in a 34-year old woman who had neither travelled abroad nor had a history of consumption of molluscs, undercooked crabs or prawns.[8] Serological tests were not done in this case, and exposure to *A. cantonensis* was not confirmed. This was followed by an outbreak of EM among 12 students vacationing in Montego Bay, that was linked to the consumption of a salad.[5] Since then, fatal infections have been reported in a child and an adult, and two additional paediatric cases have been diagnosed in Jamaica[4] (T. Evans-Gilbert, T.S. Ferguson, unpublished data).

Both *Rattus rattus* and *R. norvegicus* have been found to be infected throughout the endemic territories of the Caribbean. Within the region, snail intermediate hosts include *Thelidomus asper* in Jamaica, *Subulina octona* in the Dominican Republic, *S. octona* and *Aquebana belutina* in Puerto Rico and *Bradybaena similaris* in Cuba.[6,9] The only slug that has been identified as an intermediate host in the Caribbean is *Veronicella cubensis* from Cuba. The parasite is not very host-specific, and *A. fulica* may not have played a central role in its establishment in the Caribbean. Paratenic hosts that may serve as a vehicle for transmission to humans have not been identified in the Caribbean.

Pathogenesis

The larvae of *A. cantonensis* are inherently neurotropic. Following ingestion, the larvae penetrate the intestinal wall and migrate via the bloodstream to the central nervous system and burrow into neural and ocular tissue. Parasites are found mainly in the medulla, pons, cerebellum and in the adjacent leptomeninges; the spinal cord is also frequently involved, at least histologically. Most worms die shortly afterwards but live worms have been isolated from neural tissue before death and also post mortem. An inflammatory response develops in the vicinity of the worms, particularly dead worms. There is an associated infiltrate of polymorphs and eosinophils and sometimes a zone of necrosis and granulomatosis. It is this inflammatory response that accounts for most of the symptoms in infected patients.

Clinical Manifestations The spectrum of clinical manifestations in EM due to *A. cantonensis* ranges from a self-limiting illness with fever and headache to a severe and sometimes fatal meningoencephalitis. The majority of cases are self-limiting and resolve in about 4 weeks.[3,10,11] A rare chronic form of the disease has been described; in these cases symptoms may persist for several months. Symptoms typically develop 2–35 days after ingestion of larvae. Excruciating headache is the most common presenting symptom and is seen in more than 90 per cent of cases.[3] The pain is usually frontal but may be occipital or bitemporal. Nausea and vomiting are also frequently reported symptoms. Some patients have fever, malaise, constipation and anorexia. Less common symptoms include cough, neck stiffness, paraesthesiae, weakness of the extremities, muscle twitching, and cranial nerve abnormalities, including diplopia and facial paralysis.

Data on the clinical manifestations of EM are derived mainly from case reports and small series. In one recent case series, Slom et al.[5] reported the following symptoms among nine travellers returning from Jamaica: headache (100%), visual disturbance (92%), nuchal rigidity (83%), fatigue (83%), hyperaesthesia (75%), vomiting (67%), paraesthesia (50%), muscle pain (50%), fever

(42%), muscle weakness (33%) and diarrhoea (17%). Generally, patients have meningismus on clinical examination, including nuchal rigidity and positive Kernig's and Brudzinki's signs. In addition, patients may have alteration of mental status ranging from mild confusion to deep coma. Decreased tendon reflexes and cranial nerve abnormalities (extraocular muscle dysfunction and facial weakness) may also occur. Seizures have been infrequently reported. Paresis, paralysis and urinary retention or incontinence occur much less frequently.[5,10,11] Persistent painful paraesthesiae and hyperaesthesia have been described as 'hallmarks' of EM caused by *A. cantonensis*, and occurred among all nine hospitalised patients in the Jamaican outbreak.[5]

Case fatality rates in Thailand and Taiwan have been reported to be 0.5% and 3%, respectively.[3,10,11] In a case reported by Lindo et al.,[4] a 14-month-old boy was admitted to hospital with a history of anorexia, constipation and abdominal distension. Five days later he developed fever, hypotonia and hyporeflexia in the lower limbs. Cerebrospinal fluid (CSF) analysis revealed leucocytosis with predominant neutrophils. The child died 34 days after admission. Post-mortem examination revealed meningeal infiltration with eosinophils and portions of worms identified as *A. cantonensis* in the brain and lungs.

In the second fatal case in Jamaica, a 27-year-old man was admitted to hospital with a history of headache, fever, myalgia and malaise. Examination revealed mild nuchal rigidity and drowsiness. CSF analysis showed leucocytosis with predominant eosinophils. The patient became progressively more comatose and died after 6 days in hospital. Post-mortem and serological findings confirmed *A. cantonensis* as the causative agent (T.S Ferguson et al., unpublished data).

Laboratory Findings and Diagnosis

The laboratory diagnosis of EM is difficult. Worms are rarely found in the CSF, occurring in as few as 27 out of 259 cases and 19 out of 484 cases.[3] In Taiwan, where large volumes of CSF (up to 25 ml) were removed to relieve severe headache, larvae were found in less than 10 per cent of cases (eight out of 125).[2,12] When worms are found they must be differentiated morphometrically from other helminthic causes of EM.

Laboratory diagnosis is most often made on the basis of eosinophilic pleocytosis together with a history of eating raw molluscs. Eosinophilia exceeds 10 per cent in 95 per cent of patients and develops at around 12 days post-infection. It is therefore essential that a differential white blood cell count be carried out on all CSF samples in cases of aseptic meningitis. The CSF pressure is generally elevated (>200 mm H_2O) and the fluid is clear or slightly cloudy and is not xanthochromic. The CSF protein level is slightly elevated but glucose is normal. Peripheral blood eosinophilia is seen in most patients and is often greater than 3 per cent. This usually does not correlate with CSF eosinophilia or with the clinical course of illness.

The diagnosis is also supported by serological tests including enzyme-linked immunosorbent assays and Western blots. There are several assays available; however, they have not been widely evaluated and the results are not often ready in time for clinical input.[3,10,11] Furthermore, whilst these assays are usually found to be very sensitive, their specificities are often very low. Further improvements in these tests are needed before they can be used widely. In the light of this, the diagnosis of *Angiostrongylus* meningitis is generally made on the basis of clinical, epidemiological and CSF features, supported by serology.

Neuro-imaging with computed tomography (CT) or magnetic resonance imaging (MRI) is recommended in patients with altered mental status or focal neurological signs. However, MRI and CT are more useful in excluding other potential causes of EM than at making a definitive diagnosis of *A. cantonensis* infection of the central nervous system.[3,10,11]

Treatment

Treatment of *A. cantonensis* infection is primarily supportive. Anti-helminthics are not often given as there is concern that they may exacerbate symptoms as a result of host responses to dead worms. Despite this, both thiabendazole and levamisole have been used with doubtful effect.[3,10]

Treatment options include repeated lumbar punctures, which provide relief for patients with persistent headaches and raised intracranial pressures. While this method has been responded to produce dramatic clinical improvements, these are only transient.[5] Many subsequent reports have suggested serial lumbar punctures for the relief of raised intracranial pressure, but CSF volumes have not been reported.[2,3,5,10] The risk of cerebral herniation must always be considered if serial lumbar punctures are used. Corticosteroids have been used to reduce the inflammatory response induced by the release of antigens from dying worms. Prednisolone at a dose of 60 mg daily in adults, or 2 mg/kg daily in children, given for two weeks has been found to be beneficial.[11]

Practical Points

- Angiostrongyius cantonensis is endemic in Jamaica, Cuba, the Dominican Republic and Haiti.
- Infection with the parasite should be considered as a cause of aseptic meningitis in patients with paraesthesiae and peripheral eosinophilia, even without a history of exposure to undercooked molluscs or crustaceans.
- Clinicians must routinely request differential white blood cell counts in cerebrospinal fluid as this is a good indicator of the need for further investigations.
- Eosinophilia in peripheral blood and CSF supports a diagnosis of EM. Absence of eosinophilia does not exclude it, particularly early in the course of the illness.
- Treatment is not optimal, but serial lumbar punctures have been used to relieve headaches. Reduction of the inflammatory response using steroids also appears to be beneficial in relieving symptoms.

J.F. Lindo & T.S. Ferguson

Notes

1. P.F. Weller, L.X. Liu, 'Eosinophilic meningitis', *Semin Neurol* 13 (1993): 161–8.

2. P. Prociv, M.S. Carlisle, 'The spread of *Angiostrongylus cantonensis* in Australia', *Southeast Asian J Trap Med Public Health* 32, Suppl. 2 (2001): 126–8.

3. K. Yoshimura, '*Angiostrangylus* (Parastrongylus) and less common nematodes', in *Topley Wilson's Microbiology and Microbial Infections*, eds., FEG Cox, JP Krier, D Wakelin, 635–60, vol. 5, 9th ed. (London: Arnold, 1998).

4. J.F. Lindo, C.T. Escoffery, B. Reid, G. Codrington, C. Cunningham-Myrie, M.L. Eberhard, 'Fatal autochthonous eosinophilic meningitis in a Jamaican child caused by *Angiostrongylus cantonensis*', *Am J Trap Med Hyg* 70 (2004): 425–8.

5. T.J. Slom, M.M. Cortese, S.I. Gerber, et al., 'An outbreak of eosinophilic meningitis caused by *Angiostrongylus cantonensis* in travelers returning from the Caribbean', *N Engl J Med* 346, no. 9 (2002): 668–75.

6. M.M. Kliks, N.E. Palumbo, 'Eosinophilic meningitis beyond the Pacific Basin: the global dispersal of a peridomestic zoonosis caused by *Angiostrangylus cantonensis*, the nematode lungworm of rats' *Sac Sci Med* 34 (*1992*): 199–212.

7. P.N. Levett, K.A. Douglas, C.A. Waugh, R.D. Robinson J.F. Lindo, 'Failure to detect *Angiostrangylus cantonensis* in rats in Barbados', *West Indian Med J* 53 (2004): 58.

8. K.O. Barrow, A. Rose, J.F. Lindo, 'Eosinophilic meningitis. Is *Angiostrangylus cantonensis* endemic in Jamaica?' *West Indian Med J* 45 (1996): 70–1.

9. J.F. Lindo, C. Waugh, J. Hall, et al. Enzootic *Angiostrangylus cantonensis* in rats and snails after an outbreak of human eosinophilic meningitis, Jamaica. *Emerg Infect Dis* 8 (2002): 324–6.

10. T. Slom, S. Johnson, 'Eosinophilic meningitis', *Curr Infect Dis Rep* 5 (2003): 322–8.

11. V. Lo Re 3rd, S.J. Gluckman, 'Eosinophilic meningitis', *Am J Med* 114 (2003): 217–23.

12. C.Y. Yii, 'Clinical observations on eosinophilic meningitis and meningoencephalitis caused by *Angiostrangylus cantonensis* in Taiwan', *Am J Trap Meq Hyg* 25 (1976): 233–49.

CRITICAL THINKING AND WRITING

1. What is the writers' intention?
2. a) Comment on the use of scientific jargon and the diction in general.
   b) What does the diction reveal about
      (i) the writers' expected audience?
      (ii) the context in which you would expect to find this?
3. Comment on the writers' use of :
   a) definitions
   b) historical/background information
4. Identify two examples which the writers use. Explain the purpose for which they are included in the text.
5. Choose one writing strategy/organizing pattern which the writers use. Explain how it is used and assess its effectiveness.
6. Identify three aspects of this article which you would use to explain that it is accurately classified as exposition.

WRITING ACTIVITIES

7. Explain how this article is different from the writing you would do in your own discipline. Comment on the tone, register and overall style.
8. Do research on the Tropical Medicine Research Institute at the University of the West Indies. Present the information to your class.
9. Justify your interest, or lack of interest, in this article.
10. State three facts which you have learnt about the *Angiostrongylus cantonensis*. Write three different paragraphs in which you explain them to the following three groups.
    a) A group of ten year olds
    b) A group of concerned parents
    c) A group of teenagers

SECTION 2
ARGUMENT

INTRODUCTION TO ARGUMENT

Dear Students,

One of the purposes of a university education is to prepare students to think both within and outside of their disciplines. A course in argument at the tertiary level contributes to this goal, as it is designed to hone the thinking skills of students.

In everyday speech, people often use the word 'argument' to mean a quarrel or a verbal dispute/disagreement of some kind. However, in this text the word is not used in this way. According to Diestler,[1] when critical thinkers speak about an argument they are referring to a conclusion drawn about a particular issue, supported with reasons (4). Reinking, Hart and von der Osten[2] describe argument as 'a paper, grounded on logical, structured evidence, that attempts to convince the reader to accept an opinion, take some action, or do both' (160). Although they refer to argument as 'a paper', argument is not always written; there are also oral and visual arguments.

An argument is an attempt to persuade someone that one position on an issue is preferable to another. The argument must make a claim and attempt to justify that claim by presenting evidence. For example, if someone stated that smoking in public places should be banned, that would not be an argument; rather, it would be an unsubstantiated assertion. To develop this claim into an argument, one would need to say why such a ban would be justified.

As a university student, you need to critically analyse what you read. For argument, this means that you must identify the essential parts of the arguments presented, ensure that the justification given for each claim is true, and that the conclusion drawn follows logically from the evidence given. Sometimes in a general argument course you might be spared the task of verifying the information and instead be asked to accept it as true for the purposes of argument, but remember that when you read articles in your disciplines the veracity of the evidence provided is critical; an argument cannot be considered to be sound when the evidence on which it is based is fabricated or inaccurate.

Argumentation is an important skill and you must learn both to read and write arguments. Many of the skills of argumentation will be very useful in the world of work. An attorney-at-law uses argument every day on the job, whether in the courtroom or doing paperwork at a desk. A trade unionist must argue the case of workers at the bargaining table and also seek to analyse the proposals put forward by management, in order to protect the rights of workers. But in less obvious cases, argument is critical for everyday decisions. When someone sends you a proposal you will need to analyse the information and arrive at a decision regarding how you will proceed. Are the facts as presented true/accurate? Do the promises made look realistic in light of the information given? Are the conclusions drawn logical? The decisions you make may determine how successful you are at your job, or how much money you lose or gain in a venture. You will need to be able to decipher evidence presented in support of a claim and determine whether it is sufficient to warrant the claim made. Similarly, when you write in your job, you will often need to be convincing in order to get that proposal or budget approved; and your speeches may also need to be persuasive if you hope to get the response you anticipated. Most of you, at some time, will have to negotiate in order to get something you want/need. You probably have had to do that already with one or other of your parents or some of your peers.

How Argument Works

Argument should not be confused with psychological persuasion. In psychological persuasion, the audience is persuaded to believe something primarily through an appeal to the senses. Advertisements are a good example of psychological persuasion. In visual media (for example, television and print) the appeal is often to sight. Argument, on the other hand, is concerned mainly with reaching a conclusion through **logical** reasoning.*

In arriving at a conclusion in argument, the arguer needs to make an **inference**; pure reporting is not considered to be an argument, nor is an unsupported claim. If,

for example, you were to say that a large number of Caribbean sportsmen and women have medalled at the Olympic Games over the last two decades, that would not constitute an argument. However, you could use this to infer that the Caribbean has many talented athletes. Similarly, if you were to declare that Caribbean people are conservative, without presenting any evidence for your claim, this would not be argument either; rather, it would be an unsubstantiated assertion.

Arguments often have **inference markers**. These are words that herald a conclusion or support for a conclusion. For example, one might use the words 'therefore', 'thus', 'so', or 'then' to introduce the conclusion; 'since', 'if', 'as' and 'because' are often used to introduce evidence for a conclusion.

An argument is a series of connected statements — premises, propositions, or observations — that attempt to provide support/evidence/justification for another statement or proposition. The conclusion that a writer draws from the evidence presented must be a logical one — that is, the audience should be able to follow the reasoning of the writer. The evidence should be relevant and must be sufficient to allow the readers themselves to draw the conclusion. Good argumentative writing will consider both or all sides of a controversy. The audience is not likely to be convinced without an examination of alternative viewpoints.

When you read an argumentative piece, you need to identify the **issue or controversy** that the writer is addressing. Next, look for the **conclusion** that the writer is drawing (or wants you to draw). This is called the writer's **thesis**. A number of claims would have been made in an attempt to lead you to this conclusion; identify them, and finally find the **reasons** that are given to justify each claim.

Blooming with the Pouis

As a writer, you too need to identify what your **controversy** is and clearly outline it for your audience. This will help the audience to identify the **issue** you are discussing and understand why it is controversial. You must arrive at a position on the issue and have a clear thesis statement. There are different argumentative structures that you can use, and the placement of the thesis statement will depend on the type that is being used. What is important is that the thesis should be **clearly** stated or implied.

Issue

The issue is the question being addressed. This is different from a topic. Under the topic 'homosexuality' one might address the issue of whether homosexuals should be allowed to be legally married. The issue can also be framed as a question — *Should the law allow a person to be married to someone of the same sex?*

Controversy

A controversy is an issue on which persons do not agree. An issue that is controversial is contentious and incites arguments. A controversy can be on a small scale — something involving only two people — or it can be a wide-scale dispute involving a whole society or the world. The issues that are dealt with in argument are most likely to be controversial ones. Issues that have already been resolved would not need to be debated (except for mere academic interest). Some issues that would have sparked heated debate five years ago have ceased to be controversial, as society has arrived at a consensus about the issue, or perhaps the contentious aspects of it.

Application of Argument to the Academic Context

Most students of argument will ask themselves at some point 'Why am I learning this? Why do I need to know what an argument is?' These are reasonable questions. After all, learning must have some purpose, and such questions begin the search for appropriate answers. A quick answer to the questions is that students who master the skills of argument are better able to deal with the material they encounter in their studies. Arguments are found everywhere. They are found in everyday life — in newspapers, on the radio and television; they are found in every school, college and university subject. Academics make use of argument in many different ways. Many of the articles written in journals are argumentative. When you read a critique about a literature book, the writer is arguing. He or she is convinced about a certain perspective and hopes to persuade you to accept that perspective. If you are in the pure and applied sciences you will meet arguments about evolution and whether the current weather patterns are attributable to global warming. Social scientists will argue about the cause of crime or the importance of the family structure. A proper understanding of argument will help you to be able to assess the quality of the different arguments that you encounter and also to become competent in developing your own arguments in various academic disciplines.

In the academic realm there will be times when an author will make a claim or express an opinion but either fails to provide sufficient evidence or offers support that you will not find to be convincing. As a tertiary-level student you must ensure that you not only know the facts for the courses that you do, but that you are competent. This means that you are able to evaluate the material that you encounter and analyse it before accepting or rejecting its claims. You will, therefore, have to read critically and analytically. In addition, you need to ensure that when you write your own essays you seek to validate all your claims and to do so without using fallacious reasoning. You will be expected to write well-reasoned papers in your various courses. Although your instructors will not necessarily tell you about the rules of argument, they will recognise a well-structured argument when they get it and will reward you accordingly.

Types of Claims

There are various types of claims that can be made in argument. These include claims of fact, definition, cause, policy and value.

The claim of **fact** is a claim that something happened or exists. An example of a claim of fact is — the legal age of consent is sixteen.

The claim of **definition** provides an answer to a question about the meaning or interpretation of something, as in this statement: An athlete who receives monetary compensation cannot be viewed as an amateur.

When someone makes a claim about the cause or effect of something, that is a claim of **cause**. 'Late-night partying causes students to get poor grades' is an example of a claim of cause.

A claim of **policy** proposes a new course of action. For example, someone claiming that university students should be required to take a course in public speaking is making a claim of policy.

A claim of **value** provides an answer to a dispute over the worth of something. For example, if I claim that swimming is the best

form of exercise, I am making a value judgement about the worth of swimming and am therefore making a claim of value.

Analysing Arguments

In an effort to determine the worth of an argument you will need to analyse it. There are different aspects of argument that need to be analysed; one of them is proof. Logical argument has three types of proof: **pathos**, **ethos** and **logos**.

Pathos refers to appeals to the emotion. This should not be confused with the appeals that are used in psychological persuasion (see section entitled '**How Argument Works**'). Pathos is a rational appeal to one's emotions. This can be done by speaking to issues that the reader values or is concerned about, or by using language that evokes an emotional response. If the writer appeals to values that the reader holds dear, the likelihood that the argument will be convincing is greater than if the reader were not concerned about those values. On the other hand, if the writing contains excessive use of emotive language and lacks reasoning, one might find the piece less than convincing.

A logical argument about the risk to children that comes with irresponsible parenting might be more effective if the writer refers to the children as 'dehumanised, forlorn and forsaken'. Parallelism and repetition can also create an appeal to pathos. Both of these devices evoke an emotional response on the part of the audience. In Martin Luther King Jr's 'I Have a Dream', the repeated use of the phrase 'One hundred years later' in the second paragraph of the speech helps to reinforce the fact that one hundred years had elapsed and yet change had not occurred.

Ethos focuses on an appeal to the reader's sense of what is right or wrong. Ethos can be created as a result of the credibility of the author. The work of a credible writer is more likely to be believed by the reader than that of someone who is not perceived to be credible. The writer can also make himself/herself appear credible by using authoritative sources and crediting these sources.

Logos refers to reasoning that appeals to the intellect. There are different types of logos proof (referred to as **types of argument**). The way in which we evaluate an argument depends on the type of argument it is.

Argument types and sub-types

There are two main types of argument — **deductive** and **inductive**. A deductive argument is based on premises. If the premises are true and the argument is properly constructed, then there is absolute certainty about the truth of the conclusion. The strength of the claim is such that if the premises are true, the conclusion could not possibly be false. In the inductive argument the evidence provides only probable truth of the conclusion.

An **inductive** argument arrives at a conclusion based on an examination of data, observations or examples. The conclusion will be a **generalisation**. The reader is expected to accept the examples given as sufficient and accurate enough to arrive at the generalisation (that is to make the inductive leap to the conclusion). Since the conclusion is arrived at based on a sample, there can be no absolute certainty that the generalisation will always apply. The conclusion is at best probably true.

Deductive arguments have different sub-types, but the main type encountered in everyday discourse is the **syllogism**. A syllogism is a collection of three statements

— two premises from which a third statement (i.e. the conclusion) is inferred. For example, the argument that '*all animals must be creations, because they are biological creatures and all biological creatures are creations*' may be broken down as follows:

Major Premise:	*All Animals are Biological creatures.*
Minor Premise:	*All Biological creatures are Creations.*
Conclusion:	*(therefore) All Animals are Creations.*

A 'syllogism' with one component left out is called an **enthymeme**. The missing component could be the conclusion or one of the premises. An example of an enthymeme with a premise missing is:

'She is going to fail her courses because she does not attend classes or study for examinations.'

The missing premise can be implied — *Persons who fail to attend classes or who do not study for their examinations will fail their courses*. This is the major premise. The argument can be seen thus:

Major Premise:	*Persons who fail to attend classes or who do not study for their examinations will fail their courses.*
Minor Premise:	*She does not attend classes or study for examinations*
Conclusion:	*She is going to fail her courses.*

When the missing element cannot be reasonably implied, the conclusion does not follow from the premise and we get what is called a **non-sequitur** (a Latin phrase that means 'it does not follow').

Inductive arguments can be arrived at based on analysis of general examples or statistics. The former is usually called a **generalisation** or an **inductive generalisation**, while the latter is sometimes referred to as a **statistical** generalisation or an **argument from statistics**. Different texts will use different terms, but they are all speaking about the same thing.

An example of an **inductive generalisation** is

Boys tend to peak later than girls. Girls at age 14 have consistently done better academically than their male counterparts. However, boys at age 18 have consistently outperformed their female counterparts.

One might make an **argument from statistics** thus:

This institution has an ever increasing student population. In the last three years student enrolment figures have been 4500, 5000 and 6000 respectively.

When the generalisation is about the cause or the effect of something, it is called an **inductive causal generalisation**, a **causal generalisation** or an **argument from cause**. The following is an example of a causal generalisation:

Researchers claim that video games may be causing depression in children. Depression has increased in the sample that was studied and this group of children has also increased its use of video games.

There is some disagreement in the literature about the **argument from analogy.** In some texts the analogy is seen as a sub-type of inductive arguments, while in others the argument from analogy is classified as another type of argument.[3]

Whatever classification you use, the important thing is that an argument using analogy is one in which two situations, persons or things are compared, and the arguer claims that because they are alike in one (or more) ways, they will also be alike in other ways. The support for the claim is (a)

the assumption of similarity between the two, and (b) an observation about one of these. For example,

Many people will die of AIDS, because many people died of Small Pox some years ago.

The arguer is claiming that many people will die of AIDS because he/she knows that Small Pox killed many people in the past and assumes that AIDS is similar to Small Pox.

Analysing Deductive Syllogisms for Soundness

A deductive argument is deemed to be sound only when the argument is valid (that is, the conclusion follows logically from the premises) and the premises are true. To test the validity of a deductive syllogism, one has to evaluate whether the premises have the proper order. If all bananas are fruits and Janice's lunch is a banana, then one can conclude that Janice's lunch is a fruit. However, if we were to reverse the proper order and say instead that all bananas are fruits, and Janice's lunch is a fruit, one would not be able to draw any conclusion from the two premises. If her lunch is a fruit, it could be any fruit, not necessarily a banana. This would therefore be an invalid argument form. Remember that the premises in deductive syllogisms give an absolute guarantee about the truth of the conclusion. These latter premises would give no such guarantee. Even when the two premises have a valid form, you need to ensure that the arguer extracted the conclusion that would follow logically from those premises. The following table helps to summarise the elements that you should look for in a sound syllogism.

Features of a Sound Deductive Syllogism

	True Premises	False Premises
Valid Argument Form	**Sound Argument:** *Valid Argument Form and True Premises*	**Unsound Argument:** *Valid Argument Form but Untrue Premises*
Invalid Argument Form	**Unsound Argument:** *True Premises but Invalid Argument Form*	**Unsound Argument:** *Invalid Argument Form and Untrue Premises*

Judging the Soundness of an Inductive Generalisation

Although by definition a generalisation is arrived at on the basis of an examination of only some persons, things, and so on, a sound inductive generalisation must be based on a large enough sample of typical examples that is truly representative of the group about which the generalisation is being made. When you analyse a generalisation you need to look carefully at the sample and the means by which the sample was collected. Ensure that it is free from bias and that each item or person in the population about which the arguer is generalising had an equal opportunity to have been in the sample. In addition, make sure that the sample and the population represent the same group. For example, if the sample consists only of St. Lucians, the generalisation should be about St. Lucians and not about Caribbean people in general.

When statistics are being used to justify a generalisation, ensure that there are no statistical fallacies — for example, the fallacies of central tendency, misleading totals, misleading percentages or misuse of figures (see **Glossary**). The statistics used must be current, reliable and accurate, and also relevant to the context. Generalisations must truly reflect the evidence presented and should not distort the truth.

Causal Generalisation

Generalisations about cause are very difficult to prove. When analysing an argument from cause, verify that the writer has clearly established that a causal relationship exists. Often writers are guilty of committing the **post-hoc fallacy** because they mistake coincidence for cause. If one thing follows another, one cannot, on that basis alone, jump to the conclusion that the latter is caused by the former; one would need to prove that nothing else could explain this phenomenon.

Sometimes writers are successful in proving that a causal relationship exists between two things, but claim that the cause they have identified is the only cause when in fact it may be a contributory cause or one of many possible causes. One example of this is when some social scientists claim that poverty is the cause of crime. It is clear that poverty could not be the only cause of crime, since there are many who are not poor and yet commit crimes. If the writer has not established that there is a causal relationship, then the issues raised in this paragraph do not apply. The writer would have committed the **post-hoc fallacy** and that is what you should concentrate on.

Analysing an Argument from Analogy

Sometimes the two things, people or situations being compared, are indeed similar, but not in relation to the issue being discussed. However, for an argument from analogy to be deemed a good one, it must contain significant similarities that are directly relevant to the issue that is being discussed. In analysing an argument from analogy you need to assess the differences and the similarities. The test of a good analogy is the extent to which the similarities outweigh the dissimilarities. If the dissimilarities outnumber and outweigh the similarities then the analogy is not considered to be a good one and the argument would be deemed unsound.

Some Concluding Thoughts

- When you read an argumentative piece, you should be able to take a stance on the issue that was under discussion. You may not necessarily accept the position of the author, but you should have found some of the arguments convincing and have gained enough information about the different sides to the debate to allow you to arrive at your own position on the issue.

- Pathos is used to make an argument more convincing, but remember that inappropriate use of emotive language can detract from the logical issue. Examine the writing to see if there is an attempt by the author to manipulate the reader through the use of psychological persuasion.

- Ensure that you identify the author's main claim, and search for the subsidiary claims that help to substantiate that main claim. Each of these subsidiary claims should have evidence in its own support. Evaluate these claims and the support given for each of them in order to satisfy yourself that the argument is sound. Look at both the veracity of the information provided and the logical thread of the argument.

- Lastly, examine the credibility of the argument and the author. Is the argument believable? Does the author have the knowledge and/or authority to speak on the issue? Does he or she use appropriate sources or refer to relevant authorities?

A good argument should be convincing. That means that it must be credible, logical and based on accurate information.

Vivienne A. Harding

Notes

*   See also, p. xxix of this text for additional explanations of argumentation and persuasion.

1. Sherry Diestler, *Becoming a Critical Thinker* (Upper Saddle River, NJ: Pearson Prentice Hall 2005).

2. James A. Reinking, Andrew W. Hart and Robert von der Osten. *Strategies for Sucessful Writing*. Upper Saddle River, NJ: Pearson Prentice Hall, 2002.

3. Nancy V. Wood, *Perspectives on Argument* (Upper Saddle River, NJ: Prentice Hall, 2007) and *Strategies for Successful Writing*, treat the analogy as a separate type of argument, whereas Barnet & Bedau in *Critical Thinking, Reading and Writing* (Boston: Bedford/St. Martin's, 1999) view the argument by analogy as a type of inductive argument.

EDUCATION & SCIENCE

CHAPTER 27

COMPUTERS IN THE MATHEMATICS CLASSROOM

Claims for the role of technology are appropriately more modest in the Caribbean, and curriculum developers are constrained by what might be possible in only a minority of institutions. If this is true at a national level, it is even more the case with regional examination syllabuses such as those of the Caribbean Examinations Council (CXC) whose syllabuses so frequently become the working curriculum of high schools.

It is possible to argue that curricula should be radically transformed by the existence of the computer — in the approach to learning, and also in what it is appropriate to learn with the power of the computer in the classroom and with a technological world outside. Old skills such as numerical computation, algebraic manipulation or graph drawing might be seen as largely redundant, while using algebraic, statistical and other software, together with modelling and the handling of dynamic images in a problem-solving environment could be seen as the way forward. Such thinking is exciting and might be fruitful but may have to be left to the 'visionaries' while the majority of teachers continue working within the realities of their professional situation. Certainly, the current CXC syllabuses for mathematics at both

CSEC and CAPE levels make reference to computer use; indeed, even references to the use of calculators are somewhat constrained.

Professional experience with electronic calculators provides sobering evidence of the difficulties that professionals have, both, within mathematics education and outside, in agreeing on, or adjusting rapidly to, the influence of technology on the mathematics curriculum. The potentially much greater impact of the computer seems even more daunting, and suggests that an evolutionary and exploratory approach has to be the way forward. However, there is a need to share experience, provide encouragement and establish frameworks, if there is to be progress in harnessing the power which has become a mainstay of so much of the 21st century world in which we live. In reality, a new-look curriculum with integrated computer use can only emerge as experience, confidence and skills accrue. So let us consider some down-to-earth possibilities within the current content of the curriculum.

Within the school context we can identify a number of strands to computer use in mathematics teaching. At one extreme, the long tradition of alchemy is evident in the search for the complete package which will provide total coverage of the whole syllabus, which can be used with minimal teacher input, and has diagnostic and assessment procedures built into it. Such packages are often termed Individual Learning Systems (ILS) and various commercial companies have invested heavily to produce attractive and versatile material of this type. These systems can provide a comprehensive learning environment over the ability and age range of students. However, they make big assumptions about the long-term motivating power of such material and of the relatively limited variety of learning experiences which are involved. The apparently modest role of the teacher may appeal to some, but will not be welcomed by more creative professionals. The cost of making such a facility available to learners is high in relation to both the hardware (access to a computer for several hours a week for each child) and the software (access to such a major package for a large number of students).

At another extreme is the almost random collection of fun software for learners to play with when their serious work in class is done at the end of the day or the term. Students may get the opportunity to use computers as a reward or for enrichment, but there is little sense of integration. Computer learning is projected, perhaps unintentionally, as being outside the normal means of learning mathematics.

But much of the most significant development work evident has arisen from software designed to address particular learning needs or to provide particular kinds of learning experiences. While some of the software is quite specific, other material is of a generic nature. Indeed some of the generic software programs, such as data handling packages and spreadsheets, while not designed for education, have been adapted and tailored to the needs of mathematics education. At a more

specific level, there are programs for reading scales and for solving linear equations which are carefully structured to overcome some of the learning difficulties which experience and research have shown to be problematic. Access to these for an occasional lesson can indeed be beneficial and may be embedded in the development of the topic by the teacher, or used for remedial purposes.

Generic programs can, by definition, be used to do many things. For example, a word-processing package can be used for the writing, storing or reading of letters, reports, poetry, posters, novels, and so on. If it is to achieve a specific purpose, such as 'helping students to write poetry', then the teacher must plan appropriate ways to use it. The same applies to generic software in the mathematics lesson. Some software programs are more 'open' than others. For example, a spreadsheet package such as Excel is very open and mathematics teachers can use it to develop work on number patterns, on statistics and on aspects of algebra. Other programs are more clearly identified with mathematics, but the way in which they will be used is largely left open to the individual teacher. Graph drawing packages are of the latter kind — *Autograph* and *Omnigraph* are examples of such programs. The power of these programs rests partly in the creativity evident in their design but also in the fact that they can provide a different kind of learning experience from the traditional ones in classroom learning.

John Hayter and Mike Egan

CRITICAL THINKING AND WRITING

1. What do you think the writers hoped to achieve by writing this article?
2. What is the writer's main claim/thesis?
3. With reference to the register and content of the article, state what assumptions the writers are making about the educational background of their audience.
4. Examine the second paragraph of the article and discuss how the writers attempt to establish common ground.
5. How do the writers justify their claim in paragraph 2 that 'Such thinking is exciting and fruitful, but may have to be left to 'visionaries' ... of their professional situation'?
6. Using specific examples from the article, discuss the extent to which you consider the arguments in this article to be balanced.
7. Examine the argument in paragraph 7.
   a) identify
      i. the type of claim
      ii. the type of argument
      iii. the support provided
   b) Evaluate the soundness of the argument.

WRITING ACROSS THE CURRICULUM ACTIVITY

8. Examine the writers' discussion of Individual Learning Software (ILS) packages in paragraph 4 and write a paragraph in which you support or refute the points they make regarding the use of ILS packages in the classroom.

CHAPTER 28

BIOTECHNOLOGY – RELEVANCE FOR CARIBBEAN AGRICULTURE

The Caribbean region consists of 23 island states and four associated continental countries. The region as a whole has a population of 37.7 m and a total land area of 61 m ha of which approximately 25 per cent is under agricultural production and 11 per cent is arable. The island states account for 37 per cent of the total land area (22.9 m ha) and 94 per cent (35.6 m) of the population. Agriculture is largely based on plantation crops such as sugar cane, bananas, cocoa, coffee and tobacco. Over the past decade, globalization has had an adverse impact, with considerable loss of export markets. There is remarkable pressure on arable lands, particularly in small island states. Consequently, agriculture is carried out largely on small holdings providing little opportunity for achieving economies of scale and global competitiveness. The geo-political fragmentation of the region, where territories are separated by political ideology, language and oceanic or land barriers, poses a serious challenge for developing appropriate mechanisms for technology development, transfer and cooperation within the region. Other challenges include the fragility of the island ecosystems and associated worries of environmental degradation, poor human resource capacity in individual nations, low investments in research and lack of an enabling environment to foster innovation and entrepreneurship.

The Caribbean region has other weaknesses, which stem from the extremely diverse and fragile ecosystems and the high pest and disease pressures associated with most tropical countries. This requires crop varieties and animal breeds with tolerance to biotic and abiotic stresses and broad adaptability. The conglomeration of seed companies into larger companies has shifted focus from niche breeding to breeding for larger countries and territories. The lack of regional efforts at breeding and seed production has also placed the region in a seriously disadvantageous position. The seeds, considered to be a vehicle of innovation, have become a handicap to becoming competitive in agriculture.

The decline of the plantation sectors in many islands has led to migration of labour out of agriculture. As a result, the population involved in agriculture is declining and aging, with the additional threat of a loss of indigenous skills and food security in the region.

On the other hand, the Caribbean region has a marine coastline of 26,826 km, approximately 1.5 times larger than that of the USA, providing an enormous potential for developing its marine resources. Further, it lies between the Central American and South American megacentres of biodiversity and is considered to be a biodiversity 'hotspot', with an estimated endemism of 2.3 per cent of plant species and 2.9 per cent of vertebrate species on only 0.15 per cent of the Earth's surface. It is also considered to be a centre of diversity of numerous crops, including corn, pepper, cucurbits, pineapple, cotton and spices, to list a few. The region also houses an international collection of cocoa and other regional collections of crop germplasm. The strong tourism sector allows for developing backward linkages with agriculture and popularizing local brands and innovations. It should be emphasized that, in addition to the local knowledge residing in the indigenous peoples of the region, there is also a rich heritage inherited from Africa, India, China, Europe and the Middle East.

The high levels of literacy, comparatively high per capita GDP, relatively good income distribution and a population that is innovative in many aspects of life, provide opportunities to foster a culture of innovation. The proximity to the North American market and emerging regional economic blocks are seen as opportunities for the expansion of markets and the provision of access to technology. Linkages can also be forged between technology-rich and more financially stable parts of the region, for making greater strides.

P.U. Umaharan

CRITICAL THINKING AND WRITING

1. Identify the dominant discourse mode and the context in which you would expect to find this article.
2. What is the issue being discussed? What is the writer's position?
3. With reference to the content and diction, identify the assumptions the writer makes about his audience in terms of their level of interest in the subject.
4. How does the writer establish credibility?
5. Identify the type of argument being proposed in paragraph 1. State, with support from the article, whether or not this is a sound argument.
6. a) Identify ONE organizational strategy used in paragraph 1.
   b) Discuss the effectiveness of the strategy, highlighting how it helped the writer support his claim.
7. Using specific examples from the article, discuss the extent to which you consider the arguments in this article to be balanced.

WRITING ACROSS THE CURRICULUM ACTIVITY

9. Write a paragraph in which you provide support for ONE of the points the writer makes in paragraph 1 regarding the reasons for the adverse effect of globalization on the Caribbean.

CHAPTER 29

INEFFICIENCY OF THE EDUCATIONAL SYSTEM

The home is the first learning environment, but the school, the church and the wider society provide formal and informal educational opportunities for the intellectual, physical, spiritual, social and emotional development of the young. Education is concerned with all these aspects of development, not merely the intellectual, although it is this area which determines the form of the curriculum, the teaching methods used and the methods of assessment employed.

The education individuals receive, and their levels of attainment, have far-reaching implications for their ability to make informed choices, decisions about themselves, their families, and their occupational and social roles. The school serves as an extension of the home in terms of its socializing function — assisting children with the very difficult and complex tasks of academic competence, self-reliance in all areas of life, moral development, acquisition of social skills, motivation and personality formation. Article 29 of the United Nations Rights of the Child Convention — to which Jamaica is a signatory — addresses the aims and content of education, and stresses the development of the child's potential to the fullest, the

preparation of the child for active and responsible citizenship and the development of respect for cultural and national values.

Educational provisions for Jamaican children differ, and affect their life opportunities, their future occupational and societal roles. For the more advantaged, there are kindergarten and private preparatory schools, an academic secondary high school education in public or private schools and tertiary education at the University of the West Indies, the College of Arts, Science and Technology, or overseas. For the less advantaged, community basic schools are followed by public primary school, the possibility of a secondary high school, but the probability of a vocational/technical secondary school, and the remote possibility of tertiary education. In Jamaica, education has been considered to be the means whereby disadvantaged children can break the cycle of ignorance and poverty, and most parents identify a good education as one of the goals they have for their children. Many struggle and sacrifice to send their children to school, providing uniform, books, lunch and transportation.

A number of children, however, because of their home conditions, arrive at school tired, hungry, and unable to participate fully in the learning experience. Many are kept away from school to assist in income generation, or because there is no bus fare, or lunch money for that day. In 1988, the Grade 6 Achievement Test of the National Assessment Programme assessed 31 per cent of Grade 6 students as being illiterate. Performance in the terminal examinations of the secondary system — the Caribbean Examinations Council (CXC) — is also poor: in 1990, only 28.8 per cent of the students sitting CXC General English Language gained grades I and II, while the comparable figure for mathematics was 25 per cent.

The data point to inefficiency in meeting the cognitive objectives of the educational process. The result is that large numbers of young people are unemployed and unemployable, without any preparation for self-employment. Few of them have acquired the qualities which belong in the affective rather than the cognitive domain of educational objectives. Included among these are the ability to set and meet personal and performance goals; interact with and influence others positively; accept responsibility for work; demonstrate initiative, discipline and industriousness.

All these qualities are vital, not only for employment but also for personal and social maturity. Those who have not acquired them suffer from low self-esteem and poor ethical standards. They are easy prey for those who need unquestioning assistance in illegal and immoral activities.

The educational system has been hard hit by the Structural Adjustment Programme, and the quality of education offered to students has been seriously compromised. Errol Miller reported in 1992 a decline of 33.8 per cent in real terms and constant dollars in recurrent expenditure on education between 1977 and 1987. The physical conditions in schools are often deplorable. Classrooms are overcrowded, and school premises, often vandalized, lack proper maintenance and repair. Fewer persons are selecting teaching as a career, and it is becoming an option of last resort. Teachers are underpaid and undervalued, demotivated and disgruntled. They are often unavailable to students for valuable character-building, leadership-development activities such as Girl Guides, Boy Scouts, and extra-curricular clubs and organizations because they are busy trying to juggle two jobs in order to make ends meet.

The curriculum of schools tends to be limited, in terms of the vocational skills and life preparation courses offered to students. Although a Family Life Education programme has been developed by the Ministry of Education, it is not given sufficient emphasis, probably because it is not an 'examination subject'. Traditional subject courses may also perpetuate biases rather than enduring values. King and Morrissey in 1988 sampled history, geography and social studies texts used in CXC courses and evaluated their content. Among their findings were the following:

- non-writers and their cultures are portrayed negatively;
- survival of non-European cultural forms is denied;
- the dynamics whereby contemporary Caribbean culture has developed have been ignored;
- racial myths and stereotypes are perpetuated;
- achievements of non-white peoples have been ignored;
- Europeans continue to be portrayed as the only, or the main, actors, their customs and institutions held as being superior;

- male dominance is supported and fostered;
- use of language excludes women;
- women are portrayed in subordinate and menial roles;
- the contribution of women to Caribbean development is omitted.

The most serious instances of bias were found in books written by non-Caribbean authors, or Caribbean nationals who have lived abroad for many years and who have limited exposure to contemporary Caribbean society.

Discipline in the public primary schools is often harsh, and not destined to build or enhance the self-concept and self-esteem of children. It is not unusual to see a teacher walking around her class with a belt over her shoulder which she uses to maintain order among the forty to fifty children who may be in her classroom. There are no explicit statements on the methods to be used in the administration of school discipline, and corporal punishment is applied in several primary schools and a number of secondary schools. When children are admonished, the effect is often self-loathing rather than an appreciation of right and wrong.

In the past, parent and teacher often agreed about those behaviours which were acceptable and those which were not. Recently, however, parents have challenged teachers for wrongfully punishing their children. Such disputes reflect differences between home and school values and have consequences for the child's socialization. Guidance counsellors who can play a vital role in assisting students in all aspects of their development are not available in all secondary level schools, and are not assigned to primary schools at all.

Many young people view education as irrelevant in terms of their personal goals. The criterion by which success is increasingly being measured is money, and in the Jamaican society, wealth and education are not necessarily highly correlated. Students view their teachers, for example, as individuals without ambition or status.

The inefficiency of the educational system has serious implications for national productivity, for the ability of young people to control their lives and for the parenting of the next generation. Parents, particularly mothers who are better educated, are more likely to understand and appreciate the complex demands of parenthood, the importance of antenatal care and of sound nutritional practices. They tend to have children who are healthy, and stable, quick to learn and likely to remain in school longer. These children have a better opportunity to understand and care about the human condition, and also to contribute to a world in which new information and new technologies demand human resource capable of dealing with these innovations for the betterment of societies and nations.

Elsa Leo-Rhynie

References

King, R. and M. Morrissey, (1988). *Images in Print: Bias and Prejudie in Caribbean Textbooks.* Kingston, Jamaica: Institute of Social and Economic Research, UWI, Mona.

Miller, E. (1992) *Education for All: Caribbean Perspectives and Imperatives.* Baltimore, MD: Johns Hopkins University Press.

CRITICAL THINKING AND WRITING

1. What is the writer's main claim? What type of claim is it?
2. What is the controversy?
3. Identify the evidence used to support the following assertions and state whether or not this evidence is adequate.
    (i) 'Educational provisions for Jamaican children differ and affect their life opportunities, their future occupational and social roles.' (paragraph 3)
    (ii) 'The educational system has been seriously hard hit by the structural adjustment programme and the quality of education offered to students has been seriously compromised.' (paragraph 7)
4. a) Identify the type of argument being presented in the extract below.
    b) Say whether or not this argument is sound, giving reasons in support of your answer.
    'Discipline in the public primary schools is often harsh and not destined to build or enhance the self-concept or self-esteem of children.' (paragraph 9)
5. a) Evaluate the effectiveness of the use of statistics in the text.
    b) How does the citing of sources contribute to the writer achieving her purpose?

WRITING ACROSS THE CURRICULUM ACTIVITIES

6. Write two paragraphs in which you discuss the extent to which the assertion made in the first sentence of paragraph 2 ('The education individuals receive…') is congruent with your own life experience and observations.

CHAPTER 30

THE RIGHT TO WRITE

The Editor, Sir:

A few days ago I returned to my office to find a note with the word **ERGENT** written in large capital letters, followed by a series of exclamation marks pinned to my door. I quickly snatched the note from my door, hoping that not too many persons (and hopefully no one) had seen it and come to the conclusion that I, along with the person who had left the note, had invented some new rules of spelling. I hurried into my office to read the note. It was written by a third year student who was anxious to finalise her registration for her research course. She was '**conserned**' that we were a day away from the deadline and she had not yet received online clearance for a research course.

I was concerned that this student was unaware of the fact that she was a few months away from graduating from a world-renowned university, and had not mastered basic spelling. I was even more dismayed when the student appeared at my door a day later, because she was a mature woman who was teaching part-time while attending University. I wanted to tell her quietly that she had not earned the right to write notes with spelling errors and leave them on my door. But I knew that the note had more far-reaching implications and I shuddered as several

questions came to mind. Did she have the right to write a research paper? Was this an indication of how fraught with errors her work would be? I recognized then that these were only two errors and therefore it was probably not fair to use them to generalize about her overall ability to write. Nevertheless, they were two errors which I considered to be very grave at this level.

As I thought about this young lady's errors, I recalled a group of graduate students whom I taught a course in Writing and Research a few years ago. They were very bright people, most of whom had earned first and upper second class honours degrees in a number of highly esteemed disciplines. My job was made particularly challenging because of their view of their writing proficiency and their general attitude toward writing. Their attendance at the seminars was irregular and the scant regard they gave the course was troubling, especially in view of the fact that I did not consider all of them to be proficient in their writing skills, as they frequently made errors in the use of appropriate verb forms, noun forms, auxiliaries and spelling.

Today, some of them are employed in important jobs, or some have continued on to the doctoral programme. I still question whether or not they should have earned the right to write in those prestigious jobs by virtue of the fact that they have excelled at the content of their discipline. I hope, though, that when they write their important reports for their companies' CEOs, they will recognize the need to give attention to grammatical accuracy, coherence and the appropriate use of mechanics.

Who is responsible for producing a forty-odd-year-old woman and persons with master's degrees who have not mastered basic writing skills? The answer is many persons: all the educators at the different levels of the education system — Primary, Secondary, Tertiary. Presumably, many persons assumed it was the job of a particular person — no doubt, the English teacher. Quite presumably, the English teachers tried, some not enough, I'm sure, to teach spelling and grammar. But I am almost sure that many of the other teachers/educators paid attention to the facts — the subject content — and not enough, if any, attention was given to correct language usage.

Writing may be an activity in which, as human beings, we all believe we have a right to indulge (and we probably do), but I do not believe that we have the right to abandon the conventions of writing in any non-creative discourse – writing that is not poetry, drama, or the short story or novel. This right comes with responsibilities which we are obliged to fulfil, especially in formal written discourse.

It is time for all educators to see themselves as having responsibility for ensuring that their students develop their language competence and enhance their writing skills. No social studies, physics, history, economics, politics or management studies teacher, should award grades with only consideration for content. It is unfair to the students. Errors of grammar,

spelling, etc. must be pointed out and even penalized by all, so that all students will develop a disciplined approach to writing and commit themselves to the acquisition of linguistic and communicative competence. Something is seriously wrong when a student goes through two years of University education without her language proficiency being improved.

A few years ago, my children attended Middle and High Schools in the United States where school district Superintendents enforced the basic principles of Writing Across the Curriculum. This way they ensured that all teachers across the curriculum were responsible for improving and maintaining good writing skills among students in all disciplines. This did not place any additional responsibility on subject teachers; it simply meant that in all subjects across the curriculum, teachers paid attention to grammar and other writing skills including disciplinary conventions. Only when grammar and spelling were good was the work in its entirety considered good as well.

Here in Jamaica we need to implement this system at all levels of the educational system. If students know that they will be penalized and lose their As and Bs for grammatical errors, they will make the effort to improve in this area. If they know that it does matter in other disciplines, they will take it seriously. This is **URGENT!!!!!**

Paulette A. Ramsay

CRITICAL THINKING AND WRITING

1. Identify the figurative device employed by the writer in the title.
2. What is the controversy that Ramsay is addressing in this letter?
3. Examine the author's use of rhetorical questions. What is the intended effect on the reader? Is this an example of ethos, pathos or logos?
4. Describe the tone of the passage.
5. What is the intended effect of the use of mechanical emphasis?
6. Ramsay states: 'I recognized then that these were only two errors and therefore it was probably not fair to use them to generalize about her overall ability to write'. What fallacy was she about to commit?
7. In the penultimate paragraph, Ramsay states that it is unfair to students for teachers/lecturers to award grades with consideration for content only. What type of claim is this? What reasons does she advance for this claim? To what extent do you consider this a sound argument?

WRITING ACROSS THE CURRICULUM ACTIVITIES

8. Explain your understanding of the writer's position on the controversy. To what extent do you agree with her?
9. Use the Internet to research 'Writing Across the Curriculum'. Using at least two sources, write a paragraph (using **your own** words) in which you define 'Writing Across the Curriculum'.
10. In view of the current debate about the status of Caribbean creole languages, is it important for university students to have an excellent command of the English language? Using a deductive approach, write a short essay (no more than 200 words) in which you take a position on this issue.

FAMILY LIFE

CHAPTER 31

WOMB RIGHTS

I am sure you know that Sunday is Mother's Day and this is Child Month. Put better, this is Child Month and Sunday is Mother's Day.

I emphasize the child because that is the priority order, if this month is to mean much in terms of societal reflection and celebration.

You see, every grown female is a woman but it is a child, somewhere, that gives the status and responsibility of motherhood to a female.

Every mother, then, should be grateful for the added status that she has because of her child.

Having said that, let me quickly say that the responsibility of motherhood is awesome and so every child should be eternally grateful to mother.

Children, in this day and age especially, have another good reason to 'big up' mother. Mother probably wanted to, but decided not to abort or kill that child in the womb!

I highlight this reality against the growing sentiments and arguments in Jamaica for '*the right to terminate pregnancies*' because the woman is carrying in **her** womb a mere '*bundle of disposable cells*'.

If that right becomes law in Jamaica, then legal reform would be necessary, concerning certain national laws and human rights conventions that provide special protection for pregnant women.

Why such protection if a pregnant woman has within her womb simply a '*bundle of cells*'?

Why does article 6 of the UN Covenant on Civil & Political Rights prohibit the execution of the death penalty on a pregnant woman, if she is not in fact carrying within her womb another human person?

The abortion rights campaign has legal implications, as well, for child abuse legislation and conventions. If you can legally kill a child a few months before birth why the legal fuss if you rough up a child seriously (without killing her) shortly or some time after birth?

There is yet another dimension. The practice of abortion on demand reveals a certain brand of medical schizophrenia within the health-care fraternity.

Imagine the scene in a hospital. A team of specialists struggle to save the life of a premature baby born with birth defects that are incompatible with normal life.

In the same hospital, doctors destroy perfectly normal infants in the womb! It's a bit crazy, in my view.

Let's remember that life **does** begin for the child in the womb, not at birth. At birth the child does not '*come into being*' but simply switches '*location of being*'.

These are issues that we really should ponder during Child Month and on Mother's Day, as a matter of principle.

Clinton Chisholm
May 12, 1995

Critical Thinking and Writing

1. Identify the author's central idea/thesis/ major claim. State two logical claims made in support of his thesis.
2. The author uses pathos, logos and ethos. Identify at least one example of each.
3. Does the appeal to pathos distract the audience from the logical issue? How? If not, why not?
4. Comment on the use of language in this passage and say how Chisholm uses this to establish common ground.
5. Identify the deductive arguments in the passage. To what extent is each logical (i.e. valid or sound)?
6. This commentary was originally aired on radio and subsequently published in a collection of commentaries. How has the medium shaped the writer's style and the presentation of the subject?

Group Discussion

7. In keeping with the medium, the passage is conversational. What changes would you make to transform it to academic writing?

CHAPTER 32

OUTLOOK FOR THE FUTURE

What Jamaica is witnessing now is a crisis in human relationships clearly seen in children's lack of respect for adults; their aggressive behaviour on the roads; the abandoning of children to the streets; increasing drug use; the targetting of the most helpless in society for sexual abuse and violence; the viciousness of crimes; and the formation of gangs which terrorize communities. All are related to changing values and new priorities. The family is no longer the place where a sense of belonging, a sense of tradition, love, communication and good human relationships flourish. The absence of this anchor for individuals leaves them drifting aimlessly in a hostile society.

The problem has many facets. Individuals become parents carelessly, without recognizing the extent of the responsibility involved. They quickly become disillusioned when the day-to-day realities of what is a lifetime commitment become evident. The opportunity to establish and build a family is not regarded as such and planned for, and the commitment required in terms of time, physical, emotional and psychological involvement, is not made. The abdication of responsibility by parents and the resultant abandonment of their children, whether physically or psychologically, is at the root of the problem. Problem children are not born, they are made by problem parents.

Problem parents provide a home environment which is hostile and marred by impatience and intolerance, empty of love and caring; where there are quarrels and fights, rather than discussions and communication; where punishment is inconsistently and harshly administered; where insecurity, mistrust and despair are the predominant feelings generated among family members. Problem parents preside over broken homes: not necessarily homes broken by the separation of parents, the break-up of a marriage, or an absent parent, but homes in which, for whatever reasons, the functions of the family no longer operate, and the caring, sharing and support expected are absent.

Problem parents do not fully understand the demands which parenting will make on them and are ready and willing to give up the care and nurturing of their children to someone else. They do not recognize that although they will need and obtain help from various sources in this task, the ultimate responsibility is theirs. They take for granted, for example, the assumption of child care and rearing by one or other grandmother.

Grandmothers are not, however, as willing or as able to become substitute parents as they were in the past. Many, particularly in the urban areas, are employed or running a small business, and so have their own work lives in addition to their personal lives. Although they may assist in providing economic, and occasional or even regular child-care support, they cannot assume full responsibility for child rearing. There are many grandmothers who consider it a duty to assume some responsibility for their grandchildren's upbringing, yet often resent the restrictions this places on their own activities, as well as the fact that this involvement is expected, and taken for granted by the children's parents.

Problem parents do not recognize and accept their changed status when they become parents. They do not seek to set an example for their children or to build a climate which will generate respect for the adult by the child. Instead, differences between the generations are minimized; parents dress and act like teens, however inappropriate this may be; insolence and defiance go uncorrected; the use of indecent language is not only condoned but also engaged in by parents when speaking to children; there is no behavioural example set, no dignity preserved, no restraint exercised, no maturity displayed. Although inter-generational communication is to be encouraged, mutual respect must be integral to this communication.

Problem parents create a false foundation for their children. Parents who have struggled from poverty and have acquired the material trappings of middle and upper class life are frequently unwilling or embarrassed to reveal to children the nature of that struggle, and are ashamed of their humble origins. Their children do not meet their 'country' cousins, aunts, or uncles, nor visit the village or town where their parents were born. Instead, they spend holidays in hotels or cottages on the North Coast. This abandoning of their roots by parents creates a void in the children's lives, and they grow up in a false world detached from their Jamaican heritage. Although, in some cases, there is no family home to visit in the country, family expeditions do not allow time for children to explore the by-ways, observe, communicate and identify with Jamaican people in country towns and villages, with the result that there are many Jamaican children who are more familiar with Florida, New York, or Ontario than they are with their own country and their own people.

Problem parents provide or seek to provide immediate gratification for their children's wants as opposed to their needs. They do not allow children to experience the satisfaction of owning something towards which they have planned, worked and saved: they feel guilty if they deny their children anything they want. Thus they create the impatient generation which must gratify its needs immediately; people who must have, must do, at any cost. They become inconsiderate, demanding adults, who have great difficulty adjusting to a life in which they have to rely on their own resources and become independent. They remain dependent on their parents well into adult life, or they find devious ways of maintaining the lifestyle to which they have become accustomed.

Problem parents breed attitudes of prejudice and intolerance among children, based on factors such as social class, age, status and material possessions. Such parents instruct their children about other children who are considered to be 'unsuitable' visitors to the home, 'unacceptable' friends, not because of their behaviour, but because of factors such as their home address or racial origin. Grandparents and older relatives are considered to be the 'disposable generation', and are rarely visited or included in family activities, so the wisdom of the old, their valuable perspectives and experiences, their provision of continuity through sharing of 'old-time' stories, are lost to the young. Within the homes of such parents, there is often exploitation of domestic helpers — a lack of recognition that they too have families and feelings. They are forced into working hours and conditions which make them absent parents, and prevent them from spending quality time with their own children.

Problem parents neglect and abuse their children, often with serious consequences. Many parents do not know where to find their teenage children at night, have no curfews, or have one which is not enforced and so is not obeyed. Increasingly, we read of accidental poisoning in the home and of young children dying in fires when left alone with a lamp burning at night. There are also reports of parents sending their daughters to work in night clubs as scantily dressed dancers in order to earn money for their families, their sons to 'hustle' in the streets, and of fathers who feel that it is their 'right' to demand sexual intercourse from their daughters because they had undertaken the responsibility of their up-bringing. Many children, mainly boys, have no home apart from the streets; they have been completely abandoned by their parents. They do not go to school and, in order to eke out a living, they become involved in dangerous activities such as drug peddling, prostitution, and criminal activity.

If the family is not rescued and rebuilt within our communities and our nation, we run the risk of seeing our Jamaican youth deteriorate and become alienated to the point where they are like the street children observed and vividly described thus by Father Richard Holung in 1989:

> Food and shelter for the body, ganja for the brain: these are the only goals of our children of the street. Survival being the only wisdom means they steal, grab, fight for what they want. There is no inner desire for nobility, no search for spiritual qualities. Just physical existence and physical pleasure, and the response to the variety of goods that don't last. For this, the children of the streets will kill. (*Daily Gleaner*, 30.3.1989.)

This crisis must be averted. The national mobilization observed in the wake of physical crises such as a hurricane must also be brought to bear on this crisis which we admit exists, which may not have the immediate visible impact of a hurricane on the physical environment, but which has, and will have, even more damaging consequences on the lives of our people now, and for generations to come.

Elsa Leo-Rhynie

CRITICAL THINKING AND WRITING

1. Identify
    a) the controversy/issue that the writer is addressing in this passage;
    b) the writer's purpose.
2. State the writer's thesis in your own words.
3. What evidence does Leo-Rhynie present to justify her claim that Jamaica is witnessing a crisis in human relationships?
4. Comment on the writer's use of repetition. How does it assist her in achieving her purpose?
5. Evaluate the writer's success in supporting her position. (Does she have sufficient and appropriate evidence?)
6. Identify two generalizations in the passage. Analyse them for soundness.
7. Identify the type of claim (that is, cause, definition, fact and so on) in each of the following:
    a) Problem parents provide or seek to provide immediate gratification for their children's wants.
    b) They become inconsiderate, demanding adults.
    c) The national mobilisation observed in the wake of physical crises … must also be brought to bear on this crisis.

WRITING TASKS

8. To what extent do you agree that the changes in family structure have affected the values and attitudes of the current generation of children? Address this in a paragraph.
9. Write a short piece of no more than 200 words in which you agree or disagree with Leo-Rhynie's position on the controversy.

CHAPTER 33

❖

ARE CARIBBEAN YOUTH IN CRISIS?

Three newspapers in three different Caribbean countries recently carried reports about the challenges that youth in the Caribbean face, each making observations, which, with few exceptions, basically note identical concerns.

Cayman's *Net News* notes failure at school, increase in the misuse of drugs and alcohol, adolescent crime, and road accidents.

It further observes the kind of lavish lifestyles of kids from affluent homes, and stresses the need for teenagers to be equipped to compete in this competitive world as an issue of concern.

The Trinidad and Tobago *Express* mentions the need for career guidance for students at the Secondary Entrance Assessment level, to deal with unemployment among the youth, which stands at 12.1 per cent in the 20–24 age group. The report goes on to say that at school, children do not have a career in mind, even at the ages of 15–16 years, and some leave not knowing which career they would like to pursue.

It is suggested that knowledge of careers should begin at the Assessment level for high school so that the youth could enter the system more focused, since students even did not understand why they had to do certain subjects, or what benefit it would be to them.

The Jamaica *Gleaner* discusses the issue of whether the youth were ready for the workplace. It states that secondary and tertiary graduates often had limited job opportunities, and mentions a university lecturer saying that at the workplace there is a reduced number of good quality employees because of the kind of graduates being recruited.

There is the further observation by the managing director of a company, that graduates entering the workplace are not mentally ready to become good employees, even though they may be academically qualified. Their interpersonal and communication skills are not developed, and they do not know how to relate to their superiors.

Other concerns noted in the report were a lack of initiative, responsibility and morals, and that young employees lacked the capacity to think beyond their work roles, and were driven primarily by the monetary reward from the job.

Can we say, then, that Caribbean youth are experiencing a severe crisis?

My view is that they most certainly are. This has to do in part with the emergence of a new kind of Caribbean society which has left adults behind. This is because the average Caribbean adult, particularly the male, is on drugs, is an alcoholic, or has not mentally matured, and this is seen in the playboy image he displays in dealing with the opposite sex.

This means that even if such a person has a nuclear family, he is hardly at home to make a difference to the teenagers, in terms of representing positive values which the young could incorporate in their behaviour.

Again, the Caribbean adult, because of the new demands of the workplace, and the competitiveness of Caribbean society, is busy in his later adult years trying to earn a qualification, or additional credentials, because the workplace is requiring more qualified people. Time is therefore spent studying, which should have been done in the early adult years which were spent irresponsibly.

The attention that should have been given to the young at home was therefore lacking. We therefore have a different kind of Caribbean youth that have grown up without proper knowledge of appropriate values, and therefore with no context in which to anchor their behaviour.

Resistance and rebelliousness therefore replace good and proper values.

Furthermore, Caribbean society's heroes have become the drug lord, or dons, the gunmen, or the DJs, who are associated with quick money. Even youths from affluent homes take on this gangster culture, which is promoted by some Caribbean performing artistes, the content of whose songs leaves much to be desired. And so does the vulgar display of performances at various concerts.

These factors act as a deterrent to any serious attitude by the young towards school work, or even if some of them succeed, they are still infused with the dance hall culture. Many of the performers themselves are not well educated, and so present an image of fun, quick bucks, and the latest dress styles and cars.

This is where the irresponsibility, not yet being mentally ready for the workplace, and the poor communication and interpersonal skills have their origin. The education the youth receive has not countered these lower, short-lived cultural practices.

Coupled with this is the quality of education that the youth receive from some of the institutions they attend. Many of these institutions do not expose the young to good and proper knowledge, the best that has been thought and taught, and therefore has lasting value. Some of those who deliver the knowledge at these institutions were themselves not properly taught.

Students are therefore not exposed to high culture, but to knowledge that is intellectually feeble. This is again why they display the kind of behaviours mentioned by the three newspapers. Students leave some of these institutions with personalities that are not fully developed, and without a core of ethical principles on which to base and reinforce their conduct.

In this sense, then, Caribbean youth are definitely in crisis, one which is being perpetuated by a Caribbean society which in many instances is unsure of itself, lacking in cultural cohesion, and with political, social and legal institutions which are not trusted, and which, in many instances, are regarded as suspect by the minority of decent citizens who, despite everything else, rise above the fray.

It is only when the society undergoes fundamental change in its morals and mores, and allows positive values to permeate our various institutions, including our education system, that a new human person will emerge with the kind of desirable qualities that are the hallmark of good citizenship.

Our youth will then become the products fit to contribute positively to this new society, as well as fit to live with.

Oliver Mills

CRITICAL THINKING AND WRITING

1. What is the writer's central point and what reaction do you think he wants to get from his audience?
2. What are some of the main reasons provided in support of the writer's main claim?
3. Is this piece largely inductive or deductive argument?
4. The eleventh paragraph begins 'This means that even if …' What bias do you see highlighted in this paragraph? Do you see any other instances of bias in the essay?
5. Is the piece based largely on fact, or opinion, or a combination of the two? Provide reasons for your answer.
6. Are any opposing arguments present in the writer's overall argument? If so, list them. If not, explain how this affects the strength of the writer's argument.
7. What is the effect of the writer asking 'Can we then say' but answering by stating 'my view is …'? Does this help to qualify his comments and position?
8. Identify any flaws that you find in the writer's reasoning.

CLASS DISCUSSION

9. What are some of the complaints that you have heard about Caribbean youth? Discuss the strengths and weaknesses of some of these complaints.
10. Discuss some of the ways in which the paragraphing utilized here differs from the conventions of paragraphing used in academic writing.

WRITING ACTIVITY

11. Get a sheet of paper. On one side, list the writer's main points, and on the other, list some opposing points. Look at your opposing points. How do you think the writer might respond to some of these?

HISTORY & POLITICS

CHAPTER 34

WOMEN IN CARIBBEAN LITERATURE: THE AFRICAN PRESENCE

Such was the nature of slavery in the New World that the African slaves were allowed little opportunity to practice overtly any aspect of their aboriginal culture. Little wonder, then, that there has developed among scholars the theory that the Middle Passage destroyed the culture of the Africans who were imported to the New World during the period from 1540 to 1807. Edward Brathwaite, however, the Barbadian poet, historian and critic, disputes this theory. He claims that African culture not only crossed the Atlantic but survived and creatively adapted itself to the new environment.[1] It will be the contention of this essay that the exigencies of slavery in the New World drastically altered but did not completely annihilate the traditional role of African women in the family or in the community. Further, an examination of the literature will reveal parallels between Afro-West Indian women and their African counterparts.

In traditional Africa, religion and the family formed the nucleus around which the culture was built and the society revolved. It is no wonder, then, that in looking for African survivals and retentions in the New World, these are the two areas that usually come into focus. Outsiders sometimes express surprise at the 'seeming lack of seriousness' with which Caribbean men and women enter into alliances and bear children. They wonder, too, at the fact that many of these people do not eschew legal marriage because of any penchant for promiscuity, since many older couples have lived together for years and do adhere to all the tenets of a legal marriage.[2] Attempting to explain this phenomenon, Melville Herskovitz states that in Africa, marriage is not a matter requiring approval of the state or any religious body. The only requirements are the consent of the families concerned and the benevolent approval of the ancestors.[3] With regard to children in traditional Africa, there is no such thing as an unwanted child. Janheinz Jahn explains that when a person dies, he lives on or is reborn in his descendants. Because of this, to leave no living heirs behind is the worst evil that can befall a man, and there is no curse more terrible than to wish a man to die childless.[4] Marriage (in the African sense) and children have always been of the utmost importance among Africans; children have always been welcome, whether they were born within the recognized family unit or not. An examination of Caribbean literature will reveal that this situation also holds true among West Indians.

Women in Caribbean literature always seem to exist vis-a-vis a man (be he lover or husband) and, of course, children. Very often, these man/woman relationships are tension-filled, tenuous, and polygynous. Very often, the man in these relationships is transient, reminiscent of the period during slavery when a man was simply a breeder of slave children for his white owner. In many of the families portrayed in these works, the man, the husband, the father, simply is not there. He fathers the children and then moves on, leaving the woman solely responsible for the upbringing of the children. The female-headed family is the one most frequently found in Caribbean literature.[5]

George Lamming's *In the Castle of My Skin* (1953) offers an excellent example of the mutations that have taken place in what used to be a viable and positive family structure in traditional Africa. To begin, most of the fathers in this work are absent, including the father of the child-narrator, G. When the fathers are present, they seem to be impotent as authority figures. The mothers, then, emerge as the dominant parents throughout. This point is highlighted early in the work when the child-narrator muses, 'My father who had only fathered the idea of me had left me the sole liability of my mother who really fathered.'[6] Nor is G alone in his 'fatherless' state. It is always the women who 'have' the children. Thus we read that Miss Foster had six children, three by a butcher, two by a baker, and one whose father had never been mentioned. Bob's mother had two and [G's] mother one.[7] In attempting to explain this

phenomenon, Merle Hodge, the Trinidadian critic and novelist, states:

> [In the New World] the function of fatherhood was limited to fertilizing the female. Gone was the status of head of family, for there was no family, no living in a unit with wife and children. A man might not even know who his children were, at any rate; they did not belong to him in any sense; he was unable to provide for them .... The black man had no authority over his children, but the woman did. The children's mothers, or female child-rearers, were responsible for the upbringing of the race. Women became mother and father to the race.[8]

The absence of the father in the lives of these children leads naturally to a rather close and somewhat stifling relationship between mother and child. Thus, when the mother's pumpkin vine and fence are accidentally torn down, the child-narrator reflects:

> My mother on such occasions looked pitiful beyond words. I had often seen her angry or frustrated and in tears, but there were other states of emotion she experienced for which tears were simply inadequate. Seized by the thought of being left alone, she would become filled with an overwhelming ambition for her child, and an even greater defiance of the odds against her .... She would talk about pulling through; whatever happened she would come through, and "she" meant her child.[9]

When G, now on the threshold of manhood, is about to leave home to work on another island, the mother is reluctant to let him go. He has been the sole purpose of her life and now is made to feel guilty for leaving. In the confrontation between them, the mother says to the son:

If you grow to one hundred you're my child ... and when you see the others playing man, an' doing as they please, just tell them you sorry, 'tis different with you, 'cause your mother ain't that sort o' woman. Let them know I don't play, an' that a child is a child for me. Nothing more or nothing less.[10]

Scholars are in disagreement as to the origin of the so-called matriarchal family in the New World. E. Franklin Frazier subscribes to the theory that the female-headed black family can be attributed to the nature of slavery. He does concede, however, that the situation in the West Indies might have been different from that in North America. He claims that, unlike the United States, where slaves were scattered in relatively small numbers on plantations and farms over a large area, in the West Indies large numbers of African slaves were concentrated on vast plantations for the production of sugar. Under such conditions it was possible for the slaves to re-establish their African way of life and keep alive their traditions.[11] Herskovitz, on the other hand, who is one of the chief proponents of the theory of African cultural survivals in the New World, sees the matriarchal family as primarily an example of an African cultural retention. He states that in polygynous unions in West Africa, the woman always has been the visible head of the household. In the compound, the husband and father lived in his separate quarters; each wife and her children had their own dwelling. The wives took turns cooking for the husband and sleeping with him. Naturally the children of each household spent more time with their mother than with their father, and there developed a closer bond between mother and child than between father and child.[12] Perhaps, in assessing the situation in the Caribbean, it would be

realistic to assume that the preponderance of the matriarchal family is the result of a synthesis of an African cultural survival with the realities of slavery in the area.

One might well ask whether the apparently irresponsible behavior of the Caribbean man who casually fathers children with a variety of women and then moves on is in any way related to the custom of traditional African polygynous unions. If so, it is a custom gone awry, for the role of the man in the traditional African family was one of responsibility and importance; in the traditional African family a man's economic success was measured by the number of wives he could afford, for, in the words of Jomo Kenyatta, 'the ... customary law of marriage provides that a man may have as many wives as he can support, and ... the larger one's family, the better it is for him and the tribe.'[13] It becomes clear, then, as pointed out earlier by Hodge, that somewhere along the way, the roles of men and women of African descent in the Caribbean have changed, while at the same time retaining a flavor that is African.

The fact that a husband and children always have been of utmost importance to African women and their Caribbean counterparts has never meant that black women have been passive or powerless within West Indian society. Admittedly, as Orlando Patterson, the Jamaican sociologist and novelist notes, women in the West Indian society have always had a narrower range of occupations to choose from than their male counterparts.[14] The literature reveals, though, that black women in the Caribbean have proven, in spite of economic and social constraints, to be quite innovative in making a livelihood for themselves as well as their families. The point is, however, that they have never been encouraged to take pride or credit for any other function than that of wife and mother. It is a fact that many a young woman in the Caribbean has deliberately stifled any pretensions to a career, lest in so doing she outshine her male counterpart and thereby end up an 'old maid.' Thus, with very few exceptions there are no women writers; with very few exceptions there are no women exceptions. The portrait of women that is revealed to the world in the written and oral literature is that given them by men. Yet to reiterate, women in the Caribbean, like women in Africa, are not passive, nor are they powerless in the sense that they are dependent on men to provide for them. Often they are self-supporting, married or unmarried; often they are the sole support of their households, whether there is a man present or not. However, they are not considered 'complete' women unless there is a man in their lives. As Hodge sees it, 'the unmarried, ... or childless woman, say, in her forties, is projected as a stock joke — frustrated, nagging, disagreeable, withering away for the want of a man to rule her or offspring to prove her fecundity.'[15]

The similarities between the plight of women in the Caribbean and that of women in Africa are highlighted in the novel *Efuru* written by the Nigerian, Flora Nwapa in 1966. Efuru, the central character in the work, is a tragic as well as a heroic figure. Efuru's tragedy lies in the fact that she cannot 'hold on to a man'. She is married twice and is deserted by both her husbands. In addition, her only child dies. With the death of her daughter her failure as a women is complete. It does not matter that Efuru is an asset economically to the men in her life, that she is a successful trader and a prosperous businesswoman, that she is self-supporting and independent. Ultimately, she is judged on her success as a wife and mother.

A relative at the funeral of Efuru's daughter sums up Efuru's dilemma when she asks,

> Efuru, in what ways have you offended our ancestors? ... You were married and for a long time you did not have a child. Then the gods and our ancestors opened your womb and you had a baby girl .... A girl is something, though we would have preferred a boy .... And now, that only child is dead .... As if all this is not enough ... I hear your husband has run away with that worthless woman.[16]

The women in Merle Hodge's novel *Crick Crack Monkey* (1970) are examples of women who are self-assertive and self-sufficient. First, there is Tantie, a woman of strength in her own right, who has no permanent man in her life and no children of her own. Tantie adopts her godson, Mikey, and when her sister-in-law dies and her brother leaves for England, she becomes surrogate mother to his two children, Tee and Toddan. By the time Mickey leaves for America, and Tee and Toddan are on their way to their father in England, Tantie has already taken in one of Mikey's sisters, two of Ma's children, and Doolarie, the daughter of a disabled neighbour. Tantie, with no husband and no visible means of livelihood, is, nevertheless, a mother, in every sense of the word, to her brood.

And then there is Ma, of matriarchal African proportions. Like Nwapa's Efuru and so many of her counterparts in Africa, Ma is a market woman, selling her jellies, jams, and sweets in the village marketplace. During the August holidays, Ma has a multitude of her grandchildren (those related to her by blood and those not) come down from all parts of the island to spend their vacation with her. Ma, reminiscent of the women in Nwapa's West African village, would gather her brood on the steps on a full-moon night and tell them 'Nancy stories. In traditional African fashion, Ma attempts to inculcate in Tee, the child narrator, a sense of tradition and identity. Thus we read:

> Ma said I was her grandmother come back again. She said her grandmother was a tall straight proud woman who lived to an old age. ... The people gave her the name Euphemia or Euph-something, but when they called her that she used to toss her head like a horse and refuse to answer so they'd had to give up in the end and call her by her true-true name.... She couldn't remember her grandmother's true-true name. But Tee was growing into her grandmother again, her spirit was in me.[17]

Even the child narrator Tee is no exception to the independent and spirited women we meet in this work. Tee becomes Cynthia as she grows into young womanhood and rejects the folkways of Tantie and Ma for the middle-class mores of the urban Trinidad society in which she finds herself. It is no easy achievement for Cynthia to be accepted into this new society, for she is dark-skinned and does not blend easily into the color-conscious, light-skinned middle-class society of Trinidad. Tantie, however, is sensitive enough to know what ails Cynthia, and concealing her own pain at the young woman's rejection of her, she arranges for Cynthia and Toddan to join their father in England.

The women in C.L.R. James's *Minty Alley* (1936) are further examples of women of strength and determination who, in the face of a harsh and indifferent environment, remain in control of their destinies and are thus able to survive. Mrs. Rouse is one such woman. Like Nwapa's Efuru, Mrs. Rouse is in one sense a victim, but Mrs. Rouse is also a woman of compassion and of strength, a survivor and a heroic figure. Like Efuru, children and a husband are important to Mrs. Rouse, but she is a widow and has never had any children of her own. She circumvents these problems by 'adopting' her niece, Maisie, and entering into a common law marriage with the despicable Benoit. Mrs. Rouse makes a living for herself, her husband, and her niece by baking and selling breads and cakes. She is unfortunate, though, in her relationship with both husband and niece. After several years of marriage, during which time Mrs. Rouse virtually supported him, Benoit deserts her to marry the near-white nurse. The marriage, however, is short-lived. When Benoit becomes sick, the nurse abandons him. When he dies in the pauper ward in the local hospital, it is Mrs. Rouse who claims the body and buries him. Explaining to Haynes, the narrator, her feelings for Benoit after all that he has put her through, Mrs. Rouse declares, 'God put this fiery love in my heart for Mr. Benoit.... I try to root it out, but it wouldn't come out. God plant it there for his own purpose.'[18] Though the people at No. 2 Minty Alley laugh at Mrs. Rouse because she 'cannot hold on to a man', she emerges as a woman of strength and character, a survivor.

There is also Maisie. Maisie, about fifteen years old, has had the minimum of education and is trained for nothing. Like many West Indian children, Maisie does not live with her parents. Indeed, we are never told anything of either her mother or her father. Maisie is the bane of Mrs. Rouse's life. When Mrs. Rouse finds out that Maisie has been a co-conspirator of Benoit and the nurse, her anger knows no bounds. She bewails to Haynes, '[Maisie] brings back all my wrongs when I see her .... She knew everything, Mr. Haynes .... The girl betray my honour for vanilla ice cream and sugarcake' (p. 126).[19] Eventually, there is a violent confrontation between aunt and niece, and Maisie is forced to leave her aunt's home with only the clothes on her back. But the indomitable Maisie does not accept defeat. She chooses not to surrender to the limitations of her world. Soon after she leaves Mrs. Rouse's home, she and Haynes meet. She explains to him that she has paid twenty dollars to a stewardess who works on one of the ships that go to New York. Acting as a 'procuress,' the stewardess will provide passage for black girls because the white officers like them. When Haynes reacts with shock to this information, Maisie responds:

> Mr. Haynes, I want a job and I am going to get it. The captain and the whole crew can't get anything from me unless I want to give them. But when that boat hit New York and I put my foot on shore, if it wait for me before it leave, it's going to wait a damned long time.[20]

As can be seen, none of these women is passive or powerless. In the face of all odds, they emerge as self-assertive women who, in the final analysis, are in control of their lives. Of significance, too, is the fact that James's Maisie, like Hodge's Cynthia, comes to terms with her environment paradoxically by escaping it. Maisie's achievement, though, is greater than Cynthia's. For unlike Hodge who shows us Cynthia evolving in a rural world of love and cultural richness before being introduced into the middle-class Trinidad society, James places Maisie in the urban slums of Trinidad. Yet Maisie too overcomes the obstacles of her environment. Both she and Cynthia, for better or for worse, decide not to settle for the lives of their elders. Faced by a society that offers very few choices, they decide to create their own choices. That they

both choose a departure is both ironic and revealing.

Again, one might ask what happens to these young women once they have departed their island home. Do their roles change? Do they function independently as women in their own rights? Or are their identities still defined through their roles as wives and mothers? Claude McKay, in his characterization of Bita Plant in *Banana Bottom* (1938), does attempt to supply an answer to such questions. Through Bita, McKay portrays the evolution into womanhood of a West Indian child who has been exposed to European culture and who then returns to the Caribbean setting. Bita does not, like Hodge's Cynthia, become alienated from her roots. After eight years of education in Europe, she returns to her rural village and fits right back into place. To culminate her unique history, Bita eventually falls in love with and marries the uneducated but hardworking and dependable Jubban. Bita spurns the superficialities of the so-called middle-class society of Jamaica for the simpler and almost idyllic life of the folk peasants that McKay depicts.

With Bita, then, we have an example of a woman who, unlike most of the women we meet in the literature has been given a real choice — a choice to be truly independent, to define herself through her own achievements, to pursue a career for her own satisfaction. However, in analysing the role McKay has Bita play, one must remember one important fact: McKay, when he wrote *Banana Bottom*, had been away from his native Jamaica for almost two decades. McKay, therefore, is writing with a certain degree of nostalgia. Consequently, his portrayal of Bita and the folk peasants of rural Jamaica, on the whole, tends to be romantic and somewhat unrealistic. In contrast, the message that Merle

Hodge has for the women in the Caribbean is pragmatic and forward-moving:

> The term "career woman" has been turned into a dirty suggestion. It has associations of selfishness, abnormality and coldness on the part of the woman. The myth will have to be shattered. What we need is more and more pioneers of so-called career women, women who do not rush into starting families at eighteen, before they know themselves, and whose children, if they decide to have any, will have the full benefit of their mother's maturity and self-fulfillment; women who will never come to blame their children for getting in their way.[21]

Another role that Caribbean women play in the literature, and one that might also be related to the African cultural heritage, is that of religious leaders in the community. The traditional role of the female diviner in Africa is well known. John Mbiti writes that in some West African cultures, God calls a would-be diviner, usually a young woman in her adolescence. She wanders about in the woods, and after several days returns with the power to divine. The community then erects a shrine for her, which is referred to as the 'hut of God,' while the diviners are called 'children of God.'[22] This phenomenon has, of course, undergone many changes and reinterpretations in the Caribbean. Maureen Warner-Lewis, in an article entitled 'The Nkuyu: Spirit Messengers of the Kumina' writes a revealing and factual account of Miss Queenie, a full-time diviner and religious leader of a small following in lower Kingston. Miss Queenie, who at the time she was interviewed by the author was forty-five years old, can be viewed on one level as a symbol of the synthesis that came about between the culture of the Old World and that of the New.

Miss Queenie's maternal grandparents had arrived from Kongo as indentured laborers in Jamaica after the abolition of slavery in 1834. As a young girl Miss Queenie had had her first mystical experience which lasted for a period of twenty-one days and paralleled that of female diviners in Africa. She went on to achieve all the mystical powers peculiar to female African diviners, at the same time gaining the respect of her faithful followers.[23]

Not surprisingly, the female religious leaders we find in the fiction usually inherit this position on the death of their husbands. Examples can be found in Sylvia Wynter's *The Hills of Hebron* (1962) and Andrew Salkey's *A Quality of Violence* (1959). The women who people Wynter's work, followers of a Christian God, are in search of a dream, in search of some meaning for their meaningless lives. Prostitutes, stonebreakers, grass-weeders, cane-cutters, they have been exploited all their lives in the outside world by an indifferent society and at home by their men who have fared no better than they. When their leader, Prophet Moses, fails to fly to heaven on their behalf, he has himself tied to a cross and left to die. On his death, his widow, Miss Gatha, becomes the *de facto* leader. Miss Gatha is the only one among them who has any money, and with the drought that compounds the existing poverty, it becomes apparent that the Hebronites are more in need of physical than spiritual salvation. Miss Gatha rises to the occasion. She suffers Aloysius and then Obadiah to temporarily lead the New Believers, all the while with her eyes on the leadership for her own son, Isaac, when he comes of age. But Isaac betrays his mother, for, like Cynthia in *Crick Crack Monkey*, once Isaac has experienced life outside of his rural setting, he no longer wants any part of his former life. He secretly returns to Hebron, rapes Obadiah's young wife, Rose, and steals his mother's money. Rose is able eventually to vindicate herself and save her marriage. With the birth of Isaac's and Rose's son there is renewed hope for Miss Gatha and the Hebronites. For as her new-born grandson is put in her arms, the rain begins to fall, the long drought is over, and there is renewed life in the hills of Hebron. Hence, although Miss Gatha does not function as a successful religious leader, it is through her tenacity and determination that the people of Hebron continue.

The religion practised in Salkey's *A Quality of Violence* is Pocomania, which, according to Jahn, is a fusion of various African and Christian rites.[24] Mother Johnson takes over the leadership on the death of her husband, Dada Johnson. In this work, there is an obvious struggle between African religious practices and Christianity. The intent of the work seems to be to demonstrate that the rites of Pocomania are based on ignorance and evil-doing. In the beginning, when the followers are under Mother Johnson's influence, they accept their link with Africa and acknowledge that Mother Johnson has some special spiritual power. However, when Mother Johnson fails to save the life of a sick child, and Brother Parkins, who is the spokesman for the educated and Christian section of the community, tells the people '[Mother Johnson] is a common obeah woman: Black magic and a lot of nastiness are the things she thinks important ... ,'[25] they soon turn against her. Eventually Mother Johnson is deserted by all of her followers. Good has triumphed over evil. As she is being led to her death, one of her erstwhile followers comments, 'We going to learn her a lesson.... We going to learn her what it means to lead people into darkness. Must be back to Africa

she must be want to lead we.'[26] There is very little that is subtle in the portrayal of the African presence in this work. The African retentions, as evidenced in Mother Johnson and her followers, are absolutely rejected and explicitly denigrated. Mother Johnson is depicted as a complete failure as a religious leader.

It is obvious, therefore, that in spite of the transmutations and reinterpretations that various aspects of traditional African culture have undergone in the New World, there still exist among Caribbean people some survivals of Africanism. These survivals surface in a variety of areas, religious as well as secular. As has been shown, there are several analogies that can be drawn between Caribean women as they appear in literature and their African counterparts. The most significant analogy that the literature reveals is that women in the Caribbean like their counterparts in Africa are ultimately assessed on their success as wives and mothers, and that traditionally they have not been taken seriolsy as a viable force in either the religious or secular workings of the community, even though, as we have seen, their contributions in both areas are anything but negligible.

Leota Lawrence

Notes

1. Edward Brathwaite, 'The African Presence in Caribbean Literature', *Daedalu* 53, no. 2 (Spring 1974): 13.
2. Melville J. Herskovltz, *The Myth of the Negro Past* (Boston, 1941), 171.
3. Ibid., 172.
4. Jahneinz Jahn, *Muntu: An Outline of the New African Culture*. (New York, 1960), 108.

5. In addition to the works examined here, this family structure is found in V. S. Naipaul, *Miguel Street* (London, 1959); H. Orlando Patterson, *The Children of Sisyphus* (London, 1964); and Michael Anthony, *The Year in San Fernando* (London. 1965) among others.

6. George Lamming, *In the Castle of my Skin* (1963; rpt. New York, 1975), 3.

7. Ibid., 18.

8. Merle Hodge, 'The Shadow of the Whip: A Comment on Male-Female Relations in the Caribbean', in *Is Massa Day Dead? Black Moods in the Caribbean*, ed. Orde Coombs (New York, 1974),115.

9. Lamming, 10–11.

10. Ibid., 295.

11. Franklin Frazier, *The Negro in the Untied States* (New York, l949), 6–7.

12. Herskovitz, 179–80.

13. Jomo Kenyatta, *Facing Mount Kenya* (New York, 1965), 129.

14. H. Orlando Patterson, *The Sociology of Slavery* (London, 1967), 61.

15. Merle Hodge, 'Young Women and the Development of stable Family Life in the Caribbean', *Savacou* (Kingston, 1977): 42.

16. Flora Nwapa, *Efuru*, (London, 1966), 37–8.

17. Merle Hodge. *Crick Crack Monkey* (London, 1970), 32.

18. C.L.R. James, *Minty Alley* (1935; rpt. London.1971), 238.

19. Ibid., 126.

20. Ibid., 226.

21. Hodge, *Savacou* XLIV, no. 1,(1983): 44.

22. John Mbiti, *African Religions and Philosophy* (New York, 1970), 89.

23. Maureen Warner-Lewis, 'The Nkuyu: Spirit Messenger of the Kumina', *Savacou*, (op. cit.): 57-8.

24. Jahn, 60.

25. Andrew Salkey, *A Quality of Violence* (London, 1959), 137.

26. Ibid., 158.

CRITICAL THINKING AND WRITING

1. Two opposing arguments regarding the nature of slavery in the New World are presented in the first paragraph. What are they?

2. What is the controversy to which the writer draws attention in her thesis?

3. How does the writer employ comparison and contrast in the second paragraph?

4. What is the purpose of the writer's examination of Caribbean Literature?

5. Explain the writer's opinion regarding the preponderance of the matriarchal family in the Caribbean.

6. What evidence does the writer use to support the claim that there is similarity in the plight of Caribbean and African women?

7. What roles do Caribbean female characters play that are related to African cultural heritage?

8. In the study of different Caribbean texts, the author provides different examples/ categories of female characters. List them, and show how the author characterises each.

9. Write the main points of the conclusion.

10. Comment on the tone, and say how it aids in communicating the writer's meaning.

GROUP DISCUSSION

11. Working in small groups identify and discuss three features of the essay that would help you to improve:
    a) your research skills
    b) your ability to write arguments.

CHAPTER 35

THE ARAWAKS ARRIVED BEFORE COLUMBUS

American Indians called 'Arawaks' discovered and settled in Jamaica before Columbus arrived. They were six or seven centuries ahead of 'the Discoverer'. The Arawaks migrated in waves from their homes in eastern Venezuela and the basin of the Orinoco. To this day, Arawak-speaking Indians live in that region. From giant trees in the forest, working patiently with fire and stone-axes, they fashioned great dug-outs, some so large that they would hold forty or fifty men. They propelled them only with oars, for they did not know how to harness wind power with sails.

Slowly, generation after generation, they and their kinsmen, the fierce man-eating Caribs, made their way through the Caribbean archipelago, settling or moving on as they thought fit. They travelled light, for they wore few garments if any. They travelled with what they needed to survive: batatas (sweet potatoes), cassava bread (the Jamaican bammy) and the cassava plant, a store of maize, grinding stones for crushing the grains, and their sacred tobacco. The plant was called 'cohiba'. It was the pipe used for smoking it that was called 'tabaco'. Smoking set them dreaming of 'Coyaba', their paradise.

The Arawaks also took with them their 'zemes' — images in stone and wood — spirits that they worshipped. The name was given also to anything that had magical powers. Finally the Arawaks came to the Greater Antilles, the four large islands of Puerto Rico, Haiti 'land of mountains', Jamaica 'land of springs', Cuba, as well as to The Bahamas.

The Arawaks were the first dwellers in Jamaica of whom we have records. The description that Columbus gave of the Arawaks whom he met first in The Bahamas holds true in general for those whom he met in the other islands. As Columbus himself wrote:

> All that I saw were young men, none of them more than thirty years old, very well made, of very handsome bodies and very good faces; the hair they wear over their eyebrows, except for a hank behind that they wear long and never cut. Some of them paint themselves black (and they are of the colour of Canary Islanders, neither black nor white), and some paint themselves white, and others red, and others with what they have. Some paint their faces, others the whole body, others the eyes only, others only the nose.

They had a liking for finery and ceremony, and showed great respect to their chiefs, whom they called caciques. In each island, caciques, assisted by village headmen and sub-chiefs, exercised authority and enjoyed certain privileges and special favours. For example, caciques were allowed several wives, whereas other males were allowed only one each. The best of cassavas, sweet potatoes and maize went to them, the best of the wild coneys and iguanas caught in the forests, the best of the harvest yielded by the sea. The cacique's house was larger than the others and contained revered idols. But there was one special favour that would not seem to us as desirable as the others. This was that, if a cacique were ill or dying, he would be strangled. This was not as cruel as it seems, for other people who were ill were usually abandoned in the bush with some cassava and water.

There may have been as many as 100,000 Arawaks in Jamaica when Columbus arrived in 1494. Being coastland people rather than forest or mountain people, they built their villages on high ground overlooking the sea or river estuaries, within easy reach of the inshore waters which they harvested for the shell-fish, the mussels and the chip-chip that they loved. The shells they threw on the village middens or scrap-heaps, providing in this way the abundance of shells by which we identify the sites of the villages. The settlements were scattered at points along the north coast from Priestman's River, just east of Port Antonio, through to a populous village they called Maima at New Seville near St. Ann's Bay, and on to Rio Bueno and Montego Bay. They settled along the south coast also, at Savanna-la-mar, Bluefields, Cow Bay at Portland Bight, at White Marl on the Kingston-Spanish Town highway, on Jacks Hill overlooking Kingston harbour, and at some points inland such as Ewarton and Moneague.

The houses were small and round, with a cone-shaped roof of thatch. The circular wall of wild reeds tied together with vines, or withes, was supported by posts which were driven into the ground, with a strong centre-pole to hold the structure together. Some settlements consisted of only a few households while others had as many as forty or fifty.

The Caribs, according to Columbus's account, built better houses and were more skilled than the Arawaks. He reported that

they appeared to be more civilized than those that we had hitherto seen, for although all the Indians have houses of straw, yet the houses of these people are constructed in a much superior fashion, are better stocked with provisions and exhibit more evidence of industry, both on the part of the men and the women. They had a considerable quantity of cotton, both spun and prepared for spinning and many cotton sheets so well woven as to be in no way inferior to those of our country.

Within easy reach of their settlements the Arawaks made clearings in the forest for their food-gardens or 'conucos', no easy task because in those days primeval forest extended, on the north side, from the topmost mountain ridges to the coast. Streams were plentiful and ran sparkling to the sea. In the forest they hunted the coney (utia) and the iguana, the only wild animals in the island.

Their tools and implements were simple, for they were stone-age people and had no knowledge of iron. With stone-axes and pointed sticks and fire, they cleared and prepared the ground, and planted their staples, sweet potatoes, maize, and cassava. These, with fish and shell-fish, were their mainstay. The larder was a limited one, lacking in high-energy foods. They had no domestic animals, neither cattle nor sheep nor swine, no horses, no mules, no asses; only a sort a small dog that never barked. Sometimes Jamaicans, deafened at night by the barking of their dogs, wish that the Arawak dogs were still around.

Limited though the larder was, the Arawaks delighted in festive occasions, when they dressed themselves up in red, painting faces and bodies yellow, black and red, and wearing cloaks and head-dresses of bright feathers. They wore on arms and legs ornaments of shells which rattled as they moved. Usually there was a parade led by the cacique who beat a wooden gong. Singing and dancing followed, with offerings of cassava bread to the zeme. The priests then broke the holy bread in pieces which they distributed to the people, who kept them as charms for protection against disasters. Most fearful of these was the onslaught of the god Huracan, who brought storms in the summer, whipped the sea to fury, drove mountains of water against the land and uprooted the trees that sheltered their conucos.

After the distribution of the sanctified cassava came the drinking of fermented juice made from crushed maize and the smoking of tobacco, either as crudely made cigars or with pipes. Generally the pipe was a tube shaped like a 'Y'. The two branches were put into the nostrils, and the smoke inhaled in deep breaths. The smoker was soon knocked out.

This love of ceremony and their delight in bright colours comes out in the description left by Andres Bernaldez, of a meeting between Columbus and an Arawak cacique on the south coast of Jamaica, at Portland Bight. Bernaldez was not an eyewitness but he probably heard the account from Columbus himself. He told how a fleet of canoes approached Columbus' ship. In one of the canoes, very large, painted throughout,

> came the cacique with his wife and two daughters, one about 18 years old, very beautiful, entirely naked as is the custom and very modest …. There were two sons and five brothers and others who must all have been his servants and vassals; he brought in his canoe a man acting as an ensign who stood alone in the stern, with a cloak of coloured feathers … and on his head, a large plume and he bore in his hand a white banner.

With him were 'two or three men, their faces painted in similar colours … each with a large plume arranged like a helmet … and these men had in their hands a kind of musical instrument which they plucked …'.

The cacique wore around his neck a very delicate ornament of copper, so delicate that it looked like eight-carat gold. It was suspended from a string of thick beads of marble stone 'on which they set great value here', and on his head a large wreath of small green coloured stones. But there was no dressing up for death. We know that they sometimes buried their dead in caves, and that they sometimes put the head and certain bones in a bowl of clay, for that is where some of the best preserved Arawak skulls and finest examples of their pottery have been found. After death the soul went to a happy land called Coyaba, a place of perpetual feasting and dancing.

On the morning of 12 October 1492, the old world of Europe collided with the old world of the Americas. Columbus, in command of a little fleet of three ships, had set out from the port of Palos, near Cadiz, to sail westwards across the Atlantic in order to reach India. He stopped briefly at the Canary Islands, then on September 8 began his history-making trans-Atlantic voyage. Thirty-two days later, at about two o'clock on the morning of October 12, the lookout on one of the ships saw land and shouted 'Tierra, tierra!'

The ships lowered sails and jogged offshore. At daybreak Columbus and his men saw before them a little island in The Bahamas that the Arawaks called Guanahani and Columbus named San Salvador, Holy Saviour. That morning, Columbus went ashore in the armed boat, with his captains and with the Royal Standard of Spain and the banner of the expedition, 'and said that they should bear witness and testimony how he before them all took possession of the island … for the King and Queen, his sovereigns'. Columbus's first act, then, was to dispossess those who had first discovered and settled on the island and who had lived in it for generations.

The Arawaks gathered around the strangers in friendly fashion. Columbus said of them, 'They bear no arms nor know thereof, for I showed them swords and they grasped them by the blades and cut themselves through ignorance.' The blood-shedding, accidental though it was, foreshadowed the future. A century later there were few Arawaks left. The third sign foreshadowed slavery: 'They should be good servants and of quick intelligence and I believe that they would easily be made Christians…'. Enforced slavery, cruelty and imported diseases wiped out the Arawaks of the islands in a century and a half.

The tragic story of the genocide of the Arawaks and of the indigenous people throughout the Americas justifies our applying to them the words of a distant kinsman, Seattle, chief of the Dwarmish and allied tribes of Puget Sound, spoken in 1855 as he thought of the collision of Europe with the old world of the Americas:

My people are few. They resemble the scattering trees of a storm-swept plain. There was a time when our people covered the land as the waves of a wind-ruffled sea covers its shell-paved floor, but that time long since passed away with the greatness of tribes that are now but mournful memory.

Phillip Sherlock

CRITICAL THINKING AND WRITING

1. Identify the writer's thesis.
2. If you were told that the title represents a claim and the rest of the article serves as support for the claim, how would you answer the following?
   a) What type of claim is it?
   b) Identify three different types of evidence used by the writer to support this claim.
3. The language of this passage is very simple. Why does the writer use this simple language?
4. There is a definite pattern of opposition established in the passage.
   a) Write three pairs of words (stated or implied) that help establish this pattern.
   b) How do these binary terms help to support the claim expressed in the title?

WRITING ACROSS THE CURRICULUM ACTIVITY

5. Write your own claim — value, policy, fact or cause — about Columbus's visit to the Caribbean. List three types of evidence you would use to support your claim.

GROUP PRESENTATION

6. Work in groups to find out more about the author and his contributions to
   a) The University of the West Indies.
   b) The development of studies in history, in the Caribbean.

EXPLORING THE WEB

7. Search the web for information on early explorations by the Spanish in the Caribbean. Share the information with your class.

CHAPTER 36

=== ◈ ===

WHITE WOMEN AND SLAVERY IN THE CARIBBEAN

Caribbean historiography before the mid 1980s, unlike that of the United States, offers but whispers in response to the challenging call for major revisions to the traditional concepts and methodologies that have negated and marginalized the writing of women's history.[1] On the surface, it would appear that most Caribbean historians have displayed a surprising (or suspicious!) reluctance in adopting gender as an instrument of investigation and analysis. Interpretative inertia has resulted in the study of women's history being defined, or claimed, as a sort of 'minority' area — the special responsibility and reserve of feminist scholars. This condition, in turn, is used as part of an on-going effort to devalue feminist scholarship, and promote dissonance in relation to the dominant male-centred historiography.[2]

Fortunately, however, historians of slavery, feminist and otherwise, have succeeded in avoiding the conceptual pitfall inevitable in the perception of women as socially homogeneous. Rather, most have subjected women's experiences to investigation with respect to caste, class, race, colour and occupation. To date, the primary focus of research (and this is reflected in the structure of historiography) is the black woman, with the coloured woman running a competitive second, and the white woman trailing behind at a distance. Recently, for example, three major monographs on the subject of black women's enslavement were published, all of which addressed directly, and in detail, the experiences of the 'coloured' women, but paid little attention to the lives of white creole or European women. Scholarly articles and essays reflect a similar research bias.[3] By way of contrast, however, a major subject of post-war Caribbean historians has been the study of white males within the colonial enterprise. This work focuses primarily upon the politics and entrepreneurship of white males in shaping the Caribbean world, and suggests the insignificance of ideological, social and economic inputs from white women.

These research patterns and trends can be accounted for in three ways. First, they are endemic to an earlier imperialist scholarship that conceptually subsumed white women under their male counterparts in assessments of agricultural and mercantile activities and their corresponding colonial cultures. Studies of the rise and fall of the planter class in Caribbean societies, for instance, have not paid systematic attention to the planter's wife as a socio-economic agent. Ignored to an even greater extent is the white woman as owner of slaves, agricultural lands, and other forms of property. Second, historians and social anthropologists, inspired by considerations of cultural decolonization and nation building, targeted black women's history in search of general explanations for problems identified as resulting from the legacy of slavery; this included matters such as the perceived instability and matrifocality of the black family, and the role it played in shaping social life and community development. Third, emerging from both these types of scholarship is the notion of white women's relative unimportance to ideological formation within the history of the colonial complex.

The argument that Caribbean white women were of marginal historical importance in fashioning the colonial complex is striking, when placed alongside interpretations found within the historiography of slavery in the southern United States.[4] Here, historians suggested that white women, particularly planters' wives, represented a kinder, gentler authority within the totalitarian power structure of the plantation. Some historians have gone further and argued that the plantation mistress was the unifying element within southern patriarchy. It is through her, according to this argument, that slaves were emotionally and socially integrated into the white household, rather than rejected and used primarily as natally alienated, disposable chattel. Against the ideological background of patriarchy, the southern plantation mistress, Morrissey states, came to consider herself 'the conscience' of society, while her Caribbean counterpart is conceived within the literature as a person who 'contributed little' and 'benefitted shamelessly from slave labour'.

Recently, this perception of the Caribbean white women received an important boost from the work of Barbara Bush. In discussing the socio-sexual manipulation and exploitations of all women by empowered white males, she produces a typology in which women's societal roles were defined by race and colour, and prescribed by the ideological weight of racism within the colonizing tradition. While Bush recognizes the privileges afforded white women within the slave system, many of which were predicated upon the subjection and brutalization of non-white women, she seeks, nonetheless, to highlight the common ground where womanhood in general was the target and prey of white male patriarchal authority.[5]

Lucille Mair, pioneer in Caribbean feminist historiography, moreover, in outlining a framework for detailed historical research, reinforced the parasitic view of the white woman by stating that in Caribbean plantation society 'the black woman produced, the brown woman served, and the white woman consumed'.[6] Again, the diverse productive roles played by white women in the development and maintenance of the slave mode of production are peripheralized by the projection of a hegemonic, culturally moronic consumerism in which they were apparently imprisoned. Caribbean historiography, then, lacks a clearly articulated and empirically sound conceptualization of white women in their roles as pro-slavery agencies within the world made by the slave holders.

None of theses approaches addresses adequately questions concerning white women as economic actors, managers of slave-based households, and conduits in the process of socio-ideological transmission. As a result, the traditional conception of the slave owner as male remains unchallenged, and the socio-economic limit of patriarchy not identified.

Nowhere is there to be found within the historiography, for instance, a systematic assessment of white women's autonomous roles as economic agents and positive participators in the formulation of pro-slavery values and institutions. Yet there is no shortage of documentary evidence to show white women as accumulators of property and profits through involvement on their own account in commercial and service activities, and as ideological enforcers within the social organization of slave society. The complex pattern of women's roles, in addition, should be understood in terms of the internal evolution of colonial society, particularly in relation to its patriarchal foundations.

In 1797, Moreau de Saint Méry noted, with respect to the eighteenth century developments in the French colony of Saint-Domingue, that white women were initially the ideological victims of the male-centred colonization mission. He argued that they acquiesced under intense social pressure to support the institution of black slavery by managing the plantation household and projecting it to slaves as the centre of all legitimate power and justice.[7] In committing themselves to this socio-economic role, however, they emerged over time as critical parts of its internal logic, and became inseparable from its cultural legacy. At the centre of Saint Méry's argument is a conception of white women's removal from the process of production, and integration into the plantation system at the level of reproduction as mothers and wives. This analysis runs along the same course as that by Pollack Petchesky, who suggests that women with a large investment in reproductive relations tend to exert a conservative influence on gender-role attitudes, and in so doing become critical to the consolidation of patriarchal structures and ideologies.[8]

It would be consistent, therefore, following Saint Méry, to state that once white women's socio-economic interest had become linked to the reproduction of slavery, their consciousness and social behaviour would be fashioned by its social laws, customs, and culture. As a result, the sight of creole white women examining the genitals of male slaves in the markets before making purchases, which offended the sensibilities of some European travellers, should not be considered necessarily as evidence of social degeneration, but rather as a product of the dialectical relations between social and economic forces within the slave mode of production. Neither should such action be considered contrary to their roles as good mothers and wives within the plantation household. Rather, it suggests that white women were acting fully within the epistemological framework of slavery by ensuring that rational market choices were made. The slave plantation enterprise, it must be emphasized, was considered a principal expression of Renaissance rationality within the colonial realm.

It is important to recognize the contradictions inherent within the attempt of plantation patriarchs to import and impose elements of aristocratic and bourgeois domestic values upon the metamorphic creole culture of frontier civilization. These can be seen in their effort to insulate white women, as much as possible, from the aesthetically crudest aspects of slavery. They went about this by passing legislation and using specific aspects of social custom as moral strictures. For example, in order to protect white women from the hallmark of enslavement — field labour — Caribbean planters, by the early eighteenth century, refused to employ white working-class women as fieldhands. By the end of the century most fieldhands in the English colonies were black women.[9] Also, from the beginning of the plantation system, laws were framed and implemented in order to disassociate white womanhood from the reproduction of the slave status by linking it solely to black women. When white women produced children with enslaved black men, which was not as uncommon as generally suggested, infants were born legally free. In this way the offspring of the white women would not experience social relations as human property, nor suffer legal alienation from social freedom. White women, then, were constitutionally placed to participate in the slave-based world as privileged persons, and to adopt ideological positions consistent with this condition.

The linking of white womanhood to the reproduction of freedom meant that the entire ideological fabric of the slave-based civilization was conceived in terms of sex, gender and race. This was the only way that black slavery and white patriarchy could coexist without encountering major legal contradictions. As a result, it became necessary for white males to limit the sexual freedom of white women and at the same time to enforce the sexual exploitation of black women as a 'normal benefit' of masterhood. In so doing, white males valued black women's fertility solely in terms of reproduction of labour for the plantation enterprise, and placed a premium on white women's maternity for its role in the reproduction of patriarchy.

The 'victim' approach to the study of white women in the slave formation, however, has severe conceptual limitations. These can be identified immediately by an empirical assessment of the white women's autonomous participation in the shaping of economic and social relations. The demographic data, for instance, show the extent to which the slave ownership correlated to differences of class, race and sex. While white males were the predominant owners of slaves in the plantation sector, the same cannot be said for the urban sector. White women were generally the owners of small properties, rather than large estates, but their small properties were proportionately more stocked with slaves than the large, male owned properties. In 1815, they owned about 24 per cent of the slaves in St. Lucia; 12 per cent of the slaves on properties of more than 50 slaves, and 48 per cent on the properties with less than ten slaves. In Barbados in 1817, less than five of the holdings of 50 slaves or more were owned by white women, but they owned 40 per cent of the properties with less than ten slaves. White women were 50 per cent of the owners of slaves in Bridgetown, the capital, on properties stocked with less than 10 slaves. In general, 58 per cent of slave owners in the capital were female, mostly white, though some were also 'coloured' and black. Overall, the women owned 54 per cent of the slaves in the town. The typology of slave owning in the West Indies as a whole shows a male predominance in the rural areas, and a female predominance in the urban areas, where property sizes were relatively smaller.[10]

White women also owned more female slaves than male slaves. The extensive female ownership of slaves in the towns was matched by the unusually high proportion of females in the slave population; female slave owners owned more female slaves than male slave owners. The evidence shows, furthermore, that in Bridgetown in 1817, the sex ratio (males per 100 females) of slaves belonging to males was more than double that for female slave owners. The majority of slaves in the town were owned by male slave owners. The sex ratio of slaves belonging to males was 111, and that for slaves belonging to females 49. The sex ratio of slaves belonging to white females, when separated from other non-white females was even higher, at 53. For Berbice in 1819, slaves owned by males had a sex ratio of 132, while those owned by females had a ratio of only 81.[11]

From these data the image that emerges of the white female slave owner is that she was generally urban, in possession of less than ten slaves the majority of whom were female. That female slave owners generally owned female slaves, indicates the nature of enterprises, and hence labour regimes, managed and owned by white women. It is reasonable, then, to argue that any conceptualization of urban slavery, especially with reference to the experiences of enslaved black women, should proceed with an explicit articulation of white women as principal slave owners. Such a departure is an analytically necessary precondition for the correct identification of white women within the slave-owning ethos, and for more rigorous assessment of urban-rural differentiations within the slave mode of production. Furthermore, it would enhance a real situational understanding which is necessary for the theoretical interpretation of black women's slavery experience, by linking it also to the power and authority of white matriarchs.

Hilary Beckles

Notes

1. See for example, Barbara Bush, Slave Women in Caribbean Society, 1650-1838, Bloomington, 1990; Hilary Beckles, Natural Rebels: A Social History of Enslaved Black Women in Barbados, New Brunswick, 1989; Marietta Morrissey, Slave Women in the New World: Gender Stratification in the Caribbean, Lawrence, Kansas, 1989; Lucille Mair, Women Field Workers in Jamaica During Slavery, Department of History, University of the West Indies, Mona, 1986: Blanca Silvestrini, *Women and Resistance: Herstory in Contemporary Caribbean History*, Department of History, University of the West Indies. Mona, 1989.

2. Rhoda Reddock, 'Women. and Slavery in the Carib-bean: A Feminist Perspective', *Latin American Perspectives* Issue 40, 12: 1, 1985, pp. 63-80, Arlette Gautier, 'Les Esclaves femmes aux Antilles Francaises, 1635-1848', *Reflexions Historiques* 10: 3. Fall, 1983, pp. 409-35. Lucille Mair, *The Rebel Woman in the British West Indies During Slavery*, Kingston. 1975.

3. Beckles. *Natural Rebels*; Bush, *Slave Women in the Caribbean:* and Morrissey, *Slave Women in the New World.*

4. See for example, Catherine Clinton, The Plantation Mistress: Women's World in the Old South, New York, 1982: C.L.R. James, *The Black Jacobins: Toussaint L 'Ouverture and the San Domingo Revolution*, New York, 1963 pp. 30-31 Morrissey, *Slave Women in tire New World, p. 150*. Barbara Bush, 'White "Ladies", Coloured "Favourites" and Black "Wenches". Some Considerations on Sex, Race and Class Factors in Social Relations a While Creole Society in the British Caribbean', *Slavery and Abolition*, 2, December 1981, *pp.* 245-62; Joan Gunderson, 'The Double Bonds of Race and Sex: Black and White Women in a Colonial Virginia Parish', *Jour-nal of Southern History*, 52, 1986, pp 351-72.

5. Bush, Stave *Women.* pp.8. 134.

6. Ibid. p. xii; See Lucille Mair, 'An Historical Study of Women in Jamaica from 1655 to 1844' (PhD, University of the West Indies, Mona, Jamaica, 1974); *The Rebel Woman in the British West Indies During Slavery*, Kingston, 1975; 'The Arrival of Black Women', *Jamaica Journal*, 9:2 and 3, Feb 1975; see also Jacqueline Jones, "My Mother was Much of a Woman", Black Women. Work, and the Family under Slavery', *Feminist Studies*, 8, 1982, pp. 235–69. Marietta Morrissey, 'Women's Work, Family Formation and Reproduction among Caribbean Slaves', *Review* 9, 1986. pp. 339-67.

7. Moreau de Saint Méry, [1797], *Description topog-raphique physique, civile politique et histonque de Ia partie française de Visle Saint Domingue*, Paris, 1958, p. 10. Morrissey, *Slave Women in the New World*, p. 150.

8. See R. Pollack Petchesky, 'Reproduction and Class Divisions among Women', in A. Swardlow and A. Lessinger (eds). *Class, Race and Sex: The Dynamics of Control*, Boston, 1983, pp. 221-31; Alwin Thornton and D. Camburn, 'Causes and Consequences of Sex-Roles, Attitudes and Attitude Change'. *American Sociological Review*, 48, 1983 pp.211-27; Alwin Thornton and D. Freedman, 'Sex-Role Socialisation: A Focus on Women' in J. Freeman (ed) *Women: A Feminist Perspective*, California 1984, pp. 157-62.

9. See Hilary Beckles, *White Servitude and Black Slavery in Barbados 1627-1715*, Knoxville, 1989, pp. 115-68; 'Black Men in White Skins: The Forma-tion of a White Proletariat in West Indian Slave Society', *Journal of Imperial and Commonwealth History*, 15: 1, 1986, pp. 5-22; *Natural Rebels*, pp. 24-54.

10. Barry W. Higman, Slave Populations of/he British Caribbean, 1807-1834, Baltimore, 1984, p. 107; also, *The Slave Population and Economy of Jamaica 1807-34*, Cambridge, 1978.

11. *Slave Populations.*

12. See for the Structure of the Barbados and Jamaica white population, Hilary Beckles, *Natural Rebels*, p. 15, Also Hilary Beckles, *Black Rebellion in Barbados: The Struggle Against Slavery, 1727-1838*, Bridgetown, 1985, pp. 58-9; William Dickson, *Mitigation of Slavery [1841]* Westport 1970, pp. 439-41.

13. Parliamentary Papers, 1791, vol.34, Testimony of Evidence of Captain Cook, p.202; also, evidence of Mr. Husbands, p. 13.

14. Major Wyvill, 'Memoirs of an Old Officer', 1815, p.386, MSS. Division, Library of Congress.

15. John Waller, *A Voyage to the West Indies*, 1820, pp. 20-21.

16. A. F. Fenwick (ed) *The Fate of the Fenwicks: Letters to Mary Hays, 1798-1828*, 1927, p. 169.

17. See Bush, *Slave Women*, pp. 44, 114.

18. Waller, *A Voyage*, p. 19.

19. F. W. Bayley, *Four Years' Residence in the West Indies*, 1833, p. 493; Bush. *Slave Women*, p. 115.

20. Bayley, pp. 493-4.

21. See Bush 'White "Ladies"'.

22. Waller, p. 20.

23. Fenwick, pp. 163-4.

24. Ibid., p. 164.

25. Ibid.

26. Ibid., p. 175.

27. Ibid., p. 170.

28. Ibid., p. 169.

29. Ibid.

30. Bayley. pp. 417-8.

31. David Turnbull, *Travels in the West*, 1840 p.53.

32. Moira Ferguson (ed), The History of Mary Prince: A West Indian Slave, Related by herself [1831], 1987. p. 56.

33. Ibid.

34. William Dickson, *Letters on Slavery*, 1789, Westport, 1970, p.41.

35. St Michael Parish Register, vol. IA, RL. 1/1, Barbados Archives; see also, Richard Dunn, *Sugar and Slaves: The Role of the Planter Class in the English West Indies, 1624-1713*, New York, 1973, pp. 255-6, Census of Barbados, 1715. Barbados Archives.

36. Edward Long, *The History of Jamaica* (5 vols), 1774, vol.2, pp. 412-13; see also 278-80. Bush, *Slave Women*, p. 25.

37. Bush, Ibid.

Critical Thinking and Writing

Discussion Questions

1. Which of the following does Beckles establish in the first two paragraphs?
    a) Most Caribbean historians before the mid 1980s did not focus on gender studies.
    b) Women's history is often viewed as a responsibility of feminist historians/scholars.
    c) All historians of slavery believe that women in slavery were socially homogeneous.
    d) The lives of white and creole women in slavery have not received adequate attention by historians.
2. How, according to Beckles, does the treatment given to white women in Caribbean historiography contrast with that given to white males?
3. How does Beckles account for these research patterns and trends?

Argument Analyses

4. Identify the sentence which states Beckles's main claim or thesis.
5. Beckles makes a number of claims about the role(s) of white women in Caribbean slavery. What are they?
6. State two ways in which Beckles establishes credibility in this article.
7. Cite two places where Beckles refutes opposing views regarding the role of the white woman in Caribbean slave society.
8. Provide reasons to show whether or not Beckles is biased.
9. State two different types of evidence which Beckles uses to support claims about how white women's businesses were concentrated in Caribbean societies during slavery.
10. Characterize the diction in this essay.

Collaborative Writing

11. Critically analyse Beckles's treatment of opposing views by pointing to:
    a) how he highlights errors in the views;
    b) how he examines the evidence of opposing arguments;
    c) how he uses different types of support to strengthen his refutation.
12. Critically analyse three ways in which Beckles uses contrast in this essay.

CHAPTER 37

LIVESTOCK FARMERS AND MARGINALITY IN JAMAICA'S SUGAR-PLANTATION SOCIETY: A TENTATIVE ANALYSIS

The sugar plantation as a socio-economic institution dominated Jamaican history from the beginning of the 18th century. Both contemporary and modern writers stress the superordinate position occupied within this plantation structure by the sugar plantocracy — that class which owned and controlled most of the means and markets of production, and dominated the social and political life of the island.[1] The resultant socio-economic order, defined by George Beckford as the plantation system, constituted the empirical basis for the formulation of the classic 'plantation economy model'. [Beckford, 2] Among the stated characteristics of plantation societies are the limited possibilities for internal capital accumulation, the absence of a significant home market, monoculture, the importation of inputs, usually from the 'mother country', and the exportation of all outputs. [Ibid.][2] But some colonial economies conformed more rigidly than others to this model. Studies have shown that in contrast to Eastern Caribbean islands like Barbados and St. Kitts, Jamaica's more varied physical environment resulted in

significant entrepreneurial and economic diversification and the evolution of an important group of non-sugar producers. [Higman, 15 and 14, Shepherd 25]. While some of these, notably the 'minor staple' cultivators like the coffee farmers, catered primarily to the export market, others geared their activities essentially to the domestic market. Among those producing primarily for the local market were the penkeepers or livestock farmers who participated only minimally in the direct export trade, accumulating their capital locally. They dominated the internal trade in livestock and by catering primarily to the sugar estate market determined that plantations did not conform to the traditional 'enclave theory'. [Dupuy, 8, pp. 169-226].

However, despite their importance to the domestic economy, Jamaican livestock farmers were never successful in challenging the institutional arrangement of the sugar plantation society. They, like other non-staple producers, were relegated to secondary roles and remained ancillary to the sugar sector. The dominant sugar sector, indeed, exploited those dependent on it, thereby reinforcing its superordinate position and the marginality of other sectors.

It should be pointed out from the outset that the article is essentially exploratory. It examines the marginality construct, considers its applicability to the penkeepers, and gives an overview of the evolution and demographic composition of the penkeepers. The paper is also concerned with the interrelationships between the sugar and the penkeeping sectors and will use the example of the interaction between these economic sectors to examine the notion of the dominance of the sugar plantocracy and the subordinate position of other producers.

The Marginality Construct

Marginality and the marginalization process have been operative throughout Caribbean history and have been recognized and acknowledged in several works. Influenced, perhaps, by the functionalist or integrationist model of society, these studies present marginalization as the antithesis of integration. The overwhelming majority of historical works on marginality deals with slaves and freed people of colour. Very few deal with the poor whites.[3] More modern works focus on the gender issue, specifically the legacies of partriarchal domination [Miller, 20] or on the rural and urban poor. [Perhnan, 22; Giddens and Held, 10; Price, 23]. Thus a review of the many schools of thought leading into the marginality construct, reveals a common focus either on the underclass who remain unintegrated into the mainstream economy or on those disadvantaged because of race, legal status, or gender. Furthermore, in most cases, the marginals studied in the Caribbean context are non-white, or whites socio-economically closer to the lowest echelons of society. The Barbadian 'redlegs' for example, hardly voted prior to 1840 because of the property qualifications attached to the franchise and the fact that few of them owned over 10 acres of land. [Sheppard, 28, pp. 5-6]. In addition, existing studies tend to deal with homogeneous groups in terms of gender, race, colour or class.

This article, by focusing on the interaction and interrelationships between economic sectors, attempts to broaden the debate on marginality as it is applied to colonial plantation societies. Admittedly, it departs from the traditional and classic interpretations of marginality because it suggests that members of the lower strata of white society who engaged in penkeeping were marginalized partly because of the economic activity in which they were engaged. A further problematic aspect of the article is that it also includes in the discussion traditionally marginalized people — the freed people of colour and women. These were already marginalized because of race, colour and gender — factors which had nothing to do with their occupation. But it would seem that if those who were agriculturalists depended solely on penkeeping for the means of upward social mobility (and not, for example, on export commodities like sugar and coffee) within their group and within a planter-dominated society, then their prospects were not very great.

The other analytical problem, of course, is that because of the great heterogeneity existing among the penkeepers, it is arguable whether they can be accorded a 'group' status in the strict sociological sense of the word. However, it seems clear from the contemporary records that the larger society regarded the penkeepers as a type of group. Planters and urban consumers often blamed 'the penkeepers' for the high price of beef and 'the penkeepers' often called their members to meetings to discuss matters affecting their industry. There is no evidence to indicate that at such meetings race, colour or gender barriers prevented united action in the interest of 'the penkeepers'.

Despite these obvious problematic issues an attempt will still be made to highlight, from the available empirical data, certain characteristics of the penkeepers which could be deemed marginal. Chief among these were their occupation of marginal lands, their economic dependence on the dominant sugar sector, internal disorganization, external isolation, exclusion from the mainstream political process and their resorting to unconventional politics such as petitions. Livestock farmers were also ascribed a social position inferior to the sugar planters, particularly if they were free coloureds. Above all, as they lacked political power, they were unable to influence legislation favourable to the livestock industry and were often passed over in favour of foreign suppliers.

The Livestock Farmers: Definitions, Historical Development and Demographic Composition

Many people kept livestock in Jamaica in the eighteenth and nineteenth centuries — slaves, free people of colour, free blacks, the large sugar planters, coffee farmers and other small-scale white entrepreneurs. The article is, however, primarily concerned with those specialized livestock farmers commonly styled 'penkeepers' in the contemporary literature. [M'Mahosi, 19, p. 172]. They are to be distinguished from the slave 'penkeepers' in charge of animals on sugar estates and other units and from the overseers of livestock farms, who were also frequently styled 'penkeepers'. Large sugar planters, resident or absentee, who established satellite pens must also be excluded from this analysis.

The livestock industry pre-dated the establishment of sugar as the dominant crop and the rise of the plantation system. The earliest livestock farmers were, in fact, the Spaniards whose *hatos* dotted the southern savannah lands of early seventeenth century-Jamaica. At that time, the industry was more export-oriented, supplying dried, cured meat to passing ships and to Cuba, and lard, hides, and tallow to the metropolitan Spanish market. With the English invasion, subsequent settlement and the rise of the sugar economy, livestock farmers increasingly catered to the estates' demand for animals for draught purposes and millwork. Edward Long, for example, stressed the positive correlation between the expansion of the livestock industry and the extension of the sugar culture. [Long, 18, fol. 308]. By 1782, there were an estimated 300 livestock farms in the island. [Gardner, 9, p. 161].

The earliest penkeepers in English Jamaica were among the soldier-settlers of the Cromwellian expeditionary force. At first they established pens on the south coast, but with the competition for land resulting from the development and expansion of the more lucrative sugar industry, some were pushed onto marginal interior lands. In this regard, they were among the pioneers of the frontier society and were early numbered among the settlers in the Pedro's Cockpit area of St. Ann. The social position of the livestock farmers was early distinguished from the sugar planter class. In his seminal work on the development of creole society in Jamaica, Kamau Brathwaite outlined the main social divisions within the society and differentiated between the several categories of settlers. [Brathwaite, 6, pp. 105-150]. White penkeepers along with 'minor staple' producers were grouped among those he categorized as 'other whites' and 'small settlers', not numbered among the 'upperclass whites'. [Ibid., pp. 135-148].

Jamaica's varied topography and physical environment then, clearly provided possibilities for small-scale entrepreneurs and together with the ready market for livestock on the sugar estates, contributed to the growth of the small-settler population. By 1820, penkeepers also included attorneys and overseers in charge of estates. Attorneys and overseers, according to M'Mahon's somewhat exaggerated description, made their 'fortunes' while in charge of properties belonging to their absentee proprietors. They invested these 'fortunes' in pens, which provided not only a ready source of animals for the estates they managed but also markets for the estates' old animals which were fattened and sold to the butchers. [M'Mahon, 19 pp. 171-173].

In addition to whites from the lower strata of the segmented white group, the penkeepers also comprised free coloureds already marginalized because of their colour and legal disabilities. Before the enactment of a law in 1761 curtailing the value of inheritance, free coloureds had managed to acquire substantial property.[4] Some inherited pens. Benjamin Scott-Moncrieffe, for example, inherited Soho Pen from his father and later also acquired Thatch Hill Pen in St. Ann. [Shepherd, 25, p. 182]. Livestock farmers also included women, though Brathwaite was essentially correct in his impression that it was a male-dominated occupation. [Brathwaite 6, pp. 146-147]. Female penkeepers comprised whites, free coloureds, and freed blacks. White female farmers seemed to have been essentially widows and were less numerous among the

penkeepers than freed women. [Boa, 5, pp. 64-69]. Catherine Buckeridge from Sonning, County Berks in England, for example, was a widow and owner of a rather substantial pen — Salt Pond Hut — in St. Catherine. [Shepherd, 25, p. 183].

Free coloured and freed black women were more numerous among the female penkeepers and only a few were numbered among the sugar planting class. Anna Woodart was, arguably, the wealthiest free coloured woman in 1762, owning Dirty Pit and Hoghole pens; in St. Catherine. Freed women were also noted among the penkeepers in Westmoreland, St. Elizabeth, St. Thomas-in-the East, and St. David. The pens owned by freed women were among the smallest and were also confined to marginal lands. [Boa, 5. p. 66]. For these freed women, marginality was derived from race, colour and gender. Penkeeping offered a chance for upward social mobility within the free coloured society but certain obstacles unique to this industry frustrated their efforts.

Other distinguishing characteristics of penkeepers were that they were primarily creole born and resident.

Economic Dependence

An examination of the economic relations between penkeepers and the dominant sugar sector, reveals a heavy dependence on the sugar industry. In this regard, it must be stressed that sugar estates provided the largest outlet for the products of the pens. A small sample of 11 per cent of the pens returned in the Accounts Produce for 1820 revealed that these units earned more from the sale of working animals to the estates than from other income-generating activities such as jobbing, wainage, pasturage and the sale of food and miscellaneous items. While livestock sales represented 69 per cent of total earnings, other resources combined accounted for 31 per cent. Taken as single categories, jobbing represented 9 per cent, pasturage 4 per cent, wainage 4 per cent, provisions 9 per cent and miscellaneous items 5 per cent. On individual pens, however, livestock sales often accounted for as high as 98 per cent.[5]

The size of the sugar estate market for livestock was considerable. Large estates like Golden Grove in St. Thomas-in-the-East needed an estimated 100 'steers' (oxen) annually in addition to mules and spayed heifers.[6] Indeed, between the late eighteenth century and the early nineteenth century, the estimated annual total island demand for working animals was put at somewhere between 56,000 and 71,000.[7] At £18 (currency) each in the late eighteenth century and between £20 and £30 in the early 19th century, estates would need to spend a considerable sum on oxen alone.[8]

Theoretically then, Jamaica's sugar economy afforded a relatively substantial market capable of acting as a dynamic factor in the development of the pen sector. In reality, this dynamism was not directed towards the local livestock industry. In the first place, Jamaican sugar planters continued to import working animals, primarily from Spanish America, even after the local penkeeping industry had been well-established. Sugar planters also established their own pens or rented existing ones in an attempt to exclude the middleman supplier. The In-givings of 1815 reveal that 84 sugar planters owned 96 satellite pens serving 122 estates.[9] As their sugar states could not always use all the animals reared on such related units, planter-penkeepers competed on the local market with the specialized penkeepers. Even the section of the sugar market to which livestock farmers had access was not always stable.

During and after the period of slavery, fluctuations in the demand for livestock on the sugar estates resulting from depression in the sugar market, often resulted in bankruptcy for some penkeepers. Between 1810 and 1817, for example, George Forbes of Thatchfield Pen in St. Elizabeth was confident of making profits of between £2,000 and £2,500 from his property.[10] The decline in profitability of some estates in the mid-nineteenth century which resulted in a decrease in the demand for livestock on the estates soon wiped out his savings.[11] In the immediate post-slavery period too, the depressed state of the sugar sector affected by labour and capital shortage, caused an oversupply of animals on the market and a drop in their prices. Livestock farmers then complained of the 'death of pen-keeping'.[12] Competition from foreign suppliers and the precariousness of depending solely on the sugar estates caused penkeepers to diversify their activities and restrict their output of animals. This further contributed to the reinforcement of their marginal and dependent position.

Verene A. Shepherd

Notes

1. See the works of E. Long[18], J.B. Mcweton [21], M.G. Smith [31], E.K. Brathwaite [6], R. Sheridan [29], and B.W. Higman [14].
2. See also L. Best [3, pp. 283-326], F.L. Pryor [24, pp. 288-317] and A. Dupuy [8, p. 239].
3. See, for example, S. Boa [5], A. Sio. [30, pp. 166-182]. R.B. Allen [1, pp. 26-150]. In Allen's article, comparisons are made with the Caribbean and he suggests that perhaps free coloured marginality had to do with factors other than local, internal

circumstances. For a discussion of the poor whites see J. Sheppard [28].

4. See G. Heuman [13].

5. Jamaica Archives, Accounts Produce, lB/I 1/4154-56.

6. Simon Taylor to Chaloner Arcedeckne, 29 October 1792, Vanneck MSS, Jamaican Estate Papers [hereafter J.E.P.] box 2, bundle 10.

7. Calculated on the basis of the number of estates each year and their estimated demand for working animals.

8. Accounts Produce, I B/ 11/4/3,4,9, 54.

9. Jamaica Almanack 1815, pp.22143. Satellite pens represented about one-third of the total number of pens.

10. George Forbes to Peter Forbes, 12 Jany. 1811 and 11 June 1817. Jamaica Archives, Private Deposit (Gunnis Papers), 4/110/17.30,40-46.

11. Ibid.

12. For further Information on the experiences of livestock farmers during the Apprenticeship and post Apprenticeship periods, see Shepherd [26] and Shepherd [27].

CRITICAL THINKING AND WRITING TASKS

DISCUSSION QUESTIONS

1. What do writers of all periods emphasize about the social and political life on the sugar plantation?

2. Which members of the sugar plantation society are the main focus of attention and why?

3. Why does the writer state that the article is exploratory?

4. How does the writer use the term "marginality" in the context of the sugar plantation society?

5. What is problematic about Shepherd's "construct of marginality"?

6. Shepherd lists three different types of penkeepers. Explain these three categories.

7. In the first three paragraphs, Shepherd uses exemplification and comparison/contrast. State in which paragraph each is used and show how it strengthens the writer's essay in each case.

8. Shepherd employs a combination of discourse modes/types.
   (i) State what they are.
   (ii) Identify the sections of the article in which each one is used.
   (iii) Provide explanations/ justifications for the writer's use of each one.

ARGUMENT ANALYSES

9. Which of the following extracts from the essay function/s as the writer's main claim?
   (i) "However despite their importance to the domestic economy, Jamaican livestock farmers are never successful in challenging the institutional arrangement of the sugar plantation society. They, like other non-staple producers, were relegated to secondary roles and remained ancillary to the sugar sector."

(ii) "The dominant sugar sector, indeed, exploited those dependent on it, thereby reinforcing its superordinate position and the marginality of other sectors."

(iii) "The paper is also concerned with the interrelationships between the sugar and the penkeeping sectors and will use the example of interaction between these economic sectors to examine the notion of the dominance of the sugar plantocracy and the subordinate position of other producers."

(iv) "This article, by focusing on the interaction and interrelationships between economic sectors, attempts to broaden the debate on marginality as it is applied to colonial plantation societies. Admittedly, it departs from the traditional and classic interpretations of marginality because it suggests that members of the lower strata of white society who engaged in penkeeping are marginalized partly because of the economic activity in which they were engaged."

10. An important way to evaluate the logic of an argument is to use the ABC test. Examine the reasons Shepherd provides to support her claims about the marginal status of penkeepers by deciding whether they are Appropriate, Believable and Convincing or Complete.

11. Which of the following are minor claims made by the writer?

(i) "Planters and urban consumers often blamed 'the penkeepers' for the high price of beef and the 'pen-keepers' often called their members to meetings to discuss matters affecting their industry."

(ii) "Livestock farmers were also ascribed a social position inferior to the sugar planters, particularly if they were free coloureds."

(iii) "Penkeeping offered a chance for upward social mobility within the free coloured society but certain obstacles unique to this industry frustrated their efforts."

12. Judge the writer's credibility by commenting on the following:

(i) How she demonstrates her knowledge of the subject.

(ii) How she builds common ground with readers.

(iii) How she treats/responds to opposing views on the subject (fairly or unfairly).

13. Subheadings are generally used to fulfil a number of purposes. Choose the subheading from the text which best matches the functions listed below:

(i) Identifying features of terms.

(ii) Cueing readers into the material by summarizing it.

COLLABORATIVE RESEARCH

14. In small groups, do research about other groups which were marginalized in Jamaica's Sugar Plantation Society. Write your own claims based on your findings and present them to the class. Write the evidence to support your claims.

CHAPTER 38

A SMALL PLACE

You disembark from your plane. You go through customs. Since you are a tourist, a North American or European — to be frank, white — and not an Antiguan black returning to Antigua from Europe or North America with cardboard boxes of much needed cheap clothes and food for relatives, you move through customs swiftly, you move through customs with ease. Your bags are not searched. You emerge from customs into the hot, clean air. Immediately you feel cleansed, immediately you feel blessed, (which is to say special); you feel free. You see a man, a taxi driver; you ask him to take you to your destination; he quotes you a price. You immediately think that the price is in the local currency, for you are a tourist and you are familiar with these things (rates of exchange) and you feel even more free, for things seem so cheap, but then your driver ends by saying, 'In U.S. currency.' You may say, 'Hmmmm, do you have a formal sheet that lists official prices and destinations?' Your driver obeys the law and shows you the sheet, and he apologizes for the incredible mistake he has made in quoting you a price off the top of his head which is so vastly different (favoring him) from the one listed. You are driven to

your hotel by this taxi driver in his taxi, a brand-new Japanese-made vehicle. The road on which you are traveling is a very bad road, very much in need of repair. You are feeling wonderful, so you say, 'Oh, what a marvelous change these bad roads are from the splendid highways I am used to in North America.' (Or, worse, Europe.) Your driver is reckless; he is a dangerous man who drives in the middle of the road when he thinks no other cars are coming in the opposite direction, passes other cars on blind curves that run uphill, drives at sixty miles an hour on narrow, curving roads when the road sign, a rusting, beat-up thing left over from colonial days, says 40 MPH. This might frighten you. You are on your holiday; you are a tourist); this might excite you (you are on your holiday; you are a tourist), though if you are from New York and take taxis you are used to this style of driving. Most of the taxi drivers in New York are from places in the world like this. You are looking out the window (because you want to get your money's worth); you notice that all the cars you see are brand-new, or almost brand-new, and that they are all Japanese-made. There are no American cars in Antigua — no new ones, at any rate; none that were manufactured in the last ten years.

You continue to look at the cars and you say to yourself, Why, they look brand new, but they have an awful sound, like in an old car — a very old, dilapidated car. How to account for that? Well, possibly it's because they use leaded gasoline in these brand-new cars whose engines were built to use unleaded gasoline, but you mustn't ask the person driving the car if this is so, because he or she has never heard of unleaded gasoline. You look closely at the car; you see that it's a model of a Japanese car that you might hesitate to buy; it's a model that's very expensive; it's a model that's quite impractical for a person who has to work as hard as you do and who watches every penny you earn so that you can afford this holiday you are on. How can they afford such a car? And do they live in a luxurious house to match such a car? Well, no. You will be surprised, then, to see that most likely the person driving this brand-new car filled with the wrong gas lives in a house that, in comparison, is far beneath the status of the car; and if you were to ask why, you would be told that the banks are encouraged by the government to make loans available for cars, but loans for houses are not so easily available; and if you ask again why, you will be told that the two main car dealerships in Antigua are owned in part or outright by ministers in government. Oh, but you are on holiday and the sight of these brand-new cars driven by people who may or may not have really passed their driving test (there was once a scandal about driving licences for sale) would not really stir up these thoughts in you. You pass a building sitting in a sea of dust and you think, it's some latrines for people just passing by, but when you look again you see the building has written on it PIGOTT'S SCHOOL. You pass the hospital, the Holberton Hospital, and how wrong you are

not to think about this, for though you are a tourist on your holiday, what if your heart should miss a few beats? What if a vessel in your neck should break? What if one of those people driving those brand-new cars filled with the wrong gas fails to pass safely while going uphill on a curve and you are in the car going in the opposite direction? Will you be comforted to know that the hospital is staffed with doctors that no actual Antiguan trusts; that Antiguans always say about the doctors, 'I don't want them near me'; that Antiguans refer to them not as doctors but as "the three men" (there are three of them); that when the Minister of Health himself doesn't feel well he takes the first plane to New York to see a real doctor; that if any one of the ministers in government needs medical care he flies to New York to get it?...

Oh, but by now you are tired of all this looking, and you want to reach your destination your hotel, your room. You long to refresh yourself; you long to eat some nice local food. You take a bath, you brush your teeth. You get dressed again; as you get dressed, you look out the window. That water — have you ever seen anything like it? Far out, near to the horizon, the color of the water is navy-blue; nearer, the water is the color of the North American sky. From there to the shore, the water is pale, silvery clear, so clear that you can see its pinkish-white sand bottom, Oh, what beauty! Oh, what beauty! You have never seen anything like this. You are so excited. You breathe shallow. You breathe deep. You see a beautiful boy skimming the water, godlike, on a Windsurfer. You see an incredibly unattractive, fat, pastrylike-fleshed woman enjoying a walk on the beautiful sand, with a man, an incredibly unattractive, fat, pastrylike-fleshed man; you see the pleasure they're taking in their surroundings. Still standing, looking out the window, you see yourself lying on the beach, enjoying the amazing sun (a sun so powerful and yet so beautiful, the way it is always overhead as if on permanent guard, ready to stamp out any cloud that dares to darken and so empty rain on you and ruin your holiday; a sun that is your personal friend). You see yourself taking a walk on that beach, you see yourself meeting new people (only they are new in a very limited way, for they are people just like you). You see yourself eating some delicious, locally grown food. You see yourself, you see yourself.... You must not wonder what exactly happened to the contents of your lavatory when you flushed it. You must not wonder where your bathwater went when you pulled out the stopper. You must not wonder what happened when you brushed your teeth. Oh, it might all end up in the water you are thinking of taking a swim in; the contents of your lavatory might, just might, graze gently against your ankle as you wade carefree in the water, for you see, in Antigua, there is no proper sewage-disposal system. But the Caribbean Sea is very big and the Atlantic Ocean is even bigger; it would amaze even you to know the number of black slaves this Ocean has swallowed up. When you sit down to eat your delicious meal, it's better that you don't know that most of what you are eating came off a plane from Miami. And before it got on a plane in Miami, who knows where it came from? A good guess is that it came from a place like Antigua first, where it was grown dirt-cheap, went to Miami, and came back. There is a world of something in this, but I can't go into it right now.

The thing you have always suspected about yourself the minute you become a tourist is true: a tourist is an ugly human being. You are not an ugly person all the time; you are not an ugly person ordinarily; you are not an ugly person day to day. From day to day, you are a nice person. From day to day, all the people who are supposed to love you on the whole do. From day to day, you walk down a busy street in the large and modern and prosperous city in which you work and live, dismayed, puzzled (a cliché, but only a cliché can explain you) at how alone you feel in this crowd, how awful it is to go unnoticed, how awful it is to go unloved, even as you are surrounded by more people than you could possibly get to know in a lifetime that lasted for millennia, and then out of the corner of your eye you see someone looking at you and absolute pleasure is written all over that person's face, and then you realize that you are not as revolting a presence as you think you are (for that look just told you so). And so, ordinarily, you are a nice person, an attractive person, a person capable of drawing to yourself the affection of other people (people just like you), a person at home in your own skin (sort of; I mean, in a way; I mean, your dismay and puzzlement are natural to you, because people like you just seem to be like that, and so many of the things people like you find admirable about yourselves — the things you think about, the things you think really define you — seem rooted in these feelings): a person at home in your own house (and all its nice house things), with its nice back yard (and its nice back-yard things), at home on your street, in your church, in community activities, your job, at home with your family, your relatives, your friends — you are a whole person. But one day, when you are sitting somewhere, alone in that crowd, and that awful feeling of displacedness comes over you, and really, as an ordinary person you are not well equipped to look too far inward and set yourself aright, because being ordinary is already so taxing, and being ordinary takes all you have out of you, and though the words 'I must get away' do not actually pass across your lips, you make a leap from being that nice blob just sitting like a boob in your amniotic sac of the modern experience to being a person visiting heaps of death and ruin and feeling alive and inspired at the sight of it; to being a person lying on some faraway beach, your stilled body stinking and glistening in the sand, looking like something first forgotten, then remembered, then not important enough to go back for; to being a person marvelling at the harmony (ordinarily, what you would say is the backwardness) and the union these other people (and they are other people) have with nature. And you look at the things they can do with a piece of ordinary cloth, the things they fashion out of cheap, vulgarly coloured (to you) twine, the way they squat down over a hole they have made in the ground, the hole itself is something to marvel at, and since you are being an ugly person this ugly but joyful thought will swell inside you: their ancestors were not clever in the way yours were and not ruthless in the way yours were, for then would it not be you who would be in harmony with nature and backward in that charming way? An ugly thing, that is what you are when you become a tourist, an ugly, empty thing, a stupid thing, a piece of rubbish pausing here and there to gaze at this and taste that, and it will never occur to you that the people who inhabit the place in which you have just paused cannot stand you, that behind their closed doors they laugh at your strangeness (you do not look the way they look); the physical sight of you does not please them; you have bad manners (it is their custom to eat their food with their hands; try eating their way, you look silly; you try eating the way you always eat, you look silly) they do not like the way you speak (you have an accent); they collapse helpless from laughter, mimicking the way they imagine you must look as you carry out some everyday bodily function. They do not like you. They do not like me! That thought never actually occurs to you but still you feel a little uneasy. Still, you feel a little foolish. Still, you feel a little out of place. But the banality of your own life is very real to you; it drove you to this extreme, spending your days and your nights in the company of people who despise you, people you do not like really, people you would not want to have as your actual neighbours. And so you must devote yourself to puzzling out how much of what you are told is really, really true (Is ground-up bottle glass in peanut sauce really a delicacy around here, or will it do just what you think ground-up bottle glass will do? Is this rare, multicoloured, snout-mouthed fish really an aphrodisiac, or will it cause you to fall asleep permanently?). Oh, the hard work all of this is, and is it any wonder, then, that on your return home you feel in need of a long rest, so that you can recover from your life as a tourist?

That the native does not like the tourist is not hard to explain. For every native of every place is a potential tourist, and every tourist is a native of somewhere. Every native everywhere lives a life of overwhelming and crushing banality and boredom and desperation and depression, and every deed, good and bad, is an attempt to forget this. Every native would like to find a way out, every native would like a rest, every native would like a tour. But some natives — most natives in the world — cannot go anywhere. They are too poor. They are too poor to go anywhere. They are too poor to escape the reality of their lives; and they are too poor to live properly in the place where they live, which is the very place you, the tourist, want to go — so when the natives see you, the tourist, they envy you, they envy your ability to leave your own banality and boredom, they envy your ability to turn their own banality and boredom into a source of pleasure yourself.

Jamaica Kincaid

CRITICAL THINKING AND WRITING

1. What is the writer's major claim (stated or implied)? What type of claim is it?
2. What are some of the minor claims (supporting evidence) that the writer uses?
3. What is the effect of Kincaid's use of the pronoun 'you'?
4. 'An ugly thing, that is what you are when you become a tourist, an ugly, empty thing, a stupid thing…'
   a. What type of claim is this?
   b. What support does the writer provide for this claim?
   c. Is this a sound argument?
   d. 'The thing you have always suspected about yourself the minute you become a tourist is true'. What support does the writer provide for this claim?
5. Describe the writer's tone and explain how it contributes to the essay's persuasiveness.
6. How convincing is Kincaid's argument? Identify the strong and weak parts.

WRITING ACTIVITIES

7. Conduct a Web-Quest. Choose two or three websites and examine the manner in which your country is depicted. As a citizen how would you respond to some of the depictions? What are some of the opposing or supporting viewpoints that you would present?
8. This activity is a debate between 'tourists' and Caribbean nationals. For this activity,
   a) the class will be divided into two groups;
   b) one group will play the role of a tourist;
   c) another group will play the role of a Caribbean citizen.
   d) The tourists should describe their perceptions of and experiences in the Caribbean. The Caribbean citizens should respond to the tourists (this will involve concessions, where necessary, and providing opposing points). The tourists, in turn, should respond to the Caribbean citizens and so forth.
9. What are some of the common perceptions which you think that Caribbean people have of tourists? Write a short descriptive paragraph from the standpoint of a Caribbean person observing a tourist. Use a syntactical structure which is similar to Kincaid's.

Chapter 39

The Plight of the Guyanese Migrant Worker

I am appalled at the continued efforts to use and abuse the good people of the Republic of Guyana who travel throughout the Caribbean region seeking an opportunity to better themselves. While our leaders attend fancy meetings and drink expensive liquor while paying lip service to the idea of an integrated Caribbean, we continue to fail our Caribbean people on the bread-and-butter issues that matter most.

It is no secret that some of the people of Guyana have taken to migration as a means to better their economic lives. Such migration is not unique to Guyanese and all of us, whether Jamaican, Nevisian, Barbadian or some other nationality have at some point turned to migration as a means of bettering our lot in life.

What continues to astound me about our Caribbean people is how easily we forget. How easily we forget that remittances from the United Kingdom and the United States, the USVI and St Maarten kept Nevis afloat before we saw more affluent days. How our people flocked to the Dominican Republic to cut cane, to Trinidad and Curaçao to work in the oil industry, to the US and British Virgin Islands to work in construction and the hospitality industry. How easily we forget that Jamaicans still flock to the United States and the United Kingdom to better their lot in life.

Even the much touted Caribbean heavyweight Barbados has people flocking to the other islands of the Caribbean as an emerging professional class providing consultancies for everything from law to politics. St. Lucians now abound in places like Anguilla. Antigua has for years been a melting pot of Caribbean nationals. Why, then, are we so inclined to abuse the Guyanese people?

Just recently in Grenada, a young Guyanese construction worker, Rudolf Holligan, was forced to leave that island upon the revocation of his work permit. No reasons have been advanced by the Grenada Government as to why the young worker's work permit was revoked. Efforts by his lawyers to ascertain the true position have not borne fruit. This young Caribbean national has had to flee Grenada with his wife and 3-year-old child in tow. His sin? We do not know but I would not be surprised if it was nothing more than his Guyanese citizenship.

I picked up a young Guyanese lady here in Nevis recently and asked if she had ever visited the rest of the Caribbean, other than Nevis. She advised that she had spent a few hours in Barbados, as she was deported forthwith, upon arriving in that country for a short holiday. The infamy of the callous treatment of Guyanese at the hands of Bajan immigration officials is now a matter of well-documented regional lore.

But even when they are allowed into the country, how are they treated by our leaders and by us as a people? It is no secret that our new Premier, the Honourable Joseph Parry, referred to Guyanese, in public statements in New York while he was Leader of the Opposition, as 'breeding' faster than Nevisians and that he admired Idi Amin's handling of the Indians in Uganda. Historians would remember how that despot Amin deported nearly all the Indian merchant class from Uganda when he seized power.

More recently, the NRP (now in power in Nevis but then in full campaign mode) staged a march through the streets of Charlestown claiming that they were protesting electoral irregularities. Interestingly, virtually all of the names objected to were citizens of Guyana who are living among us and therefore eligible under Nevis law to vote. That is the treatment meted out to our Caribbean brothers and sisters by our Caribbean leaders.

And how are they treated by our people? In Nevis, it is an open secret that Guyanese workers are routinely forced by unscrupulous employers to pay for their own work permits even though the law prescribes that work permits be paid for by the employer. Even where some workers have done that, those same employers turn around and report them to the immigration authorities if those workers try to augment their income by engaging in any other work on the island. Suddenly, workers who would have been forced to pay their own permit fees, are subjected to deportation even before those permits expire. And we sit by and do nothing because it seems that the sin of these, our Caribbean brothers and sisters, is that they are Guyanese.

I wish to say for my part that talk of CSME and greater integration in our region is meaningless unless we can address the real bread-and-butter issues of our people. Until the Guyanese national can feel as secure in Nevis as he does in Berbice, we are wasting precious time and resources talking about greater integration in the region. CARICOM musings about Haiti and the Dominican Republic buttress the point. If we cannot embrace Guyanese who speak our language, who play our cricket, who revel in our calypso, who attend our University of the West Indies and whose history is our history, how can we ever hope to embrace Haitians and Dominicans?

Our Caribbean civilization must demand more of our Caribbean leadership. We as a people must demand better of ourselves. We cannot hope to oppress our Caribbean brothers and sisters at home and demand that America treats us humanely. We cannot abuse Guyanese and look to traipse into St. Thomas, St. Maarten and Tortola as if we have a right there. We cannot demean our migrant workers and demand that we be treated with respect when we too travel to other countries seeking sustenance. When our leadership says that Guyanese are 'breeding' too fast, and marches against them through the streets of Charlestown, we are embarking on a slippery slope to oblivion.

Nevisians are part of the Caribbean civilization and that Caribbean civilization is in large measure built on migration. Let us not conveniently forget our own and continuing history of migration in some ill-conceived superiority complex over the Guyanese people. Let us embrace our Guyanese brothers and sisters and welcome them to this beautiful island where peace and prosperity abound. It is the right thing to do.

Mark Brantley

CRITICAL THINKING AND WRITING

1. a) What is the controversy which Brantley is addressing?
    b) What is Brantley's main claim and what type of claim is it?
2. At the end of the argument the writer declares 'It is the right thing to do.' What type of claim is this?
3. Comment on the effectiveness of Brantley's tone.
4. 'I picked up a young Guyanese lady here … of well-documented regional lore.' Analyse the soundness of the argument presented in the sixth paragraph.
5. Is this piece largely an inductive or a deductive argument? Provide support for your answer.
6. 'It is no secret that our new Premier the Honourable Joseph Parry referred to Guyanese in public statements in New York while he was Leader of the Opposition as "breeding" faster than Nevisians and that he admired Idi Amin's handling of the Indians in Uganda. Historians would remember how that despot Amin deported nearly all the Indian merchant class from Uganda when he seized power.' Analyse this analogy.
7. What types of appeal does the writer use to engage his audience? Provide examples.
8. Identify the argumentative structure which the writer uses to organize his essay.
9. How does the use of diction in argumentative writing generally differ from its use in expository writing?

WRITING ACROSS THE CURRICULUM ACTIVITIES

10. List and discuss some of the controversies which exist in some of your disciplines and which presently exist in your country. What positions do you hold on these controversies?
11. Using one of the topics below, write a thesis and a counter thesis:
    a) The CSME
    b) Political Leadership in Caribbean Countries
    c) The University of the West Indies

CHAPTER 40

PUTTING ON THE DOG

The readers of the *Gleaner* do not know this, but for the last five years I have been writing Cargill's column for him without getting any credit for it. So this morning I am writing my man's column under my own name.

Although my man is fairly decent I have been living a bit of a dog's life. All I get to eat every single day is turned cornmeal with a bit of liver or some cheap mince added, and that is a very boring diet. Indeed, I am forming a society to work for canine equality for I think it is unjust that we dogs should be regarded as inferior. Everybody is seeking equality these days and I see no reason why dogs should not do so too.

I discuss many things with my man. I have learned quite a lot of English, words such as 'Sit' or 'Lie down' or 'Shut up' and for his part my man has learned a lot of dog language. In fact, one of the aims of my society is to develop a proper understanding of dog language. If people can propose that what my man calls *yahoolish** should become a second language in Jamaica, I see no reason why *poodlese* should not become a third one. It is, after all, at least as understandable.

One of the things that I have been discussing with my man is the welcome news that there is a large campaign afoot to eliminate screw worms. I am particularly interested in this for screw worms are a very grave danger to all animals and particularly to dogs. I understand that the main way of overcoming the screw worm threat is to introduce into Jamaica large numbers of infertile male screw worms. As I often hear my man complaining of human overpopulation I have suggested to him that the problem could be similarly solved by introducing into Jamaica thousands of infertile human males.

I might add that I have my doubts about the success of the screw worm scheme for the simple reason that I don't think it will matter how many infertile screw worm males are introduced for there will always remain a few fertile screw worm males lurking about somewhere. I think that it is very possible that these few fertile males will become in great demand as the females go in search of a genuine old-fashioned screw. My man feels that there would be the same difficulties if a similar scheme were introduced for humans.

Exodus

I wonder if the humans in Jamaica have noticed that while the exodus in the 70s was dramatic and much more publicised, the present human exodus is proceeding very quietly but with equally devastating results. Indeed, my man tells me that the only thing that is limiting it at present is the shortage of visas to prosperous countries. As a dog I regret this human exodus for the number of dogs left without homes is rapidly increasing.

It is true, of course, that owing to the fact that there is no hydrophobia in Jamaica, dogs are allowed to migrate anywhere without special permission. But this doesn't help us for we are not allowed on jet planes unaccompanied. This seems to be unfair for while there are no mad dogs in Jamaica there are lots of mad people. Indeed, the Government, too broke to feed them, is putting hundreds out from the asylum onto the streets where they will become more dangerous to people than even the most disagreeable of dogs.

I am worried about this too, for it is not only mad people that the Government can't afford to feed but apparently it can't afford to feed its prisoners too. The prison warders who told us about that have been punished by the authorities for letting that cat out of the bag. It is not only dogs who dislike cats.

Public Life

I have sometimes thought about entering public life but my man who is the same colour as I am tells me that it would not be wise, as both white dogs and white people are not well accepted by creatures of a darker hue. So, perhaps my society should agitate against racism. At any rate white dogs would give the people in Jamaica a choice. For nowadays all they can do is to swap black dog for monkey.

I end my column with one final protest. The only education open to dogs in Jamaica at the moment is to teach them to sniff the baggage of human passengers to detect ganja or cocaine. This is creating considerable trouble for my fellow dogs. Many of them, after months of sniffing, become addicted. Fortunately for me I don't have to do anything like that, though I must say that I find the constant smell of my man's tobacco smoke rather unpleasant.

I have asked my man to stop smoking but he tells me that he has been smoking without interruption for 65 years and hasn't yet dropped dead of it. My man is a stubborn fellow. I hear it said constantly that a dog is a man's best friend. I wish the contrary were true, for man is not always a dog's best friend. Still, my man is comparatively decent to me and I will continue to write his column for him though he insists that I am not again to use my own name.

We used to think that Morris Cargill was the Gleaner's senior columnist, writing for more than 45 years!

Morris Cargill

* '*yahoolish*' is a term used by Cargill to refer to Jamaican Creole.

CRITICAL THINKING AND WRITING

1. Cargill writes on a number of issues. What are they? What is his attitude towards these issues?
2. What is the writer's tone in this passage?
3. Discuss the effectiveness of the strategy of writing from the dog's point of view.
4. Analyse the analogy in paragraph 3.
   a) What is the claim?
   b) On what basis (grounds) does the writer make this claim?
   c) Is the analogy appropriate? Why, or why not?
5. What point is Cargill making about the Jamaican male in paragraph 5?
6. Identify the fallacy in Cargill's attempt to justify his smoking habit (penultimate paragraph).
7. Examine Cargill's use of the word 'contrary' in the penultimate paragraph ('I wish the contrary were true'). Suggest a word that would be more suitable.

WRITING ACROSS THE CURRICULUM ACTIVITIES

8. Out of class assignment: Go to the library and research Morris Cargill — his life and his work. Compare this article with another one written by him and write a short piece in which you state your opinion of his work. Ensure that you justify your claims.
9. Choose any of the issues raised by Cargill in this article and write a response in which you oppose his argument.
10. Cargill suggests that there is racial discrimination in Jamaica. To what extent do you see evidence of racial discrimination in your country? Write two paragraphs on the topic 'Racial discrimination is alive and well in my country' — one in which you support your position on the moot, and another in which you present a counterargument which you successfully refute. (Optionally, you may choose to use a Rogerian structure — that is, write an objective counterargument and then a paragraph in which you advance your own position).

a
tl
an(
pre
in m
emot
black 1

CHAPTER 41

SHACKLED TO THE PAST, TRAPPED IN THE PRESENT

THE ENSLAVEMENT of our people for almost four centuries destroyed our ethnic, national and social identities. Many of the problems we face, such as underachieving males, interpersonal violence, fragmented social systems, dysfunctional family patterns and a preponderance of single female-headed households, are part of the psychosocial legacy of slavery, and are experienced by many post-slavery societies.

Colour and class

Out of slavery evolved a class system which was determined by colour. Blacks were denied their humanity and deemed inferior to all others. Consider the aphorism, 'If you are white you are right, when you are brown stay around and when you are black stay back.' Are we then surprised that in 2004 the 'browning' is still glorified, that many still aspire to marry someone of a 'browner' hue, that our people continue to bleach their skins and that the brown or white person is still preferentially treated in many quarters? That in many families the darkest person is abused emotionally and physically and anything is degraded?

Family

The plantation system was designed to generate wealth for one class. A stable family life was never encouraged: men were separated from their women and children from their mothers. The dominant family patterns, characterized by visiting relationships, a preponderance of single-headed households and absent fathers have evolved out of slavery.

Denigration of the human being

The West Indian negro slaves were devalued. In 1928 Lowell Ragatz wrote,

he had all the characteristics of his race. He stole, he lied, he was simple, suspicious, inefficient, irresponsible, lazy, superstitious, and loose in his sexual relations.

Such was the perception of slaves and their descendants. These are concepts many still have of blacks, especially poor black persons. Many of these traits, described as negatives, were some of the strategies used to survive slavery. These strategies were considered adaptive but have become maladaptive in modern society.

Violence

Slavery was characterised by hard labour, brutal punishment and constant separation from loved ones. Here are some examples from the literature, of how humans were punished: 'flogged him, had him rubbed in salt pickle, lime juice and bird pepper'; 'gagged him, locked his hands together, rubbed him in molasses and exposed him naked to the flies all day, and to the mosquitoes all night'; and 'a slave caught eating cane was whipped and another slave told to defecate in his mouth.'

Punishment by the master was harsh and brutal, and the life of the black slave was worth nothing. Such was the level of dehumanisation, indignity and enforced powerlessness. It has generated resentment for authority and a devaluation of human life. Are we surprised at the high levels of interpersonal violence and the lack of respect for human life in Jamaica?

Sex and power

Power and sex were integrally linked in the plantation system. White men and higher-ranked black men exploited the black woman. Historian, Barbara Bush noted that 'the sexual exploitation of slave women by white men represented a natural extension of the general power of white over black'. According to one historical review, a white overseer had sexual encounters with 87 different women in one year.

The greater the sexual exploits of the black male slave and the more children he had, the more valued he was. Black women also manipulated relationships with white males as they saw themselves as being able to achieve social mobility by sleeping with white men and having 'brown children' who could achieve social mobility by virtue of their colour.

Male Responsibility

The black male was encouraged to sire as many children as possible on the plantation. The fact that men would have their women and children separated from them discouraged the development of strong emotional bonds in families, and fostered 'the irresponsible black male'.

As we grapple with the scars left by slavery, we equally need to devise strategies to overcome them. This society must go through a period of deconstruction and break from the psychological chains that shackle us to our past. This deconstruction is necessary as we reconstruct ourselves into a caring, just, and less violent society.

Wendel Abel

CRITICAL THINKING AND WRITING

1. What do you consider to be the writer's purpose in writing this article?
2. What is the writer's thesis?
3. What criteria would you use to judge the credibility of this article?
4. How does the writer justify his claim that 'Many of the problems we face such as underachieving males, interpersonal violence, fragmented social systems, dysfunctional family patterns and a preponderance of single female-headed households, are part of the psychosocial legacy of slavery and are experienced by many post-slavery societies.'?
5. How do the sub-headings assist the reader?
6. Is this a balanced article? Justify your answer with specific examples from the passage.
7. Examine the following argument:
   'Punishment by the master was harsh and brutal, and the life of the black slave was worth nothing. Such was the level of dehumanisation, indignity and enforced powerlessness. It has generated resentment for authority and a devaluation of human life. Are we surprised at the high levels of interpersonal violence and the lack of respect for human life in Jamaica?' (Paragraph 6).
   a) What is the claim, and what support is provided?
   b) What type of argument is it?
   c) Evaluate the soundness of the argument.

WRITING ACROSS THE CURRICULUM ACTIVITIES

8. In paragraph 4, the writer claims: 'These strategies were considered adaptive but have become maladaptive in modern society.' Write one paragraph in which you agree with this statement, and one in which you refute it.
9. Write one paragraph in which you present and develop a causal generalisation that illustrates the idea that 'the enslavement of our people for almost four centuries destroyed our ethnic, national and social identities' (paragraph 1).

MUSIC
& CULTURE

CHAPTER 42

CARIBBEAN MUSIC AND THE DISCOURSES ON AIDS

AIDS, music, and youth culture in the Caribbean represent a rich site for further enquiry. Although adolescents and youth constitute a high-risk group for AIDS, AIDS discourse in the Caribbean has not yet put into perspective the relationship between music, leisure practices and the disease. In this respect, I believe that this paper in its broadest application will facilitate a much-needed, wider discourse on the disease. In particular, it should serve as a critical resource document for the Caribbean, on account of its interventionist engagement within (what to my mind and best knowledge is) a domain of discursive silence.

Within the first decade since the discovery of AIDS, there was the perception in the Caribbean that the lack of information and awareness about AIDS globally, meant that youth were at risk of perpetuating the transmission of the disease through homosexual activity, unprotected sex, intravenous drug use and the sharing of needles. An opinion, which is still current in popular belief, is that the music of youth culture supports the very practices which can lead to AIDS. This popular belief can be heard on radio call-in programmes, in the press and in everyday conversation. But, to date, 'serious' cultural studies investigation has not sought to discuss the nature of the interface between music, youth culture and AIDS....

The decade of the 1980s represented a period of ignorance and curiosity about AIDS in the Caribbean. AIDS has always been a mysterious and hence a mistrusted disease within Caribbean society. Although it was being suggested by the medical profession that the disease could only be spread through the exchange of blood or semen, there still loomed a societal skepticism, which was based largely on the perception that researchers themselves, worldwide, had been unable to come to terms with the nature of the disease. Since it was initially propagated in the Caribbean that the AIDS virus was transmitted primarily (only?) by homosexual contact, AIDS was perceived to be a disease of homosexual men. Although this view is not held as commonly as it used to be, there is still the lingering suspicion in the region that it is this homosexual practice which is responsible for the widespread scourge of AIDS.

The reaction to AIDS within the music of popular culture in the Caribbean in the 1980s in many respects reflected this larger societal ignorance and skepticism about the disease. On his 1985 album *A Touch of Class*[1], Sparrow treats the topic of AIDS in the song 'Ah Fraid the AIDS'. The song reflects both fear and mistrust of the disease. It expresses the perception that the disease was started by homosexuals. There is a fear that it is endangering romance. The lyrics also make reference to the impact of the disease on all and sundry, like Rock Hudson, who is seen to have been justly rewarded for his homosexual proclivity. Sparrow's song therefore reflects a number of concerns which were being felt within Caribbean society. His title, carefully chosen, conveys the message of caution and trepidation at this post-modern epidemic.

Also in 1985, in the neighbouring island of Barbados, a fellow calypsonian, Viper, tackled the disease of AIDS. Unlike Sparrow's song, his did not focus on the AIDS epidemic solely. The song 'Jesus' nonetheless analysed the body social, spiritual and political of the Caribbean and concluded that the panacea was Jesus. Next to Gabby's 'De List', which I want to make mention of subsequently, Viper's song has sparked the most debate and controversy on the AIDS question in the Kaiso genre in the 1980s.

In the manner of picong, Viper's persona refers to an earlier question by Trinidad's Winston 'Gypsy' Peters of 'where do we go from here?', an enquiry which reflected the general lament of social degradation in the region. The growing drug problem and unemployment were major concerns. There has undoubtedly been greater commentary on the drug problem in the Caribbean than there has been on AIDS. Whereas the drug problem has been viewed as an overt menace to society, as being the central instigator of the whole range of ills in society, AIDS has been viewed as the 'silent killer'; since its means of transmission has been considered to be almost exclusively through sexual contact. AIDS has largely been perceived in the 1980s as a domestic, 'private' affair. So as a result, there has been a general reaction of fear, condemnation and silence with respect to the disease, especially in the public domain. That is why Viper's song is so vital to our examination of AIDS in popular Caribbean music discourse. Whereas clerics were in large numbers condemnatory of promiscuous sexual activity and some criticized homosexual activity, few were as committed and overtly forthright as Viper's persona. I have made this reference to religion since Viper's song proposes to enter the debate at that level. It remains as one of the most outspoken, and committed songs on sexual practices, AIDS, and its eradication, within the domain of Caribbean popular music in the 1980s period. It enters this discourse when Caribbean gospel music proper was still flirting with cover versions of North American gospel by Amy Grant, Petra, Sandi Patti, and the Imperials. It enters the discourse some ten years before other gospel artists would begin to touch the subject of the AIDS disease. There did not exist then, and there still does not exist in Caribbean gospel, the lyrics of 'local'/social awareness. It is within this background and context therefore that Viper's song enters the discourse on socio-religious issues within Caribbean society. The discomfort which some felt about this song also had to do with it being performed in the calypso forum. Was it gospel? Was it calypso? Where was its place? This was another aspect of this song's subversive qualities.

Dem homosexuals such undesirables that we
have down in de city
Contaminating and destabilizing all de youths
with them philosophies
Dem prostituting worse than the women
So let we shun them or better yet bun them
AIDS is a problem and we don't want them
If yuh get de point help me clear de joint
cause we don't need prostitution we don't need
cheap trick
woman don't sell your body for no kinda kicks
we don't want blue movie we don't need sex
show
woman respect your body don't do um no more[2]

In the song's controversial second verse, its persona clearly associates the spreading of the AIDS virus with homosexual and prostitution activity. A primary concern is with the effect of the sexual practices (which it treats) on the bodies and minds of the young within society — a point which in the mid-1980s was lost within the song, though. When one examines the overall structure of the song, of which I have only represented its second verse here, the song is seen to be built on stating the problem, noting its effects and positing a solution. It is the solution of 'shunning' homosexuals and their activity or 'bunning' them which commanded the greatest interest in the song. At the level of 'high' national debate this attitude was deemed to be distasteful. At the informal level, Viper's presentation represented the philosophy of many more individuals. This attitude was rooted in the 'local values that have been shaped by a fundamentalist reading of biblical scriptures.'[3]

For a long time the unofficial discourse on AIDS, which is the 'discourse of the people', sought to reflect their concerns, pose their questions and also to challenge the claims of the official organizations within the Caribbean. Viper's song brought more clearly

into focus the existence of these discursive poles. It proposed to be the carrier of the feelings of the general populace. This reading of the song and its discursive polemics was lost in the fray of heated discussions on the rights and wrongs of 'bunning' human beings.

Many 'official' commentators on Gabby's song 'De List' in the 1980s have also deemed it to be in poor taste. It has been suggested that the song was ill-conceived and just like the rumour on which it was built, the song's function has primarily been destructive. What many of these criticisms have not taken into consideration, though, is the context, the time at which the song appeared (that is, in the years of almost total ignorance concerning AIDS). Other calypso specialist critics read the Gabby song purely and literally as a historical documentation. Few, if any, have seen it as a warning, and as being representative of a cry of a helpless susceptible populace somewhat in the vein of Viper's 'Jesus'. Fewer still have considered it as a plea on behalf of the populace, for a much more candid and informed exposition by all agencies on the question of AIDS.

The song focuses on a much rumoured list of male partners which an AIDS patient allegedly made before he died. The song reputes the victim as being a 'young fellah':

Nuse Babbleow say yuh won't believe it
They try to keep de thing a secret
But that don't suit Bajan character
dem know we mout ain't have no cover
Big names popular names
So now even married women saying they insist
De hospital show them all de names pun de
list[4]

The song seems to locate the point of initial impact for the spreading of AIDS in homosexual relations. The insistence by married women that they see 'de names pun de list', however, is a reflection of the realization (which comes to popular song in 1985), that the spread of AIDS is not restricted to any single form of sexual contact. The futility which the song conveys surrounding the request to see 'all' the names, further signifies the clandestine constitution of the virus. For me, this represents the perception of an epidemic gone wild. Hence the cutting pains 'like razor blades' correspond with the lethal incisions within the body social of the Caribbean, and the innate psychological fear and suspicion which the insidious AIDS disease has created at the heart of Caribbean society. In retrospect, some ten years after the dissemination of this song, it must be assigned this new reading, in the light of the overall development of the discourse on AIDS in the music of popular Caribbean culture ....

By the late 1980s, there began to be a shift in popular Caribbean music in terms of the treatment of AIDS, at least more so in the calypso domain. There began to be a shift away from the earlier association of AIDS and homosexuality. There now seemed to be a proliferation of songs which (if only in passing) carried a message of warning.... So by the late 1980s and early 1990s, AIDS was being integrated as yet another of the region's social ills. Songs like Arrow's 'Death for Sale' on his 1991 *Zombi* Soca album[5] were therefore cryptically cautioning 'Don't buy death in sex', as it went on and dealt also with other social problems like drugs, unemployment and materialism.

Dancehall has been much more notorious than any other Caribbean popular music form in terms of its perceived supporting of activities which can give rise to the AIDS epidemic. 'Slackness' and dancehall have been synonymously associated in mainstream perception. The recent slating of a show in St Lucia with the dancehall queen Patra, and its ensuing debate, are reflective of the attitudes which society holds towards dancehall, and some of its artistes. The Patra controversy brought to the fore the lingering perception in mainstream society that such acts as Patra's are the promoters of promiscuity, illicit sex and by extension AIDS. The calypsonian, the Professor, commented on this in his 1995 song 'Patra':

> *Chorus:*
> *Patra they balling*
> *Patra all that I hearing*
> *She wears nothing under*
> *When yuh come over you show us*
> *Kingston Harbour*
> *The things that you do encouraging raper*
> *Show some decency anytime you come to this country*
> *If you want money employment here man ain't easy*
> *I work with sanitation and I cleaning*
> *The streets of corruption.*[6]

There has tended to be much emphasis on the themes of sex and drugs, and on abusive language, throughout the history of dancehall and its derivative reggae. When this emphasis is compounded with the apotheosis of the play of bodies in the actual dancehall context, then one begins to better situate mainstream perceptions of the relations between the lyric and the act in the actual performative context. Looking through the catalogue of an artist like, say, Shabba Ranks, one could identify many songs which this conservative reading of popular music culture might regard as supporting lyrical tracks for the perpetuation of practices which lead to AIDS: 'Twice my Age', 'Love Punany Bad', 'Girls Wine', 'Kill

Me Dead', 'Wicked in Bed', 'Mr Loverman', 'Hardcore Lovin' to list a few.[7]

Although this has been the general perception of dancehall and its function within popular culture, dancehall artists have been particularly tough and homophobic when it comes to what they see as misplaced sexual proclivities. In a sense, these artists have maintained what has been called their 'fundamentalist' reading of homosexuality. This many of them still perceive as being punishable by death, and one way is through the AIDS disease.

Buju Banton's song 'Boom Bye Bye'[8] is emblematic of this attitude. It has attracted many comments both favourable and negative. In the international world of music and business the response has been negative. When Shabba Ranks appeared on international television in support of this view on homosexuality and AIDS, after his signing to Epic, he too was threatened with being taken off tour and was forced to retreat to a much more amicable and politically correct position on homosexuality and AIDS:

Boom bye bye in a battie boy head
Rude boy no promote nuh nasty man dem ha fe dead!

In the mid-1990s Caribbean music was continuing to reveal a further shift in its treatment of and attitude to the AIDS epidemic. Although some elements of roots reggae and dancehall held fast to the 1980s popular outlook and attitude, by and large Caribbean music tended towards a more 'sober' attitude .... The song which best exemplified this new attitudinal orientation though, was done by the band 'Touch' out of St Vincent; it was their highly infectious song 'A Sex World.'

Sex education make it a part of our productive school curriculum And this one it should be planned
School's where they meeting there's where they courting
There is where most dating begins among other things
Teachers likewise parents have a role to play
In preparing the children for the cruel world out there
This knowledge is vital all the way.
Not now when the fact they likely to get in trouble
On this course of life you one responsible
You feel the more they know the more they'll want to experiment
Hey, they'll find out some how don't keep them ignorant
No, no. [9]

I have made reference to this song because I think it offers a notable contrast with the earlier song by Viper, especially in terms of lyrical and performative tone. Viper's lyrics are loaded with fear and revulsion, his persona would distance him/herself from what s/he perceives to be the 'AIDS culture'. Touch's song appears much more controlled and its persona situates him/herself inevitably as being part of the culture which AIDS impacts: 'our curriculum'; 'A Sex World ... we're living in'. Whereas Viper's attitude is tough and militant, almost, Touch assumes the voice of the sage teacher who is in control of the subject matter and its discourse...

As with most other phenomena which are practised in the body social and culture of the USA, this Industry–AIDS interface has also trickled down into the Caribbean. This has seen some artists being enlisted to perform in conjunction with anti-AIDS agencies, to promote 'safe sex' through the use of condoms. Buju Banton assumed this role of superstar/teacher in 1996 where his

'Operation Willy' (the title of his 1993 AIDS-awareness song) became the slogan for shows within the region:

Ragamuffin don't be silly
Rubbers pun you willy
AIDS a go round and we don't want catch it. [10]

In spite of the popularity of the show among youths at one such show held in Barbados, it was still felt by a significant portion of the mainstream of the population that there existed a serious contradiction between the stated objective of such concerts and the underlying signification of dancehall's iconographies. The skepticism about this method stems partly from the residual feeling of lack (of power) which Caribbean society still feels in the face of AIDS. It is also reflective of the diverse views which the Caribbean region holds with regard to social practices, youth culture, music and music culture.

One of the most positive advances, as regards the relationship between popular artists and AIDS education, is the recent initiative by a group of artists who have formed themselves into an organization called Artists Against AIDS. The first major project undertaken by this association was the composition and recording of a song which promotes the importance of the preservation of life. A music video accompanies the song. The video performances are not pretentious. The performers are not over-presented, hence the message is foregrounded to a position of fuller presence within the discursive space of image, sound and lyrical text.

The proceeds from the sale of the production are intended to be used in the fight against AIDS. What is more positive about this initiative is the fact that it is driven by the artists themselves. It therefore appears less pretentious than other performances, like some of the ones I have mentioned before. The artists in this most recent venture appear more credible and hence appeal much more to the sensibilities of those who hear and see them ....

Few Caribbean youths are won over to AIDS-awareness by the distribution of condoms on the night of such shows. These audiences can see through the thin synthetic covering which the performers at such shows don for the duration of the performance. The artist must not be viewed as someone who can be used, and used for a one night performance in the hope that he/she will win over others. The artist her/himself must be viewed as someone who can be won over. When this is done, then the kinds of initiatives which I have just alluded to will be born. These should prove more effective in affecting awareness, education and prevention.

Curwen Best

Notes

1. Sparrow, 'Ah Fraid de Aids', A *Touch Of Class*. B's BSR-SP 041.1985.
2. Viper, 'Jesus' c.1984.
3. Peter Manuel et al, *Caribbean Currents* (Philadelphia: Temple University Press, 1995) p.178.
4. Gabby, 'De List', *One In The Eye*. ICE BG11001. 1986.
5. Arrow. 'Death For Sale', *Zombie*, Soca Arrow 035.CA 1991.
6. De Professor, 'Patra', 1995.
7. Shabba Ranks, *Caan Dun: The Best of Shabba*, VP Records VPCT 1450. 1995.
8. Buju Banton, 'Boom Bye Bye', *Simply the Best vol. 9*. 1993.
9. Touch, 'A Sex World', 1993.
10. Buju Banton, 'Willy' (Don't Be Silly), *Voice of Jamaica*, Mercury 314518013-419931.

CRITICAL THINKING AND WRITING

1. a. What is the controversy that Best seeks to address?
    b. What is his position on it?
2. Why, according to Best, is Viper's song vital to the examination of AIDS in popular Caribbean music discourse?
3. What is the writer implying when he claims that Caribbean gospel music was 'flirting' with North American gospel music?
4. Does the writer do justice to both sides of the debate, or is there evidence of bias?
5. In the last paragraph, the writer argues that 'Few Caribbean youths are won over to AIDS awareness by the distribution of condoms on the night of such shows.'
    a) What type of claim is this?
    b) To which 'shows' is he referring?
    c) Why are the youths not 'won over'?
    d) Does Best provide sufficient empirical evidence for his claim that 'few youth' are won over? If so, what is the evidence? If not, what kind of evidence might he have given?
6. What is the predominant argument type used in this article?

COLLABORATIVE ACTIVITIES

7. To what extent are the attitudes towards AIDS as espoused by this writer reflective of your perceptions of the reality in your own society?
8. This article was written almost a decade ago. Locate current songs on the topic from different Caribbean countries and examine the lyrics. To what extent are Best's opinions portrayed in the lyrics of the songs you have examined? Is there any indication (based on these lyrics) that there has been a change in the discourse on AIDS in Caribbean popular music? Prepare a position paper to be presented in class.
9. In groups of four, prepare an argument supporting the moot 'AIDS victims should receive state aid', and one argument opposing it.

CHAPTER 43

A REVIEW OF PAULETTE RAMSAY'S *AUNT JEN*

Paulette Ramsay's deceptive novella tells the story of Sunshine, a young girl growing up in rural Jamaica in the 1960s to 70s. Deceptive — because the simple prose of Ramsay's child narrator (Sunshine herself, writing her story in the form of letters to a mother in England who never answers) masks and reveals several layers of reality that make for a complex, finely nuanced story. *Aunt Jen* is a subtle exploration of the issues of migration, exile and diaspora from a point of intersection between Caribbean migration in the early days and the present. Ramsay's narrative specifically explores the effect of these issues on children, a group given scant if any attention, both in our traditional readings of the Caribbean bildungsroman and in the current preoccupation with adult gender and cross-border identity in diaspora studies. *Aunt Jen* is an important work, as it is children who suffer the greatest fallout from new migration trends between the Caribbean and the North American and European metropoles. Ramsay's careful modulation of the child narrator's voice exploits the familiar strengths of the bildungsroman. On the one hand, there is the irony created in the interplay between the child's naïve response to inconsistent adult behaviour and the evidential detail that allows the reader to assess and judge that behaviour. On the other hand, there is the searing critique that is generated as the child grows older and is able to make her own appropriate judgements. In Ramsay's treatment, the circumstances of the child's loss of innocence infuse the narrative with a heartbreaking poignancy that barely skirts the edges of tragedy. In the end, Sunshine's resilience, nurtured by family and community support, rescues her from a tragic fate and speaks of the refusal of tragedy that is pointed in the Caribbean mode of carnival.

One haunting example is seen where Sunshine begins to apprehend that her mother, Aunt Jen, is probably never going to answer her letters, and does not in fact care much for her. The child's grief, anger and sense of violation express themselves in a series of rewritings of the same letter. The rewrites show her struggle between these emotions, a kind of despairing hope that she may yet be wrong, and the good manners that she has been taught and which dictate that one's elders should be respected. Here respect in Jamaican/Caribbean cultural terms means keeping silent about one's true feelings where their expression might not show the adult in a good light. Much later we learn that Sunshine has not in fact sent the letters, and they remain primarily an index of her growth into the experience of loss that accomplishes maturity. Sunshine's withholding of several letters links to ideas of vocality and silence, which are the basis on which the young girl's maturation takes place. The progression of the novel as a series of unanswered letters in which she tells of her upbringing nurtured by the taciturn but strong and supportive presence of her grandfather, and the voices of church, community and grandmother (Ma), creates Sunshine as the product of a liminal space between opposites, silence and vocality and between absence, presence, exile and community. If her struggle to come to terms with her mother's silence forces her to discover a strength she had not known herself capable of, it is the community that gives her the sure foundation from which that strength springs. The interplay is marked by her increasingly frequent quotation of Ma's pithy (biblical and proverbial) sayings as a way of battling the enigma of Jen, side by side with increasing assertions of her independence of Ma's world view as she grows towards adulthood. It is marked too in the inversion of power by which she keeps Aunt Jen on tenterhooks when the latter (it seems) finally writes back: she makes Jen wait upon her own silence, while she decides whether she will accept the invitation to come to England after Ma's death. Finally, she refuses, and explains why: 'When I got up out of that bed [of silence] I felt strong and I kept hearing Ma's voice, "Sunshine you will be awright"' (97). The supreme irony of *Aunt Jen* is that Jen's silence in answer to Sunshine's appeal causes the young girl to incorporate aspects of her mother into herself. The letters shift from being a hope of meeting to being a form of indictment, punishment and self-vindication. Her final missive, ending coldly and politely, 'Thank you for the photograph. You do not look like me or anybody I know' (98), thus acquires a double edge, justly punishing Jen while revealing her own growth into a fine taste for cruelty.

Ramsay's text is realistic, not idealistic: Sunshine is scarred as well as liberated. The intersection of speech and silence is also the space where Sunshine discovers the paradoxical significance of letter writing: both a space of self-expression and a space of being-alone-in-the-world; more importantly, the space of her own development as an artist — 'writing is [now] in my bones and when anything strange happens, the first thing I think of doing is to write about it so I'm writing to you' (78).

Being-alone-in-the-world then appears as the artist's necessary crucible, in which she is protected by the organic relation to community which Caribbean writers have seen as indispensable to authentic representation. *Aunt Jen* strikes us as authentic. The life of the community is rendered in vivid scenes that might strike us as sometimes extravagant, but this very extravagance is Ramsay's understanding of the fine line between tragedy and comedy, pain and laughter, which is the Caribbean carnivalesque. One example is the hilarious episode in which Miss Clara's daughter's coffin disgraces her churchgoing mother by falling open to reveal baby nappy, baby pin, olive oil and other paraphernalia of superstitious burial, causing Major Rankine to lose her false teeth and flee, crying 'Lord Jesus, thave me, thave me!' The comedy of the episode masks and makes bearable the fact that this funeral is one of many that move towards a painful climax from the middle of the book: Uncle Johnny's after he is mown down by a tractor; Gramps's from a stroke in his yam field, alone with nobody to give [him] a little water or rub him head or him back; and Ma's, from grief over the loss of her son and husband. That the novella escapes melodrama despite being packed so full of tragic episodes in so short a space, is due to Ramsay's skill as a storyteller: she manipulates her plot with dexterity to achieve suspense, surprise, acceptance — catharsis, even. We are completely unaware, until the fifth letter, that Aunt Jen is Sunshine's mother and not some possibly mythical aunt or aunt-figure. Yet once the revelation is made we recall subtle clues that prepared us for the revelation. The epistolary mode allows not only for a nuanced movement between history and autobiography, memory and immediate moment, but also for ellipses that moderate our reception of the tragic episodes. Sunshine's letter to Aunt Jen on 5 March 1971 ends:

> Good news. When you come you will be able to talk to Uncle Johnny. Ma and Aunt Sue just came from the hospital and they say he woke up after I left. We are all so happy. We will go to see him tomorrow (26).

The ellipsis between this and the next letter is marked by the date, 16 March 1971, and the dumb silence of the opening sentences: 'Dear Aunt Jen, we buried Uncle Johnny yesterday, in the pouring rain'. The poignancy is emphasized by the fact that the good news of the earlier letter is rendered as a PS. Throughout, Ramsay balances pain in deft gradations ranging from the speechlessness of 'Yesterday we buried Uncle Johnny' to a naked outburst such as

> Dear Aunt Jen, so you tek we fe popppyshow. You do not have any respect for us and you seem to think we have no feelings so you can keep disappointing us over and over again .... You have become

like a poison in our blood. Right now I hate you I hate you for bringing shame on us (77).

Silence is the liminal space in which Jen herself is drawn. The final letter, written after a gap of many years by Sunshine's daughter to Aunt Jen, indicates that the latter finally showed her hand in an unbelievably cruel way, successfully contesting Gramps's will and robbing Sunshine of her inheritance. Yet the revelation does nothing to dispel the sense of mystery that surrounds this figure who never appears except in Sunshine's dreams and in things she is supposed to have done and has not done or has done badly: her failure to turn up at the airport after she has promised to come, following Gramps's funeral; her failure to send her photograph; her ghostly presence when Sunshine is in a coma and therefore unable to see her; that ghostly presence behind her father who suddenly appears and behaves in ways that possibly mimic Jen herself. Those letters that suggest that Jen finally wrote complicate the picture, as we are never sure whether she actually wrote or whether Sunshine fantasized her replies, first as a way of inventing Jen, and later as a means of exorcising her by simulated punishment. Jen is a portrait of questions as complex as identity itself. Her portraits invert the customary direction of the gaze in migration fictions, in which it is the migrant who looks back at those at home through the lenses of memory. If the judgement of this deserting mother is harsh, the harshness is mediated by the field of open questions and by Sunshine's dreams which raise the possibility, among others, that Jen suffers from an inability to negotiate the alien, patriarchal migratory space. The dreams are in themselves a major source of mystery and paradox, as they combine subconscious longing with surreal intimation and revelatory truth, and as they invent Sunshine as much as they invent Aunt Jen.

Caribbean literature, theory and criticism valorise speech and denigrate silence in traditional discourses of identity and counter-colonial politics. In *Aunt Jen*, Ramsay joins Marlene Nourbese Phillip (*Looking for Livingstone*) in a provocative reflection on the paradoxes of silence in ways that allow silence to be a site of positive enabling. Ramsay's treatment brings to the fore other muted aspects of Caribbean experience: that mothers as well as fathers are sometimes wilfully silent and absent; and conversely, that the rural Caribbean experience is full of examples of father figures (Gramps, Uncle Roy, Uncle Johnny) who are positively involved in children's lives. *Aunt Jen* finds resonance with other recent West Indian women's fictions (of Brodber, Senior, Collins) that traverse the Caribbean language continuum, consummately blending English with Creoles and vernaculars. Language maps and celebrates the multiple voices of the community and charts Sunshine's maturation as she moves from a proper toeing of the English line in the early letters (no doubt she has been taught letter writing in school), to an increasing use of the Creole as she grows older and finds her own voice as person and as writer.

Aunt Jen is a delightful read.

Curdella Forbes

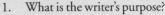

CRITICAL THINKING AND WRITING

1. What is the writer's purpose?
2. Identify the conclusion and grounds for the argument in the first two sentences.
3. '*Aunt Jen* is a delightful read.' What type of claim is this? Identify other types of claims in the piece.
4. Does the writer present or acknowledge any opposing views?
   a) What does this suggest about the strength of her argument?
   b) How does the context explain the absence of opposing views?
5. How does the last paragraph help the writer to achieve her purpose?
6. To what extent is this piece convincing?

WRITING ACROSS THE CURRICULUM ACTIVITIES

7. In this passage Curdella Forbes writes about Ramsay's exploration of migration and its effects on a young child.
   a) What are some of the effects that you have noticed that the migration of their parents has had on children in your society?
   b) Write a short paragraph directed at your peers explaining some of the challenges children face.
   c) Rewrite this piece for one of your college instructors. Did you make any changes in style, tone, diction, etc?
8. Forbes states that '*Aunt Jen* is a subtle exploration of the issues of migration, exile and diaspora from a point of intersection between Caribbean migration in the early days and the present.' Do some informal research about the African Diaspora on the world wide web.
9. Were your sources credible? How did you decide on the credibility of your sources?

CHAPTER 44

ON REGGAE AND RASTAFARIANISM – AND A GARVEY PROPHECY

The time was October, 1986; the place Brisbane, Queensland — an Australian state whose political conservatism and backwardness are a source of despair and incomprehension to most other states of a country that works hard, if at times a little naively, at being one of the Commonwealth's more liberal and tolerant nations.

I was walking over the bridge that connects the new multimillion-dollar cultural centre to the city of Brisbane proper and was feeling depressed, having just left the art gallery after searching in vain for even one aboriginal painting. Three-quarters of the way across, my eye was suddenly caught by a lone graffitto, a proclamation in black despoiling the pristine whiteness of the bridge: BOB MARLEY. I stopped dead in my tracks — and all of a sudden found that I was smiling, my depression momentarily gone. What price JA! (Marcus Garvey would have approved, too).

The influence of reggae spreads far wider than America or Europe. It has become a political weapon of racial isolates such as the Australian aborigine and of countless others of the world's dispossessed.

Michael Manley in his introduction to *Reggae International* — the most comprehensive and best researched book on reggae to appear to date — draws attention to the revolutionary nature of the Jamaican art form as compared to calypso and blues, and its acceptance as part of international culture despite the competition of 'the bromides and anodynes' of synthetic escape music which exist at the other end of the popular music spectrum. He hazards the guess that its success owes much to the originality of Bob Marley whose gifts helped it to gain international acceptance; but, he says,

it must also be true that the protest of reggae, *the positive assertion of moral categories* [my emphasis] goes beyond parochial boundaries. Among other things reggae is the spontaneous sound of a local revolutionary impulse. But revolution itself is a universal category. It is this, possibly, which sets reggae apart, even to the international ear. (Manley 1983)

Reggae and Rastafarianism

The source of this revolutionary impulse of which Manley speaks was undoubtedly Rastafarianism which had grown out of, and was continuously renewed by, the teachings of Marcus Garvey. The relationship between the two has been thoroughly expounded by Smith et al. (1960), Barrett (1977) and others and need not be gone over here. It is my assertion that the doctrine of Rastafarianism and the militant black consciousness of Garveyism would never have spread with the rapidity they have done, both here and in other parts of the world, were it not for reggae and the African-American musical tradition.

However, it has been the custom of most writers on reggae (especially non-musicians) to approach the lyrics and the music as if they originated from the same source and constituted an organic whole. The belief has grown up that reggae and Rasta are one. This is not exactly true.

Let me say from the outset that what follows here is in no way intended to detract from the contribution of Rastafarianism to reggae. It is merely intended to clarify certain unexamined assumptions which keep being repeated in order to emphasize the Rastafarian aspect of the form. That aspect needs no special pleading. Its record, as far as lyrics and performers are concerned, is unassailable.

When we listen to and analyse reggae, we find that, musically, it owes less to Rasta than to rhythm-and-blues, overlaid with indigenous elements such as mento and Pocomania and to the genius of certain individuals, particularly drummers and bass guitarists who set down patterns that others imitated to the point where they became entrenched traditions.

Nyabingi, the authentic Rastafarian music which, as Kenneth Bilby and Elliot Leib recently pointed out (1987), is most likely derived from Kumina as well as Buru, is based on the use of bass drum, funde and repeater. It is an 'inward-directed' religious music with a rhythm pattern quite different and distinct from that of reggae. And according to Yoshiko Nagashima's researches, orthodox Rastafarians 'even look down upon the reggae beats which show the **mixed** influence (hence 'impure' to Bynghi-oriented . . . Rastafarians) such as the spiritual Gospel, mento and revival songs ...' (Nagashima 1984, p.181).

Musically there is also a clear line of demarcation between the R & B-derived popular tradition that is reggae and the Rastafarian secular tradition, typified by groups such as Light of Saba, which is rooted in drumming, instrumental improvisation, group singing, dance and the conscious incorporation of 'Africanisms'. In Jamaica it has never attracted the numbers of adherents that reggae has.

This is not to say that Rastafarian rhythm patterns are not used in reggae. Occasionally the funde and repeater are added to the percussion section, or Rastafarian rhythm patterns will be utilized by the traps player or bass or rhythm guitarist, but these will be exceptional rather than customary. Reggae is an extremely traditional music that has been content to use a few basic rhythmic constructions. It does not lend itself to experimentation, except in the hands of exceptional groups such as Third World, who have the technical mastery and the solid international reputation that allow for innovation.

Among musicologists, nowadays, some clarity is beginning to emerge from the obfuscation which has been poured out by writers who take a mainly sociological or ideological approach to the Jamaican popular music tradition. Ska is now recognized as a regional variant of abroad U.S. style, namely, rhythm-and-blues, in which the shuffle rhythm is exaggerated by placing greater weight and a heavier instrumental texture on the up-beat. (Witmer, 1977, pp.105–13)

As for rock steady and reggae, we find that the instrumentation (lead, rhythm and bass guitar, drum set, keyboard and solo voice with vocal backing and optional reed and brass instruments) is exactly the same as that found in North American pop rock of the late 1950s and early 1960s. And many other features such as multiple ostinati patterns, the doubling of the bass guitar by the electric guitar one octave higher, the peculiarly playful vocal timbre and the use of call and response structures are all to be found in African-American music of the late sixties and early seventies.

A French musicologist, Denis Constant Martin, recently observed in a study on reggae (1983), that Rasta owes more to reggae than reggae owes to Rasta. It is an observation that invites careful consideration by all scholars of Jamaican music.

It is ironic that the Rastafarian message should have been proclaimed by means of lyrics superimposed on a fundamentally Afro-American commercial form transformed into a Jamaican one largely through the addition of traditional features derived from mento and Revival, both of which were rejected by Rastafari.

It is equally ironic that, without the electronic media and the pop music industry, Garvey's message might have been confined largely to intellectual circles and their comparatively limited range of influence. In the space of ten or twelve years, more has been done for Rastafarianism and Garveyism than would have been previously possible in a century if they had been dependent primarily on books or even on the spoken word. Manley also brings out this point in the article previously cited.

Once more, we return to the realization that there is no more powerful communicator of messages than music. The pen may be mightier than the sword, but music is a hell of a lot mightier! Because it is oral and rhythmic and has an instant impact, it tends to pass language barriers with consummate ease; when it is transmitted by means of the electronic media to all corners of the globe, it becomes an irresistible force.

Thus, Garvey's message of black pride and hope for the dispossessed as articulated by Jamaica's Rastafari has reached the ears of millions who might otherwise never have come in contact with either concept. Garvey's time has come, thanks to black American music, Jamaican reggae music, Rastafarian ideology and Western technology. The last named constitutes the greatest irony of all, for it is Western technology that is helping to bring one of Garvey's main prophecies to inevitable fulfilment.

> The power and sway we once held passed away, but now in the Twentieth Century we are about to see the return of it in the rebuilding of Africa; yes, a new civilization, a new culture shall spring from among our people, and the Nile shall once more flow through the land of science, of art, and of literature, wherein will live black men of the highest accomplishments. (Garvey, 1967 p.34)

When Garvey refers here to Africa, it is less likely that he is referring to a geographical location than to a civilization that, in its new form, will have worldwide influence. It is largely music that is responsible for preparing the way for that new culture whose effect will be felt almost on a global scale.

African-American Music

Anyone who is alert to musical developments worldwide must realize that African-American music is about to take the pre-eminent position which European music once held. It can be observed on a macrocosmic level (the number of countries — even Communist ones — where African-American music has not penetrated are the exception rather than the rule) and on a microcosmic level: in most societies where African-American music is present, it soon becomes the music most listened to by the greatest number of people.

Is there a reason for this?

I feel that there is. From the time when Western beliefs presided over the dissolution of the ancient unity of music, song and dance — a destruction that was initiated by the early Christian church — and when the Western scientific world view adopted the Cartesian separation of body, mind and spirit, there has nevertheless developed a concomitant and growing need for a return to human wholeness, unity and communality, especially in urban societies.

This is a need that the purest black culture has always satisfied. In religion, education, healing, the arts, the unity has always remained. But of all black culture, especially that in the New World, black music is the artistic manifestation that has remained most intact. Throughout the diaspora it has preserved its essential unity, even when it has mixed with white culture — its syncopations and rhythmic drive continuously urging the body to assert itself and move, its compositional patterns and social mores continuously urging a communal sharing that has been lost in Western urban civilization. Its inherent approach to time as a circular rather than a linear element denies the Western search for goals which is termed 'progress' and subconsciously asserts the importance of time in action over action in time. The message has already been picked up and understood, either consciously or subconsciously, by those who have suffered most from the dehumanizing effects of goal-oriented societies hellbent on 'progress'.

No changes occur suddenly. They are always preceded by a long period of preparation and gestation. For years, black music has been preparing — and continues to prepare — the way for the acceptance of black culture, black attitudes, a different worldview.

One cannot help feeling that, if Garvey were alive today, he would look on this amazing modern phenomenon and recognize it as the manifestation of a prophecy reaching fulfilment.

Surely that great new civilization of which he spoke will come from this hemisphere where the African slave was brought forcibly centuries ago and where he has become a cultural catalyst and a cultural leader with all the potential of changing the face of the world.

Pamela O'Gorman

References

Barrett, Leonard. *The Rastafarians*. London: Heinemann/Sangster. 1977.

Bilby, Kenneth and Elliot Leib. 'Kumina, the Howellite Church, and the Emergence of Rastafari Traditional Music in Jamaica'. *Jamaica Journal* 19:3. 1986.

Garvey, A.J., ed. *Philosophy and Opinions of* Marcus Garvey, 2nd ed. London: Frank Cass and Co. Ltd., 1967.

Manley, Michael. 'Reggae, the Revolutionary Impulse', Introduction to Stephen Davis and Peter Simon (eds.), *Reggae International*. London: Thames and Hudson. 1993.

Martin, Denis Constant. *Aux Sources du Reggae*. Paris: Editions Parentheses. 1983.

Nagashima, Yoshiko S. *Rastafarian Music in Contemporary Jamaica*, Tokyo: Institute for the Study of Languages and Cultures of Asia and Africa.

Smith, M.G., Roy Augier and Rex Nettleford. *Report on the Rastafari Movement in Kingston, Jamaica*. Mona: University of the West Indies. 1960.

Witmer, Robert, 'African Roots: The Case of Recent Jamaican Popular Music', Proceedings of the Twelfth Congress of the International Musicological Society: Berkley, California, 1977.

CRITICAL THINKING AND WRITING

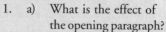

1. a) What is the effect of the opening paragraph?
    b) Why do you think O'Gorman began in this way?
    c) For what context do you think she was writing?
2. a) What is the writer's purpose?
    b) What is her thesis?
3. Is the writer fair in her treatment of the contribution of Rastafarianism to reggae? Explain, citing examples from the text.
4. The writer claims that *Reggae International* is the 'most comprehensive and best researched book on reggae to date'.
    a) What type of claim is this?
    b) Does she attempt to substantiate this claim? If so, how?
5. To what extent do you consider the writer to be credible? Justify your answer.

WRITING ACTIVITIES

6. Vocabulary building. Use each of the following words in a sentence. (Write a separate sentence for each word). If you do not know the meaning of the word or are not familiar with its usage, look it up in a dictionary.
    a) Obfuscation
    b) Musicologist(s)
    c) Macrocosmic
    d) Microcosmic
    e) Syncopations
    f) Mores
7. a) Formulate a claim about a Caribbean music form. State the type of claim (fact, cause, and so on).
    b) Develop a paragraph in which you support your claim. State clearly the type of argument (analogy, syllogism, and so on) that is being used.

Chapter 45

'Dutty Wine'

Tanisha Henry died last week. She had been at what I understand is called a 'school uniform' party in St. Catherine, and had participated in a 'Dutty Wine' competition. The newspapers report that while taking part in this activity, she fell, was hurriedly taken to hospital, and was pronounced dead.

The tragic circumstances of Ms Henry's death, at age 18, have prompted much grief. The circumstances have also prompted concern, for it is argued that the Dutty Wine dance was the cause of her death. Against that background, some persons have publicly called for the banning of Dutty Wine, while others have said that Dutty Wine contests should be prohibited by the Government.

Understandable

The sentiment behind the pro-banning perspective is perfectly understandable. From what I have seen on television, the Dutty Wine is a vigorous, strenuous, whirlwind of a dance, in which the head and other parts of the body are subjected to extraordinary contortions. To the untrained eye, this is something that could well cause bodily harm. I note, though, that two medical experts have expressed divergent views on whether the Dutty Wine could possibly have prompted Ms Henry's death, and autopsy results are reported by the *Gleaner* to have been inconclusive.

Should Dutty Wine be banned? First of all, there needs to be some care in assessing cause and effect. A man jogs briskly down the street, collapses and dies. There may be a sense in which the jogging may be said to have caused his death, but this, by itself, would be a far too simplistic conclusion. And the mere fact that the death followed the brisk jog does not mean that the jogging had anything to do with his death: *post hoc ergo propter hoc* is not really helpful in this case.

So then, before we join the calls for banning Dutty Wine or Dutty Wine contests, we would need to be sure that there is a causal connection between death and the dance. Now, supposing for argument's sake, that this way of moving the body really can produce death or serious bodily harm, should it be banned?

Expression

Dancing is a form of expression. And the state should be slow to ban forms of expression. In fact, without being too legalistic on the point, the Constitution says that everyone is entitled to freedom of expression, a form of words that suggests, on the face of things, that I should be left alone to Dutty Wine all I want. But the Constitution also goes further: it allows the state to circumscribe my freedom of expression if, for instance, this is reasonably required 'in the interest of defence, public safety, public order, public morality or public health' or to regulate 'public entertainments'.

The question, then, is whether any of these grounds for restriction would apply in the case of the Dutty Wine. Obviously this dance gives rise to no questions of defence or public safety, and I rather suspect that in most cases, a Dutty Wine will not undermine public order. But what about public morality? This is a tricky category, not least because your general approach to the morality of 'wining up' yourself may well change as you grow older.

The best possibilities, therefore, would be for the dance to be banned as a threat to public health, or as a means of regulating public entertainment. But even these categories are not without problems. On public health, go back to my cause and effect point, for we are not sure how dangerous Dutty Wine may be to the body. And can we really argue that the over-enthusiastic head-spinning in Dutty Wine is inherently more damaging to health than heading a tough football towards the goal, or participating in a regulated boxing fight? As to public entertainment, we should note that this would not allow the banning of Dutty Wine *per se*, but it might allow a ban on Dutty Wine contests.

But, you know, even if the law could be used to ban the dance or the contests, I have mixed feelings. The state should be reluctant to interfere with individual, personal activity, and should only do so where this activity is unquestionably harmful to others or to the society. I would need to know more about the real medical effects of Dutty Wine before I could support a state ban. But, in the meantime, I would discourage those around me from Dutty Wining.

Stephen Vasciannie

CRITICAL THINKING AND WRITING

1. What is the issue being debated in this article?
2. What is the writer's stance? What justification does he provide for his position?
3. To what extent does the writer acknowledge or address opposing views?
4. What argument structure does the writer employ to organise this article?
5. The writer mentions '*post hoc ergo propter hoc*'. What is the meaning of this expression, and what is its relevance to the context?
6. Where does the burden of proof lie?
7. What is the warrant on which Vasciannie bases his position?
8. In paragraph 6, Vasciannie argues that 'Dancing is a form of expression. And the state should be slow to ban forms of expression.'
   a) What conclusion does he expect you to draw from this paragraph?
   b) What criteria would you use to judge the validity and soundness of this argument?
   c) Explain why you would consider this argument to be sound or unsound.

WRITING ACROSS THE CURRICULUM ACTIVITIES

9. Write a brief response (no more than 200 words) to Professor Vasciannie's article which could be submitted to the same newspaper for publication as a follow up article. You may choose to agree or to disagree with him.
10. Write an introduction and a conclusion for an essay in which you support or oppose the claim that 'The state should not legislate against any form of entertainment carried out on private property'.

CHAPTER 46

VILE VOCALS

The hue and cry raised in the Barbadian media in response to an April 2000 Caribbean Broadcasting Union (CBU) *Talk Caribbean* television programme on Jamaican dancehall/dub lyrics is an excellent example of the hysteria that frank discussion of popular culture often provokes. Especially when the cultural product is exported and, in the process, stripped of its 1ayers of indigenous meaning, it becomes subject to much misinterpretation in its new context of appropriation. The public outcry in Barbados against dancehall music and its articulate apologists noisily demands censorship of the 'muck, the raw incitement to rebellion and violence which loom large on the "dub" menu.' Mixed metaphor aside, this quote from the *Barbados Advocate* editorial of April 11, 2000, denotes the purist construction of national identity in elitist Barbadian discourses. 'Barbados' is conceived immaculately; 'Jamaica' is synonymous with sin.

The contemptuous headline of the editorial, 'Vile Vocals', and its combative subtitle, 'Unofficial War in Bim', are an aggressive declaration of intent to defend Barbadian hegemony against the encroachments of Jamaican culture in its many treacherous forms. Indeed, 'Vile Vocals' refers not only to the 'impure' content of the lyrics,

but also to the moral depravity of the 'bastardized' Jamaican Creole language in which the villainous vocals are voiced. Any attempt to encourage Barbadians to learn Jamaican so that they can be sure of the meaning of lyrics they are condemning is itself misconstrued as an immoral act.

This impassioned editorial exemplifies the irrationality that undermines much of the public discourse on Jamaican 'dub' music in Barbados today. Beginning with an attack on the Creole language in the United States – a language that is indeed related to Jamaican Creole – the plantocratic editorial asserts that acknowledging the intrinsic worth of Creole languages as useful is an acceptance of the 'supposed intellectual inferiority' of their habitual speakers. In Jamaica one hears this reductionist argument all the time. One of its most disdainful exponents was Morris Cargill, the senior columnist of Jamaica's centuries-old newspaper, the *Gleaner*, who died in 2000. Cargill was notorious for his attacks on Jamaican Creole, which he scornfully termed 'yahoolish.' Listen to his dog, who ostensibly wrote a column for him that was published on February 25, 1999:

> one of the aims of my society is to develop a proper understanding of dog language. If people can propose that what my man calls yahoolish should become a second

language in Jamaica I see no reason why poodlese should not become a third one. It is, after all, at least as understandable.

The *Talk Caribbean* programme clearly illustrates a Barbadian failure to understand the preferred language of Jamaican dancehall lyrics. One of the panelists on the programme, David Ellis, an upstanding broadcaster at the Starcom Network News radio station in Barbados, defines dancehall lyrics as essentially unintelligible, especially to older ears. The base beat becomes the sole signifier:

> It is a music with a reggae base whose lyrical content is very difficult to understand. I think many people sum it up that way. And that's the challenge that many people in the Caribbean have with it. Older people just do not understand the lyrics. And it is in that environment that some younger people exploit the ignorance.

I agree with Ellis that age is a key variable in determining the intelligibility of dancehall lyrics – in Jamaica as much as elsewhere in the Caribbean. Dancehall is, essentially, a youth music. And the youths who chant verbatim in tune with the performances of their favourite superstars celebrate communal rituals of mutual understanding. But other factors must be taken into account in explaining why dancehall's 'lyrical content' is so difficult for some listeners, many of whom would even deny that there is any 'content' in the lyrics. An immediate obscurity arises: the audience's incompetence in the Jamaican Creole language. Then there are the limitations of (un)intelligibility that class arrogance imposes. And there are the prejudices that intolerant religious passion aggravates.

Despite Ellis's disclaimer, he nevertheless proceeds from a position of near-total adult ignorance to vilify lyrics that he obviously does not understand. For example, condemning Mr. Vegas's 'She's a Ho' because of its vulgar use of the earthy, African-Americanized Anglo-Saxon word 'whore', Ellis fails to hear the DJ's strident critique of prostitution. Incidentally, like many a whore, the word 'whore' itself has gone down in life. The *Oxford English Dictionary (OED)* gives its etymology as the Latin 'carus', meaning 'dear'. And it is true that many dearly beloved whores, especially at the top end of the market, are very dear indeed. The dictionary notes that 'whore is now confined to coarse and abusive speech, exc[ept] in occasional echoes of historical expression, as the whore of Babylon.' Polite society prefers the latinate 'prostitute', 'Pro + statuere to cause to stand.' In these feminist times, even prostitute is no longer politically correct; the preferred term is the gender-neutral 'sex worker', an occupation that is no less precarious for the euphemism.

The exporting of Jamaican dancehall lyrics to Barbados and the wider eastern Caribbean reveals the problematic cultural politics of national identity in the so-called Anglophone Caribbean – despite the best efforts of CARICOM to consolidate an updated 'federal' politics. Contesting the viability of regional definitions of cultural identity, conservative nationalist discourses are asserting themselves with renewed authority. The censorious, purist rhetoric of the *Advocate's* editorials and the surprising xenophobia of Curwen Best's declaration that Jamaican dancehall music is the quintessential Caribbean music of death exemplify this disturbing trend. Gordon Rohlehr's dismissal of both rap and Jamaican dancehall music as 'songs of the skeleton' is also troubling. Furthermore, as local cultures in the Caribbean and elsewhere respond to the homogenizing imperative of the globalization epidemic, they are tempted to assert cultural autonomy as a self-protective vaccine. But whereas the elite in Barbados, for example, are terrified of the invasive 'Trojan horse of a counter-culture' from Jamaica, the masses of the region's youths, both at home and in the Caribbean diaspora, embrace Jamaican dancehall music and its language as a celebratory discourse, asserting a shared identity of cultural affiliation.

Carolyn Cooper

CRITICAL THINKING AND WRITING TASKS

1. In 1-2 sentences, state Cooper's main purpose in writing this article.
2. Identify the central idea/thesis/major claim.
3. Analyse Cooper's argument by answering the following questions:
   a. What is she opposing?
   b. What do you think is the main reason for her opposition?
   c. Cite two reasons that she presents in support of her argument.
   d. Underline the sections in which she acknowledges points that are not in support of her own argument. Discuss how she handles these.
4. How does Cooper attempt to establish common ground with her audience?
5. Identify the type of argument used in the last sentence of the third paragraph ("If people can propose...understandable"), and
   a. state the conclusion and the grounds
   b. analyse its soundness.
6. Does Cooper provide satisfactory evidence in support of her claims? Justify your answer by referring to the text.
7. What types of appeals does the writer make?

WRITING ACTIVITY

8. Write one of each of the following types of claims relating to the issue under discussion:
   a. Policy
   b. Fact
   c. Cause
   d. Definition

CHAPTER 47

MIGRATION AND REMITTANCES: A CASE STUDY OF THE CARIBBEAN

The issue of remittances arises only because there was a prior decision to migrate, thus, the analysis of remittances cannot be divorced from an analysis of the factors which motivate migration. It is this analysis of migration that provides part of the rationale for fixed remittances. This brief section of the paper cannot do justice to the multi-faceted issue of migration and its motivating factors. Thus, rather than focus on the factors which determine migration for its own sake, this section of the paper would examine the influence of the motivating factors on the decision to remit.

In spite of the voluminous literature on migration and the importance of remittances to many developing countries, there are very few attempts to develop a systematic theory of remittances. The Seminal works of Lucas and Stark (1985) and Stark (1991) are notable exceptions. Lucas and Stark (1985) divide theories of remittances into three groups, that is, Pure Altruism, Pure Self-interest and Tempered Altruism or Enlightened Self-interest.

In the Pure Altruism model, the migrant derives utility from the utility of the rest of her household in the country of origin. The utility of the household depends on its per capita consumption. The migrant's utility function depends on her own consumption and on the weighted utility of the rest of the household in the country of origin. The migrant's utility function depends on her own consumption and on the weighted utility of the rest of the household in the country of origin. The migrant chooses the level of remittances that maximizes her utility function. This model yields two testable hypotheses, (1) remittances increase with the migrant's wage level; and (2) remittances decrease with the level of income of the household (that is, remittances to less well-off households would be higher). The impact of household size on the level of remittances can be either positive or negative depending on presence of economies or diseconomies of scale in consumption, the rate of decline in marginal utility of home consumption and whether the migrant has a preference for a subset of the household in the home country.

Pure self-interest generates three motives for remittances. The first arises from the belief that if she takes care of the family a larger portion of the family wealth would be bequeathed to her. This motive predicts that the larger the remittances, the larger the potential inheritance. The second motive is to build up assets at home such as land, houses and livestock, which would necessitate that a family member act as an agent to purchase the assets and maintain them in good condition. The third motive may arise from an intent to return home at a later stage which would require investment in fixed assets, in a business or in community projects if the migrant has political aspirations. The last objective illustrates the difficulty of separating altruistic and self-interest motives.

Neither of the two theories above is sufficient to explain the extent and variability of remittances. Thus Lucas and Stark developed a theory that views remittances as part of an inter-temporal, mutually beneficial contractual arrangement between the migrant and the household in the country of origin. Such contractual arrangements are based on investment and risk. In the case of investment the family bears the cost of educating the migrant worker who is expected to repay the investment in the form of remittances. This motive not only predicts that remittances could be higher for more educated workers but also that remittances from children of the head of the household would be higher than from in-laws and even spouses.

The risk motive gives rise to a much richer theoretical analysis which utilizes portfolio investment theory. In most developing countries both financial markets and insurance markets are not well developed. In addition, income, especially agricultural income, is subject to a significant variability due to natural disasters, hurricanes, droughts et cetera. In these circumstances the decision to migrate is a rational decision to reduce risk by diversifying the household's stock of human wealth over activity and space. Provided that the shocks that affect the host country and the country of origin are not highly correlated positively, it would be mutually beneficial for the migrant and her family to enter a co-insurance contract. The migrant would remit relatively more when the home country is beset by natural disasters and similarly the family would take care of her obligations at home or even make transfers to the migrant if she becomes temporarily unemployed.

Such contractual arrangements are voluntary and hence, must be self-enforcing. The mechanism for self-enforcement could be mutual altruism, which explains why such arrangements are usually struck between members of a household. The aspiration to inherit, the desire to return home and the need to have reliable agents to assist in the accumulation and maintenance of assets are additional considerations for self-enforcement.

A number of well documented observations about migration and remittances can be explained by this theory of Enlightened Altruism. These include:

The Structure and Performance of the Economy

(i) A high ratio of Agriculture to GDP is associated with higher rates of migration. Agricultural income is more variable and hence the greater need for co-insurance;

(ii) The decline of an industry induces higher migration since income prospects in the home country would decline, hence the need for spatial diversification;

(iii) Economic downturn in the host country reduces the flow of remittances (insurance payments), but this may be moderated by drawing down the stock of accumulated wealth;

(iv) Natural disasters in the country of origin induce a larger flow of remittances. This is also predicted by pure altruism but enlightened self-interest would predict that such flows would be higher for households with more assets.

Education

(i) Migration would be higher among the more educated members of the household, not only would their job opportunities and income prospects be greater, they represent the stock of human capital which is part of the policy of diversification;

(ii) The level of remittances from the more educated is greater, not only because their earning would be higher, but also because the remittances represent higher implicit loan repayments to the family, which has invested in their education.

Wendell Samuel

References

Bascom, W. 1990. *Remittances Inflows and economic development in Selected Anglophone Caribbean Countries.* Working Paper No. 58 of the Commission for the Study of International Migration and Cooperative Economic Development, Washington D.C.

Central Bank of Barbados. *Barbados Balance of Payments 1994.* Barbados.

Chaderton, and W. Samuel .2000. 'Return Migration and Implication for Public Policy in St. Kitts-Nevis'. Paper prepared for ECLAC (Port of Spain).

Eastern Caribbean Central Bank. 1995. *Balance of Payments.* Saint Kitts.

Guengant, J. 1993. "Wither The Caribbean Exodus: Prospects for the 1990's". *International Journal,* Vol. XLVIII, Spring, : 336–53.

Henry, R. 1990. 'A Reinterpretation of Labour Services of the Commonwealth Caribbean'. Working Paper No. 61 of the Commission for the Study of International Migration and Cooperative Economic Development, Washington D.C.

International Monetary Fund. 1995. *Balance of Payments Compilation Guide.* Washington D.C.

International Monetary Fund. 1995. *Balance of Payments Statistics* Yearbook. Washington D.C.

Lucas, R.E., and O. Stark. 1985. 'Motivations to Remit: Evidence from Botswana'. *Journal of Political Economy,* Vol. 93, no. 5: 901–18.

Simmons, A.B. and J. Guengant. 1992. 'Recent Migration Within the Caribbean: Migrant Origins, Destinations and Economic Roles'. In *The Peopling of the Americas,* Veracruz, 419–41.

Stark, O. 1991. 'Migration in LDC's: Risk, Remittances, and the Family'. *Finance and Development,* Vol. 28, no.4 (December): 41–4.

Stark, O., J.E. Taylor and S. Yitzhaki. 1988. 'Migration, Remittances, and Inequality: A Sensitivity analysis Using the Extended Gini Index'. *Journal of Development Economics,* Vol. 28: 309–22.

Wahba, S. 1991. 'What Determines Workers Remittances?' *Finance and development,* Vol.28, no.4 (December): 41–4.

CRITICAL THINKING AND WRITING

1. You have recently migrated to the United States, acquired a job and have started sending a large portion of your salary to your family in Jamaica (you may choose another Caribbean country). Your friend (in Jamaica/other Caribbean country) is however very concerned about the level of your remittances. Write a 300 word letter in which you explain your motives which are based on the *Pure Self Interest Model* outlined in the article.

2. Your twelve year old niece is upset that the level of remittances normally sent by her mother from Canada has been drastically reduced. Explain to her why this is so, using the *Pure Altruism Model* as a reference point.

SECTION 3
MIXED MODES

CHAPTER 48

—— ◈ ——

THE MANIFESTATION OF TAWHID: THE MUSLIM HERITAGE OF THE MAROONS IN JAMAICA

Introduction

The process of *reconquista* in Spain ended with the final conquest of the last Muslim possession, Granada in 1492, as Columbus with his Andalusian mariners embarked on his adventures in the Atlantic. While Christian demands for religious homogeneity led to the forceful conversion or exile of the Muslim population from Spain, the natives in the West Indies perished in millions, due to diseases and 'cruelties more atrocious and unnatural than any recorded of untutored and savage barbarians'.[1] Black slaves brought from Spain's house of Muslim captives to work in the mines and in the production of sugar died as rapidly as the Indians, but as they continued to be replenished from Spain many resorted to Jihad, or holy wars, against the indignity of slavery. A common resistance to the slave system, and one which was perhaps the most vexing to the owners, was the flight from servitude to establish their own communities based on their tradition and culture in inhospitable and inaccessible areas. They became the *cimarrones*, or the Maroons and Maroon communities, also called *Quilombos*, in Brazil became a common feature in the New World plantation economy. *Marronage* initiated by the Spanish Maroons became the nucleus of the Maroon society in Jamaica under the British.

The presence of Maroon societies in the New World plantation economy is well documented. The history of the Maroons constitutes an important aspect of the historical study of Jamaica particularly because of the British recognition of their societies as separate entities beyond the jurisdiction of the British colonial government and their continuance into the present. However, there is much misinformation, misconception and misrepresentation regarding Jamaican Maroons. The Islamic heritage of the Maroons has not been studied, despite all the indications that Blacks directly brought to the West Indies from Spain were of Moorish background who were believed by the Spanish Government to be facilitating marronage.[2] Evidently, many African slaves who subsequently joined the Spanish Maroons also professed the Islamic faith, as they came from West Africa and the Sub-

Saharan region which saw the rapid spread of Islam from as early as the tenth and eleventh centuries. Between the tenth and the eighteenth centuries, a succession of Sudanic Kingdoms — Ghana, Mali, Kanem, Songhay, Hausaland and Dogomba — were organized under the banner of Islam, incorporating Madinka, Fula, Susu, Ashanti, Hausa and other nations. The present paper attempts to focus on the Islamic heritage of the Maroons and examines the political and social structures from an Islamic perspective.

The omission regarding the Muslim background of the Maroons, like the misrepresentations, may be due to several factors. Historians are handicapped by the absence of written documents by the historical Maroons. The imperative of secrecy to maintain their strategy, and their marronage perhaps, precluded written history and hence restricted knowledge of their perceived goals, their religious beliefs, their social and cultural traditions and their economic and political structures. The uncertainty which historians encounter regarding the ethnic background and the faith of the historical Maroons was in all probability due to the deliberate intention to maintain secrecy regarding the Islamic belief. The Muslim Blacks knew too well the wrath of Christendom's Europe towards Islam. Spanish Islamic people had been sold into slavery since the thirteenth century as Christian Spain began to reconquer its lost possessions from the Muslims. In addition, the hatred of the crusaders was fresh in the memories, particularly of those who came from the Iberian peninsula. Many African Muslim slaves who subsequently joined the Spanish Maroons had experienced similar or worse experiences in the hands of the Christian slave traders or the Christian plantocracy, aided and abetted by the established Christian Churches.

The absence of any written history by the Maroons has led researchers to rely on official documents, eyewitnesses' accounts and on planter historians. With the then prevalent mentality, almost all were biased and written from their ethnocentricity and coloured by their economic interests. Hence, the official documents and the histories are corrupt, inaccurate, inconsistent and unreliable for the proper reconstruction of Maroon history in Jamaica, without which the history of Jamaica remains incomplete.

Although the etymology of the word 'Maroon' is uncertain — *Marron* to the French — it is a generic term used to designate fugitive slaves from plantations in the New World. It is commonly accepted that it comes from the Spanish *marran*, a sow or young hog. Initially, the hunters of wild hogs were called marrans, distinguishing them from the buccaneers, who hunted wild cattle and horses.[3] Consensus opinion seem to suggest the view that it derives from the Spanish word *cimarrón*, which originally referred to domestic cattle that had escaped to the wilderness. Subsequently, the term is used almost exclusively to embrace runaway slaves. 'Cimarron' and its derivative, 'Maroon', seem to be peculiarly New World terms when applied to runaway slaves. In other words, Maroons according to the established authorities are no less than domesticated animals or wild hogs.

Moors in the West Indies

The extensive colonial possessions of Spain created an elusive and exaggerated notion of the Spanish empire as a source of wealth and as a market for goods and slaves among the European slave traders — Portuguese, Dutch, English and French. Spain in the West Indies did not need and could not afford to buy slaves in the sixteenth and the seventeenth centuries. Spain had just regained her sovereign rights after almost eight centuries of Islamic rule. The massive displacement of population as a result of the forceful expulsion of the Moors imposed upon the Spanish government a labour of resettlement, which stretched manpower resources to the limit. Moorish Andalusia had to be colonized as well as the areas which were previously uninhabited. The policy of forceful expulsion or exile of the Moors at a time when manpower was limited worked in favour of the Spanish government. Evidently, the export of Moorish captives to foreign slave markets increased.[4] Although it is not precisely clear regarding the specific foreign markets, the destination of the Moorish captives was the newly acquired empire in the New World. Since Spain was not involved in the Atlantic slave trade, one of the policies of the four slave-trading powers was to secure a share or a monopoly in the supply of slaves to the Spanish colonies. Hence, Spain could not have been exporting its own Moorish or Black slaves to any foreign markets other than its own colonies, where the need for labour was so acute. The Spanish slave trade to the West Indies was thus initiated not from West Africa, but from Spain by the King of Spain on September 3, 1503.[5]

Jamaica was one of the final destinations for many of these Moorish captives who are referred to as Black slaves from Spain. The exporting of such Moorish captives contradicted the directives of the Spanish Crown which did not consent to the immigration of Moors, heretics, Jews, re-converts or new converts to Christianity.[6] Black slaves born within the power of Spaniards were allowed to be exported, but under the circumstances of the time, Christian Black slaves in Spain were inadequate to meet the demand. Also, many who had accepted Christianity became crypto-Muslims and tried to reconcile the secret practice of Islam with the outward profession of Christianity.[7] To be a crypto-Muslim became a common characteristic even among the African Muslim slaves who were forcefully baptized by the slave owners on the plantations.[8] Besides Moorish captives who came to Jamaica and elsewhere in the New World as slaves, Moors from Spain were also included in the voyages of discovery and conquest.[9]

The Spirit of Marronage

Given the background of the Moors, who were not only once conquerors, establishing empires over three continents, but were also culturally enlightened people, resistance to subordination or subjugation in various forms by them became a common feature in the New World. Evidently, no sooner had they set their feet in the West Indies than they fought unceasingly for their freedom. The unspoiled Virgin islands in the Caribbean were to be the grounds of resistance and freedom for many of these proud Moors through whom Europe acquired the techniques to reign over the contemporary world. Many resorted to running away to the hills and forests, as they correctly perceived that the islands were largely unknown to their masters. Hence, they had little to fear from immediate repercussions. Within two years of the initiation of the Black slave trade from Spain to the West Indies, it had to be temporarily suspended on the ground that the Blacks ran away and made common cause with the Indians.[10] In 1521, the Spanish government tried to contain marronage by prohibiting the inclusion of Moors in the voyages of discovery and conquest, as they were believed to be encouraging slaves to run away. Such a directive is indicative of the importance of the Moors as part of the discovery and conquest entourage long after Columbus. In short, Moors also came as conquerors and discoverers. Furthermore, it implies the existence of a Moorish Islamic community in the New World since the coming of Columbus.

Moors in Jamaica

Although the immediate response of the Blacks in Jamaica is imprecise, slave revolts and resistance across the Caribbean would suggest that the scenario was no different. For the Spanish Black fugitives, the topography and ecology of Jamaica were also conducive for their hideouts and establishments. Since the prohibition of 1521 applied to all the new territories of Spain, it is likely that Spanish Maroon communities had already been established in Jamaica by 1523, when the first set of African slaves purchased from the Portuguese arrived in the island. The presence of 107 free blacks, substantiated by the census of the island taken by the Spaniards in 1611, further strengthens the argument that Moorish or free Black communities, referred to as Maroon communities, were in existence long before the British occupation of Jamaica in 1655. Bryan Edwards suggests that the blacks had formed their own communities and attacked the British intermittently.[11] Though the number is uncertain, a few Moors apparently, enjoyed the trust of the Spaniards, as they were left in authoritative positions in Jamaica at the time of the British occupation. Following the British occupation of Jamaica, as most of the Spaniards had left the island chiefly for Cuba, the slaves from the Spanish settlements joined the then existing Spanish Maroon communities or formed new societies of their own. Since the Spanish Maroons were creoles, they were for the most part the direct descendants of the Moors from Spain.

Spanish Muslim Maroons

Some of the uncertainties regarding the ethnic background of the Maroon leaders at the time of the British conquest can be clarified to some extent by an analytical study of their names.[12] Christian names given to Blacks, whether free or slaves, often had little religious significance to the persons, but they accepted them for social approval or to avoid physical torture. The name of Don Christoval Arnaldo de Ysassi, a Jamaican born Spaniard who was appointed the Governor of Jamaica by the Spanish King in 1655, is indicative of his Moorish origin. It is a corruption of the Arabic word Ysassa, meaning one who enjoys political authority or, in short, ruler. Apparently, de Ysassi or Sasi as the British called him was the title bestowed upon him for his political position. Such an appointment also demonstrates that white Spaniards were often dependent on Blacks, free or ex-slaves, during political and military crises, perhaps because of their superb sense of strategy and a shared common political past. Some historians have disputed Ysassi's claim of Black loyalty to him, although it would appear from the evidence that such loyalty was not wholly lacking.[13] The Spanish lieutenant general of Jamaica, Don Francisco de Leyba testified in Madrid in 1659 that the black settlements in the hills were obedient to Ysassi, though they governed themselves.[14] It would seem that Leyba and Ysassi both had a common Moorish background. Leyba is an Arabic term meaning intelligent or lienine. His war-like and administrative qualities might have won him this title. The Christian names, i.e. the first names of both Ysassi and Leyba although they appear to be

European Christian names, may have meant very little to these Spanish Jamaican leaders in their real lives, since most Moors who were under the control of the Spaniards were forcefully baptized.

Despite the numerical strength of the British with their superior weaponry, the defensive fight put up by Ysassi's contingent was reported to have caused heavy casualties to the British and caused alarm among the conquering forces at the uncertainties of their hold over Jamaica. The British officers appealed to soldiers and planters from the other islands to come to their assistance because they feared that they would not be able to keep the place for long.[15] Ysassi, however, eventually had to flee to Cuba with most of his men, in the face of stiff British opposition, and with very little of any Spanish assistance coming from Cuba. Perhaps the Spaniards in Cuba feared that military help extended to Christopher de Ysassi might lead to the formation of an independent black state of Jamaica and challenge the established status quo of the plantocracy in the New World.

Similarly, Juan de Bola, invariably called de Bolas, Lubola by the British or Juan Lubolo by the Spaniards, also appears to have been of Muslim origin. Bola, a name common among the people of Yoruba, whether Muslims or non-Muslims, in Arabic means 'the respectable'. Juan de Bola was the head of one of the three main black groups of Maroons. He commanded the respect of one of the biggest settlements of free Blacks who were regarded to be not only guerilla warriors but also agriculturists, and were settled in the Clarendon hills. Two hundred acres of cultivated crops, which was considered the largest single source of locally grown food, is indicative of the high stability of the community.[16] These free Blacks either were the descendents of the first generation of Moors who came as part of the conqueror party or directly came from Spain subsequent to Columbus. Bola has been accused of betraying the Maroon cause to the British. Perhaps he was a more pragmatic Maroon leader who realized that the stability and safety of his settlement required a policy of accommodation with the British. The first duty of Muslims is to maintain peace, which is the essence of Islam. The 'Declaration' by the Jamaica governor and Council, officially called 'a charter to the said Negroes', issued February 1, 1662/3 saying, 'Bola and all the Negroes ...' recognized the freedom of Bola's people with thirty acres of land granted to anyone eighteen years old and above.[17] This acknowledgement of the freedom of the Maroons in Bola's community may suggest that the British did not want to unnecessarily antagonize such a stable and self-sufficient Maroon society at a time when their first priority was security.

Very little is known of the head of the Karmahaly band of Maroons, Juan de Serras. However, his name and his style of leadership are possible indicators of his Islamic faith. Serras, a corruption of the Arabic term Sarra, meaning happiness, complemented his style of leadership. With all the uncertainties regarding his background, Juan de Serras may have been a Spanish creole, a creolized black, or a Moor from Spain. Evidently, he was a man of extraordinary ability.[18] Apparently, he had established an efficient and disciplined organization based on a hierarchical ordering similar to those founded by the Muslim rulers in al-Andalus and in the early Caliphate days, rather than modelled on European feudalism. Although a warrior himself, he carried the title of governor, as most rulers did during the Caliphate rule. His governorship also suggests that he had the authority to govern both the civil and the military aspects of his administration. The position of a sergeant-general, who was the next in command, is indicative of the importance of the military force. Serras governed his people with consensual authority, known in Arabic as *shura* or consultation. Such governance was still unknown to Europeans but established and practiced by the Muslim rulers in al-Andalusia for over eight hundred years, and in the Islamic world, as enjoined by the *Qur'an*.[19] Serras evidently recognized those with particular skills in his group and delegated functions accordingly, thus suggesting an understanding of his people and their acceptance of his leadership.[20]

The policy of consensual leadership apparently made the Karmahalys more united against their enemies, the British and other Maroon groups. Recognition of talents, and his consultation with the people on their wants, further helped Serras to promote the freedom and equality of the people. His behaviour, attitude, and the importance which he attached to his duties as sovereign towards his subjects, speak of his Islamic roots and his knowledge of Islam.[21] Far from the centre of the Islamic world and in the midst of a most brutal plantation society — i.e., military feudalism combined with the worst form of slavery — it is most probable that Serras's strong background and devotion to Islam had influenced his consensual leadership.

The Karmahalys, settled in the impenetrable north and north-eastern interior of the island, posed the greatest threat to the British. Within ten years of British conquest, the first formal declaration of war was made against the Karmahaly Maroons and others who were called the Rebellious Negroes.[22] Serras, himself an astute diplomat, with the assistance of his appointed emissaries, was able to defuse the tense situation, and gain time to secure his position. The Council Proclamation of 1668 gave the Karmahalys the freedom of movement to trade for necessary provisions. The permission 'to pass and repass in any part of this island without trouble' also implied that they could deploy their people at strategic points to challenge the British.[23]

The Karmahalys, inhabiting mainly the eastern parishes of St Georges, St. Thomas and Portland, are believed to have avoided all possible confrontation with the planters from the end of the seventeenth century until the beginning of the eighteenth century. However, it would appear that with the coming of new African slaves into the island, runaways from the plantations increased either taking refuge in the Spanish Maroon communities or forming separate communities in the neighbourhood. Clashes with the colonial authorities thus became inevitable. In addition, slave rebels from the estates in Clarendon and St Elizabeth developed their societies in the hills in the leeward part of the island. The evidence suggests that many of the runaways were of Islamic faith. Hundreds of Muslim slaves were brought to the Caribbean from West and Central Africa.[24]

The establishment of the Din of Allah, or Islam, oral testimonies seem to suggest that the Spanish Maroon leaders and the subsequent African Maroon leaders had founded their communities to establish the Din of Allah, or Islam, to guide them in this life, or *Dunya*, for the hereafter *Aakirah*. The terms *Din* and *Dunya* are *Qur'anic* words, which form an integral part of the vocabulary of some of the living elderly Maroons in Mooretown, Portland.[25] However, the Maroons are not aware of the significance of these terms in Islam nor of their origins.

Increasing slave rebellions on the plantations and the existence of Maroon societies as a source of reference for the runaways led to an intensified effort by the colonial government upon the requests of the planters for the extirpation of the Blacks in rebellion and of the established Maroon communities. Repeated attacks by the British troops on these communities led to defensive responses, or Jihad, from the Maroons, ultimately compelling the Colonial authorities in Jamaica to sue for peace and conclude treaties, first with the Leeward Maroons led by Cudjoe and subsequently with the Windward Maroons headed by Quao. The Leeward treaty, formally concluded on March 1, 1738/39, is referred to in the official documents in various ways, such as 'Agreement with Captain Cudjoe Vera Copia' or as 'Articles of Pacification with the Maroons of Trelawney Town' or as 'Articles of Agreement betwixt Coll. Guthrie Lieut. Sadler and Capt. Cajoe.'[26] The Treaty begins 'In the name of God Amen' which in *Qur'anic* terminology is *Bismillah*, i.e. 'In the Name of Allah'. [27] Historians have failed to study such a beginning from an Islamic perspective but have researched ancient Italian practices to look for precedents. Even the African background of the Maroons served as no indicator to the researchers to examine one of the most dominant religions of West Africa or Andalusian Spain, i.e. Islam, and study Maroon beliefs and institutions. All actions of a Muslim should begin with *Bismillah* to ensure good and meritorious conduct. This pious beginning undoubtedly speaks of the Islamic faith of Cudjoe and the other Leeward Maroon leaders who must have insisted upon its inclusion before signing the agreement. Such an introduction to a treaty or contract was never the precedent in Christendom's Europe.

The Arabic names of Cudjoe, meaning a shy person, and of his brother Ghani, denoting self-sufficiency, further strengthen the argument supporting their Muslim background. Ghani is one of the attributes of Allah, the Self-Sufficient, and is a common name among Muslims throughout the world, including Muslims of Akhan origin. Apparently, the Anglo-Saxon corruption of Ghani rather than Gyani, is Johnny.[28] The names of Cuffee and Quao, the two Maroon leaders from Moore Town (the Windward maroons), are also suggestive of Islamic background. Quao, invariably spelt as Quoha, Quaba, Quoba, Quaco and Quaw by contemporary authorities such as Philip Thicknesse, Lieutenant Governor of Jamaica, and in official documents, seems to be a corruption of the Arabic word *Quwah* which denotes another of the attributes of Allah, the Most Strong. The name of Cuffee who was the other Windward Maroon leader, is also a *Qur'anic* word used to specify another attribute of Allah, the Efficient. These Maroon leaders referred to each other as brothers. Present Maroon leaders claim that they were all brothers and that Granny Nanny was their sister.[29]

The use of the term 'brother' among the Maroon leaders is also indicative of the presence of a strong feeling of Islamic brotherhood, which is one of the basic principles of Islam — equality and brotherhood. Evidently, the claims made by both Moore Town and Accompong (Leeward) groups that Nanny was the sister of Cudjoe may imply blood-related sister or 'sister' of the same faith, Islam. The terms 'brother' and 'sister' are common in Islamic societies, denoting a common family, i.e. the Muslim *umma*/community. The value of human brotherhood is a fundamental element in the value system of Islam. Human brotherhood in Islam is based on an unshakable belief in the Oneness and Universality of Allah, the unity of mankind, the worshippers, and the unity of religion, the medium of worship.[30] Historian Mavis C. Campbell sees the use of the term 'brother' by the Leeward Maroon leaders as Ashanti tradition.[31] However, she fails to take note of the fact that much of the Ashanti Empire had come under the direct influence of Islam as early as the tenth century.

The Maroon leaders appear to have followed the *Sunnah*, i.e. the tradition of Prophet Muhammad in choosing those with the best skills, military or otherwise, for the good of the entire society. Following the tradition of the historical Maroons, the present Maroon communities continue to have a 'Chief who is unanimously elected by the elders and is regarded to be the most righteous person in the society.'[32] Race or past social background did not have an impact on the choice of leadership. So also was the leadership of the Maroons based on integrity and transparency, as required under Islam.

Adoption of Islamic Aadaab/Etiquettes of Greeting and Meeting

Oral tradition suggests that the historical Maroons of Moore Town adopted Islamic Aadaab (etiquettes) of greeting and meeting. Moore Town is built on land granted by the British to Granny Nanny in 1740. The Islamic greeting *Assalaamu Alaikum*, meaning 'peace be upon you' still continues as the official Council greeting among the 26 Council members in Moore Town.[33] The present Maroon Councillors are unaware of the significance of the greeting in Islam and consider it as a traditional greeting adopted by the historical Maroons such as Nanny and therefore to be adhered to with respect. The

existence of such a tradition leaves no room for further argument on the authenticity of the Islamic heritage of the Maroons of Moore Town.

The adoption of the Islamic greeting suffices to show that the historical Muslim Maroons of Moore Town differentiated themselves from the non-Muslim communities since the Islamic greeting is confined only to the Muslims. In Islam, a non-Muslim should be greeted with *Assalamo-Ala-Manittaba'al Huda*, i.e. 'Peace be on him who performed allegiance'.[34] The Islamic greeting of the Council members of Moore Town would further suggest that Granny Nanny, the great Jamaican heroine, was a Muslim. It was under her leadership that the windward Maroons fought against the British and were granted five hundred acres of land in the Parish of Portland for her people in 1740. After the British had reduced Nanny Town, which was founded by her, to rubble in 1734, Granny Nanny and her people apparently founded their community in and around Moore Town, which was then called New Nanny Town.[35] Past and present Maroons in Jamaica have revered Nanny as 'Granny' Nanny. She was in a position to revoke Quao's decision and impose her own. The acceptance of Nanny's decisions is indicative of her skills in military strategies and her political acumen. According to oral testimony, it was under the directives of Granny Nanny that the Maroon Council was formed for the governance of the Maroons. In Islam, since it is important to take counsel, the historical Maroon leaders formed Councils, a tradition still maintained today for the governance of the Maroon people. Furthermore, following the *Sunnah*, Granny Nanny never assumed political leadership, but blessed her people with her spiritual piety. The present ethnic diversity which exists within the Moore Town Maroon community also suggests that the community by then comprised people belonging to different ethnic groups from West and Central Africa but professed Islam, which appears to be the unifying force. The continuation of *Assalaamu Alaikum* among the Maroon Councillors even today speaks of the pervasiveness of the greeting among the historical Maroons and the unity of the Muslim *Umma* (community).

Although popularly called Granny Nanny, her real name according to oral tradition was Sarah. Sarah is a *Qur'anic* term meaning 'happiness.' Like many other Muslim women, such as Hazrat A'isha, Hazrat Umm' Umara, Hazrat Umm' Atiyya, Granny Nanny or Sarah was a courageous and skilful warrior who fought galantly for the defence of human dignity, the basis of Islam. The early Muslim women warriors fought in battles alongside with men often protecting men such as Prophet Muhammad.[36] Apparently, Granny Nanny, considered by the Maroons as the most illustrious woman, who never lost a battle with the British, had the commanding ability in the battlefield as well as the political acumen to unite the community together. The name Nanny Town, is perhaps indicative of her leadership and the respect she earned from her people. Under Granny Nanny's military leadership the Maroons sometimes killed the entire British contingent, such as at the battle in Seaman's Valley in 1729, where 600 invading troops lost their lives. Out of such disastrous British defeats arose myths that Nanny was a witch practising witchcraft.

Islamic Family Practices

The fragmentary evidence regarding the family structures among Maroon communities is also suggestive of Islamic practices. Although polygamy practised among the Maroons has been seen by historians as an African custom, in Islam, polygamy is allowed under specific circumstances. Monogamy is the general rule in Islam, while polygamy is the exception, particularly in the aftermath of war, when widows or orphaned girls need protection. The Maroon communities, it would appear, had more women and children than men, who were either abducted from the plantations or escaped and were provided protection by the Maroons.[37] To contain social ills, such as prostitution and to enlarge their communities, the Maroon men would appear to have followed the Islamic prescription which permits polygamy but limits it to four women. There is no accurate account as to the number of wives a Maroon man had. That the Maroons despised the unlawful sexual pleasures carried out in the plantations is exemplified by the severity of the punishment meted out to those committing adultery, as required under Qur'anic laws. While adulteresses were severely punished in Cudjoe's community, in Nanny Town an adulterer was put to death, even if it happened to be the headman.[38] In Islam, adultery or fornication has been expressly made unlawful.[39]

Allahu Akbar is uttered in many of the practices of Islam, signifying that man is only a creature of Allah and that Allah is Supreme. The knowledge and the literal translation of the phrase *Allahu Akbar* by the present Maroon leaders of Moore Town testify to the community's traditional foundation in Islam.[40]

Jihad, both inner struggle for self-purification and the wars against slavocracy, resulted in recognition of Maroon rights within territorial limitations by treaties. It is believed that Granny Nanny was not only against Cudjoe's treaty with the slave regime but she was also disappointed with Quao for signing the treaty on behalf of the Windward Maroons.[41] Granny Nanny, it would appear, was fighting to establish the Islamic concept of freedom. Within the framework of this Islamic concept there is no room for religious persecutions, class conflict, or racial prejudice. The individual's right of freedom is as sacred as his right of Life; hence freedom is the equivalent of Life itself. The existence of the slave system was the antithesis of the concept of Islamic freedom. The Maroon Treaties perhaps appeared to Granny Nanny as the denial of the Unity of Allah, since slavocracy would still continue outside the Maroon territory and that Maroon behaviour and policy towards other runaways would be monitored by the slave system. However, the order of succession of Maroon leadership, as stated in the Treaty, speaks of the unity and the prevailing consensus among the Maroons.

With the signing of the Treaties, the historical Maroons were faced with a dilemma. On the one hand, the *Qur'an* prohibited the breach of the treaty provisions, and on the other hand, runaways from the plantations had to be facilitated or accorded shelter. Apparently, Cudjoe and Quao accepted the offer of peace and cessation of hostilities in accordance with the *Qur'anic* commands.[42]

The Islamic Act of Prostration

Dallas's account of Cudjoe's behaviour during his meeting with Colonel John Guthrie and Captain Francis Sadler when the peace offer was made is highly unacceptable in the context of Islamic procedure, which was followed but completely distorted and misunderstood by Dallas and subsequent historians who rely on his work.[43] It is highly

unlikely that Cudjoe, the warrior leader who apparently, had organized both the Leeward and the Windward Maroons under his command to fight against the slave system in the island, would have 'kissed the feet' of Guthrie. In all likelihood Cudjoe immediately prostrated himself on the ground to thank Allah for the peace offer. This is implied in the same account, which says, 'The rest of them following the example of their chief, prostrated themselves....' In Islam, prostration is the highest manifestation of humility and self-surrender to Allah.[44] This posture of prostration performed by Cudjoe in glorification or seeking Divine favours seems to have been misinterpreted and ridiculed by Dallas. It is customary among Muslims to prostrate oneslf to express gratitude to Allah, or to seek mercy, beneficence or blessings.

In Islam, after establishment of peace with the conclusion of treaties with the enemies, it is one of the greatest sins to violate the terms.[45] Although Cudjoe, Quao and the historical Maroons are ridiculed by historians for assisting the slave authorities for the return of runaways, it would appear that the Maroon leaders, in accordance with the Qur'anic commands, abided by the treaty provisions which guaranteed peace for their communities. Cudjoe would appear to have negotiated well with the enemies, winning for those who had fled their masters 'within two years last past' two options. [46] On being granted full pardon and indemnity, they could return to their masters or remain under Cudjoe's authority. Apparently, Cudjoe worked for the freedom of all runaways within his community, Muslims and non-Muslims, in accordance with Islam.[47] With reference to Muslim runaways, Cudjoe simply applied the Islamic principle of universal brotherhood.[48] It would be logical to suggest that Muslims, or those who accepted Islam, remained in his community and non-Muslims were returned to their masters for reasons of the security, and harmony of Cudjoe's people. In addition, Islam must have been the criterion for extending membership to post-treaty runaways to Cudjoe's or Quao's communities.

Conclusion

The argument put forth by some historians that there was 'a lack of any philosophy of freedom ...' among the Maroons can be refuted on grounds that the Islamic concept of freedom was the basis of the Maroon struggle against slavocracy.[49] Furthermore, the tendency was not towards ethnic exclusivity, as sometimes claimed. The Maroon communities, both in Accompong in the Leeward, and in Moore Town in the Windward, areas are not ethnically homogeneous, but consist of various ethnic groups, such as Yoruba, Coromantine, Hausa, Akan and Fulani.[50] Islam united the heterogeneous society to form the Muslim *umma*, apparently to fight against the oppressor, *Bucra*.[51] Indeed, the unity of the Maroon Muslim *umma* to fight for the cause of righteousness, piety and good conduct is the greatest manifestation of Tawhid — the Unity of Allah.

Sultana Afroz

Notes

1. Eric Williams, *From Columbus to Castro: The History of the Caribbean, 1492–1969* (London: André Deutsch, 1983), p. 34.
2. Ibid., p. 67.
3. Edward Long, *The History of Jamaica* (3 Vols., London: Frank Cass, 1970), Vol.2, p. 338 n. (first published, 1774).
4. Felipe Fernández-Armesto, *Before Columbus, Exploration and Colonization from the Mediterranean to the Atlantic, 1229–1492* (Philadelphia: University of Pennsylvania Press, 1987), p. 58.
5. Williams, pp. 41–42.
6. Ibid., p. 41.
7. Ira M. Lapidus, *A History of Islamic Societies* (Cambridge: Cambridge University Press, 1994) (first published, 1988) p. 389.
8. Sultana Afroz, 'The Unsung Slaves: Islam in Plantation Jamaica — The African Connection'. *Journal Institute of Muslim Minority Affairs*, Vol. 15: 1& 2, January & July 1994, p. 161.
9. Williams, p. 67.
10. Ibid., p. 66.
11. Bryan Edwards, *The History, Civil and Commercial, of the British Colonies in the West Indies*, 2 Vols., (Dublin: Luke White, 1793), Vol. 1, p. 153.
12. The names of the Spanish and African Maroon leaders have been translated by Sheikh Musa Tijani Kayode, Central Masjid of Jamaica, Kingston, Jamaica. Sheikh Tijani, a native of a Yoruba speaking clan, teaches Arabic and Islamic Studies in Jamaica.
13. Mavis C. Campbell, *The Maroons of Jamaica 1655-1796*, (Trenton, New Jersey: Africa World Press, 1990), p. 18.
14. Frank Cundall and Joseph Pietersz, *Jamaica under the Spaniards: Abstracted from the Archives of Seville* (Kingston: Institute of Jamaica, 1919), p. 81.
15. 'The State Papers of Jon Thurlos, 1655–1658', Vol.4, cited by Carey Robinson in *Fight for Freedom* (Kingston: Kingston Publishers, 1993), p. 12.
16. S.A.G. Taylor, *The Western Design: An Account of Cromwell's Expedition in the Caribbean* (Kingston: Institute of Jamaica, 1965), pp.185–86.

17. Colonial Office (C.O.) 140/41, Council Meeting, February 1, 1662/63.
18. Campbell, p. 25.
19. The Holy *Qur'an*, 42:38.
20. The Holy *Qur'an*, 49:13.
21. Azneer Al Syed, *The Spirit of Islam* (London: Darf Publishers, 1988) (first published 1902) p. 261: and Numani, Professor Shibli, Al-Farooq *Omar the Great, the Second Caliph of Islam*, Translated into English by Maulana Zafar Ali Khan (lmrnad Publications, 1898) p. 219.
22. C.O. 140/1, Council Meeting, August 15, 1665.
23. C.O. 140/1, Council Meeting, March 28, 1665.
24. Robert R. Madden, *A Twelve Months Residence in the West Indies During the Transition from Slavery to Apprenticeship*, Vol. 1 (Philadelphia: Carey, Lea & Blanchard, 1835), pp. 99-101.
25. Interview with Leopold Shelton and Milton Shelton, Maroons of Moore Town, Jamaica, August 6–8, 1994.
26. The National Library of Jamaica (Institute of Jamaica).
27. Abdul Wahid Hamid, *Islam the Natural Way* (London: Muslim Education and Library Services,1989), p. 176.
28. Campbell, p. 46.
29. Interview with Colonel C.L.G. Harris, Moore Town, Jamaica, January 14, 1999.
30. Hammudah Abdalati, *Islam in Focus*, (American Trust Publications, 1975), p. 36.
31. Campbell, p. 62.
32. Interview with Colonel C.L.G. Harris, Moore Town, January 14, 1999.
33. Meeting with Colonel C.L.G. Harris and some Council members, Moore Town, August 7, 1994.
34. Maulana Ashraf Ali Thanwi, Bahishti Zewar, Tr. M. Mansoor, *Khan Saroha Heavenly Ornaments* (New Delhi: Sayeed International, 1997), p. 290.
35. Interview with Colonel Harris, January14, 1999.
36. Muhammad Saeed Siddiqi, *The Blessed Women of Islam* (Lahore, Pakistan: Kazi Publications, 1982).
37. Campbell, p. 53.
38. Ibid., pp. 48 & 50.
39. The Holy *Qur'an* 17:32.
40. Interview with Colonel Harris. Moore Town, August 7, 1994.
41. Campbell, pp. 51 & 178.
42. The Holy *Qur'an*, 8:61 & 62.
43. R.C. Dallas, *History of the Maroons*, 2 Vols. (London: T.N. Longrnan and O. Rees. 1803), Vol 1, p. 55.
44. Al-Hadis, *Mishkat-ul-Masabih*, Vol. 3, p.284.
45. The Holy *Qur'an*, 23:140.
46. Campbell, p. 130.
47. The Holy *Qur'an*, 90:11-13.
48. Riyadh-Us-Salaheen, Compiled by Imam AbuZakariya Yahya Bin Sharaf An-Nawawi, Tr. S.M. Madni Abbasi (New Delhi: Kitab Bhavan, 1994), p. 647.
49. Campbell, p. 131.
50. Interview with Colonel Harris, Moore Town, January 14, 1999; see also C.O. 140/4, September 29, 1686. I Page 10 April 1, 1999.
51. Bucra, the corruption to the Arabic word Baqarah or 'cow', is often used to denote the fossilization of human beings. While the planters found comfort in being called Bucra, the Maroons and slaves amused themselves in such mockeries. Self-sufficiency, as *Sura Al-Baqarah* in the *Qur'an* states, prevents men from seeing that spiritually they are not alive, but dead. Such was the view prevalent among the Maroons and the slaves towards the plantocracy.

CRITICAL THINKING AND WRITING

1. What is the author's thesis?
2. Read Afroz's introduction (this ends with her intention) and her conclusion.
   a) How do the introduction and conclusion reinforce the message in the body of Afroz's essay?
   b) Read or skim through the essay. Were the introduction and conclusion good indicators of what was explored in the essay?
   c) What does this suggest about the way in which introductions and conclusions should work together in any piece of writing?
3. List some of the elements that Afroz uses to create unity in her writing.
4. What tone does Afroz adopt in the first three sections of this passage?
5. Focusing on the first three sections, characterize the intended audience. Provide evidence to support your answer.

WRITING TASK

6. Choose a religion and write an expository paragraph stating how this religion was introduced to your territory or to the Caribbean.

WEB SEARCH

7. Do some research on the world wide web to find information about different types of religions present in the Caribbean.

CHAPTER 49

JAMAICA'S MUSLIM PAST: DISCONCERTING THEORIES

Some weeks ago, Gordon Mullings issued a challenge to historians to comment publicly on the claims put forward by Dr. Sultana Afroz, a member of the Department of History at the Mona campus of the University of the West Indies, regarding the high number of Muslim slaves who came to Jamaica and the Muslim foundations of the island's Maroon communities. Although not a historian by training, I have researched both African and Caribbean history enough to put forward my views with some degree of confidence.

There is no doubt that there were Muslims among the enslaved brought to the Caribbean. My oral interviews in the 1960s with Trinidadian descendants of such persons bore testimony to this — findings which were published in the *African Studies Association of the West Indies Bulletins* 5 and 6 (1972, 1973), later republished in my *Guinea's Other Suns* (1991). These foreparents had come from the Hausa, Fulani, Yoruba, and Mandingo ethnic groups of West Africa. Of these groups, the Mandingo of the Senegambia region were most associated with Islam. The religious ideas of these Muslims, as well as the writing skills in Arabic which several of them possessed, had in fact caught the attention of

European planters, among them Jamaican-based Bryan Edwards (1819).

In fact, their numeracy and writing skills allowed them to secure jobs as storekeepers and tally clerks on estates. But many of the Africans who had come into contact with Islam before migrating were not literate in Arabic, and it is the literacy of those who belonged to families of established Muslim priests and scholars which most readily attracted the attention of European commentators.

Attended Muslim Schools

Having attended Muslim schools, they were able to recite short or long sections of the Koran, as well as write Arabic words and letters. Indeed, Jonas Mohammed Bath of Port of Spain, Trinidad, wrote several petitions in English and Arabic during the 1830s on behalf of other Muslims who wished to be repatriated to their native lands.

In a 1974 article, Carl Campbell set out the life story of Mohammedu Sisei of the Gambia, who had arrived in Trinidad as a demobilised West India Regiment soldier in 1816 and who, through the agency of the

Royal Geographical Society of England, did return to the Gambia.

In an almost similar vein, Magistrate R.R. Madden of Jamaica alerted anti-slavery and Africa colonisation interests in London to the Arabic autobiography (1830s) of Abu Bakr al-Siddiq, otherwise called Edward Donlan in Jamaica.

Moravian and Baptist missionaries collected other autobiographies; and European and American missionaries commented on the arguments they conducted with Muslims regarding the relative positions of Jesus, Abraham and other sacred figures shared by the Christian and Islamic orders of divinity. There is therefore, in the travelogues and histories of the eighteenth and nineteenth centuries, mention of Muslim Africans, but the comment is consistently made that the presence of such persons was small.

Of course, Europeans did not understand much about the lives of the slaves. So other evidence must be adduced to bring to light fuller understandings of the Caribbean past. An important strand of evidence lies in the data on sources and destinations of the Caribbean's enslaved populations.

Orlando Patterson's ethnic ratios of slave imports into Jamaica given in *The Sociology of Slavery* (1967) have been consistent with the findings of later analysts such as Curtin, Higman, Eltis and others. Between 1655 and 1700, after the British seized the island, the main slave sources were the Gold Coast and the Senegambian Windward Coast composed of today's Guinea-Bissau, Guinea, Sierra Leone, Liberia, and the Ivory Coast.

In the first half of the eighteenth century (1700–1750), the Windward Coast and Angola at the south-eastern extreme of the slaving zone parted with 27 per cent, and 33 per cent came from the Slave Coast (today's Togo and the Republic of Benin, previously called Dahomey), while the neighbouring Gold Coast yielded 25 per cent. By the second half of the eighteenth century, there was a noticeable shift toward the Niger and Cross deltas of today's Nigeria and Cameroon, but between 1790 and 1807 when the traffic was outlawed, there was a rapid increase in slaves exported by the British from the Congo and Angola.

By contrast, Afroz, in her 1995 article on 'The Unsung Slaves: Islam in Plantation Jamaica' identifies Jamaican slaves as being Mandinka, Fula, Susu, Ashanti and Hausa, without indicating their relative strengths vis-a-vis other significant ethnicities such as Igbo-Ibibio from the Niger and Cross River deltas, Ewe-Fon from Togo and Dahomey, and people from Congo and Angola. Four of her five named categories came from cultures which had been either minimally, partially, or heavily converted to Islam between the eighteenth to the nineteenth centuries.

In a similar non-rigorous manner, by her 1999 article 'From Moors to Marronage: The Islamic Heritage of the Maroons', Afroz moves from indicating that Muslims (called Moors) in Spain were among the earliest Spanish settlers in the Americas to speaking of Jamaica's Maroon settlements as being 'Muslim'.

Thereafter, her article continues to make extravagant claims for Muslim influence among them, the fact that Windward and Leeward Maroon links are couched in 'brother' and 'sister' terms; that Maroon communities are governed by councils; that Nanny's other name, reputedly Sarah, is Muslim; that since *Salaam aleikum* (peace be with you) has been used by the Moore Town Maroons, and since this term is confined to greetings among Muslims rather than by Muslims to non-Muslims, then this serves as proof that Muslim culture dominated Moore Town and that Islam was its 'unifying force'.

Regarding the salutation, studies on residual and dying languages show that grammatical forms in their original languages become abridged when languages are used by isolated minority groups who are under pressure to acquire the dominant languages of an exile environment; and the infrequency of usage also leads to a non-observance of the social conventions which govern the use of particular phrases or words, such as the appropriate differentiation between pronouns which are emphatic versus non-emphatic, familiar versus respectful.

Since speakers of a language most often speak it among themselves, Arabic speakers would most commonly use 'Salaam aleikum', rather than 'Assalamo-Ala-Manittaba'al Huda' which Afroz indicates is the proper greeting from a Muslim to a non-Muslim.

Furthermore, the shorter, less complicated phrase would be the one most likely to be remembered in a situation of exile, where an immigrant language is in disadvantageous competition with other languages.

As for the other claims, these are similarly untenable as proof of intense Muslim influence. African cultures in general use certain basic kinship terms, such as 'father' 'mother' 'brother', 'sister', 'uncle', 'aunt', 'husband', 'wife', to signal relationships among individuals for which European languages add 'in-law', 'adopted', 'half', or use words such as 'cousin' or 'friend'.

In like fashion, all over Africa alliances between communities, villages, and ethnic groupings are rationalised in terms of descent from common ancestors, thus making the groups 'brothers' and 'sisters'.

Another distortion is Afroz's assertion that Akan day-names such as Kojo, Kwao and Kofi are Arabic. These names are so embedded in the Akan tradition of the Fanti (Coromanti) and Ashanti that in their ancient and cryptic

drum poetry and religious verse, one of the aspects of God, Nyankopong or the Great Ananse, also bears Kwaku, the birthday-name for those born on Wednesday. And Mother Earth is named Asase Yaa, the final name being given to females born on Friday.

Given the fact that Islam did not become a serious political force in the royal court of Ashanti until the second half of the 1700s, it is surprising that names so deeply embedded in the Akan and Ga cultures to the east and west of the Volta River and extending from the savannah lands bordering the Sahel in the north and southward to the Gulf of Guinea coast could be Arabic in their source.

Muslim Influence

This is because Ashanti was one of several West African kingdoms where Muslim influence was confined to the royal court, rather than an aspect of mass popular culture and worldview.

Islam had penetrated sub-Saharan Africa from North Africa in the eighth century. Its first host was the ancient kingdom of Ghana in the vicinity of present-day Mali. It was introduced by Berber traders who opened up the trans-Saharan gold trade from Ghana to the Mediterranean.

Over the next 11 centuries, the international contacts stimulated by the trade in gold, slaves, salt, and kola, and the need of sub-Saharan rulers to communicate with the Arab world of traders, lawyers, and scholars, led African kings to recruit Arabic speaking scribes-cum-merchants as diplomats and interpreters at their courts.

This process took place at different times at varying locations from west to east across the savannah belt of West Africa, and in some cases this collaboration led to the conversion to Islam of court elite.

By cultural osmosis, and sometimes by upsurges of Islamic religious militancy, the village-level leadership, and later commoners, eventually became converted from various forms of African animistic religion and ancestor veneration to the monotheism and international religious culture of Islam. In contrast to Ashanti and Yoruba, by the fourteenh century Islam had already extensively penetrated into the urban culture of the Senegambian peoples.

The contention that the final segment of Juan de Bolas' name was a Yoruba name originating from Arabic is another glib assertion. In the first place, the Yoruba did not figure in the slave trade till the late seventeenth century whereas de Bolas or Lubolo or Libolo lived in Jamaica in the mid-seventeenth.

Furthermore, 'Bola' is easily decoded as comprising two Yoruba segments of meaning. Then the assignation of Sarah as Arabic might be more helpfully denoted as Semitic, that is, common to the languages of the Red Sea, such as Hebrew and Arabic. This applies to names like Abraham/Ibrahim, Solomon/ Suleiman, Miriam/Miramu, and so on. 'Sarah' having entered into English language and culture through Biblical influence, it would be preposterous to claim that every British girl who bore the name Sarah or Sally was Jewish, just as the slaves who carried such names cannot be identified as either Muslim or Jewish on that ground.

Another custom deeply embedded in African culture was prostration on the ground by the subordinate in deference to a superior. It was already the practice in Central Africa when the Portuguese arrived in the Congo at the end of the fifteenth century, and the northeastern segment of the vast Congo Basin only felt the effects of Islam approaching from East Africa in the nieteenth century.

Prostration in its full form, in which the subject lies full-length on the ground face downward in the presence of the superior in social status or age, or in truncated forms which involve touching the hands to the earth, is widely practised among several peoples of West Africa and predates Islamic intervention. Maroon Kojo's act of prostration during the signing of the Treaty with the British in 1739 cannot therefore be ascribed to Islamic influence, in the light of the acts of respect and social distance which are indigenous to so many African cultures.

Another instance advanced by Afroz to assert the Islamic affiliation of Jamaican Maroons is the initial phrase of the Treaty drawn up between the British authorities and the Leeward Maroons led by Kojo (Cudjoe). The Treaty begins with the words 'In the name of God, Amen,' the equivalent to Arabic *Bismillah*, 'In the Name of Allah'. Afroz asserts that 'such an introduction to a treaty or contract was never the precedent in Christendom's Europe.'

On the other hand, the phrase in the Treaty occurs at the beginning of some British wills, and possibly was a reflection of the testator's religious faith. To cite two instances I know of, it occurs at the start of a will made by Sarah Hart in St. Elizabeth in 1822 and registered in 1834, and in a Scottish will registered in 1818, which begins: 'Follows the Probate of the Defuncts last will and testament: In the name of God Amen. I Robert Douglass of Mains...'. Indeed, it is clear that Kojo did not himself draw up the wording of the Treaty; the British would hardly have allowed him that privilege. He was a formidable military tactician, but his signing the Treaty with an X indicates that the writing styles of legal documents was outside of his specialisation and that he wrote neither in Roman nor Arabic letters.

Questionable Device

Yet another questionable device in Afroz's two articles is the application of the term *Jihad* to label acts of war and rebellion on the part of slaves and Maroons in Jamaica, Suriname and, by association in the same sentence, Haiti. Because two Suriname Maroon leaders bear names which she identifies as Arabic, her deduction is that their military actions constituted jihad.

Such an attribution cannot be made unless proof is adduced as to the motives for their actions. Similar over-reading affects her designation of the 1831–32 Jamaican slave rebellion as inspired by motives to effect an Islamic jihad.

No such evidence emerged in the several inquiries into the prolonged event and no Muslims were specifically singled out as pivotal to the action. Were Sam Sharpe and his principal lieutenants Muslim, then it is strange that they did not use the forum of their trials, their interviews with pastors, or their execution gibbets to proclaim their Islamic faith.

All the same, there might well have been either crypto- or active Muslim believers among the hundreds of slaves who participated in the uprising. The sole piece of evidence that suggests a link in the mind of a contemporary slave was recorded by magistrate Madden regarding Muhammad Kaba of Spice Grove estate in Manchester who in Jamaica also carried the names Robert Peart and Robert Tuffit.

Given the repression by government, militia, and anti-missionary civilian elements, that followed the widespread devastation of the uprising, Kaba's wife destroyed a letter in Arabic which had been hand-delivered to Kaba in 1831 from a Muslim friend in Kingston. It was believed to have been written in Africa by a Muslim cleric and it 'exhorted all the followers of Mahomet to be true and faithful, if they wished to go to Heaven.'

What else it said is not recorded. But Kaba's wife thought it might be incriminating at a time when in several parishes local militia and army personnel were carrying out house-to-house searches and were posted outside churches, while slaves were being put to death on the slightest suspicion of disloyalty.

Indeed, Brother Pfeiffer, a German Moravian pastor, had been arrested in St. Elizabeth on January 7, taken on the 9th to Mandeville in Manchester and tried, and came within an inch of being executed, in addition to which Craton (1982) alludes to some events in Manchester on the night of January 11, 1832 which led to the army shooting six and executing two, so that there was reason for alarm by Kaba's wife, especially as Kaba had become a Moravian and so might have come under special scrutiny at this time.

If the letter to Kaba advanced the cause of jihad, it might have had the effect of triggering rebellion, in the way in which Muslim slaves rose against bondage in the city of Salvador in Bahia, Brazil, in January 1835.

In the Brazilian case, there was evidently a sufficiently large Muslim community of Yoruba and Hausa slaves united by a supra-ethnic religion to have made this prospect feasible, despite the fact that these two ethnicities had been engaged in a religious-political war in Africa since the end of the 1800s and this was feeding the nineteenth century slave trade with many war captives.

But there has not so far emerged evidence of concentrations of Yoruba or Nago in Jamaica sizeable enough to have spread their influence and shaken the system, though there are known to have been pockets of Nago in the post-slavery period in Hanover (where etu is practised), at Abeokuta in Westmoreland, in St. Mary and St. Thomas, and of course, there may have been a settlement at Naggo Head in St. Catherine. But there did appear to have been loose interconnected groupings of Muslim slaves, generally referred to as 'Mandingo' who debated the authenticity of Christianity even as they joined various Christian religions.

This network takes vague shape in the writings of magistrate Madden, even though he clearly did not comprehend the complexity of the religious lives of individuals such as Peart/Kaba.

Kaba's religious questionings also gained the attention of the Moravian clerics John Lang and Henry Buchner, while the recent discovery of a notebook with pastoral advice on prayer, fasting, and marriage written by Kaba in Arabic sheds more light on his spiritual conflicts and preoccupations. The contents of that notebook were discussed by Yacine Daddi Addoun and Paul Lovejoy in a paper on 'The Arabic Manuscript of Muhammad Kaba Saghanughu of Jamaica, c. 1823' at the Caribbean Culture conference at Mona in January 2002.

It is very useful that the understanding of Caribbean history should have the benefit of analysts who know the Arabic language, religion, and culture. It allows the researcher so equipped to spot information which another would miss. As for example, when Afroz (1999) informs us that the Koranic terms Din and Dunya still form 'an integral part of the vocabulary of some of the living elderly Maroons in Moore Town, Portland.'

Unfortunately, the writer does not divulge precisely in what context or what sentences these terms were used, or whether the words were suggested to the speakers and responses thus elicited.

This lack of proper supporting evidence undermines the validity of her discovery ...

Maureen Warner-Lewis

CRITICAL THINKING AND WRITING

1. How does Warner-Lewis establish herself as a credible writer?
2. a) What is Warner-Lewis's purpose in this piece?
   b) What are some of the elements in the piece which help you to identify the writer's intent?
3. What is the dominant organizing principle of Warner-Lewis's piece and why do you think she chose to use it?
4. Identify some of the techniques that Warner-Lewis uses to ensure that her piece is coherent.
5. How would you characterize Warner-Lewis's tone? Provide support from the passage.
6. Warner-Lewis's article appeared in a newspaper, while Afroz's was written for an academic journal. How is the use of rhetorical devices in the two articles (register, tone, diction, syntax and so on) influenced by the context?

WRITING ACROSS THE CURRICULUM ACTIVITIES

7. List some of the strategies which Warner-Lewis provides for evaluating a writer's credibility. In groups, evaluate an article, using some of the methods which Warner-Lewis points out.
8. What are some of the religions that are present in your society?
   a) Choose one religion and write a paragraph about it, choosing your focus.
   b) Identify the organizing principle which you will use and explain why it will be effective.
9. Do a reverse outline, then a summary of this passage in no more than 150 words.

CHAPTER 50

THE MEAL IS THE MESSAGE— THE LANGUAGE OF BRAZILIAN CUISINE

Everyone has to eat to live, but each society defines in its own way the significance of the act of eating, and stipulates what should be consumed regularly and what must never be eaten for fear of turning into an animal or a monster.

Strict rules define the relationship between the food consumed and the condition of the person who consumes it. All Brazilians know that they should fast before taking communion, in order to maintain the assumed state of purity compatible with the host which they receive into their bodies. They behave very differently, however, when they entertain their relations or friends at home for Sunday lunch. On these occasions they carefully choose the food that will help them to define the social situation they wish to create.

If I am invited to eat a *feijoada*, a *cozido*, or a *peixada*, I expect to take part in an informal ritual of meal-sharing in which there will be a connection between what is eaten, the way in which it is eaten, and the people with whom it is eaten. These dishes consist of a variety of ingredients (either meat or fish, combined with vegetables and flour) from which the guests help themselves and make their own mixture of the various items offered on the table, Brazilian-style, establishing a parallel between the act of eating and the ideal of 'mixing' socially those who eat together.

Brazilians have strict rules for matching a meal to those who eat it. I should never think of inviting home the Governor of my State for a *feijoada*. A more classic menu would be appropriate on such an occasion and might include such dishes as roast chicken with salad, or meat cooked in a more cosmopolitan style. However, there is nothing wrong in having a cup of coffee or a snack with strangers; in this case you eat standing up in a downtown snack-bar or *balcão*. This is a mode of eating in which the utilitarian concept of 'eating to live' takes precedence over the moral or symbolic aspects of a meal. During a slap-up meal with your friends, on the other hand, Socrates's adage is forgotten and instead of eating to live you live to eat.

In Brazilian cooking and hospitality a great effort is made to combine the 'universal' aspects of food (such as its nutritive and energy value, its capacity to sustain the organism and its protein content) with its symbolic characteristics, since 'man does not live by bread alone' and the act of eating has great social significance. All this is connected with 'totem commensality', as the French anthropologist Claude Levi-Strauss described a system in which people and their mood, the surroundings, the food, and even the way of preparing the meal, must all be in harmony.

This no doubt explains why in Brazil a sharp distinction is made between the concept of 'food' and the concept of a 'meal'. In the language of Brazilian cuisine, these terms express a fundamental semantic opposition between the universal and the particular. Brazilians know that all edible substances are 'foods' but that not every food is necessarily a 'meal'. In transforming food into a meal the preparation is of critical importance, but a degree of ceremony is also required. When preparing a carefully organized and well-thought-out meal, no Brazilian will be satisfied with simply buying top-quality produce and then obediently following a cookbook recipe. He will take great pains to prepare the ingredients and season them properly. Since the quality of the meal, served copiously and with care, expresses consideration for the guests, it would be inconceivable for a Brazilian to serve pre-cooked convenience foods, as is now the practice in Anglo-Saxon countries.

The meal is also a means of expressing and asserting a national, regional or local identity, or even the identity of a family or an individual, depending on the context. Essentially, the act of eating crystallizes emotional states and social identities. Outside my country I can use a regional dish to express my national identity, but within Brazil I identify many regions and even families through the way in which they prepare and serve certain foods. In a genuine system of 'totem meals' social identities can be expressed. Every Brazilian knows that the people of the Northeast are as fond of flour as mice are of cheese; that *tutú con linguiça* (a dish based on sausage and beans) is typical of Minas Gerais State; and that *churrasco* is the favourite dish of the *gauchos* of the South.

And so, when speaking of Brazilian cooking both the modes of eating and the groups of people who are invited to share certain kinds of food must be taken into account. There is no doubt that in some contexts meals acquire a personality of their own, which explains the enormous importance of meals as offerings in Brazilian traditional cults. Thus there are foods associated with the sacred (or the profane), with sickness (or health), with virility or femininity, with childhood or with maturity.

Sitting down at the table is supposed to put an end to disputes. Brazilians believe that some dishes and some situations (the Carnival, for instance) are, like some women, irresistible, so that the very presence of certain dishes should be enough to create a degree of conviviality and bring harmony to those who are assembled around the table.

But the symbolism of meals also provides an opportunity to examine a highly complex question which is usually overlooked in 'anthropologies of eating' — the search for a rational explanation for the culinary peculiarities that are found in every society. Every society has dishes it would almost be ready to die for. It is not fortuitous that North American society has an individualistic culinary model according to which everyone tucks into a solitary meal from a tray in front of a newspaper or television set. There must be some connection between the fast food and junk food industries, self-service restaurants, and the values of self-reliance and independence which under-pin society in countries such as the United States.

But what is happening in countries like Brazil where traditional cuisine exists alongside modern, more individualized patterns of food consumption? There is no doubt that in these countries, the modern practice of eating an individual food product such as a hamburger, either alone or with strangers, coexists with traditional eating habits which reassert themselves at banquets held in that atmosphere of friendliness and conviviality to which people are still strongly attached.

The Brazilian example reveals that these two practices are not mutually exclusive. On the contrary, they can reinforce each other; dual eating habits seem to exist in societies of this kind. One practice is an expression of 'modernity', while the other can provide a focus for personal relationships. In Brazil there is, indeed, an impersonal, individualized, public cuisine, in contrast to traditional home cooking which keeps people in touch with the basic social relationships that give form and meaning to life.

On the whole, however, the concept of the meal as an act of sociability is inseparable from family, friends and colleagues, in other words, from all close relationships. In this connection it is worth mentioning that all Brazilian national dishes such as *feijoada*, *peixada*, *cozido*, *vatapa* (a dish based on manioc flour or rice with fish or meat) and *cararú* (typical of Bahia State), specifically combine solids with liquids, meat with fish, and dried vegetables with green vegetables.

In Brazilian cooking the utmost importance is attached to combining ingredients which in other countries are served separately. Brazilians pay close attention to the arrangement of the table and carefully blend black beans with assorted meats, cabbage, oranges, *torrezno* (pieces of bacon) and white manioc flour, all of which are eaten in a rather curious manner, taking a little here and a little there and mixing everything up in the centre of one's plate.

Echoing the layout of the table, where the main dish is surrounded by accompanying dishes in a perfectly-defined hierarchy, the centre of each plate is reserved for the principal item of food, as though gradations were emphasized at all levels. The ideal of Brazilian cooking is to assemble appropriate dishes and guests on an important occasion in a harmonious ceremony which is the main symbol of sociability in Brazil.

Does this arrangement of the table (where there is always a leading figure and supporting actors), table manners (the main dish is served first, then the others) and even the method of eating, have a direct correlation with what I would call 'intermediate meals', an embodiment of the ties which for centuries have enabled so hierarchical a society to absorb and harmonize values from other cultures? It is similar to the effect achieved by humbly and subtly blending in the same dish black beans and white manioc flour to form an intermediate mass that is as delightful as a mulatto skin.

Roberto DaMatta

CRITICAL THINKING AND WRITING

1. a) At which audience do you think this essay is aimed?
      i. general
      ii. expert
   b) Explain your choice of (i) or (ii) using evidence from the passage to support your answer.
2. What is the thesis of the essay? Do you think it has been stated at an appropriate point in the essay? Justify your response.
3. Is the writer's purpose to entertain or inform his audience? Provide evidence from the passage to support your answer.

STRUCTURE, STYLE AND STRATEGIES

4. How effective do you consider the introduction to be? Does it create interest in the essay?
5. What does the writer achieve by using comparison–contrast in the second, third and fourth paragraphs?
6. What do you think the writer hopes to accomplish in the paragraph beginning: 'This no doubt explains why in Brazil a sharp distinction is made between the concept of food' and ending, 'as is now the practice in Anglo-Saxon countries.'?
7. The writer uses several Brazilian words and phrases. What is the effect of these foreign language words in this English essay?
8. How does the writer explain the phrase 'anthropologies of eating'?
      i. Cite one culinary model which he provides to support his definition.
      ii. State two claims which he makes about that culinary model.
      iii. What are the strengths and weaknesses of these claims?
9. The writer explains two types of 'eating practices'. What organizing principle does he use to present them; and how do they communicate the ideas of 'separateness' and 'coexistence' which the writer claims both practices express?
10. DaMatta views food and the preparation and serving of food as having different symbolisms. Identify two symbolisms of meals or the preparation of meals which he provides and explain how these symbolisms work.
11. Critically examine the relevance of the title of the essay to the content.
12. Describe the diction used and say why you think the author employs this level of diction.

WRITING ACROSS THE CURRICULUM ACTIVITY

13. The writer states: *"The meal is also a means of expressing and asserting a national, regional or local identity, or even the identity of a family or an individual, depending on the context. Essentially, the act of eating crystallizes emotional states and social identities."*
    Write a paragraph in which you support the statements and one in which you oppose them.
14. Write two paragraphs in which you explain the social significance of food in your country.
15. Find a foreign student or lecturer on your campus. Discuss the symbolism(s), if any, which the preparation, serving and eating of food have in their country. Share what you have learnt with your class.

CHAPTER 51

TROPHY AND CATASTROPHE

Mr. Chairman, Your Excellency the President, Ministers of Government, members of the Diplomatic Corps, friends and fellow-travellers in this vale of tears and laughter: I would like first of all to say my sincere thanks for the honour which you have conferred on me by inviting me to address such a gathering on such an occasion.

The establishment of the Guyana Prize for literature in such hard times as these is an act of peculiar grace, equalled only by that first memorable Carifesta of 1972, which was also a Guyanese initiative. It isn't often — with all due respect to the Commonwealth Prize, the Booker Award or the W.H. Smith Award — that the Caribbean writer finds a serious sponsor. Even in the area of research, it is generally easier to find a sponsor for research into our chaotic politics or our foundering economies, than into our remarkably vibrant literature. Thus both creative writer and academic suffer in a situation where it is not unusual for publication to lag behind creation for ten years or more.

During the 1950s and 1960s, Caribbean writing attracted the British publishing houses. It was new and passionate, and signalled the eruption into visibility of the colonial person who, if he had never quite accepted his servitude, had at the same time never quite articulated his deepest and most burning necessity in a fiction and language that was unmistakably his own. Part of the interest of the British publisher no doubt lay in the fact that a relatively easy market existed for writing that was new and strange. There was, also, a curious pride and proprietorship; for this new writing was seen as demonstrating the flexibility of the English language. Despite the astringent satire which it directed at colonial education, the new literature was taken as proof of the virtues of that education which, against all odds, had taught inarticulate Caliban to speak.

One has only to read those inane reviews that used to appear in the *West Indian Committee Circular*, the journal of the old Sugar Interest, to realise that our literature was being promoted as a quaint curiosity, or as a marketable commodity whose meaning did not, and could not possibly matter. At a 1971 conference, I heard more than one of our writers remark that it was only the advent of West Indian critics and reviewers such as Edward Kamau Brathwaite who, since 1957, wrote long essays in *Bim*, that they gained a sense of what their work meant to the community for whom it was intended.

After the novelty of the 1950 to 1965 period had worn off, and Reid, Mittelholzer, Lamming, Selvon, Naipaul, Salkey, Hearne, Harris and Walcott had been established as our most important voices, the willing sponsorship of British publishing houses was, it seems to me, tacitly reduced. One waited for a second wave of writers to follow in the wake of the first, but this did not happen, for several reasons. Firstly, the writers of the fifties had said most of what it was possible to say about the folk life, politics and landscape of small impoverished societies. Secondly, the early elation had begun to encounter the hard realities of self-government and independence, and an already serious vision had darkened considerably by the mid-sixties. Thirdly and most important, new writers were finding it increasingly more difficult to get published, the publishers being more concerned with the easier task of promoting already established voices, than with risking money and energy on the encouragement of fresh talent.

If we think of the writers who emerged between 1965 and 1970, we would find that Jean Rhys was a survivor from nearly four decades earlier. Edward Kamau Brathwaite had been publishing poems in *Bim* since 1948 and was, like Walcott, only three years younger than Lamming. Michael Anthony and Earl Lovelace were among the few to be given exposure and encouragement in the immediate post-Independence period, while poets such as Dennis Scott and Mervyn Morris who had developed their own styles, would have to await the emergence of those brave little West Indian publishing houses, New Beacon and Bogle-L'Ouverture, who in the post-1970 period have borne the brunt of the new publishing. I must have at least one hundred poets in slim collections, which have

been either self-published or the results of the efforts of *Savacou*, *Bim*, Karia Press or the Extra-Mural Department of UWI.

While the presence of local and foreign-based Caribbean publishers is a sign of independence, there is a limit to the exposure which the small publisher can give to a writer. Sometimes an entire genre suffered from an inadequacy of promotion, as was the case with drama, which after the series of one act plays published by the UWI Extra-Mural Department from the late fifties to the mid-sixties, went into a slump until the seventies, when the Walcott plays began to appear. At present, Walcott's main publisher is not British, but American.

Relief of a sort came with the short-lived Allison and Busby, who republished Lamming and C.L.R. James, and promoted the novels of Roy Heath. Relief of a sort has also come from **Casa de las Americas**, the Cuban publishing house which in 1976 extended their annual literary competition to include writers from the Anglophone Caribbean. Guyanese writers such as Noel Williams, Angus Richmond, Harry Naain and John Agani, have won the Casa prize. Edward Kamau Brathwaite has won it twice, once for *Black & Blues*, a collection of poems, and in 1986 for *Roots*, a collection of essays.

Very recently, through the agency mainly of West Indian publishers, we have seen the healthy and exciting emergence of several women writers such as Merle Collins, Grace Nicholls, Erna Brodber, Velma Pollard, Olive Senior, Lorna Goodison, Christine Craig, Pamela Mordecai, Jean Goulbourne, Jean Binta Breeze and Opal Palmer. I think, indeed, that it is safe to predict, that our most significant voices for the next two decades will be female. There are several reasons for this. First: the time demands it. All over the world women have been coming into visibility, and edifying, in ways as significant as their male counterparts, the fundamental reality of human existence. Caribbean women are part of this universal re-definition, this transformation of reality. Second: the emergence of women writers in the Caribbean indicates that the other half of Caribbean sensibility is seeking fulfilment through self-expression. If the male writers sought their liberation of spirit in the face of rigid colonial structures, the female writers seek theirs in the face of equally rigid patriarchal ones.

The third reason our next wave of writers may well be women, lies in the contempt for things of the sensibility which our societies have unconsciously bred in the minds of young men. Young men have absorbed a notion of development based on the idea of science and technology, to the exclusion of the Arts. It is quite normal in a class of say, sixty literature students at UWI, to find only three males. While there is no necessary or inevitable correspondence between studying literature as an academic discipline and becoming a creative writer, it is still true to conclude that over the last fifteen years, far more women have been exposed to a wider range of literature than their male counterparts. Given this exposure and the already described need for self-definition, the women will be carrying the major burden of our writing in the near future.

Popular artistic forms such as the Calypso, Reggae and the emerging 'Dub' poetry, are still largely dominated by young men. The Calypso, contrary to some opinions, is neither dying nor deteriorating. If there are fewer narrative calypsoes, there are more celebratory ones. The Calypso today also contains a range of political recall, as well as an analytic grasp of the political moment, that is equal to, if not greater than what obtained in the age of Atilla. It provides us with an index of popular

attitudes to an increasingly bewildering social experience, and has had to wrestle with growing problems of madness (Terror's 'Madness', 1974), drug addiction (Duke, Sparrow, Explainer, Singing Francine, among others, have all sung on this theme) as well as unemployment, corruption and vagrancy.

The darkening social experience since Independence has changed the nature of calypso laughter which, in the process of adjusting to bewildering paradox, has become a very complex thing. Chalkdust's 'Learn to Laugh' advocates bitter mirth. It disturbs precisely because it unmasks the source of laughter, revealing it as chaos, bitterness and helplessness, as well as its function: masking, evasion and dereliction of the intolerable responsibility for setting the situation right. The language of some calypsoes has returned to the singalong simplicity of the old-time kalinda chants, while that of those singers who have accepted a burden of self-definition, has become more metaphorical, more dense, and more capable of expressing a wider range of feeling.

But calypsonians, like most other creative artists, face extreme problems when it comes to having their records produced. The young singer, like the young writer, may find that there is no one who is prepared to invest in an unknown voice, or that an investor may not offer fair terms.... Tales of the exploitation of singers can fill a book. Plagiarism for commercial gain has been a major concern. Also, subtle or overt political censorship has existed in some Caribbean territories; such censorship places an additional pressure on the singer, whose revenues are inevitably affected when his songs are not played on the radio. A paradoxical situation is often created, where one sector of the community blames singers for composing trivial party songs, while another sector damns them for telling too much depressing political truth.

It should be clear that all categories of artists need help of some sort. There is pressing need not only for awards such as the Guyana Prize for Literature, but also for a CARICOM Publishing House, which should belong equally to the public and private sectors in the Caribbean, and which, utilising the infrastructure that already exists in abundance throughout these territories, should publish school books, literary, academic and historical texts, as well as the burgeoning music of the region. There is no reason why, equipped with skilled panels drawn, as CXC panels are, from all over the region, a CARICOM Publishing House should not be able to select work that has merit and quality: work that is vital to our perception of self and possibility; work too, that is informed by that critical intelligence which will be necessary for our self-knowledge and our location of the Caribbean self in the world of the cosmos.

Such a CARICOM Publishing House can become a means whereby we may ingather our wandering wits, or, to use Martin Carter's arresting image: 'collect our scattered skeleton.' No regional cultural policy will emerge without something like it. We need institutions that are more permanent than Carifesta, which, indeed, will give us something to celebrate whenever Carifesta comes around. A CARICOM Publishing House should also serve to stem the annual outflow from the region of millions of dollars, which is what we as a region pay foreign publishing houses, by presenting them with our captive primary and high school markets.

The act of writing poetry, prose or drama is, now that we know the extent that science and technology are controlled by the metropole, one of the most crucial necessities and possible frontiers for development in the Caribbean. We cannot control the price of oil; we cannot control, try as we may, the price of bauxite; nor can we control the American quota for sugar. But we can control our exploration and presentation of ourselves. The Arts are probably the only area in which sovereignty is possible; though even here the burden of autonomous statement is exacting as frightening a toll as the region-wide collapse of our economies. This is not only because of the difficulties artists experience in getting their work published, but also because of the difficult conditions in which the average citizens of these territories have been existing for some time.

At times, these conditions objectify themselves, crystallize themselves, as it were, into moments of terrible atrocity, that have wrung from the poet, novelist and playwright outcry after outcry. Since Independence, we have had guerillas and gundowns, the Malik affair in Trinidad — we all know the literature that grew out of that catastrophe: Vidia Naipaul's essay, 'The Killings in Trinidad' and his stark best-selling novel *Guerillas*, which became very popular in North America, a country so much engaged in the conversion of fact into fiction, that many people there can no longer distinguish between the two. Trinidad, which is very similar to America in this respect, converted the Malik affair into the Carnival Ole Mas Band, BENSON UNDER HEDGES.[1]

Jamaica has since Independence been conducting its fixed dialectic of gunmen; its unending, fratricidal conflict between the duppy and the duppy-conqueror. This conflict has concretised itself in the sacrificial waste of the 1980 elections when well over five hundred people were killed.

The Jamaican tragedy has given rise to several poems. One has only to read Brathwaite's Kingston poems as 'Springblade', 'Starvation', 'Dread', 'Wings of a Dove', 'Sun Song' and 'Kingston in the Kingdom of this World' to see how this tragedy has affected the expression of one of the region's leading writers. The Orange Lane fire is directly alluded to in his 'Poem for Walter Rodney' where he makes the connection between two atrocities, twinning the cities of Kingston and Georgetown. Recognising in contemporary Jamaica patterns, and structures of mind as old as the slave plantation, Brathwaite has shown in some detail how what he calls 'the return of the status crow' has produced 'the resurrection of the dread'. The poems of Dennis Scott, Brian Meeks or Kendel Hippolyte, Scott's play *Dog*, the reggae songs of Marley and the murdered Peter Tosh, the Dub poetry of Linton Kwesi Johnson, Mutabaruka, Jean Binta Breeze and Mikey Smith, the latter who couldn't believe that children were being deliberately thrown into the Orange Lane fire, but was himself soon to be stoned to death by people who disagreed with his political views: all provide us with a range of artistic responses to Jamaican atrocity, and define the bleak spiritual landscape out of which many Caribbean writers operate.

One of the duties of the Caribbean State should be to provide the citizen and artist with the necessary space within which he can operate, even when the citizen and artist see through and beyond the structures and devices of the State. Where such space does not exist, literature creates it through protest, or through the imaginative territory which it liberates in quest of living-room for the spirit. The creative voice in the Caribbean has always challenged the political reality or unreality, fostered by ideologues for or against the prevailing political order. When this happens, the creative voice may find itself confronted by the ignorant machinery of an oppression which, when it is not fostered directly by the State, may be tacitly permitted to happen because of the indifference or neglect of the State. The word may then find itself in chains.

Edward Kamau Brathwaite's 'Kingston in the Kingdom of this World' dramatizes the outcry of the voice against such imprisonment. The poem's voice is simultaneously that of a Christ figure awaiting trial and crucifixion; that of the artist, whose authority of sunlight, vision, music, dance and the illuminating power of the imagination is pitted against the incarceration of the State; and that of the Dogon Nummo, the primal creative word and voice and spirit of Africa, rotting in a Jamaican jail.

Guyana has matched the rest of the Caribbean in atrocity. We had the mind-blowing Jim Jones Affair being enacted in the Guyana forest of the night, involving a handful of white masters of the religious word and nine hundred black slaves to it. This atrocity has produced about a dozen prose accounts, including one from Shiva Naipaul who, imitating his elder brother as he usually did, also squeezed a novel out of the catastrophe. There were also two or three American movies, one of which was significantly entitled *The Guyana Tragedy*. Popular response in Guyana was provided by two songs, one by Nicky Porter and the other by the Trade Winds, who summarised the Jim Jones catastrophe with the couplet:

He tell them to think and they thinking
So he tell them to drink and they drinking.

What the Caribbean mind cannot comprehend, it converts into a macabre carnival of humour, behind which still lurks the cadaver of evaded catastrophe. Here the Trade Winds are, perhaps unconsciously, establishing the link between centralised propaganda, mind-control and self-destruction, and suggesting a lesson pertinent not only to the Jim Jones commune, and their ilk, but also to the Guyanese nation as a whole.

Guyana can also boast the death of Walter Rodney which, like the Grenada fiasco three years later, was a devastating body blow to an entire generation; the literal reduction to ashes of passion, energy, commitment, courage, laughter and intelligence. That death has evoked an entire anthology of poems, as well as collections of papers from conferences and seminars on the meaning of the life's work of this outstanding Caribbean historian, and international personality, who could not find a job at the University of Guyana. That this could happen under a regime which four years earlier had had the generosity, scope and vision to inaugurate Carifesta, is perhaps the most astounding paradox to have been produced in a country of astounding paradoxes.

Moving as all these elegies to Rodney undoubtedly are, I would have preferred other poems and Rodney alive. I would even have preferred him to have rejected what Linton Kwesi Johnson termed 'History's weight', and obeyed the advice which Wordsworth McAndrew offered him in a 1976 poem, written in reaction to his being denied the job at the University of Guyana. McAndrew at that time had already intuited a sort of doom, and advised Rodney to leave a country which could or would not find use for either his academic excellence or political commitment. McAndrew himself, by far Guyana's best and most active folklorist, who almost single-handedly provided a forum for scores of new Guyanese short stories and unearthed the customs, sayings and practices of Guyanese from all corners of the land, took his own advice and left Guyana. The warehouse manager where he first sought work in New Jersey gave him a simple arithmetic test which he expected him to fail. When Mac returned after a few minutes, the manager exclaimed in that mixture of amazement and contempt with which Prospero is sometimes grudgingly forced to acknowledge Caliban as a being capable of intelligence: 'Gee: He got them all right.' Our national talent has been to make the real man into a small man. As the voice in 'the Kingdom of this World' laments: 'He is reduced, he is reduced'.

In the sponsoring of Literature by State and School, it is worth reminding both State and School of the strain under which writers exist, particularly when they are politically critical of the State. In Trinidad five poets were among the 1970 detainees, and Jack Kelshall, whom Guyanese of the early sixties might well remember, became a poet after he was wrongfully imprisoned in the 1970s. Martin Carter had, of course, experienced this under the British nearly two decades earlier.

Under such stasis, such unchange, some writers have chosen the amnesia of alcohol. Others — Mittelholzer, Leroy Calliste, Eric Roach, the painter and folklorist Harold Simmons, the poet and teacher Neville Robinson — committed suicide. It is a dangerous thing, often a fatal thing, to even possess sensibility in such an age, where there are so many ways that a person can be destroyed. We live in societies in the Caribbean where the price of a certain type of commitment is certain arrest; of a certain quality of feeling is possible self-immolation.

The grimness of the age has affected the styles and modes of functioning of both the State and the individual. If many individual sensibilities have succumbed to despair or become fixed in automatic attitudes of protest and resistance, the State has tended to ossify into rigid authoritarian attitudes which are really the mask of a fundamental impotence.

Surveying West Indian societies since Independence, one is forced to conclude that we remain colonial in how authority reacts to critical challenge; that certain aspects of our consciousness have become paralysed in ancient attitudes of crippledom; that sadly, it has proven easier to mummify entire nations than the individual corpse.

Our neo-colonial situation of simultaneous freedom and mental enchainment is one of deep and perplexing paradox. In Trinidad in 1986 it was possible for black policemen to unleash an unprovoked attack on black people demonstrating against the anti-black racism of South Africa's Apartheid State. The same Trinidad moved a vote in the United Nations to enforce sanctions against South Africa. Faced with such inconsistency, deeply rooted in our colonial past and blossoming daily in our neo-colonial present, the mind of the artist and critic alike seeks naturally to express and explore paradox.

I have consequently, named this address 'Trophy and Catastrophe'. If the catastrophe refers to these societies in which we now live and breathe and have what remains of our being, the trophy refers to the Guyana Prize for literature. I hope the prize is only the beginning of a new dispensation for writers, and that the graciousness which inspired this inauguration will also inform the political future of the Guyanese people.

Gordon Rohlehr

Note

1. Benson was the name of the English woman found murdered in Trinidad, and buried in a garden.

CRITICAL THINKING AND WRITING

1. What is the main point which the writer is trying to make in this piece?
2. What knowledge have you gained about the development of literature in the English-speaking Caribbean?
3. This piece is predominantly exposition. What other discourse mode does the writer utilize?
4. What do the writer's word choice and allusions suggest about his intended audience?
5. How is the piece organized overall (for example, general to specific, most important to least important, and so on)?
6. 'It was new and passionate and signalled the eruption into visibility of the colonial person who, if he had never quite accepted his servitude, had at the same time never quite articulated his deepest and most burning necessity in a fiction and language that was unmistakably his own.' Identify the figurative device that the writer uses here and comment on its effectiveness in helping him achieve his purpose.
7. a) Identify, (from the passage), the reasons the writer names his speech 'Trophy and Catastrophe'.

    b) How might an article's title serve as a signpost?
8. This extract is a speech that was intended for a listening audience. Indicate two ways in which the writing has been shaped by the context.

WRITING ACTIVITIES

9. In this passage, the writer utilizes a range of organizing principles. Identify some of those principles. What does this suggest about the varied ways in which your paragraphs may be organized in any piece of writing? Write a piece utilizing more than one organizing principle.
10. The writer refers to various situations which occurred up to the year that he delivered this speech. Do any of the concerns that the writer raises still exist as major issues in the Caribbean?

CHAPTER 52

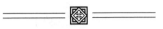

U-ROY THE ORIGINATOR

The man who established the deejay style as a legitimate musical form was U-Roy, born Ewart Beckford. Frustrated at seeing crowds respond ecstatically to his art while having nothing to show for it — his best performances vanished into thin air and he was regarded in musical circles as nothing but a glorified record spinner — U-Roy decided to etch his work on vinyl. In late 1969, under the urging of King Tubby, whose set U-Roy was working on, he got some studio time at Duke Reid's and chanted over some old Treasure Isle hits. The result is history.[1]

Within the space of months, the face of Jamaican music was irrevocably altered. U-Roy controlled the top three spots on both RJR and JBC charts simultaneously, an unprecedented feat, with 'Wear You To The Ball', and the presciently titled cuts 'Wake the Town' and 'Rule the Nation'. Spurred by his success, a slew of imitators rushed into the recording studios. Other system deejays like Prince Far I and Dennis Alcapone decided to also put their sounds on record. Catchier and clearer than most of his contemporaries, Dennis Alcapone had a number of hits like 'El Paso', 'Power Version', 'Mosquito One', 'Alcapone Guns Don't Argue', 'Judgement Day' and 'Teach the Children'.

Singers of middling success eyed deejaying as a chance to break through. One of these,

Scotty, was the most successful of U-Roy's direct successors, scoring a string of number one hits like 'Skanking in Bed' and 'Sesame Street', the only one well remembered being the famous 'Draw Your Brakes'.

'Wear You To The Ball' is the most celebrated deejay tune of all time, and justifiably so. It was not U-Roy's first hit; 'Wake the Town' came out a few months earlier. But it was 'Wear You To The Ball' which made the greatest impact, and established the deejay sound. The dancehall masses had known about deejaying for years. But being recorded on vinyl meant dissemination to the nation, rural and urban, uptown and downtown. As it had so often before, the sound of the Kingston ghettos spread across the entire Jamaica.

Naturally at the beginning it seemed just another fad, a novelty craze like the twist or cha cha. But the public kept demanding and buying deejay discs and the sound became an established part of local music. Many derided it as 'not really music', a charge you still hear today. But protest as the naysayers might, it became increasingly obvious that the deejay sound of the Jamaican ghetto had developed an almost completely new art form.

Most of the songs didn't make any sense at the start. What was important to the public was a driving beat, bouncy deejaying and a catch phrase — something as trite as Dennis Alcapone's signature 'Ah wa so, El Paso' could make a deejay's reputation and stay on everyone's lips for months. 'Wear you to the Ball' is often cited as the form's apex, but is basically a radio deejay pattern — a mixture of exhortation, commentary on the song, braggadocio and nonsense.

What counted was not so much what was said as how it was said. One of the big differences between U-Roy's records and his predecessors' was that he brought all the excitement of his dancehall chanting to vinyl 45, an almost hysterical vocal timbre rising and falling as the song demanded. And he played with the song's rhythms — sometimes bouncing off the beat, sometimes off the singer's voice, sometimes sliding in between both and weaving his voice into the melody and rhythm, sometimes obliterating all background sound with punishing verbal barrages. As U-Roy says to younger deejays who ask advice: 'Be sure that you're not running away from the riddim and the riddim's not running away from you.'[2]

Even though the early recorded deejays, Comic, Stitt, and even U-Roy, chanted in the kind of pseudo-American accent used by set and radio deejays, it wasn't long before nearly all deejays were toasting in full-blooded 'patwah'. The great appeal of deejaying to Jamaicans is that deejaying reproduces habitual, everyday speech mannerisms. Singers are forced to alter their vocal patterns to suit the song's melody — indeed that is what good singing is all about, joining one's voice as closely to the melodic line as possible. So singing produces a sort of generic vocal structure, and national accents tend to virtually disappear in traditional western song.

But the deejays expressed their emotions in the staccato vocal patterns and vernacular language of everyday Jamaican conversation,

and this gave their music an unprecedented emotional immediacy. No subconscious translation was needed — the rhythmic chanting bypassed the conscious ego and went straight to the brain, generating a gripping, visceral excitement not found in 'regular' singing.

This new phenomenon was to have international as well as local repercussions. Once deejaying was established at home, wide-travelling Jamaicans began taking it abroad. And more than most immigrants, Jamaicans bring a part of home to their new surroundings.

Clive Campbell moved to the Bronx in New York with his family in 1967 at the age of twelve. In 1973 he assembled a sound system like the kind he had grown up with in Kingston and began throwing parties. The set was called Herculord and Campbell assumed the name Kool DJ Herc. Modeled after the huge sets necessary to compete in the heated sound system battles of Jamaica, Herculord was far more powerful than anything around, and blew the competition away, establishing a ghetto-wide reputation. He murdered the competition with his 'clean', distortion-free sounds, shattering frequency range, and massive volume.[3]

The exact details and chronology of what came next are lost in the mists of time because no one was really paying attention to what was only one of a million musical trends happening. But Herc probably sensed that while American blacks didn't really respond to the reggae rhythms he and his emcees toasted to, they liked the chanting. Even if they couldn't understand what the Jamaicans were saying and didn't talk like them, something in these verbal broadsides touched a chord. Chanting over funk and disco hits was the next natural step and black American youngsters began adapting the form to their slang and rhythms of speech.

According to Afrika Bambaata:

[Herc] knew that a lot of American blacks were not getting into reggae. He took the same thing that the deejays were doing – toasting — and did it with American records, Latin records with a beat. Herc took phrases like what was happening in the streets, new sayings going around like 'rock on my mellow', 'to the beat y'all', and would call out the names of people who were at the party, just like the microphone personalities who deejayed back in Jamaica.[4, 5]

Herc began leaving the deejaying to his MC Coke La Rock while concentrating on 'mixing'. Using identical copies of a record on twin turntables, Herc would cut back and forth on the 'break' part of a song where the instruments jammed. The break was the sonic climax that always sent his listeners wild, but it was too short. By cutting back and forth on his twin turntables, he created a continuous 'break beat' and thus the first 'hip hop' rhythms. In his book *The New Beats*, S.H. Fernando points out unmistakable similarities between dubbing and sampling, and says Kool Herc and Coke La Rock were to the fledgling hip-hop scene what King Tubby and U-Roy were to dancehall in Jamaica.[6]

One amusing aspect of rap's beginnings is how closely it paralleled the early days of Jamaican sound systems. Not only did they use toasters to give dances a live feel, but Kool Herc and his imitators, like Afrika Bambaata and Grandmaster Flash, would often have system battles where rivals set up near each other and tried to blast away the opposition with superior wattage — shades of Tom the Great, Trojan and Downbeat in the downtown Kingston 1950s! And, hilariously, Herc would often soak his records in water and remove the labels to stymie potential competition![7] Coxsone must have remembered 'Lator For Gator' and chuckled when he heard this. Duke Reid is probably still laughing in his grave.

There's another interesting facet of Herc's early days. As someone who was there notes: Nobody ain't never thought of playing no records like he was playing before that. And all of them shits was sitting in your house — all your mom's and pop's old records. Soon as Kool Herc started playing, every motherlover started robbing his mother and father for records.[8]

It's a very Jamaican trait to keep playing songs you like no matter how old they are. Curiously, Herc had denied the Jamaican connection with rap: 'Jamaican toasting? Naw, naw. No connection there. I couldn't accept it. The inspiration for Rap is James Brown and the album "Hustler's Corner" by the Last Poets.'[9] But this album came out in 1973, years after deejaying had been established as a legitimate musical form in Jamaica. And 'Rapper's Delight', the first big rap record, didn't come out until 1979.

It's natural that Herc would wish to be seen as 'an originator, never an imitator' (U-Roy's signature phrase) and that black American kids who had adopted rap as 'their' music should maintain they had created it. But the Jamaican link (and interestingly the earliest rap star, Grandmaster Flash, had Barbadian parents who collected both American swing and West Indian records[10]) aligned with the similarity of musical methods and deejaying's unquestioned chronological precedence, make the conclusion that rap evolved from deejaying undeniable.

Of course some would say that Jamaican deejay music evolved from the southern black R&B radio disc jockeys, who in turn, developed their style from jazz scat singers.

And they may be right. But it was the Jamaican deejays who first turned chanting/toasting/scatting into a commercial musical form that stood on its own and pushed all accompaniment into the background — where people bought the records because of the rhythmic talking.

As many commentators point out, deejaying and rapping can both be considered an extension of the West African oral tradition of the griot or storyteller, who recited the history of his tribal community, sometimes to the accompaniment of talking drums.[11]

Deejay music in Jamaica was going through countless changes in style and form years before rap music was recognized as anything more than a novelty. One thing became clear: the same immediacy that made deejay so potent, also meant it wore badly. More than most other popular music forms, deejay music seems to be a music of the moment and loses its appeal quickly. A smash hit that sounds utterly compelling one month, can wear tiresomely trite the next.

And so it was with deejays too. Indeed the history of nearly every deejay has been one of overnight fame, massive popular appeal and almost complete oblivion. Better management has enabled deejays to last longer of late. Lt Stitchie, Papa San and Admiral Bailey can still pull crowds after almost ten years in the business. But a hot new deejay still begins looking over his shoulder rather quickly.

One offshoot of deejay music which has garnered much interest in academic circles is dub poetry. To quote Jamaican poet, Professor Mervyn Morris, circa 1982:

The term dub poetry was promoted early in 1979 by Oku Onuora to identify work then presented — often at the Jamaica School of Drama — by himself, Mikey Smith and Noel Walcott. The dub poem, Oku has said, "is not merely putting a piece of poem pon a reggae rhythm; it is a poem that has a built-in reggae rhythm – hence when the poem is read without any reggae rhythm (so to speak) backing, one can distinctly hear the reggae rhythm coming out of the poem." More recently, however, Oku has been arguing that any verse that refers to or incorporates music rhythms belongs in the family, poetry into which music rhythms have been dubbed, so to speak: dub poetry.[12]

One of Jamaica's best known dub poets at present is Mutabaruka, who is also a health food businessman and radio talk-show host. Muta's resonant baritone and striking appearance — his leonine dreadlocks have a natural white streak in front — have gained his work a lot of attention, even though he resists the label of 'dub poet' because it refers to only one aspect of his work.[13]

Linton Kwesi Johnson, who emigrated from Jamaica to England when eleven, is probably the most famous and highly regarded dub poet. LKJ's best work is considered to be 'Dread Beat an' Blood'. According to *The New Trouser Press Record Guide*:

'Dread Beat an' Blood' was a call to arms, a dark commemoration of police harassment and social repression of blacks told in a forceful but strangely spiteless manner. Speaking his poems over Johnson uses the patois of the streets to speak to his audience, calling for brotherhood and vigilance. The clean, supple, vibrant music and incisive pointed words make it a powerful and memorable political statement.'[14]

Kevin O'Brien Chang and Wayne Chen

Notes

1. 'U-Roy: Words of Wisdom', *The Beat* (1989).
2. Dave Marsh, *The First Rock & Roll Confidential Report* (US: Patheon Books, 1985), 79–80.
3. Afrika Bambaataa 'The Rap Attack', *The Beat* 5: 4 (1986)
4. *The New Beats*, 10.
5. Ibid., 44.
6. Ibid.
7. Ibid., 7–8.
8. Ibid., 8.
9. *The Beat* 5: 4 (1986).
10. Dave Marsh, *The First Rock & Roll Confidential Report*, 79–80.
11. *The New Beats*, 32.
12. Stephen Davis and Peter Simon, *Reggae International*, 189.
13. Ibid., 191.
14. *The New Trouser Press Record Guide*, 30.

CRITICAL THINKING AND WRITING

1. Whom do you consider to be the writers' anticipated audience, based on the details presented in the essay?
2. While the article, as the title suggests, highlights U-Roy's role as the 'originator' of the deejay style, it deals with much more. Select the sentences which present other important aspects developed in the article:
   a) The impact of U-Roy's singing on Jamaican music.
   b) U-Roy's role in taking the music of the ghetto across Jamaica.
   c) The meaning of 'Wear You To The Ball'.
   d) How dub poetry developed from deejay music.
   e) How rap music influenced deejay music.
   f) The parallel between the development of deejay music and rap music.
3. What general statement is supported by the details of the essay? How successful are the writers in supporting this statement?
4. Discuss three purposes for which the writers use illustration.
5. Comment on the writers' use of language (music related words, colloquialisms, creole expressions).
6. Identify the figures of speech used in the following, and explain how they help to intensify or expand meaning in the text:
   a) 'U-Roy decided to etch his work on vinyl.'
   b) 'The face of Jamaican music was irrevocably altered.'
   c) '…sometimes obliterating all background sound with punishing verbal barrages'.

WRITING ACTIVITIES

7. Write two paragraphs about a Caribbean musician with whose work you are familiar. Attempt to use a style similar to that of the writers of the passage (especially in terms of how they combine formal and informal language).
8. Write two paragraphs for a student newspaper providing information on any form of Caribbean music which you know well.

CHAPTER 53

EMANCIPATE YOURSELF FROM MENTAL SLAVERY

PART I

Dear Mr. Garvey,

Emancipation anniversaries are the affirmation of our right to renewal at the personal and community levels. I liked how Emancipation anniversaries entered into the way the Universal Negro Improvement Association and African Communities League structured their organizational life. Your annual conventions in the 1920s and 1930s, which brought together representatives of black communities in Africa and the Diaspora to discuss our condition and plan for the future, were held in the month of August. In another letter I will ask you about the organizational challenges you faced in attempting to network, without the Internet, over 1,000 UNIA divisions in 38 countries.

I have been asked to give the Emancipation 2000 lecture at the Boulevard Baptist Church and this coincides with the 60th anniversary of your death in London in 1940. 'Emancipate yourself from mental slavery' is a phrase made popular by Bob Marley in his famous 'Redemption Song'. Marley, who like you hailed from the parish of St Ann, was born five years after your death and he died in 1980. His music has had a powerful global outreach. 'Redemption Song' is the last tune on the *Uprising* album by Bob Marley and

the Wailers. That album came out in 1980 and I still have my copy of the original long-playing record. So it is twenty years now that we have been listening to this profound message of revolution. Bob got hold of your speech and put the line to very creative lyrics and music and has directed us to the philosophical and historical depth of your conceptions. But it takes much more than very good music to get there.

The word 'revolution' has now become commercialized, and advertisers use the word to describe new fashion in designer jeans, shirts and shoes. It has also been used to describe the new information technology. On another level it has become associated with violence used to overthrow the state. But the way you fought mental slavery implies a kind of mental emancipation that is revolutionary on a profound level because it means releasing the shackles on our minds, cutting through the doctrines of racial inferiority to arrive at our human potential.

The Idea of Mental Slavery

Professor Barry Higman, an Australian scholar of West Indian history, has written that this idea of mental slavery goes back even further than your speech in 1937. Little did you know that the phrase you used in 1937 in an address in Menelik Hall, in the town of Sydney, in the province of Nova Scotia, Canada, would have been picked up and given new life. This is part of the reason why I feel confident in writing this letter because in many ways you have taken on a second life in our minds. But the life in our minds takes on many forms and some of these forms do not reflect what you meant by mental freedom. So we sport the red, black and green, of the Universal Negro Improvement Association, have your image on coins, and have streets and schools named after you. But do we really know what you stood for, and what mental emancipation continually demands of us?

Professor Higman has identified one source of the term 'mental slavery' in a letter by one Sydney Moxsy of Dry River, Hayes, Clarendon, which was published in the *Daily Gleaner* of 31 July 1919 under the caption 'Manual and Mental Slavery'. Professor Higman says that Moxsy

> believed that slavery was of at least two kinds, the mental and the manual. Manual or "body slavery" was forced on people through the enslavement of "one man to another", whereas "mind-slavery" was either created or permitted by people themselves, and was therefore more a matter of sorrow than of anger. All human beings were potentially subject to mental slavery, said Moxsy, and, in words foreshadowing Garvey and Marley, he claimed "none but the individual himself can alleviate it." The trouble was, he argued, that whereas people would readily help to free others from manual slavery they "will not make any personal effort to free themselves from the slavery of their own passions; or from that slavery of custom and carelessness which permits of extravagance and waste" (Higman 1998: 9–10).

Moxsy had a moral approach to mental slavery but he put his finger on the important concept of self-liberation.

Professor Higman suggests that you might have got the idea of mental slavery from Moxsy. Maybe you got a copy of the *Gleaner* in New York in 1919 during your demanding travel schedule throughout the United States and, somehow, in your 1937 speech you decided to use it; or maybe it is sheer coincidence that you and Moxsy used the same formulation. I wonder how useful speculation is on this matter when we have no idea of the conversation you were having during the August meeting of the second Regional Conference of the branches of the Universal Negro Improvement Association in the United States and Canada. Moreover you had just finished giving your lectures in the School of African Philosophy which was meant to train new leaders. The oral tradition is very strong with us. But I am glad you were a journalist and printer and so much of what you wrote and spoke is with us today. Since I started writing this letter I found that in the *Blackman* newspaper of November 22, 1930, you referred to mental and physical subjugation in Liberia as you commented on twentieth century slavery and the antislavery movement there. If we dig deeper we'll probably find the term in wider use during the nineteenth century and the early twentieth century. What does it matter? What matters now is the relevance of mental slavery to your grandchildren and great-grandchildren in the year 2000.

Professor Higman notes:

> Perhaps part of the attraction of the mental slavery model in recent times has been its apparent usefulness in explaining continuing social inequality, the perceived failure of independent politics and the new

forms of international bondage associated with globalization and the "free" market. It goes together with the idea that neo-colonialism is simply another form of slavery and that Jamaican (black) people are still not truly free, something Rastafarians have regularly contended (Higman 1998: 11).

Mental Emancipation

You said

We are going to emancipate ourselves from mental slavery because whilst others might free the body, none but ourselves can free the mind. Mind is your ruler, sovereign. The man who is not able to develop and use his mind is bound to be the slave of the other man who uses his mind, because man is related to man under all circumstances for good or for ill (Hill 7:791).

You have taken the discussion to the general level of man. Those who read you purely in racial terms miss where you are heading. Your discussion about mental slavery and mental emancipation takes place at a more general level, which is why you argue that under all circumstances the persons who develop their minds will dominate those who do not. By the way, I also found out that one of the most frequently used words in your *New Jamaican* newspaper of 1932–1933 was the word 'mind'. You recognized that whether it was the renaissance art of Europe, the Pyramids of Egypt or the engineering genius of the Panama Canal, it had to start in the mind. The idea of mental emancipation in your work is connected to a conception we took from you in 1969 when some of us started the *Abeng* newspaper. As a banner on the front page of a few early issues, we used your phrase, 'We want our people to think for themselves.' This

is no easy thing to do and requires daily application. Thinking for ourselves implies that we have a sense of self and selves, implies community, and also that if we don't think for ourselves we follow those who think. Coupled with this is the challenge of confidence in self. You placed such a big emphasis on this and in fact your entire work is premised on this idea of how we think and whether how and what we think advances or hinders our goals.

Coming from the experience of plantation slavery and continued in the post-slavery years of colonialism has been this idea of inferiority, of us being of less capacity than white people. This was no easy battle to wage given the fact that the Western world, its universities, research institutions and philosophers all said the same thing. Immanuel Kant, the German philosopher and one of the sources of Western modernity, said 'this fellow was quite black from head to foot, a clear proof that what he said was stupid' (Eze 1997: 38). The Western traditions of modernity from left to right of the political spectrum all shared variations of this view. The problem you identified was not whether white thinkers had this view but whether black people believed it as well. Some people of African descent who resisted this idea seized educational opportunities and tried to demonstrate through hard study that they were as good as the whites, and struggled for acceptance. Yet when some of these educated blacks came to hold power in Africa and the Caribbean they implemented the same laws, institutions and practices that upheld slavery and colonialism, and thus continued oppression on their people. So education does not necessarily resolve this problem of self-contempt. In fact it can compound it. Moreover, in any group, regardless of race, education and wealth place people among the pool from whom power-holders are drawn, and power can be and is abused, anywhere.

One of the things that mental slavery still means is vulnerability to new forms of the virus of racial self-contempt, from the days of slavery to the twenty-first century. Each generation during slavery and after slavery engaged this issue. The fact that I am writing you on this matter of mental slavery is evidence that it is still an issue in Jamaica.

Peter Abrahams, the South African-Jamaican writer, in his recent memoirs has made an observation that will shock some of his readers. While recognizing the strengths of the Jamaican people, he points to the depth of black self-contempt in Jamaica.

> We had adopted and applied to ourselves the judgements and values whites had used to justify the way they treated blacks. We had, to a greater extent than I had seen elsewhere, become the frontline of black self-contempt. Black mothers told their own little black daughters they were ugly because they were too black. African hair was "bad" hair; African features were ugly; ugly fat lips, ugly broad noses. You are black therefore you are worthless (Abrahams, ms. 2000: 252).

It is true that many of us reject these stereotypes but there are too many who subscribe to many of these racist values. There are too many men who state their preferences in terms of a brown shade and too many women who bleach to please them; too many who live as if 'nutten black nuh good.'

This problem of racial self-contempt is not only a Jamaican problem. It is an international problem that bears on the children of Africa outside of the continent itself. Talking to black people in Brazil or in Central America we hear variations on a familiar theme. It is ironical that in many of these places Jamaican black people are held up as torchbearers of

freedom from racial inferiority because of your reputation as well as the reputation of Bob Marley.

What is most disturbing about Abrahams' observation is that this type of mental slavery operates on the level of the way many of us think in day to day relations with our families, in our communities, and which bear on judgements we make about each other.

It would be a mistake, however, to think that Jamaica is at the same stage on this issue in 2000 as we were in the 1930s. There is no legal barrier to a black Jamaican taking up any position in the island, whether in the state or in the private sphere. A lot of black Jamaicans are positive about themselves and many of us who have lived abroad, as in your time, feel inferior to nobody and have demonstrated this in outstanding achievements in many spheres, whether in Jamaica or in different parts of the world. There are many more opportunities for us to demonstrate our potential than in your time. In fact, the present generation has no idea of the world as it was during the first half of the twentieth century. Black Jamaicans who have come into money are very eager to demonstrate it by the expensive cars they drive and the 'great houses' they build.

But at the same time that there have been changes from the white-skin dominance of the colonial era, there continues to be a widespread view that it is better to have light-skinned people in positions of leadership and authority. This is due to the fact that some people still associate being black with negative social behaviour such as criminality, violence, corruption and inefficiency. If that premise is accepted, it follows that you need people with light skins to be in charge.

Anyone who follows world events will realize that criminality, violence, corruption and inefficiency are in no way functions of race or colour. Criminality, violence, corruption and inefficiency abound in China, India, in Europe, as well as in the United States and Latin American and are rooted in the working of human nature and in particular social circumstances. They are not the product of pigmentation.

Yet mental emancipation must engage with the Achilles heel of racial self-abasement in the Jamaican psyche, which keeps on reasserting itself. Colour stereotyping is the single most important mental obstacle to the realization of our human potential. The people who deny that this is a problem are often the same people who give preference to their children with a lighter skin, who have preferences for lighter people, who bleach themselves or who in daily conversations pass judgements on people based on skin colour. The ascription of social value to skin colour is an idea rooted in old slave relations.

PART II

To What End Do we Struggle for Mental Emancipation?

To what end do we struggle for mental emancipation? Our struggle for mental emancipation is connected to your discussion early in the 1937 speech on world civilizations. We discussed African civilizations, then went on to other civilizations, identifying Persian, Greek, Babylonian, Roman and European civilizations. You identified some of the artifacts and scientists of the early twentieth century. Too often we look at what took people hundreds and thousands of years to build and we are awed by the achievements but we lose sight of the essential point that they represent the finest in human potential for particular periods of time. To be civilized

is to realize our human potential. This is long-term thinking, but the start of a new century is a good time to at least think about your challenge. In the same 1937 speech you also said, 'The only way you can be happy is to lay the foundation in one generation for the succeeding generation' (Hill 7: 793). You were the conscious beneficiary of the experience of previous generations. One can be the beneficiary of something without being aware of it. Consciousness of complex and contradictory legacies, and being able to build on the positive and to root out the bad grass from our mental yards was part of your challenge.

The closest I have come to thinking along this line is the discussions started by Thabo Mbeki, the South African President, on the African Renaissance (Mbeki 1998). What you were calling on us to do, together with the people of Africa and the Diaspora, is to conceive of and build an alternative civilization. Our struggle for mental emancipation represents the affirmation of our capacity to deal with the problems facing us today. Mental emancipation also has to oppose the idea of human expendability.

Human expendability has been one of the fundamental assumptions underlying the formation of the Caribbean. We ought not to forget that the Tainos were victims of a genocidal violence in Jamaica from the sixteenth to the eighteenth century. And this violence extended to the entire indigenous people of the Americas. The Guyanese writer, Jan Carew paid attention to this but it is often neglected in our historiography (Carew 1994).

The issue of human expendability is due to the fact that too many Jamaicans whether black, brown, yellow or white, write off other Jamaicans, particularly poor black Jamaicans. It is this that contributes to the justification of arbitrary executions that take place by agents of the state, by dons, by gangs and by mobs. The privileged sectors of society ignore the execution of young black men in inner-cities. And young black men execute with impunity those who don't belong to their corner, street or community. This idea of expendability is a variation of notions of expendability developed during slavery: that a slave's usefulness was a function of his or her contribution to labour processes and property accumulation. This rationale for slavery was well developed by Eric Williams, the Trinidadian scholar and the first Prime Minister of Trinidad and Tobago, in his classic book *Capitalism and Slavery*. Our post-colonial political ideologies also contributed to ideas of human expendability particularly in the context of the Cold War struggles between communism and anti-communism. In Africa and the Caribbean, black people killed each other on ideological grounds based on Marxism-Leninism, socialist or pro-capitalist positions, and political movements and parties justified this slaughter. But we don't need ideologies to kill each other. Disputes between a man and a woman, as well as disrespecting someone in the thousand and one ways this can take place, can easily lead to murder today.

Mental emancipation never ends if ending it is a process of realizing our human potential. That requires effort, work, discipline and self-confidence. It requires literacy, the foundation of modern and expanded knowledge. Your emphasis on reading and on opening up ourselves to where the world is in our time continues to be relevant. The story you told in 1932 to an audience in Kingston still rings true today: you spoke about returning from England with books on Africa and Economics and leaving them in your office. No one touched them; but, you said, if you had left a farthing it would have disappeared. But in addition to our individual efforts,

civilization concerns the circumstances of our everyday life: peace, the right to live, freedom from fear and poverty, the right to speak and disagree with others, freedom of movement. These are civilizing because they are profoundly part of the conditions necessary for this realization of human potential. This takes us into some comments on political changes in the twentieth century bearing on our struggle for civil liberties and sovereignty.

In 1937 you were in your fiftieth year, and by 1940 you were gone. You missed the Second World War and the important changes that came after it. India gained independence, China had a revolution and this was the beginning of change in Asia and Africa. The West African nationalists, Kwame Nkrumah and Nnamdi Azikiwe, who learnt so much from your work, and spoke so highly about you, returned to the Gold Coast and Nigeria to lead independence movements. Well, South African independence was to take a much longer time and it was only in 1994 that majority rule was achieved under the African National Congress led by Oliver Tambo and Nelson Mandela. Today, the colonial empires that dominated the world in your time no longer exist. But what is remarkable is that Europe carved up Africa during your lifetime and when this dismemberment seemed destined to last for centuries, you felt that an international campaign could be waged to free Africa. Imagine what you had to face: empires that seemed permanent, and global racism bolstered by law and huge armies. The dimensions of this carving up never fail to astonish me. The Europeans acquired in the late nineteenth century

30 new African colonies or protectorates, covering 16 million sq. km (10 million sq. miles). They had divided a population

of approximately 110 million Africans into 40 new political units, with some 30 per cent of the borders drawn as straight lines, cutting through villages, ethnic groups, and African kingdoms (Appiah and Gates 1999: 1683).

Reparations

On the centenary of Emancipation in the West Indies in 1934, you wrote in the *Black Man* magazine about the handicaps faced by the descendants of transatlantic slavery:

> The West Indian Negro to a certain extent has accomplished much in the one hundred years. They, like the American Negroes, who were freed in 1865, through the good efforts of Abraham Lincoln, and the force of national urgencies, were set loose upon the world without a cent in their pockets or a bit of land to settle on that they could call their own. From the beginning they have had to fight their way up to where they are today. Some have done well, but the great majority are almost where they were when they came off the plantations. They were property-less and almost helpless (Essien-Udom and Amy Jacques Garvey, 1977: 92).

At Emancipation, the West Indian planters got twenty million pounds and the enslaved got nothing. The West Indian planter interests estimated that their slaves were worth 40 million pounds. In the folk tradition in the West Indies this injustice has not been forgotten, but there has never been any sustained movement to claim reparations or compensation. The twenty-first century is not too late to correct this error, where we who are free do our ancestors and ourselves an injustice.

Meanwhile, in self-help efforts to lift ourselves economically, the late nineteenth and early twentieth centuries saw massive migrations from the Caribbean outward to Panama, Cuba, Central America and the United States. These migrations were in response to the economic disaster faced by the post-emancipation free African populations in the West Indies. But you analysed a further impediment in our efforts to achieve civilization, the goal of social and economic emancipation. You argued that 'millions of Negroes of the United States have not yet formulated a programme of racial preservation, nor have they any settled racial outlook. They are still drifting in the white man's civilization' (Ibid). So we come back to notions of civilization and the route of realizing our potential through individual, family and collective vision.

The movement you led sought to reshape the world created by colonialism and imperialism. For the oppressed to think about reshaping the world, we have to create new fundamentals. And one vital element lies in the assertion of our humanity. Of the last two centuries, the nineteenth century was the century of the struggle against slavery; the twentieth century has been the struggle for political rights and sovereignty. The twenty-first century challenges us to again determine our place in the world, reckoning with issues of justice and fundamental economic opportunities for our people. These goals can be arrived at not by chance but by conscious decision and collective effort to change the world we live in, to meet our aspirations. At the start of the twenty-first century, let us continue to seek guidance from you, as you in your time emancipated yourself from mental slavery.

Yours in the struggle for mental emancipation.

Rupert Lewis

References

Abrahams, Peter. 2000. *The Coyaba Chronicles*. Ian Randle Publishers, Kingston.

Appiah, Kwame and Henry Louis Gates (eds.) 1999. *Africana: The Encyclopedia of the African and African America Experience*. Basic Civitas Books, New York.

Carew, Jan. 1994. Rape of Paradise, *Columbus and the birth of racism in the Americas*. A & B Books Publishers, New York.

Eze, Emmanuel Chukwudi. 1997. *Race and Enlightenment. A Reader*. Blackwell Publishers Ltd. Oxford.

Garvey, Amy Jacques and E.U. Essien-Udom (eds.) 1977. *More Philosophy and Opinions of Marcus Garvey*. Frank Cass and Co. Ltd., London.

Higman, B.W. 1998. "Mental Slavery: The History of an Idea." *Jamaican Historical Society Bulletin*. Vol.11 No. 1. (April).

Hill, Robert ed. 1990. *The Marcus Garvey and UNIA Papers*. Volume VII (November 1927-August 1940). University of California Press, Los Angeles.

Mbeki, Thabo. 1998. *Africa – The time has come*. Tafelburg Publishers, Johannesburg.

CRITICAL THINKING AND WRITING

PART I

1. Critically examine the effectiveness of the use of the epistolary form.
2. What is the function of the second paragraph?
3. State the writer's thesis.
4. How does Lewis demonstrate that he is knowledgeable about Marcus Garvey?
5. Explain two meanings of 'mental slavery' which Lewis presents.
6. Analyse the argument presented in the last paragraph of Part I.
   i. Identify the main claim and state the type of claim that it is.
   ii. What evidence does Lewis present to support his claim?
   iii. What minor claim does he make?

PART II

7. What are the main points presented in Part II?
8. Provide three examples which show that Lewis wants his audience to understand that he shares or identifies with Garvey's ideologies.
9. Explain the dichotomy or pattern of opposition which Lewis establishes in his speech. Cite pairs of words and phrases to strengthen your explanation.
10. Irony is an important rhetorical strategy employed by Lewis in his discussions. State two ways in which Lewis employs irony and comment on its effectiveness in each case.
11. Lewis skilfully integrates discourse modes in his speech, moving smoothly between argument and exposition. Assess the usefulness of this approach in holding the attention of a listening audience.
12. Examine two important ways in which Lewis establishes his credibility in this speech.

WRITING ACTIVITIES

13. Write a letter to Marcus Garvey in which you express your opinions about ideas of racial inferiority and mental enslavement among people in your country or in the Caribbean in general.
14. Explain your understanding of the term 'mental slavery', its origins and manifestations in the Caribbean.
15. Write three succinct paragraphs in which you present counterarguments to the claim that self-hate and mental slavery are still prevalent among black people in the Caribbean.

GROUP DISCUSSION

16. In small groups, discuss the aspects of Lewis's speech which you, as a listener, would find interesting.

CHAPTER 54

THE SOVEREIGNTY OF THE IMAGINATION

I was the child of a fundamentalist Christian home, which literally believed and lived by the precepts of the Sermon on the Mount. We were among the poor, the merciful, the meek, the peacemakers. Survival in the most adverse conditions had certainly made us, in some way, the salt of the earth; and I was persuaded by an ambitious mother that I would, by some miracle, become a light that would shine before men. There is some argument about this prediction, but my presence here may be some consolation that there has been illumination of some kind. The negative aspect of this legacy was just as powerful. Sin was not a word whose meanings invited argument. It was a kind of barometer that measured a great variety of activity, or intended action — which it was with me. I always suspect the means whereby the rich accumulate their wealth, and I am inclined to agree with Balzac that every great fortune begins with a crime.

My home forbade any form of betting, and although I have a great curiosity about the psychology of gamblers, I have retained to this day a strange, emotional block about gambling. There was, in the early Christianity of that house, a moral force that enabled me to see much later what was essentially right about the social thought of socialist philosophy; the poor as the key for change, the oppressed and exploited as the ultimate inheritors of the earth, the present as a battleground for the possessions of the future. Christians and socialists are inseparable on this emphasis on the human expectations of the earth. But Christianity never provided me with a critique of my relation to where I was born, or the social forces shaping my beliefs. My early education in Barbados was a total product of Christian indoctrination. I use the terms 'total' and 'indoctrination' because no one in the role of teacher had ever drawn our attention to the historical truth that Christianity was only one of several great religions, or that Christians then, as they do now, represented a minority of the world's population.

The fictional account in *In the Castle of My Skin* of boys' speculation on slavery and the Garden of Eden may be a pretty accurate reflection of what was a genuine popular belief among the poor at the time. And I quote:

> The Queen freed some of us because she made us feel the Empire was bigger than the Garden. That's what the woman meant — the Queen did free some of us in a kind of way. We started to think about the Empire more than we thought of the Garden, and then nothing mattered but

the Empire. Well, they have put the two of them together now — Empire and Garden. We are to speak of them the same way — they belong to the same person; they both belong to God. The Garden is God's own garden and the Empire is God's own empire.

The entire globe was the spiritual property of the Christian God. This religious proposition was supported by a secular doctrine that presented the British Empire as the political custodian of all human destiny. We were made aware of rival powers — French and German perhaps, but these did not exist as human entities in their own right. They were interlopers who represented a heretical challenge to what had been divinely ordained as the limits of human reality: the Christian God, as creator of the universe, and the British Empire as His temporal trustee.

In this respect, it is not an exaggeration to say that both church and school were agents of an intellectual and moral deception. I would not argue that it was their conscious intention to play this role; it is more likely that they were functioning as institutions which had been conditioned to reflect and support the prevailing values and demands of those who ruled the society. The religious functionary, irrespective of denomination, became associated in my mind as being an accomplice in the support and preservation of the existing status quo. And in Barbados that meant racism, economic exploitation, and a profound contempt for all that was black. Even amongst its ranks the Church refused to disturb this social arrangement, and found a sacred text to approve its conduct. Paul writing to the Romans, notes: 'Let every person be subject to the governing authorities, for there is no authority except God, and those that exist have been instituted by God. Therefore, he who resists the authorities resists what God has appointed.'

This cultural conviction can become toxic as you move from origins to unknown territory, territory which you assumed you had known. In 1950 when I went to England, migration was not a word I would have used to describe what I was doing. We simply thought that we were going to an England which had been planted in our childhood consciousness as a heritage and a place of welcome. It is the measure of our innocence that neither the claim of heritage nor the expectation of welcome would have been seriously doubted. England was not, for us, a country with classes and conflicts of interest like the island we had left. It was the name of a responsibility whose origin may have coincided with the beginning of time. This has happened elsewhere in peculiar ways; in Sierra Leone a colleague of mine asked a sixteen-year-old student: 'What do you think the letters BBC stand for?' And she replied, 'Before the birth of Christ.'

Later I would shudder to think how a country so foreign to our instincts could have achieved the miracle of being called 'mother'. It has made us pupils to its language, its institutions; baptized us in the same religion; schooled boys in the same game of cricket with its elaborated and meticulous etiquette of rivalry. Empire was not a very dirty word, and seemed to bear little relation to those forms of domination we call imperialist. The English themselves were not aware of the role they had played in the formation of these black strangers. The ruling class was serenely confident that any role of theirs must have been an act of supreme generosity, and like Prospero they had given us language and a way of naming our own reality. But the English working class was not aware they had played any role at all, and deeply resented our arrival. It had come about without any warning; no one had consulted them. Occasionally I was asked: 'Do you belong to us, or to the French?' I had been dissolved in the common view of worker and aristocrat. So even English workers could see themselves as architects of Empire.

Much of the substance of *In the Castle of My Skin* is an evocation of this tragic innocence. Nor was there at the time of writing any conscious effort on my part to emphasize the dimension of cruelty which had seduced, or driven by force of need, an otherwise honourable black people into such lasting bonds of illusion, such toxic forms of cultural conviction. For it was not a physical cruelty that we knew. Indeed the colonial experience of my generation was almost wholly without violence — no torture, no concentration camp, no mysterious disappearance of hostile natives, no army encamped with orders to kill. The Caribbean endured a different kind of subjugation: it was a *terror of the mind*, a daily exercise in self-mutilation. Black vs. black in a battle for self-improvement. This was the breeding ground for every uncertain self. But there was one area of ground where certainty had taken the form of the legend.

George Lamming

CRITICAL THINKING AND WRITING

1. What kind of binary opposition does the writer establish in the first paragraph?
2. How does this dichotomy affect the language used in the second paragraph?
3. In this essay, the writer reflects on different experiences and issues. In your own words briefly state two such topics on which he reflects in paragraphs 2 and 3.
4. Examine paragraphs 5 and 6 ('The entire globe…..what God has appointed').
   a) Identify the
      i   main claim;
      ii   secondary/minor claim;
      iii support given for the claims;
      iv   type of claim made in each case.
   b) Comment on the writer's use of irony in paragraphs 6 and 7.
   c) Discuss the significance of the title to the content.

WRITING ACROSS THE CURRICULUM ACTIVITIES

5. Lamming claims that 'it is not an exaggeration to say that both church and school were agents of an intellectual and moral deception.' To what extent do you think that this is true in your society today? Write a short essay (no more than 300 words) in which you present both sides of the argument and take a position.
6. Using the library, internet or other sources, obtain information about George Lamming and his writing. Write a brief speech in which you attempt to **persuade** your audience about the value of his work.

CHAPTER 55

THE LEGACY OF OUR PAST

Language is a very important part of the legacy of colonialism in Jamaica. Had it not been for the failure of an expedition sent out from England by Oliver Cromwell to capture Hispaniola in 1655, our linguistic heritage would probably have been quite different. For when the invaders found their original destination too well defended for their mission to succeed, they seized poorly guarded Jamaica instead. So began our long association with the English language. The Spaniards fled, leaving behind a few African slaves who had escaped to the hills. There they formed the nucleus of the group whose descendants and those of other runaways who later joined them are still known as Maroons. More slaves were almost immediately brought in by the English to work on their sugar estates. The slave trade flourished under British rule, as over the next two centuries the island became a leading source of sugar and rum. It was abolished in 1807 and full emancipation was achieved in 1838. It was the slaves' need to communicate with the Europeans and with each other that led to the establishment of the Creole that has survived alongside English and is known on the island today as Patois or the 'dialect'.

Status and Functions of English and Creole

The prestige naturally accorded English as the language of the colonizers was underscored by the contrast between it and the seemingly malformed speech of the slaves, which was attributed to Africans' alleged lack of intelligence. English has to a large extent maintained its unique position. As the official language, Standard English is still expected in the conduct of government business, in the law courts, the schools, the mass media, in religious worship and in all other contexts where written language is required. Its use is still associated with the elite, which up to approximately fifty years ago consisted of mainly the white and near-white members of the population. Creole, on the other hand, is still associated with the poorest members of the society, who are mostly black, and with rural as contrasted with urban dwellers. Its speakers are seen as exclusively labourers, small farmers, domestic helpers, small craftsmen and others belonging to the same social class as these.

In reality, the use of Creole is not confined to the groups with which it has traditionally been associated, as it is also used on occasion by members of all classes in moments of relaxation, as a vehicle for the expression of emotions (e.g. joy, anger, surprise, excitement, pain), the description of personal experiences and the exchange of jokes, among other things. Besides, no longer confined to comedy on the stage, Creole has almost superseded English in the theatre and it is no longer unusual in advertisements in the press and on radio and television. Creole speakers dominate in talk shows on radio, in which callers are allowed to express their opinions freely. The lyrics of the Reggae music now popular throughout the world are in Creole for the most part. Creole has long since been the universal language of newspaper cartoons and in them it is put nowadays in the mouths of members of all social classes, from the Prime Minister to the man-in-the-street. Politicians on the campaign trail deliberately make use of Creole in their speeches in an attempt to identify with the mass of prospective voters. Creole is used at times even in the pursuit of official business, for it is not unusual nowadays for even well educated Members of Parliament to intersperse their speeches in the House with Creole and, more often than not, their informal asides are also in Creole. Few, however, are conscious of the extent to which their actual linguistic behaviour contrasts with the traditional ideal that they would very likely claim to uphold.

The increased functions of Creole have provided Jamaicans with an additional resource in some domains. The fact is, however, that English is still considered the normal means of communication in most of these. For example, while Jamaicans accept as natural the use of a few Creole words or phrases in a speech in Parliament, they would be very surprised and probably outraged if the speaker gave the entire speech in Creole. Nor is the speaker himself/herself likely to consider doing so. Nevertheless, there are some political representatives whose attempts at Standard English regularly fall short of the mark.

The greater use of Creole has reflected social realities to a great extent. For example, its use in stage plays set in Jamaica and involving Jamaican characters who would normally speak Creole is more natural than the alternative. So is the verbatim reporting in the newspapers of statements made by eye-witnesses and other interviewees, although there have been letters condemning the practice. Again, it is noticeable that the language selected for commercials on radio and television often varies according to the target audience. Thus, whereas only a few years ago advertisements for motor cars were entirely in English, those on radio and television now use Creole as well, catering to the recently acquired ambition of even not very well-off Jamaicans to own a 'deportee' (a used car imported from Japan).

In the field of literature, two distinct traditions may be identified: the oral tradition exemplified by Louise Bennett's 'dialect' poetry, and the written tradition which includes the work of novelists like Orlando Patterson, dramatists like Trevor Rhone and poets like Mervyn Morris. The latter is basically in English but they all use Creole from time to time to make their work more true to life. For example, the novelists and dramatists use Creole for dialogue where this is what their Jamaican characters are likely to have used in real life. A few poets write in Creole but English is the language used mainly or exclusively by almost all of them.

Especially in the last decade or so, there have been sporadic efforts on the part of some members of the public to write Creole using ad hoc spelling. This has been manifested in posters on public display, billboards, newspaper columns, occasional newspaper headliners and letters in the press. The obvious wish of some persons to use Creole in writing and the unsystematic way in which it is now done leave the door open for a generally accepted writing system for Creole.

Code Switching

The use of more than one language in a single stretch of speech or writing is referred to as code switching by linguists. This phenomenon is typical of the way in which Jamaican bilinguals manipulate the two languages at their disposal in everyday interaction. Code switching is very common in everyday informal interaction in Jamaica among persons of all social classes. It may be witnessed in discussions between acquaintances on a wide range of subjects, some serious, others not. A typical example comes from a nurse, overheard addressing no one in particular in a hospital room. Her exact words were:

'*Dem a kaal im bot im* can't be found'. It is also illustrated in the words of a popular song:

'*Wa mi a go tel mi wife*, when I get home?'

The speaker in Parliament who uses a Creole word or phrase in a speech delivered mainly in English is also code switching. So is the writer who uses Creole for dialogue in his/her novel or play. Talk show hosts also exhibit code switching when they adjust their speech to that of their Creole-speaking callers.

The following two extracts taken from the *Gleaner* newspaper, provide examples of how code switching is exploited for specific purposes in some cases:

1. 'There its chairman has taken to sleeping on the job. As a matter of fact, *im draw snore inna di place.*' [1]
2. '*I man* didn't quarrel with anybody ... *I man* just *make* sure the people-*dem* get water, light, hospital beds, telephones and roads.' [2]

In the first case, the writer, a newspaper columnist who has made several derogatory statements about Creole and those who study it, used a Creole phrase to convey her solidarity with fellow Jamaicans who, like her, opposed the appointment of a Canada-based judge to chair the Commission of Inquiry into riots in Western Kingston in July 2001. By switching to Creole, she was letting her readers know that she was one of them and at one with them.

The speaker in the second case is the Prime Minister of Jamaica. The *Gleaner* newspaper reported this part of his speech verbatim. On the eve of elections he, too, was expressing solidarity with his hearers. However, he was not focusing on Jamaicans as such in his use of the Creole plural indicator *dem*, for example, but was rather identifying himself with the masses, the stereotypical speakers of Creole, including as he did so a special appeal to Rastafarians signaled by the repeated phrase *I man*, a characteristic feature of their speech.

Attitudes to the Language Varieties

Jamaicans, even those of us who would not be fully understood in most of the English-speaking world, resent any suggestion that the language we speak is not always English or that our spoken English differs in some respects from what would be heard in other parts of the Anglophone world, and not only as regards pronunciation. Indeed, many persons were incensed when the film, *The Harder They Come*, which had been produced in Jamaica in the 1960s, was given sub-titles for the benefit of English-speaking audiences abroad. Since the vocabulary of Creole is largely derived from English, Creole is usually dismissed within Jamaica as nothing more than badly pronounced English. In other words, its speakers are usually considered by other Jamaicans to be speaking English, but doing so badly. It is also not surprising that the promoters of a scheme to introduce call centres linking Jamaica with the United States did not foresee that language differences were sufficiently important to be taken into account despite the fact that they required applicants to be high school graduates.

The unique status accorded English is clearly revealed in the assertion of a columnist writing in the *Gleaner* that Jamaicans 'have no language because they stubbornly refuse to master Standard English'.[3] The views she expressed are firmly held by the vast majority of Jamaicans, even by many who admittedly enjoy the poetry of Louise Bennett, the pioneer writer of verses in the 'dialect'.

The ability to speak and write Standard English remains the mark of an educated person as English is the sole official medium of education. Mastery of it is the most usual route to the acquisition of social status. On the other hand, the use of Creole is seen as indicating a lack of intelligence, mainly because its stereotypical speakers are often illiterate. There are still some persons who think that the main purpose of teaching English is to eradicate Creole, despite the evidence that Creole has survived such efforts for well over a century. Children who are overheard speaking Creole are often admonished for 'speaking badly' and urged to 'speak properly', i.e. to speak something that passes for English in our society. In addition, whereas English is associated with good breeding, disciplined behaviour and moral probity, Creole speakers are seen as necessarily exhibiting a lack of breeding, poor moral standards and coarse behaviour. In other words, the perceived intrinsic qualities of both English and Creole are transferred to their speakers.

There is, of course, no logical justification for this. If speakers of English are often relatively disciplined in their behaviour, this is a result of their socialization, not of the language they speak. Similarly, what is perceived as rough behaviour on the part of some Creole speakers is directly traceable to their socialization, not to intrinsic properties of their language. Otherwise, all speakers of the same language would inevitably behave in the same way, which is obviously not the case. Some of the commercials and news reports on radio and television, however, reinforce the stereotype that Creole speakers are rough and ill mannered. This is unfortunate as there are many Creole speakers who exhibit a sense of discipline, just as there are many English speakers who do not.

Code switching may also bring out the contrasting social status of English and Creole in Jamaican society. For example, an educated professional may unconsciously switch from the Creole being used with close friends to English when joined by someone he/she wants to impress. He/She may feel ashamed at the possibility of having been overheard speaking Creole by this individual. This and the earlier examples of code switching highlight the ambivalent attitude to English in Jamaica. It is not the language which Jamaicans choose when we wish to express our Jamaicanness. On the other hand, it is the language we use when we wish to signal our membership of a higher social class and in doing so to distance ourselves from those Jamaicans who speak only Creole. The attitude to Creole is equally ambivalent, as was earlier implied.

Two Recent Developments

Two particularly significant developments relating to the status of Creole must also be noted here. In the late 1990s, a start was made on a project to translate the Bible into Creole under the auspices of the Bible Society of the West Indies in partnership with the United Bible Societies, a world body. The usual argument that Creole has no established writing system could not be advanced, since the work was confined to audiocassettes. In its place, those who opposed the scheme resorted to name-calling. The late *Gleaner* columnist, Morris Cargill, led the attack. He referred to the sponsors of the plan as 'a bunch of well-meaning idiots' and even as 'jackasses'.[4] As is illustrated in Chapter Five of this book, *Language in Jamaica* the project in question had several precedents in various parts of the world, evidence of its recognized practicability, at least from the point of view of the missionaries and others who supported it. Besides, the very King James Bible which Cargill admired and was so afraid Jamaica was about to lose, and which undoubtedly is to be admired for the aesthetic quality of its language, represented a similar attempt in the early seventeenth century to spread the Word among those Englishmen and women who could not read Latin, the prestige language of that day.

An even more revolutionary development took place in December 2001, but strangely enough, it excited little comment in the press. A recommendation from the Joint Select Committee of the Charter of Rights Bill to set up an agency 'to formally propose and standardize the existing system for writing Patois' was tabled in Parliament.[5] This was intended to lead to the eventual inclusion in the Constitution of a guarantee against discrimination on the grounds of language. After hearing a submission from Professor Hubert Devonish, the House agreed that before any constitutional change could be considered, the agency should be established to assist in setting standards for public organizations involved in the provision of health services, social services, education and public information, in the move towards ensuring communication with all sections of the public.

Pauline Christie

Notes

1. Dawn Ritch, the *Sunday Gleaner*, November 4, 2001.
2. Speech by Prime Minister, P.J. Patterson, reported in the *Gleaner*, August 9, 2002.
3. Dawn Ritch, the *Sunday Gleaner*, September 9, 1994.
4. Morris Cargill, the *Sunday Gleaner*, June 30, 1996.
5. Reported by Vernon Daley, the *Gleaner*, December 28, 2001.

CRITICAL THINKING AND WRITING

1. What is the writer's intention?
2. Identify, in each paragraph, the developmental strategy used. Choose two strategies and comment on how they help to communicate the writer's meaning more effectively.
3. What main pattern of opposition is established in the text? Explain, using words and phrases from the text, how it functions.
4. Explain three ways in which the writer has demonstrated her knowledge of the subject.
5. To what extent would you say that the writer is fair?

COLLABORATIVE WRITING

6. In groups, discuss three situations in which you would have to make a choice regarding language variety. In what ways would SUBJECT, AUDIENCE, and CONTEXT determine your choice?
7. Choose from the list below the function(s) of language that have been fulfilled in this passage and explain how this has been done.
   - Instrumental
   - Informative
   - Regulatory
   - Heuristic
   - International
   - Personal
   - Imaginative
8. Write a 300-word letter to your friend in England expressing your attitude to Creole.

CHAPTER 56

GENDER AND ATTITUDE TO ENGLISH

Ellis (1994) surveys the body of research available on gender differences in second language acquisition and concludes that it is conflicting and problematic. He cites Labov (1991) as one such example, where women are viewed as the speakers of the most standard form of the native language, and yet the most likely to innovate in acquiring a new language; the dichotomy is of constancy and change. Ellis reconciles the problem by suggesting that, in learning a new language, women might be more open to new forms and also more willing to reject inter-language variation and move toward the target. In cataloging some of the inconsistencies in the research, especially in second rather than foreign language learning, Ellis hits on the notion of gender as 'culture'.

> The "female" culture seems to lend itself more readily to dealing with the inherent threat imposed to identity by L2 learning (p. 204).

In so doing he is aligning himself with the strand of research that sees attitude as the key factor in male second–language learning behaviour. The use and sense of the 'threat' has resonance here, because the suggestion is that the language learning space is open and dangerous to know — in it children's actions and choices are 'performative' acts about how things are seen in public — boys need 'to guard the gendered boundaries' of recognizable masculinities (Dutro 2002, 383).

In a different context, but occupying the same domain, is Ibrahim's (1999) study of French-speaking continental Africans in settler communities in Canada. This is a complex study, in terms of the layers of identities mediated by multilingual migrant learners. Ibrahim charts how these students negotiate these layers and emerge is that culture positioned as Black, using Black/African-American youth culture and its language, Black English as Second Language (BESL) as the primary means of identification. The study suggests that attitude toward the second language, even specific varieties, affects the efficiency of the learning.

A Gendered Experience: English in Jamaican Schools

How do boys and girls experience language/English teaching in Jamaican schools? Craig (1983) remarked on the huge unrealistic demands of the Jamaican curriculum, so the implication is that for all children, language teaching needs to be improved. The two most recent curriculum initiatives in school, the Reform of Secondary Education (ROSE) and the revised primary curriculum are recognizing the necessity to innovate. For boys in language classes, the experience seems to be demotivating and unproductive. Evans's (1999) observation of boys' persistent difficulty with reading in primary, all-age, and comprehensive schools shows an area of stark, significant, and debilitating contrasts between boys' and girls' reading performance, with girls reading more confidently and spelling more accurately. The boys might see themselves represented in texts but this has not helped their achievement, because the representations are of gender-demarcated roles, sustaining the patriarchal archetypes of action heroes (Shaw 2000). In their reading books, boys were the principal characters, the centre of attention and the source of all the lively action. These are roles that Evans (2001) shows affect boys; participation in class, as it informs their sense of how males are expected to behave, and what they demand of the teaching/learning environment.

Craig (1971) confirmed some differences that he thought would impact on Jamaican children learning English, which foreshadowed Schumann's conclusion of psychological distance through language shock, as a factor for explaining lack of second language acquisition. He found that boys saw English as the language of the effeminate, mimicking falsetto tones to indicate the lack of toughness displayed by speakers of English. Foreshadowing Ellis also, Craig's study showed that girls' speech changed more extensively toward the prestige norms than boys'. This gender difference in language use and perception about English seems to be borne out in Jamaican popular culture. Cultural forms such as performance poetry and especially deejay (DJ) music are very popular. Both offer dominance to males in areas where the Jamaican language is celebrated. The boys have thus found other ways to be and new avenues of advancement — all challenges for the teacher of English. One teacher had this to say:

> The role of the teacher has been eroded by new models like the DJs. A lot of young people follow them. It is easier to follow them than what the teacher is saying. Perhaps if we could DJ in English we would have more success…. Children's focus is totally different nowadays … it's a struggle indeed (Bryan 1998, 131).

This teacher is suggesting that alternative ways of operating are being forcefully put forward within the culture, and this relates as well to alternative examples and models of language behaviour. The DJ needs no English to achieve a substantial measure of improvement, and so the teacher has to compete for relevance.

Recent Research on Jamaican Boys and English

From the foregoing we can see that there is a commonly held assumption that boys, especially adolescent boys in Jamaica, do not like English. They are alienated from its culture and norms and the ideological baggage implied. If this is so then English teaching must be a demotivating experience for both teachers and children. A small-scale research was carried out to investigate some of these assumptions, namely the question of attitude to English — and going beyond Schumann — to look at attitudes to the language and a school subject, with the attendant issue of motivation (Shaw 2000). The aim was to determine whether there were gender differences in attitudes: if the tendency reported by Craig still held sway and if it applied to adolescents. The study was limited to a group of 83 students in three traditional high schools in urban Jamaica (Kingston and St. Catherine). This is a significant research base, because, as adolescents are often presented as those most alienated from English, potentially the most difficult students to engage in an English language class. In addition, Grade 10 is a critical year, as it offers the last full year of English teaching before the Caribbean Examinations Council (CXC) examination that determines so much of the life chances of the students.

The research questions asked were:

1. What are the students' attitudes toward English as a subject?
2. Are there gender differences in the attitudes toward English as a subject?
3. What are the students' attitudes toward reading as a component of English?
4. What are the students' attitudes to writing tasks?

The second question is clearly the focus in a discussion about gender differences in language and literacy learning. However, questions 3 and 4 are also very relevant to our concerns as they deal with the specifics of literacy teaching and the literacy tasks that are to the school and society, manifestations of the successful acquisition of English.

Findings on Jamaican Boys' Attitudes to English

As this study was based on questionnaires the usual circumspections about self-report need to be observed: students were being asked in a school setting about a school subject. In addition, this sample of students would include more middle-class children from homes where there might be some higher expectations of literacy than would be found in the general population. The impact of class on attitude was not a focus of the study, but nevertheless, the investigation remains valuable as we have no other local study of adolescents' attitudes toward this critical school subject.

This group of students understood the power of English. They concurred with Chevannes' (1999) assertion about the importance of English, and with a whole body of language education and literacy theorizing that recognized the importance of language in learning across the curriculum. The study found that among the group, as a whole, there were favourable attitudes to English, which the majority found interesting, enjoyable, and not difficult.

The importance of English went beyond school subject and included its usefulness for university/college, for work, and for demonstrating a level of education. With such power and influence acknowledged, it was not surprising that 88 per cent reported that English improved their confidence, while 84 per cent said it helped them to express their ideas fluently.

When the data was disaggregated to take account of gender, some differences were noted. A significantly higher number of females indicated that they enjoyed English and liked their English classes. We will return to the number of boys who do not like English classes later in this paper. With respect to English as an avenue for social interaction, only 63 per cent of boys, for example, thought knowledge of English aids social recognition. Girls were, significantly, more likely to report that English improved their confidence, and facilitated social recognition. Curiously, only five per cent of boys thought English was necessary after school even though they thought it critical for jobs and important for university. There seems to be a subtext to these particular statistics, where boys have to use one code in school, a code they know to be important in this particular domain, but intend to leave it behind in their own personal sphere. As Ibrahim (1999) indicates, language choices are 'performative acts of desire and identification' (p. 364) and 'one invests where one sees oneself mirrored' (p. 365). The notion of 'investment' here is resonant of the social exchange theory as an explanation for accommodation in language choice, where a speaker makes a decision to change and shift because of a calculation that greater benefits will accrue from the movement. Certainly, the instrumental banking metaphor is present and is not surprising in second-language learning, where extrinsic motivation and the expectation of material rewards is said to be an important variable in achieving success (Ellis 1994).

Another aspect of English as a school subject that showed interesting differences was teaching methods. The boys again displayed the inclination to highlight a general tendency in the findings. For example, the whole group showed some dissatisfaction with teaching methods. Only 36 per cent reported that lessons and methods were clear, and barely half found the materials interesting. However, when gender was added to the data the picture looked more stark, with far more girls than boys finding the lessons and methods clear and the materials interesting. When we further add consideration of Miller's thesis of the feminization of teaching, we can see that these findings affirm our earlier comments from Evans (2002) about the gendered experience of boys in English classrooms as being de-motivating and unprepossessing. In plain truth, boys are not very happy being there and this must provide a major challenge for educators.

TABLE 56.1
FAVOURABLE ATTITUDES TO ENGLISH AS LANGUAGE AND SCHOOL SUBJECT OF A GROUP OF GRADE 10 JAMAICAN SCHOOL STUDENTS

Favourable Attitudes to English as Language and Subject	% Female	% Male	% Combined
English is			
• Interesting	95	85	82
• Enjoyable	95	65	75
• Not difficult	88	79	70
English is useful for			
• University/college	95	75	86
• Work	98	100	94
• Demonstrating a level of education	88	97	83
• Improving Confidence	100	89	88
• Aiding fluency	93	89	84
• Social recognition	85	63	58
English is necessary after school	98	5	94
I like my English Classes	81	46	79
Lessons and methods are clear	61	36	36
Materials are interesting	90	56	52

These comments will help us consider the third and fourth questions of this piece, namely the main activities of the English classroom. Evans has already indicated some painful experiences of reading among younger children. How do these grade 10 students view reading and writing, and what do they want from their classes? Analysis of student's open-ended responses revealed that they had broad reading interests in a variety of fiction and nonfiction genres. They disliked long, difficult, and boring books, and not surprisingly, some literature books, which would probably have been the set examination texts. If this is the case, the data must be suggesting that not enough account has been taken of students' age, culture, gender and therefore interests when we choose texts for syllabi in Jamaica. Year after year we continue with texts such as *To Kill A Mockingbird* or *The Scarlet Letter*, backed by the same tired forms of media support, without recognizing changing orientations of those obliged to sit the examinations. How much longer will we continue to kill a mockingbird?

Although a few of them reported that they disliked writing, most of the students indicated that they enjoyed a variety of writing tasks, chief among them short story writing. The writing tasks they found most boring were essay-writing and summaries: the two staples of the examination system as we know it in the Caribbean. At the same time, students seemed to be saying that they enjoyed the tasks that required that they generate and create something unique. The research allowed them an opportunity to say what kind of teaching they thought would be successful. They opted for using drama; explaining procedures clearly, step by step; making the tasks interesting and enjoyable; and relating the tasks to students' interests and background. No educational advice could

be clearer! The suggestions have implications for planning and for a learner-centredness that includes language, gender and culture.

Beverly Bryan and Gwendolyn Shaw

References

Chevannes, B. 1999. *What We Sow and What We Reap*. Kingston, Jamaica: Grace Kennedy Foundation.

———. 2001. *Learning to be a Man*. Kingston, Jamaica: University of the West Indies Press.

Christie, P. 1982. 'Trends in Jamaican English'. In *UWI Ling: Working Papers in Linguistics*, 50–73. Kingston, Jamaica: UWI, Mona, Department of Language, Linguistics and Philosophy.

Craig, D. 1983. 'Teaching Standard English to non-standard speakers: Some methodological issues'. *Journal of Negro Education* 52, no. 1: 65–74.

Daly, C. 1999. 'Reading Boys'. *Changing English* 6, no. 1: 7–18.

Dutro, E. 2002. 'But that's a Girl's book: Exploring Gender Boundaries in Children's Reading'. *The Reading Teacher* 55 (4): 376–84.

Ellis, R. 1994. *The Study of Second Language Acquisition*. Oxford: Oxford University Press.

Evans, H. 1999a. 'The Construction of Gender and Achievement in Secondary Schools in Jamaica'. *Caribbean Journal of Education* 21, no. 1 & 2: 3–24.

———. 1999b. *Gender and Achievement in Secondary Education in Jamaica*. Planning Institute of Jamaica, Policy Development Unit.

———. 2001. *Inside Jamaican Classrooms*. Kingston, Jamaica: University of the West Indies Press.

Gilborn, D., and H. Mirza. 2000. *Educational inequality*. London: OFSTED.

Ibrahim, A. 1999. 'Becoming Black: Rap and Hip-Hop, Gender Identity and the Politicas of ESL learning'. *TESOL Quarterly* 33, no. 3: 349–69.

Millard, E. 1997. *Differently Literate: Boys, Girls and the Schooling of Literacy*. London: Falmer Press.

Mills, M. and B. Lingard. 1997. Masculinity Politics, Myths and Boys Schooling: A review essay. *British Journal of Educational Studies* 45, no. 3: 276–92.

Robinson, S. 2000. 'An Investigation into the Factors which Contribute toward Higher than Average Attainment for some African-Caribbean children in a Birmingham Primary School'. MA thesis, Faculty of Education, University of Central England.

Schumann, J. 1978. *The Pidginization Process: A Model for Second Language Acquisition*. Rowley, Mass.: Newbury House.

Shaw, G. 2000. 'An Analysis of Jamaican Tenth Graders' Attitude toward the use of English Language as a Subject'. MED project, School of Education, University of the West Indies.

Shields, K. 1989. 'Standard English: The Case of Competing Models'. *English World-wide* 10:1.

CRITICAL THINKING AND WRITING

1. State, using evidence from the text, the main claims presented by Ellis and Ibrahim regarding gender differences in second language acquisition.

2. i. What organizing principle do Bryan and Shaw use to demonstrate the ways in which English Language learning is a gendered experience in Jamaican schools?

   ii. How effective is the use of this principle/strategy?

3. Identify and explain two ways in which the writer uses the data presented in Table 54.1.

4. What do you consider to be the main strengths of the essay? Support your answer with evidence from the text.

5. Provide a detailed characterization of the writers' intended audience.

COLLABORATIVE WRITING

6. In mixed gender groups comprising three to four persons, interview each other to find out the attitudes of males and females in the groups toward English Language Learning. Write two paragraphs in which you present your findings regarding the gender attitudes of your group, toward English Learning.

7. Attitude toward English and Creole

   a) Work in pairs to discuss the use of language in your country. Interview each other regarding your respective attitudes toward the use of the standard and non-standard forms of language in both writing and speaking.

   b) Write an expository essay of approximately 800 words in which you highlight the main differences identified in the attitudes toward both language forms.

DISCUSSION

8. What are the strengths of this essay?

9. Has this essay changed any misconceptions you may have previously held? If so, explain.

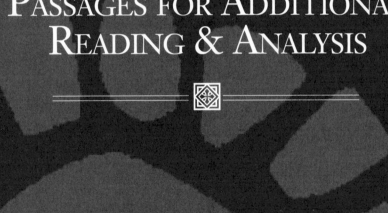

SECTION 4
PASSAGES FOR ADDITIONAL
READING & ANALYSIS

CHAPTER 57

HENS CAN CROW TOO: THE FEMALE VOICE OF AUTHORITY ON AIR IN JAMAICA

'A whistling woman and a crowing hen are an abomination to the Lord.'

As far as I can remember, the immortalisation of the whistling woman and crowing hen as aberrations in Jamaica was my introduction to overt gender stereotyping. The largely female-dominated home and school environment of my youth in the 1950s and 60s emphasized the need for any educated and independent person to be self-actualised, regardless of gender or marital status. I therefore took it for granted that educated women of my generation should be responsible for regulating their lives, and for a long time, I just assumed that all educated women in other societies had equal possibilities. *Naiveté* regarding the 'biblical' injunction was my lot as well; it took me quite some time to realise its cultural genesis and significance on the one hand, and the extent to which, at the same time, it implied an element of choice for the female on the other. It was the presence of whistling women in my environment which eventually promoted my recognition of the fact that women, even though being enjoined not to indulge in what

was condemned as inappropriate behaviour, are nevertheless able to whistle.

This preamble is intended to underscore the fact that, in a similar vein, many of the currently accepted generalisations relating to perceived gender differences in language choice, style and conversational strategy, are highly culture-specific — a point which, in my view, bears constant repetition. Jespersen's 1922 observations about women's language preceded a large body of writing in the 1970s and early 1980s (reviewed in Holmes 1991), some of which, based on intuition and personal observation, was perhaps less careful at definition and empirically rigorous than would normally be desirable, but still not to be condemned wholesale. It did, after all, direct attention to a topic worthy of discussion and research. Certain generalisations, many of which still have currency today, were promoted: women were said to be more conservative and status conscious in language choice (Gal 1978; Labov 1972; Trudgill 1974), reticent in presenting their views and hesitant in their delivery, while being less willing to take and keep the floor, and less confident about their right to speak (Lakoff 1975; Zimmerman & West 1975) than male participants in cross-sex conversation. Women were also found to display greater politeness linguistically than male conversants (Brown, 1983; Holmes, 1984; Lakoff, 1975). Many of the analyses made direct correlations between gender and these speech characteristics, which some regarded as the consequence of woman's powerlessness (Lakoff 1975; O'Barr and Atkins 1980).

Research in the late eighties and nineties has suggested that the behaviours noted above, and widely attested for white, middle class women, may have roots other than gender, or in factors interacting with it: in social networks (Cheshire 1982; Edwards 1988; Milroy 1980); social rank (Ochs 1987); speech roles and genres (Sherzer 1987; Schieffelin 1987); and power relationships (Eckert 1989; Woods 1988). It is, further, the contention of this paper that more attention needs to be paid to the real differentials in gender across cultures/subcultures (c.f. Coates and Cameron on 1988; Phillips, Steele & Tanz 1987), and, additionally, to variation in linguistic style within the same gender, created inevitably by the individual's multidimensional space (LePage and Tabouret-Keller 1985), and/or particular speech acts.

That women make their voices heard to differing degrees, depending on the society of which they are a part, is easily illustrated. Modern-day Asian, Indian and Arab societies, for example, boast a tradition of respect for elders and males — the result, essentially, of patriarchal organisation — displayed in language and other rituals which, like all cultural values, are subject to modification. It seems highly unlikely that at any point in time, however, regardless of the rate of change,

women who live in those societies will be as outspoken as their second and third generation counterparts in Jamaica, for the most part a primarily female-dominated, matrifocal society, in which women from all strata regard it as their right to express themselves in any context of their choice. And yet, when these very Jamaican women migrate to Britain or America, they are likely, in public at least, to be less vocal and assertive than they are on home ground. In each case, the gender is the same; it is the context which is directly responsible for the differences which surface, and which influences a speaker's choice of strategies 'for the linguistic construction of her social relations (not just to men but to other women as well)' (McConell-Ginet 1988: 96).

If the general organisation of a society influences the ability or inclination of its women in general to speak, it is their response to specific situations — the intensity of their feelings about a given topic, or the importance they attach to airing and/or having their views about it accepted — which will influence the degree to which they will be assertive (some may say aggressive) in their delivery. Since the perceived relationships between participants, as well as the necessity to save face, also influence stylistic choices, a conversant who wields the greater power may choose, for contextual or pragmatic reasons, to allow the other participant to exercise dominance at a particular point in the conversation. S/he may select one of a number of options: to merely put forward a view, to require analysis or approval from another participant, or to take part in an altercation about the issues raised. In each case, speakers make choices based on interpretation of the practical situation which has presented itself, and allocate to themselves the power with which they feel comfortable at that time. As a function of the particular context, rather than of their gender *per se*, they elect to be active or passive participants in verbal interaction, and to project a particular persona they select from their repertoire.

It is, therefore, detailed analysis of the exigencies of a specific society, context or event which is likely to uncover the influences on the language choices and use to which a particular speaker or set of speakers subscribes. Descriptions and comparisons of language behaviour situated in a variety of communities are required to flesh out the skeleton which at present exists.

Women, Power and Talk in the Jamaican Community

In Jamaica of the 1990s, women are overtly powerful in many respects. The society is primarily matrifocal, with women of all strata heading families in which, more often than not, they function as single parents. The burden of large numbers of children whom they could ill afford has been one endured particularly by women of limited economic means who were persuaded by their mates that artificial birth control was to be shunned, and that their only salvation was in multiplying (as a fulfilment of God's will, their lot, or old-age pension possibilities). Public education programmes and expanded availability of family planning methods in clinics have been liberating forces for many such women, who are increasingly unwilling to accept the myth that such methods are really designed to 'kill off black people.'

In the educational system, boys do worse than girls, both at high school and at university, where they have been outnumbered since 1982. Women are a growing percentage of the faculty of the university as well. The first ever female (full) professor, a Guyanese historian, Elsa Goveia, was appointed in 1961— significant because, at that time, faculty were primarily foreign and male, and female professors unheard of.

In commerce and banking, traditional strongholds of men, women are rapidly making incursions into the job market, and more gradually gaining recognition at levels previously male-dominated: presiding over major financial and commercial conglomerates, for example. As traders, women have always been powerful, having assumed primary responsibility for garnering the funds generated from the farm, for instance. This independence inherent in trading activity was particularly highlighted and exploited in the 1970s, when some self-employed women (hairdressers, dressmakers, etc.), finding the austere economic situation especially stressful, and their clientele waning, participated, with traditional higglers, in exporting spices and ground provisions to neighbouring Caribbean countries in exchange for items of clothing and canned food, toiletries and a variety of other necessities and luxuries which were otherwise in short supply or unavailable. They formed themselves into associations, became taxpayers, were recognised officially as 'Informal Commercial Importers', and used the healthy profit they generated from these activities to fulfil their responsibilities and buy real estate. Other women responded to the economic squeeze by leaving the stability and low remuneration of jobs in the teaching and nursing professions and the civil service to enter the life insurance and real estate fields, where they are increasingly assuming power and wealth.

The above sketch is not meant to deny or underestimate the real problems of domestic violence, low remuneration, inexcusably poor working conditions or lack of respect to which women are subjected on a daily basis; it is to assert the real gains towards independence, attitudinal and financial, which many women of all strata have made, and the extent to which they are a force to be reckoned with at this point in time.

The primary vehicle which women in Jamaica use to express their growing independence is TALK. It is an institution in the island, which, in spite of her high profile in the Caribbean, has not attained as high levels of literacy as those of some of her neighbours, and is still, in essence, an oral society. Talk is the primary means of disseminating information, passing on traditions and shaping attitudes and values in the wider society; the advent of talk shows has done much to reinforce its impact.

It is important to note that in the realm of public talk, however, it was the educated, well-modulated voice which, prior to the mid 1970s, almost a decade after the introduction of talk shows, was most likely to be heard expressing opinions or debating issues on radio or television in Jamaica. Since English was the sole accepted language of public/formal discourse, and the majority of Jamaicans were not proficient in it, they were automatically excluded from air talk. Further, access to telephones was severely limited, especially in the rural and poorest urban areas.

Installation of public telephones throughout the country, emphasis on phone-in talk shows in radio programming, and provision of toll-free lines to them, have resulted in not only an expansion of the possibilities available to ordinary people to air their views, but also the *de facto* erosion of diglossia on two fronts. Instead of confining themselves to the official language, English, as they did in the early days of such shows, most talk-show hosts now code-switch regularly to Creole for a range of pragmatic purposes (Shields-Brodber 1992b). One such

purpose, the encouragement of those with little or no proficiency in English to focus on their message rather than its form, has resulted in an increasingly large number of men and women being heard on radio, not only in talk shows, but in newscasts as well (Shields-Brodber 1992a), discussing issues of local and international importance in Creole. No longer intimidated by traditional standards of linguistic inappropriateness on air, average citizens are therefore no longer disfranchised as far as public/formal discourse is concerned.

This paper will examine some aspects of the content and style of conversation by women on air in Jamaica. The argument is that, in the confidence they exude, and in their management of conversational interaction, these women display characteristics which, if current stereotypes in the literature are to be believed, may well relegate them to the category of 'crowing hens'.

The Message and its Theme

Phone-in radio discussion is an anonymous, public activity. Because of its voluntary nature, and the immediacy of most of the concerns aired, callers are generally very vocal, displaying a high level of conviction about their point of view, and their right to air it. Women are no less confident than men in these respects; they outnumber men 3-1 as regards participation in programmes aired during the day, and are continually heard berating women whom they judge as passive, unwilling to participate in action, or ignorant about their individual and collective responsibility to make a difference in society.

A most striking characteristic of the message initiated by women on air is their constant eschewal of the victim mentality, and their reiteration of calls for women, whatever their station, to assert their independence, and maximise all the possibilities for self-actualisation available. Constant exhortation to take charge of their lives is a regular part of their message as well. The detached observer is the exception, perhaps because of the direct impact, on those who phone in, of the problems discussed.

There is a stridency to the tone of the message which is comparable to 'male language' in the literature. In addition, the approach by women to discussion and analysis on radio is decidedly confrontational, with caustic and disparaging remarks frequently issuing from their tongues, sometimes with encouragement from their hosts. Apart from slander and name-calling, there are very few constraints on what is permissible. On a regular basis, for instance, on-the-job household helpers (domestics) can be heard using their employers' phones to publicly castigate those very same employers — and presumably, if they follow the advice of moderators, sometimes report them to the Ministry of Labour also — with no apparent fear of recrimination (although workers in foreign-owned and operated factories who use the same strategy do not fare as well, it seems). Women are extremely vocal in castigating public figures or denigrating institutions which represent stances with which they disagree, hurling forceful, disrespectful epithets, or barely masked threats, with impunity:

1. **C(F)** I am not in any way supportive of any political party. I've never voted; and I'd like to issue a warning to the gentleman, Mr. S. (M.P.) who spoke about colour, to be careful. An' I'd advise other people, so that what happened in the seventies will not be repeated. And he should get a paint brush an' some black paint — before he talks. *[P502292/344]*

Callers who similarly exploit their anonymity to name and then chastise public figures are neither rebuked nor cut off; they direct their ire, in the unambiguous terms of their choice, at Members of Parliament:

2. **C(F)** Mr. G. was very irresponsible an' spiteful; making mischief — a big seasoned politician or Prime Minister.

3. **C(F)** Hear Mr. X (Prime Minister) saying we mus' turn to religion I — I wish he would take that an' stuff it. Yes. They don't accept Bible leaves in the supermarket. *[P50292/406]*

Women are no less reticent than men in creating and exploiting opportunities to articulate their views unequivocally, however uncomplimentary and abusive they may appear.

A preference for militancy and uncompromising action is shown by female callers of all ages. A self-styled 'youngster' subscribes to coercion for remedying what she considers idleness in young males:

4. **C(F)** My suggestion is that there are a lot of people in the ghetto where I am living (.)[1] guys on the road(.) they are on the corner sitting down(.) they have nothing to be done(..) Isn't it(.) Sometimes things can be done by force(.) It has to be done(.) I know force is not perfect to do anything but sometimes there is no other alternative(.) Use these guys by force(.) take them off the street (.) put them somewhere where production can be made beneficiary to the country(..) These things 'ave to be done drastically (.) it is not communist(.) but is a fact

that sometimes force ave to come into acts.

H(F) But ma'am, you think that if you put them an' you tell them that they have to work, they will?

C Yes. (.) I think sometimes what Jamaican youngsters (.) you can get nothing from them (.) Have you ever been driving an' see where there is a give a way sign(.) an nobody ten's to give you the bligh, you 'ave to take it? [AH277592/005B]

Apparently ignorant of her *faux pas* as regards occasionally ill-chosen vocabulary and her demonstrated limited resources as far as SE structure is concerned, this speaker makes her point emphatically and confidently, clearly persuaded of its legitimacy. Hers, like many others, is the voice of antagonism and confrontation, rather than of compromise. Women are in the vanguard of the movement towards action rather than complacency in the face of adversity, and towards women taking charge of their own destiny, even when confronted with power and authority which, superficially, may well appear to be greater than theirs. There is no evidence, in this context, of women being willing to make compromises or displaying any insecurity whatsoever as regards their message.

Managing Conversational Interaction: Interruption

Another indicator of the tendency of women on air in Jamaica to 'crow' is found in their management of conversational interaction. Although there is an accepted parity (similar to that described in Stanback 1985) rather than asymmetry between men and women in these conversations, and dialogue is built on a premise of essential equality among participants, on many of those occasions in which dominance and overt control are exercised, it is the female who exercises them, often resorting to interruption as a tool.

As I noted in an earlier paper (Shields-Brodber 1992b), interruption of a speaker in midstream or before is a technique many employ in both single and cross-sex conversations. It may occur close to a TRP; however, it also occurs at places where sometimes it is not possible to predict what the completed turn will be — i.e. at a place where it is clear that no concession to the other participant/point of view is intended. In cases such as these, the interrupter's sole concern is with delivering his/her opinion as emphatically and assertively as possible, however boorish s/he may appear in the process.

The literature presents the male as inevitable interrupter in cross-sex interaction, even when he is in the overtly powerless position; with some analysts regarding gender in this context as overriding other indices of social power (West 1984). It also presents interruption as a disruptive force which allows the interrupter to eclipse the turn of the speaker on the floor, thereby effectively silencing the competition.

Public radio discussion in Jamaica does not lend support to these analyses. Women, whether they be host or caller, interrupt men regularly, capturing and dominating the floor thereafter:[2]

5.   **C(M)**... Not that I am defending us, you know, but is the fac' that we are such a little poor country with the majority of people who are very poor who is seeking that visa to better they life, so — so they are feeling that probably if our officials sort o' criticise the US too much

H(F) Well you know but we

C Then it may jeopardise ⌜their efforts
H   ⌞I don't think it will make a scrap of

  ⌜difference
C ⌞Why, how you mean, Miss H

H   You — you can't No — sir. You cannot tell me
    that there is an⌜ything
C   ⌞But, Miss H, you know how many Jamaicans
  are — Jamaicans there relying on their children an' thing at
  home to sen' a little dollar fo' them ⌜that
H   ⌞So what

C they can ⌜survive
H   ⌞So you are tellin' me that because of that (.) if the
  (.) the (.) that there could be environmental damage that could ultimately destroy
  our country an' so we mus' keep our mouth shut simply because some people
  want to get a visa to go to the United States? You know the United States is not
  goin' to stop Jamaicans from gettin' visas because the (.) the (.) the Jamaican
  delegation criticises (..) The Jamaican delegation is not the only one (..) in the
  Third World countries tend to be the most affected by the environmental
  degradation because when you rip up the rain forest in Brazil (.) when you dump
  chemicals in countries (..) in Third World countries which will bring all kind of
  disease an' destruction to the environment in those countries (...) you are not
  going to tell me because you might require to have flour an' rice comin' from a
  large country you mus' allow your people to be poisoned by chemicals an' have
  you envir (...) your environment destroyed =

C So what you are ⌜sayin' that
H   ⌞we mus' have a little bit of pride, man
  (..) you (..) know jus' because you are gettin' something don' mean that you mus'
  keep you mouth shut

                                                        [HI 1692/086]

The person interrupted may, as does the male caller in the above example, become hesitant, or virtually silent for a time, especially if the interruption is a direct response to his/her presentation, which it may serve to elaborate, whether by requesting clarification, expanding the content or contradicting the point, etc. A clear disruption of the turn, at least for the moment, is often intended, and might well be achieved, to the extent that the speaker on the floor responds directly to the interrupter's intervention. In such an instance, however, the original conversation is modified or suspended only for the duration of the clarification, with the original speaker reassuming authority on the floor thereafter.

The negative evaluation attached to interruption as discussed in the literature does not necessarily apply in Jamaica to examples such as these. In fact, in a community where dexterity and one-upmanship in verbal interaction is highly valued, the speaker who interrupts merely provides a challenge to be matched by the one s/he attempts to upstage. This means that, in many cases, the consequence of creating total silence in the one interrupted does not materialise; most often, both speakers continue making their contributions simultaneously, incorporating a response to any potentially damaging point made by the other party. The speaker who eventually yields the floor is not necessarily the one who was interrupted; but rather, the one who first completes his/her point to his/her satisfaction. In cross-sex conversation, women in Jamaica are as able as men are to manage the floor and exercise and retain dominance thereon.

Tentativeness and Linguistic Insecurity

What has been established so far is that women callers to phone-in talk shows, as they do in society, wield power and exude confidence. This does not mean that signals of tentativeness are always absent from their speech, however. Even when the message is as unambiguous as the above examples are, pauses (see example 4), tags and other markers of tentativeness do occur:

6. **C(F)** If (...) there are plans to disconnect the light (...) I think one
of the cheapest ahm fuels available is kerosene oil (..) domestic kerosene oil =
H   Yes ma'am
C   We used to use it an' there is a law of demand an' supply which
says (...) even though there may be a mon (..) a monopoly (....)
H   Yes ma'am

C   We (...) if they don't have enough individuals (....) to support their business (..)
they are going to lose (..)
H   Yes ma'am
C   OK (.) so (..) we allow them to disconnec' it (...)
H   Yes ma'am
C   It is a very difficult decision to make but I am callin' on the women of Jamaica (....) Why? The women of Jamaica are the ones who are experiencin' the greatest pressure
H   Yes ma'am
C   OK (...) We are the strongest (..) ok (..) an we can influence what happens (...) We don't have to go out and carry on in any vulgar fashion (.) we don' have to block roads (.) but we have a right to know how things are done

In instances such as the above, the analyst may be tempted to view hesitation markers as necessarily signalling a speaker's lack of confidence in herself or about her message; however, they are often, instead, an indicator of an excessive concern with form, and concomitant pressure caused by attempts at production of 'standard' English. The location of these markers — i.e. at the beginning of the turn where callers usually converge with their host's SE usage, or at points where speakers are apparently experiencing some difficulty expressing their sentiments in English — underscores their unmistakable function as markers of linguistic insecurity. As the turn progresses, and speakers are able to overcome their anxiety about form to the point of sometimes reverting to JC, the reduction, and in some cases, absence, of hesitation signals, is usually marked:

7. **C(F)** A heard the radio when they talk about a lady with 5 children
   H(M) Yes

C Eh heh (.) What I would like to tell woman on a whole (.) you see (.) try go out dere an' do something from them (.) for they self (.) you understand (.) try an' fin' work if it even a domestic work (.) you understand (..) Don' siddown an' wait on man (..) From them find themself with 2 or 3 children an' the man [ron gain li:v dem mos riilaize se bwai a dem alo:n you understan no] (..)
   [has run away, they must realise that they are on their own you understand?]

H Yes

C Don' try an' let another man give tham another child (..) I have life very hard (.) you see (.) in the past (.) and right now I am a domestic helper an I am comfortable now (.) without a man

H Yes

C I work an' help myself (.) You understan? An I [fi:l se] woman can do the same thing *[believe that]*

H Yes

C Having over the children them and turning it over to society

H mh hm

C dr _____ dem h_____ (.) dem kom an _____ *the children are hungry; they come and they say they don't have*

   _____ (.) *this and they don't have that for the children*
                                    [WI 7129/025]

In the preceding example, frequent pauses act as an organisational device for the speaker to formulate her point in English before actually articulating it. The length and frequency of the pauses, and the repeated employment of the tag 'Okay' are interpreted by the other participant as a continuing request for approval, requiring a minimal response which acts as a supportive mechanism to indicate her comprehension of the point. The male host obliges, doing what has been called women's work (Fishman 1983).

One mechanism employed by the speaker in example 7, and highlighting her struggle to produce 'correct' English in order to meet the demands of formal language use which she deems appropriate to the context, is her reinforcement of word-final t/d consonants with schwa — a feature of deliberate, formal English produced by many Jamaicans who are striving for conformity to traditional norms (Shields 1984). The percentage of women who persist, like the one in example 7, in attempting to present their opinions, however inadequately, in Standard English, despite the problems which it creates, is much larger than that of men — supporting the analysis that some women may well be more committed than men to using the status language in contexts in which tradition has deemed it appropriate.

Pauses are not solely characteristic of presentations in which speakers are obviously experiencing difficulty with the language of their choice, however; they are also an organisational device for many who seem to have no problem expressing themselves in English. Pauses and/or tags often function in this context to provide space to facilitate, during conversation, the processing and sequencing of overlapping strains occurring simultaneously in the speaker's head. They thus serve as an organisational strategy for quick thinking — on the feet, as it were.

The preceding discussion highlights the fact that when signals of tentativeness occur, they are not necessarily indicative of a speaker's insecurity; but that even when they are, their genesis can be traced to linguistic rather than gender/power factors operating in conversation.

Code Shifting to Jamaican Creole — Women as Innovators?

Attempts such as those exemplified by example 7, in which speakers attempt to present their contribution in SE, are not surprising in view of the generally accepted research finding that women respond to the overt prestige associated with more standard forms (reviewed in Labov 1990), and the fact that SE has been the traditionally accepted prestige language in Jamaica. However, it is the exception rather than the rule which sees Jamaican female talk show participants who are emphatic about their point, and not particularly comfortable in English, trying to battle with its use. More often than not, after the initial pleasantries and introductory remarks, in which she converges with the language of her host, such a speaker shifts into JC for the duration of her turn, reverting to English, if at all, only to signal the end of the conversation.

8. **C(F)** I had a similar problem too, if you remember (..) I have been on this programme about the National Water Commission(.) Now I'd advise the gentleman to call New Kingston (.) Knutsford Boulevard where the 'ead office is, and speak to Miss X [ju si wa mi a tel ju se *do you understand what I am saying?* Di likl tir\ we mi: av deun wata komi/an ds wid *The little thing I had down at the Water Commission with* dsrn pirpl ds an wsn mi: (.) an wsn mi: Jo: mai likl self an *those people; and when I -*

when I showed my little self and se bwai mi ne get ne jestis ja se ju nue (.) mi a ge du *said, 'I haven't received justice here, you know; I am going to do* sempm bad ju nuo: ju si mi sta:t get di dsestis (...) *something bad, you know, I started to receive justice.* bet stil mi: hav a likl prabkm bika: mi a get a bil *But I still have a little problem because I am still getting bills* ft tu: teuzan ad dalaz (...) an mi aft kal dem jeside *for more than two thousand dollars, and I had to call them yesterday.* a tel ju se dem plies de ju si dem warn sem boneut / *am telling you that those places, you see, need to be burned out,* man bikaiz ef dem ne ri:li get ne beneut (.) ju nuG (.) *man because if they are not really burned out, you know,* ne ak/an (.) netn (.) ne (.) ne (.) nebadi ne nspsk nebadi *no action, nothing, no - no nobody respects the other person* again ju nue again, you know.

H(M) Why you talk so wicked? *[WI 6192/001]*

The above example illustrates the general pattern (which is probably spontaneous): movement from the initial careful, didactic and basically expository mode using SE, to a more emotional or graphic presentation employing JC. It also underscores the likely effect of the shift — an engagement of listeners in a personal response to the proposed solution (in this case, the closure, and total revamping of the Commission) graphically encapsulated in the metaphor of conflagration.

The gradual erosion of diglossia in Jamaica, accelerated by programmes such as phone-in radio talk shows, can also be related to the role of women on two fronts: the impact, on the one hand, of educated, SE-speaking female hosts who code-switch regularly from English to Creole for a variety of pragmatic purposes, and/or acts of identity, and who thereby provide a certain legitimacy for the use of JC in public/formal media, and, on the other, of callers with demonstrably weak mastery of English, who shift to JC in a manner similar to that illustrated in example 8.

While SEJC switching is increasingly a part of public/formal educated speech, shifting (i.e. remaining in the Creole language) is often a marker of uneducated speech. Its occurrence in public discourse marks the beginning of a new sociolinguistic era in Jamaica; the frequency of its use by women emphasises their role as innovators of change from below — at the subconscious level — since reversion to Creole not only indicates the speaker's preoccupation with her point but also her lack of inhibition about the language in which it is most emphatically made, though traditionally stigmatised. The complicity of some female hosts in establishing and reinforcing the change is evident to anyone who listens to radio talk shows.

Conclusion

As far as the sound of public/formal discussion in Jamaica is concerned, there can be no doubt that many female participants display language choices and conversational attributes regarded as typically male in much of the literature, and therefore contributing to my characterisation of them as 'crowing hens'.

Many explanations for the manifest capacity of women such as these to 'crow' suggest themselves — not least the possibility that, in perceiving and asserting the power and authority which they wield in their community, such women have indeed mastered what may well constitute an abomination for females in other cultures: the

art of crowing. Another explanation does, however, suggest itself. It is also conceivable, though too often not acknowledged, that the essence of crowing, universally applicable to cocks exclusively, is yet to be defined.

Notes

1. (....) indicates a pause of about 5 seconds duration, with fewer dots indicating shorter pauses.
2. [indicates the point at which overlapping speech begins.

Kathryn Shields-Brodber

References

Cheshire, J. 1982. *Variations in an English Dialect: A Sociolinguistic Study*. Cambridge: Cambridge University Press.

Coates, J. and D. Cameron, eds. 1988. *Women in Their Speech Communities*. London & New York: Longmans.

Eckert, P. 1989. 'The whole woman: Sex and gender differences in variation'. *Language Variation and Change* 1: 245–68.

Edwards, V. 1988. 'The speech of British Black Women in Dudley, West Midlands'. In *Women in their Speech Communities*, ed., Coates & Cameron, 33–50.

Gal, S. 1978. 'Peasant men can't get wives: Language change and sex roles in a bilingual community'. *Language in Society* 7: 1–17.

Holmes, J. 1984. 'Hedging your bets and sitting on the fence: Some evidence for hedges as support structures'. *Te Reo* 27 : 47–62.

———. 1991. 'Language & Gender'. In *Language Teaching*. Cambridge: Cambridge University Press : 207–20.

Jespersen, O. 1922. *Language: Its Nature, Development & Origin*. London: Allen & Unwin Press.

Labov, W. 1972. *Sociolinguistic Patterns*. Philadelphia: University of Philadelphia Press.

———. 1990. 'The intersection of sex and social class in the course of linguistic change'. *Language Variation and Change* 2: 205–54.

Lakoff, R. 1975. Language & Women's Place. New York: Harper & Row.

LePage, R. & A. Tabouret-Keller. 1985. Acts of Identity. London: Cambridge University Press.

McConnell-Ginet, S. 1988. 'Language & Gender'. In Linguistics: The Cambridge Survey IV. Cambridge University Press, 75–99.

———. R. Borker & N Furman, eds. 1980. Women and Language in Literature & Society. New York: Prager.

Milroy, L. 1980. Language & Social Networks. Oxford: Blackwell.

O'Barr, W. & B. Atkins. 1980. 'Women's language or powerless language?' In Women and Language and Literature & Society, eds., McConnell-Ginet et al, 93–110.

Ochs E. 1987. 'The impact of stratification and socialization on men's and women's speech in Western Samoa'. In Langauge, Gender & Sex in Ethnographic Perspective, eds., Phillips, Steele & Tanz, 50–70. Cambridge University Press.

Phillips, S., S. Steele and C. Tanz. 1987. Language, Gender & Sex in Ethnographic Perspective. Cambridge: Cambridge University Press.

Sherzer, J. 1987. 'A diversity of voices: men's and women's speech in ethnographic perspective'. In Phillips et al (eds.): 95–120.

Schieffelin, B. 1987. 'Do different worlds mean different words? In Phillips et al (eds.): 249–60.

Shields, K. 1984. 'The significance of word-final T/D CCs for syllable structure in Standard Jamaican English'. Paper presented at 4th biennial conference of the Society for Caribbean Linguistics, Mona Jamaica.

Shields-Brodber, K. 1992a. 'The folk come of age: Variation and change in language use on air in Jamaica'. Paper presented at conference of Association of Commonwealth Literature and Language Studies. Mona, Jamaica.

———. 1992b. 'Dynamics and assertiveness in the public voice: Turn taking and code-switching in radio talk shows in Jamaica.' Pragmatics 2 (4): 487-504

Stanback, M. 1985. 'Language & black woman's place: Evidence from the black middle class'. In For Alma Mater, eds., Treichler, Kramarae & Henley. Urbana: University of Illinois Press.

Thorne, B. and N. Henley, eds. 1975. Language & Sex: Difference and Dominance. Massachusetts: Newbury House.

Treichler, P., C. Kramarae & N. Henley, eds. 1985. For Alma Mater. Urbana: University of Illinois Press.

Trudgill, P. 1974. The Social Differentiation of English in Norwich. Cambridge: Cambridge University Press.

West, C. 1984. 'When the doctor is a lady'. Symbolic Interaction 7, no. 1: 87–106.

Woods, N. 1988. 'Talking shop: sex and status as determinants of floor apportionment in a work setting'. In Coates and Cameron (eds.): 141–57.

Zimmerman D. C., and C. West. 1975. 'Sex roles, interruption and silence in conversation'. In Thorne & Henley (eds.) 105–29.

CHAPTER 58

'SOY UNA FEMINISTA NEGRA'—SHIRLEY CAMPBELL'S FEMINIST/WOMANIST AGENDA

In this essay, the intention is to show how, in her attempts to redefine herself as a black woman in a society which has established categories of identification for blacks, Shirley Campbell's project intersects with other theories which emphasize cultural and racial politics, along with sexual politics. This is to say, that while she embraces a broad feminist ideological position, she also undertakes a complex process which may be referred to as a feminist/womanist agenda as she is careful to give attention to the uniqueness of the socio-cultural context out of which she writes, while drawing on different black theories, in her attempt to exercise power in her writing.

Keywords: Feminista negra; womanism; Afro-Costa Ricans of West Indian descent; racial politics; Black feminism; reconstruction of identity

Yo soy una feminista negra ... reconozco mi posición como mujer negra en una sociedad que discrimina y limita el acceso a determinados espacios y recursos, basada en el color de la piel y la pertenencia étnica. Reconozco además, que aún dentro del movimiento feminista, mi posición está condicionada por el color de mi piel y mi condición histórica y cultural como mujer negra. (Campbell)[1]

... we have had the male view of the Caribbean and we have recognized now that these male views have been sometimes only sexual: a view that has limited women to sex. I believe women writers or black women writers in the Caribbean and everywhere give a special touch to their literature. I'm not talking as a feminist because I wouldn't say I am one ... let's talk with Alice Walker's term [womanism] which I love very much .... (Morejón).[2]

The poetry of Shirley Campbell is part of a growing corpus of writing by Afro-Hispanic women who consciously privilege the black female experience. In doing this, they dismantle traditional images of black women in Latin American and Caribbean literature, by projecting multi-dimensional images of black women, along with the multi-faceted experiences which characterize their realities. They project positive images of black women, correct omissions and redress misconceptions to which even some black women themselves have acceded. Their main objective is to deconstruct popular or traditional perceptions of the black woman and reconstruct a new identity that is in keeping with what they themselves know to be true of their own existence or reality.

The two epigraphs which introduce this essay, indicate that the leading Afro-Hispanic writer, Cuba's Nancy Morejón, and the younger Shirley Campbell differ in their choice of nomenclature for their respective agendas. Nancy Morejón, who consciously writes to subvert the tradition set by male writers in the Caribbean whose portrayal of black women 'has limited them to sex', has expressed her own preference for Alice Walker's term 'womanism'. Campbell, however, prefers the term *feminista negra* — 'a black feminist'.[3]

An examination of both terms shows that they do not refer to two entirely disparate projects, but rather to two complexly intersecting agendas. A brief consideration of the major tenets of womanism underscores the fact that it considers socio-cultural and racial specificities as important elements in gender analysis in the African American context and places emphasis on the importance and strength of the black woman as well as her cultural contributions to society. Morejón adopted this theory to explore racial and gender issues within Cuban revolutionary politics, to develop her project of showing that gender, racial and cultural politics are interlinked and connected. Shirley Campbell's use of the term *feminista negra* implies that she is also concerned with racial politics as much as she is with gender politics. It suggests, further, that like Morejón, she is involved in a complex agenda that rejects ethnocentrism and the 'imperializing tendencies' of European and Euro-American feminisms, preferring an agenda in which the specificities of cultural, racial and gender politics as they relate to Afro-Cuban and Afro-Costa Rican women, respectively, are considered.

An Afro-Costa Rican of West Indian descent[4]

Shirley Campbell is a third generation Afro-Costa Rican of West Indian descent and one of a small group of Afro-Costa Rican female writers, who have emerged during the last three decades, producing literary works which draw attention to the problems of being black and invisible in Costa Rica. Campbell was born in San José in 1965, 15 years after the West Indian community in Limón was granted citizenship and allowed to vote and move freely about in Costa Rican society.[5] Despite being raised in San José — a predominantly Hispanic/White city, Campbell grew up to recognize and accept Limón, the province in which the Afro-West Indian culture in Costa Rica is concentrated, along with its history and culture, as central to her origins and heritage.[6]

Campbell's poetry is similar to, but different from the creative works of earlier Afro-Costa Rican writers, Quince Duncan and Eulalia Bernard. The similarity is evidenced by their commitment to validating their unique culture, and their attempts to subvert Eurocentric attitudes to race in Costa Rica. The point of departure lies in the centrality of the black woman to Campbell's poetry. She is unrelenting in her attempts to place the experiences and concerns of the black woman at centre stage in her poetry and to reformulate the identity of the Afro-Costa Rican woman of West Indian descent.

Campbell claims that experiences in Costa Rica have made her sensitive to the prevalence of Eurocentric approaches to ethno-racial matters in Costa Rica. Her experiences in different parts of the country have confirmed, furthermore, that her position as a black woman of West Indian descent, keeps her on the margins of society. Indeed, Afro-Costa

Rican women are at the base of Costa Rican society, as they are denied access to participation in politics and positions of power, in a country that insists that it is the whitest in Central America. They are victims of racism and practices which devalue, disparage and depreciate them as human beings.[7] According to Campbell, this situation in which societal norms and prejudices present several obstacles for blacks is a 'traumatic experience' for all blacks, but for black women in particular, who are among the most economically and socially underprivileged, and the least able to access the means by which to alleviate the conditions in which they often live. Moreover, black women often struggle to feed and educate their children in situations of extreme economic deprivation.

Activist and Social Worker

Shirley Campbell, who is an anthropologist by profession, having earned her Bachelors Degree from the Universidad Nacional in Costa Rica, has taken practical steps to assist in the process of alleviating the problems or changing the status of Afro-Costa Rican women. In addition to her participation in several social programmes aimed at improving the general levels of cultural awareness and literacy levels of Afro-Costa Ricans, she has worked in NGO Health projects designed to educate poor Afro-Costa Rican and indigenous women, so as to enable them to take practical steps to empower themselves. The latter project involved conducting workshops designed to sensitize them to the importance of education, physical health and other issues related to preserving themselves as vital women, who are able to make important contributions to the development of their children and their communities. Additionally, she has been Founding Director of the Group for the Promotion and Diffusion of Afro-Costa Rican Culture, a group that is insistent on validating the cultural heritage of the members of the Jamaican diaspora in Costa Rica. In this role, she undertook the mission of seeking to explode the myths about the people of Limón for the benefit of the Afro-Costa Ricans themselves — as well as for outsiders — and thereby raise awareness about the centrality of their African heritage to their own sense of identity.

A Black Feminist

Campbell's declaration of being 'una feminista negra' shows her awareness of the fact that feminism is a theoretical concept that is essentially based on the notion that gender, and not race, is the main concern in the struggle against patriarchy. It shows, furthermore, that she recognizes that there is a distinct difference between the ways in which white Costa Rican women and Afro-Costa Rican women of West Indian descent experience patriarchy. White Costa Ricans may encounter gender and sometimes class discrimination, but they are not subjected to discrimination on the basis of race as are black Costa Rican women. So while Campbell embraces feminism in its broad ideological terms, she simultaneously recognizes that the feminist movement in Costa Rica must admit that the problems of black women cannot be subsumed under one all-encompassing term or movement, unless the specific ways in which race, class and gender converge and intersect in the oppression of black women in that country are acknowledged by such a term or movement. Hence she deems it necessary to declare herself 'una feminista negra' — a black feminist, a term which also implies that heritage is important in her poetry, in the same way that gender issues are. Perhaps, given the official position on race relations in Cuba, it is neither necessary nor prudent for Morejón to use a term which overtly and explicitly draws attention to the racializing intent of her work.[8] For Campbell, however, it is necessary to show unequivocally that her own agenda is explicitly concerned about the social position of black women in Costa Rica, especially as she writes in a context in which the truth about racism, and the depreciation of Afro-Costa Ricans and their culture has not been admitted.

Campbell's construction of black feminism may be said to relate not just to Alice Walker's or Morejón's womanism, but also to broader theories of black feminism that have been articulated by black-conscious feminist critics such as Patricia Collins, Cheryl Wall and Barbara Christian, who concur in the view that feminism must consider the ways in which issues of race, diaspora and nation aid in reinforcing marginal versus central positions in society. Collins for her part, identifies several core theories that characterize black feminist thought. These include the rejection of the objectification of black woman as 'other', the adulation of motherhood as an empowering experience, the ability of love of self to enable black women to resist oppression and the general oppression of black women on the basis of a complex matrix of domination involving race, class, gender, sexuality and nation. While Collins does not claim to speak for or establish homogenizing principles for all black women, the similarities in the experiences of other black women allow them to identify with some of the values and principles that she promotes.

As a 'feminista negra', Campbell deliberately presents a discourse of oppositionality to the Eurocentric attitude to black women of West Indian descent in Costa Rica and highlights her black consciousness by underlining the importance she attaches to her definition of herself as a black woman. In a manner similar to Morejón, she demonstrates that pride in her Afro-Caribbean culture, history and traditions are important for self-empowerment in a context sustained by oppression based on race, gender and class. Other important issues that are in keeping with this position as 'una feminista negra' include the focus on the resilience of black women, the validation of black motherhood and the affirmation of black beauty. In expatiating on these issues in her work, she imbues them with a humanizing message, or a message that emphasizes the worth of all human beings. In order to present her ideological position, she skilfully incorporates a wide range of rhetorical modes and literary devices such as accumulation, polysyndeton, metaphor, understatement and anaphora, all of which create a forthright poetic persona and subjective poetry.

The purpose of this essay is to demonstrate that Shirley Campbell seeks to redefine herself as a black woman in a society that has established categories of identification for blacks, and so her project intersects with other theories that emphasize cultural and racial politics along with sexual politics. In other words, while she embraces a broad feminist ideological position, she is determined to bring black theories aimed at presenting more balanced and realistic images of the Afro-Costa Rican women of West Indian descent. In doing so, she undertakes a complex process that may be referred to as a feminist/womanist agenda. Campbell is fully aware of the specificities and uniqueness of the historical and socio-cultural context out of which she writes; therefore she carefully draws on different black theories in her attempt to exercise power through her writing.

In Campbell's project of redefinition or reconstruction of identity, the Afro-Costa Rican woman is situated as subject, to counter society's claim of her as Other. This is achieved in the central way in which Campbell's creative verses attempt to draw attention to different aspects of the lives of Afro-Costa Rican women and their contributions to society. The section, *'Las mujeres y los hombres'/* 'Women and Men' of *Naciendo* (Campbell, 1988) is replete with images of the resilient, indomitable black woman who is fearless and untiring in her efforts to face the harsh realities of her society, undaunted by suggestions or prospects of defeat. The poetic persona is fully aware of the social and economic challenges she often faces, including the deception of a lover, but she forges ahead despite the obstacles life presents. The moral wisdom, social awareness, perseverance and strength of the black woman are made particularly emphatic through the following terse lines which reveal an intriguing use of understatement, to depict a strong black woman who understands her context and role as provider for her children. Her resolve to be a source of love, affirmation and strength, especially for her children, is very forcefully portrayed:

The poem derives its complexity from its own internal contradiction. The resilience of the woman is established by the definitive phrase *'no llora.'* However, the phrase that immediately follows this suggests that this is not a firm resolve on the part of the woman, to not cry, but she may do so under the stress created by different problems. The poem becomes even more problematic in the last two lines, which suggest that when the love for her children is exhausted she will cry. But to accept that her love for her children will be exhausted one day is to undermine the image of the strong woman who has accepted her lot. It would be more consistent with the image of the black woman who is not defeated by circumstances, to interpret *'se le agate'*, expressed in the subjunctive as it is, as a suggestion that such an occurrence may, or could take place, but there is no great probability or certainty that it will. This would support the construction of the image of a black woman of endurance and fortitude that is projected in the rest of the poem. In other words, because it is highly unlikely and perhaps not possible that her love for her children will be exhausted, she will not cry, therefore the early declaration, *'no llora,'* is the

le ha tocado ser negra	It is her lot to be black
como los duros pecados	like hard sins
y arrancarse los ojos	and she looks away
para no mirar	so as not to see
la tierra adolorida	the suffering of the land
y esta mujer no llora	and this woman does not cry
se guarda el llanto para después	she holds back weeping for later
para cuando no le alcance	for when she has no man in her life
el hombre para la vida	to help her
y se le agate el amor	and when her love for her children
para los hijos.	runs out.

(*Naciendo*, p.38)

characteristic which the writer would want the reader to privilege.

The following poem shows how the black woman often becomes overwhelmed by her circumstances but draws on her inner strength to sustain her:

Mañana	Tomorrow
la verás derramarse	you will see her weep
entre sus lágrimas	between her tears
la verás arrinconarse en su espacio	you will see her withdraw into her space
protegiendo su melancholía	hiding her sadness
la verás llorand	you will see her cry
con sus hijos rotos	with her broken children
y su espalda curva	and her curved back
la verás desfigurar su tiempo	you will see her disfigure her time
y desbocarse contra su ira	and lash out in her anger
la verás llorar	and you will see her cry
llorará con la fuerza ajena	she will cry with the uncontrollable force
de cualquier mujer	of any woman
con la angustia suya	with her own anguish
por la muerte.	about death.
Más luego la verás buscarse la melancolía	Later you will see her without sadness
remendar sus hijos	mend her children
con su nuevo tiempo	with her new time
mirarse la piel	look at her skin
con su hermosa sombra	with its beautiful darkness
y seguir viviendo.	and she will go on living.

(*Naciendo*, p.34)

The poem develops through the contrast presented between the reactions of the persona in the first stanza and her restored sense of self and inner strength when she again decides to assert her agency, take control of her emotions and find strength in herself, in the second stanza. The adverb '*Mañana*' at the beginning, functions as a kind of generic term for the times when the persona will succumb to the pressures of life. The pain and suffering because of problems such as her children's difficulties and perhaps delinquent behaviour suggested by the term '*hijos rotos,*' and the anger and grief that this creates is conveyed by the uncontrollable manner in which she cries.

However, the image of her suffering with dignity, '*protegiendo su melancolia*', as she tries to hide her tears, suppresses the notion of her as a helpless victim who openly exhibits her pain and suffering for all to see. The conviction that these feelings of defeat are usually short lived is emphasized by the term '*Más luego*', followed by the positive and self-affirming acts she performs for herself and her children. This contrast is further sustained by the endings of both stanzas. The first ends with a focus on the grief and fear of death with which she battles, while the second emphasizes her determination to be a victor, overcome her difficulties and resolve to live despite the challenges of life. The reconstructed image is of one who weeps as she is affected by the obstacles she faces in her marginalized position, but in the end she emerges victoriously as she makes a conscious decision to exercise subjectivity as a black woman and be sustained by the sense of pride and fortitude with which she associates her race: '*mirarse la piel/con su hermosa sombra/y seguir viviendo*'.

It may be argued that the use of the future tense in the stanza in which this reconstructed image is created is problematic as, from a semantic point of view, the future tense (in this poem) is tantamount to a prediction, and, because this tense is not considered as necessary for future situations, its use makes the stanza systemically weaker than the present tense would. It is true that the future tense lies less in 'the domain of what is known than the present or the past' (Huddleston, 2004, p. 81). However, these claims would also have to be made about the first stanza, which is developed in the future tense. It seems then that even if the future tense is seen more as having affinities with 'may' in both stanzas, it works in an interesting manner to strengthen the poet's position. The overall prediction involves one in which a positive reassertion of self is anticipated for the black woman. In other words, whatever negative situations confront the woman, she will not be permanently overwhelmed.

This image of the strong black woman is indeed constructed in the 'feminist/womanist mode.' It is a portrayal that shows the woman asserting herself in the feminist mode, but it also finds resonance in the characterization of the Africana womanist:

> … the Africana womanist comes from a long tradition of psychological as well as physical strength. She has persevered centuries of struggling for herself and her family…. Reflecting upon her historical strength, particularly during the time when Africana people experienced the most severe blows of servitude, she embraces with open arms the rich legacy of her sisters' enduring strength out of both awesome courage and true love for her family (Hudson-Weems, 1998, p. 66).

Through her portrayal of the strong black grandmother, Campbell underlines the perseverance, moral wisdom and strength of the black woman, characteristics that have helped to preserve the Afro-Costa Rican society. Moreover, she reformulates the identity of the black grandmother who is historically known for her overwhelming struggles in her role as nurturer of the black race as she often takes responsibility for her grandchildren when their parents are absent for one reason or another. She is traditionally a figure deserving pity for the suffering she encounters in this role. However, in the poem, '*A una abuela negra cualquiera*' (in *Naciendo*, 1988), Campbell depicts a resilient black grandmother who, though battered by the hardships of life perseveres, with dignity:

"A una abuela negra cualquiera"

La vieja levanta un trozo de sueños
en el camino del día
y un trozo de melancolía
de la que aún recuerda.
Se trenza el pelo
como hizo alguna vez
con su vida
y empieza a caminar,
Bajo ese sol indiferen.e
y sin misericordia
bajo la degollante
mirada del dia.
Bajo los zapatos del cielo
que ya no mira
por donde camina.
Se ha detenido
a recoger un trozo de llanto
y en esta esquina oculta
que cayó de su cartera
se mira solo desde nuestra acera
su infinito rostro
cargado de sonrisas.
Camina erguida
aprisionando los besos
de todos los hombres necesarios
golpea o acaricia a los hijos
entre su llanto
y su felicidad con límites
se enamora a veces
de algún viajero
para descansar la vida
desnudando los sueños
sin verdad posible.
Se ha fabricado un altar
bajo la casa
donde no le limiten
la esperanza
señalandola
(como si Dios tuviera límites)
Camina erguida
aprisionando los besos
los hombres
y los hijos necesarios
para que su piel cercada
de mujer
y de otras
sea eterna.

"To Any and Every Black Grandmother"

The old lady evokes a sprig of dreams
in the passage of the day
and a sprig of melancholy
which she still recalls.
She tresses her hair
as she did before
with her life
and begins to walk.
Beneath that sun indifferent
and merciless
beneath the strangling
mien of the day
Beneath the walkway of the sky which no
longer sees
where she walks.
She has paused
to gather a sprig of grief
which fell from her pouch
and in this sequestered corner
she is beheld only from our path
her ageless face
wreathed in smiles.
She walks erect
imprisoning the kisses
of all men indispensable
she flogs or caresses the children
midst her grief
and her circumscribed happiness
and she is enamoured at times
of some traveller
to take surcease of her life
baring her dreams
without possible truth.
An altar has been built
beneath the house
where they may not limit her
her hope
signalling her
(as if God had limits)
She walks erect
imprisoning the kisses
men
and children indispensable
so that her skin circumscribed
as woman
and by others
may be eternal.[9]

(Naciendo, pp. 40-41)

The term 'cualquiera' suggests that this is a poem written in honour of all or any black grandmother who has sacrificially contributed to the preservation of the black race through her devotion to her grandchildren. This is a ballad-like poem, as it depicts the grandmother's life and experience in a descriptive-narrative discourse mode. Its rhyming scheme, rhythmic syllabic arrangements, its reliance on words, on rhetorical and metrical accents, create a memorable and emphatic poem which employs several metaphors to add to the immediacy and poignancy of the images related to the grandmother and her situation. The realities of her situation are so harsh that even nature seems to be an accomplice in emphasizing her misery. Through the use of pathetic fallacy, the writer suggests that society is indifferent to the plight of the grandmother — 'Bajo ese sol indiferente y sin misericordia' (p. 40). This grandmother weeps for there is much to weep about — but she weeps privately and with dignity, as is suggested by the metaphor: 'Se ha detenido a recoger un trozo de llanto que cayó de su cartera' — She stops to pick up a tear which fell from her bag.' A similar image of the black woman weeping with quiet dignity was seen in a previous poem and so suggests that for Campbell the extent to which pain and suffering are treated quietly and privately is a crucial measure or indicator of the subjectivity and spirit of fortitude of the black woman. It is perhaps Campbell's determined effort to subvert certain stereotypes of the 'pity-seeking black woman'. This grandmother, therefore, is undaunted by the difficulties she faces, as is seen in her smiling face: 'su infinito rostro/ cargado de sonrisas' — 'her infinite face filled with smiles'.

The grandmother carries recollections of a painful past such as the personal relationships with men who were needed to help provide some of the things she could not provide for herself and her children, the romances that offered empty promises, the occasional moments of happiness that made her sometimes caress her children, and the pain that made her punish them to give vent to her frustrations. Despite this life of inconsistencies and deprivation, the grandmother never loses hope. The altar she builds underneath her house is testimony that, besides her own inner strength, she has a private source of strength and secretly knows that there is hope for her. Through this image of a grandmother who is challenged and discouraged, but is not defeated by her socio-economic conditions, but remains positive and undefeated, Campbell promotes empowerment for the black woman, and suggests that she does not always capitulate as society expects.

In her position as 'feminista negra', Campbell holds a conventional view of motherhood and therefore regards it as an important part of the female experience. For Campbell, motherhood is an important means of self-affirmation, an act of liberation and an opportunity to nurture black children and educate them to become self-conscious black persons. Campbell expressly states:

> One of the things I enjoy most about being a woman is the experience of motherhood. I would not change that for anything. This experience is seen also as a responsibility. A responsibility which carries special relevance when it has to do with the rearing of black boys and girls in a society like ours.[10]

This view of motherhood is not only personal but draws on traditional African culture in which emphasis is placed on the role of mother as nurturer, protector and provider. It is consonant with black feminism that promotes 'strong pronatalist values' (Hill Collins, 2000, p. 196).

Indeed, in Campbell's poetry the black mother is empowered through her manifestations of black consciousness and is imaged as fulfilling a social responsibility and political vocation when she educates and nurtures her children. Motherhood is the source of inspiration for many poems in *Rotundamente negra* (Campbell, 1994) that celebrate the joy and fulfilment that are derived from giving birth. In these poems, the individual voice of the mother seems to become a collective voice that speaks for black mothers, who understand that in a situation of marginality, self-representation and the re-evaluation of an experience such as motherhood is empowering. In Poem III of *'La tierra prometida'*, 'The Promised Land,' Campbell's poetic persona celebrates motherhood and the happiness she derives from the experience of nurturing and interacting with her daughter Tiffany. The relationship in which she nurtures her child, loves her and receives her love in return, provides the persona with new insights into her life and deeper understanding of human existence:

(Ella	(She
es probable que no me entienda	probably does not understand me
entonces la amo mas	but I love her more
yo entiendo mas mi existencia).	and I understand my existence better).
(me encuentro	(I find myself
contándote de pronto	telling you soon
que somos negras	that we are black women
y esa es la tarea encomendada	and this is the task given to us
el fin de nuestro camino.	the purposes of our journey.
Somos negras	We are black women
y mientras lo entendamos	and as long as we understand this
tendremos siempre besos para dar	we will always have kisses to give
y las manos limpias	and clean hands
para ser besadas)	to be kissed).

(*Rotundamente negra*, p.22)

Through the use of an inclusive language established by the first person plural forms '*somos, tendremos,*' the poetic persona draws on her own experiences to address other black mothers. She points to the need for them to accept the important role of mothering and enjoy the fulfilment and rewards with which it is accompanied.

The persona in Poem V of *'La tierra prometida'*, further elaborates on the idea of how the experience of giving birth allows for a greater understanding of life. Following the birth of her child the persona believes that there is no challenge or obstacle that she cannot surmount. The words *'ahora'* and *'ya no'* emphasize that the experience of giving birth and establishing a relationship with her child promote a new image and definition of self, as the persona is now confident and feels empowered to face difficulties, and accepts that she must now live not just for herself, but also for her children:

Estoy segura ahora	(I am sure now
de que ya no temo	that I no longer fear
y no temo porque el temor	because fear acts against one
se vuelve contra una	and it is that I am no longer one
y es que ya no soy una	but three
sino que soy tres	one part for me
una parte para mí	and two parts for
y dos partes para los niños.	my children).
. . . Pero de verdad	. . . But truthfully
ya superé el tiempo del temor ...	I have overcome the time of fear...

('Poema V', *Rotundamente negra*, pp. 29-30)

In Poem IX of the section *'La tierra prometida'*, 'The promised Land', the past with its insecurities and fears, even of God, which the poetic persona experienced *'Antes'*, 'before' giving birth to her children, is contrasted with the joy that is now being experienced following childbirth. Motherhood is depicted not only as liberating the poetic persona from fear, but also as providing the opportunity to write liberatory verses. With the birth of each child comes new vibrancy and vitality and her life is filled with simple, but significant reminders of children, such as commonplace biscuits and sweets. The experience solidifies her faith in God and in life, and gives her the courage to face life:

Antes le temía a Dios	Before I feared God
y al Diablo	and the devil
temía salir de noche	I feared going out at night
y de día	and by day
temía morir en el sueño	I feared dying in my sleep
y vivir	and living
yo tenía miedo.	I was afraid.
Pero un día llegó Tiffany	But one day Tiffany arrived
y cuando crecía	and as she grew
no quiso dormir sola	she did not want to sleep alone
porque no le gustaba la oscuridad	because she did not like the dark
y durmió conmigo	and she slept with me
luego llegó NaKei	then came NaKei
y cuando quiso caminar se cayó	and when he wanted to walk he fell
y entonces tuvo miedo.	and then he was afraid.
Un día yo tuve una hija	One day I had a daughter
que llenó la esperanza	who filled hope
de ganas de sonreír	with longings to smile
que llenó el sol de galletas	which filled the sun with biscuits
y de dulces.	and sweets.

('Poema IX', *Rotundamente negra*, pp. 45)

Campbell reconstructs the voice of the Afro-Costa Rican woman to counter the perception that her role is limited or unimportant. She creates an impression of the important role of the black mother in raising the consciousness of her black children and helping them to understand the realities of their situation. The persona is wise and able to offer wise counsel to other women. In 'Poem XI' of the same section of *Rotundamente negra*, the poetic persona advises a black mother on how to educate her child about oppression and the hardships which he/she will encounter as a result of his/her black skin. The counsel given speaks to the ways in which black women's knowledge and experience with oppression and racism must inform their rearing of children in societies in which hegemonic attitudes to race predominate. The poetic persona is aware that the values that need to be imparted to the unborn black child will help him/her to understand the domains of power in Costa Rican society,

foster positive self-definition and ultimately empower him/her to be unfaltering in the struggle against the institutionalized invisibility of blacks.

But in addition to this encouragement to educate black children to understand how their blackness results in their marginalization, it is important for them to understand first their own humanity and the humanity of others. This adds an interesting dimension to Campbell's poetry as it reveals that she is not promoting the rejection by blacks of others on the basis of race and ethnicity, but admits that true self-acceptance begins with respect for humanity in general. This is to say that while she seeks to correct the rejection of blackness and end racial prejudice against blacks, she simultaneously understands that the dignity of all humanity must be recognized as 'an important step toward human dignity and survival' (Hudson-Weems, 1998, p. 31).

Cuando nazca vestido con el color de la tarde y no te importe que sea varón o niña es más importante que sea humano ...	When he/she is born dressed in the colour of afternoon and it shouldn't matter if it is a boy or girl it is more important that he/she is human. . .
Cuando nazca vestido con el color de las huellas de las pisadas inmensas decile que es Negro como es . . . compañero . . . que debe endurecerse el pecho para ser humano y tragarse de pronto las lágrimas para seguir andando y no olvides decirle que se detiene a luchar en las duras esquinas revolucionarias	When he/she is born dressed in the colour of well trodden paths tell him/her that he/she is Black as he/she is . . . friend . . . that he/she should harden his/her chest in order to be human and swallow quickly his/her tears to continue walking and don't forget to tell him/her to stop and fight on the tough revolutionary corners

bastara con que aprenda	it will be sufficient if he/she is learning
que este	that this
su mundo	his/her world is made up
de seres humanos.	of human beings.

(*Rotundamente negra*, pp. 137–8)

Campbell's revaluation of motherhood counters and rejects the position taken by certain branches of Western feminism that view motherhood as an obstruction to women's progress, and reject the traditional role of women as mothers. The subversion of this view of motherhood and her revaluing of black motherhood is at the core of her feminist/womanist writing. Her positive representation of mothering leaves no doubt that she is committed to her position that motherhood is honourable and redeeming for the black woman.

The collection *Rotundamente negra* also reveals a determined attempt to revalue the concept of race, by rejecting the non-black model that is usually promoted as beautiful. This rejection of whiteness as ideal beauty is achieved through the depiction of the poet's pride in the beauty of blackness. This way, the poet creates a space for marginalized persons/women of Afro-Costa Rican descent to assert their identity and to exercise their subjectivity. Campbell, who is fully aware of the prevailing Eurocentric standards of beauty in Costa Rica and the 'dominant images which derogate black women', claims that the collection was written as part of her determination to proclaim her blackness, despite Eurocentric attitudes and historical events which have made black people ashamed of their blackness and so hide behind different descriptions and try to pass discretely without being noticed. For her, the way to combat this derogation of blackness is to revalorise it

and proclaim its beauty — '*decirme a mi misma, soy Hermosa, me amo tal cual soy, amo mi piel, mi pelo, mi* historia': 'I tell myself, I am Beautiful, I love me as I am, I love my skin, my hair, my history.'[12]

This is exactly what she achieves in 'Poem XIII' of *Rotundamente negra*, a poem which is one long excellent sentence which leaves no doubt that the persona is determined to situate herself as a black woman and as subject, counter to society's claims of her as Other. The persona is effusive and animated in her valorizing of black beauty and acceptance of her negroid physical features to redefine the ways she sees herself and the way society regards her. The language of the poem is simple and direct and the repetition of key words and phrases like '*me niego rotundamente*', 'I unequivocally refuse', the intimate register and the use of possessive forms give force to the poem and establish clearly that Campbell is undertaking a complex process of subjective representation of self, designed to exercise agency, as she boldly navigates the margin to centre situation.

Me niego rotundamente	I unequivocally refuse
a negar mi voz	to refute my voice
mi sangre y mi piel	my blood and my skin
y me niego rotundamente	and I unequivocally refuse
a dejar de ser yo	to desist from being me
a dejar de sentirme bien	to desist from feeling good
cuando miro mi rostro en el espejo	when I behold my face in the mirror
con mi boca	with my mouth
rotundamente grande	unequivocally large
y mi nariz	and my nose
rotundamente hermosa	unequivocally beautiful
y mis dientes	and my teeth
rotundamente blancos	unequivocally white
y mi piel	and my skin
rotundamente negra	valiantly black
y me niego categóricamente	and I categorically refuse
a dejar de hablar	to desist from speaking
mi lengua, mi acento y mi historia	my language in my accent and of my history
y me niego absolutamente	and I absolutely refuse
a ser parte de los que callan	to be part of those who keep silent
de los que temen	of those who fear
de los que lloran	of those who weep
porque	because
me acepto	I accept myself
rotundamente libre	unequivocally free
rotundamente negra	unequivocally black
rotundamente Hermosa.	unequivocally Beautiful.

('Poema XIII', *Rotundamente negra*, p. 144)

It is clear that the persona wants a full appreciation of every part of her negroid body and so each part is named, and described in a systematic and positive method designed to conjure up an image of the total black body and the persona's satisfaction with it exactly as it is.

This unmistakable love of self expressed by the poetic voice recalls an important connection between self-love and empowerment that has been advanced by some black feminists such as Patricia Collins and June Jordan. The latter is of the firm view that African-American women need self-love or self-respect to propel them towards self-determination and political action and that through self-love black women in general can resist multiple types of oppression (Jordon, 1981, p. 141). While their views refer to black women in a different socio-cultural context from Campbell's, the principle is one which is applicable, as Campbell also seems to be promoting a similar type of self-affirmation and empowerment based on love of self, as an important aspect of expressing subjectivity.

The persona declares her refusal to be silent about her history and her cultural and racial heritage, as she recognizes that real liberation and self-knowledge are derived from fearless uncompromising self-acceptance and belief in the beauty of one's ethnicity. The reference to 'mi lengua' is arguably the persona's allusion to the Afro-Costa Rican's language that is often ridiculed and their culture that is also debased. The reference to languages also underlines the fact that it is important for Campbell to address the specific issues arising from her local Afro-Costa Rican context. The employment of polysyndeton is particularly effective in this poem, as it forcefully illustrates that every aspect of this black woman's body is valued and celebrated as beautiful and that her blackness in its totality is being affirmed. The accumulation of short, clipped phrases and the use of the anaphora bring the poem to a powerful unapologetic peak, as the poetic persona makes it clear that self-acceptance and an ideology grounded in black consciousness and the redefinition of blackness, are also an important means of asserting agency and liberating self.

It is arguable that an integral part of Campbell's agenda is achieved through her advancement of a humanizing process. This process has been defined by Richard Jackson as a move:

> which lies in part in the rejection that white is always good and non-white bad, savage and barbaric, . . . [but also] in the move to bring ethnic balances to the larger Latin-American sensibility while injecting it with persistent calls for a cultural and political independence and for sanity in race relations as well (Jackson, 1988, p. 68).

This humanizing quest has been witnessed elsewhere in Campbell's poetry, but is more fully expressed in the poem, *'Declaración de hermandad'* (in *Naciendo*), which communicates a firm belief in the sisterhood of all women. The poetic persona identifies and empathizes with the pain, suffering, disappointment and joys that women in general experience at different times in their lives. The persona acknowledges the differences in the racial, historical and cultural heritage that particularize the experience of women, but concedes that there is ultimately a point at which the needs, fears, concerns and love of children unite all women. The implication is that there should be solidarity among all women and acceptance of a kind of sisterhood that transcends racial and social contexts. This bears out the fact that even though she is black-conscious, she is not racist and does not reject other human beings on the basis of their race, but believes that the dignity of all human beings must be protected. This does not in any way dilute Campbell's message for blacks in general and black women in particular, but rather, it galvanizes it, as indeed, blacks cannot expect to perpetuate the same negative values that they reject in others. It emphasizes, moreover, that while Campbell writes from an Afro-Costa Rican consciousness, she must be mindful of the issues that complicate her situation as one who claims to be feminist, albeit a black feminist, and also the various roles and spaces she must negotiate in her struggle from a marginalized position.

When Shirley Campbell writes in a feminist/womanist mode, this allows her the boldness to speak, rather than to remain silent and become an accomplice in the continued pretence about the invisibility of blacks in general and of black women in particular in Costa Rica. Indeed, her works allow her to express ideas about blackness that are important to herself as well as to other Afro-Costa Ricans of West Indian descent. Moreover, writing in this mode is empowering for Campbell in her quest to redress the construction of race, gender and class in Costa Rica. Campbell is obviously not only interested in self-empowerment, but also in creating an identity that is empowering to other Afro-Costa Rican women of West Indian descent. Indeed, her unique poetics draw from black feminist and other Afro-centric womanist agendas, as well as the concern for humanity and undoubtedly 'provide mental, emotional and spiritual liberation' for Campbell (Martin-Ogunsola, 2003, p. 433). Without a doubt, she joins the many other black female writers in Latin America who endeavour to create a type of black female discourse which is all encompassing in its forms.

Paulette A. Ramsay

Notes

1. Personal interview with Shirley Campbell, 2002. Translation: 'I am a black feminist . . . I recognize my position as a black woman in a society which discriminates and limits access to certain spaces and resources on the basis of skin colour and ethnicity. I recognize also, that even within the feminist movement, my position is influenced by the colour of my skin and my historical and cultural condition as a black woman.'
2. Nancy Morejón, 'A Womanist View of the Caribbean,' in Boyce Davies and Savory Fido (1982, p. 266).
3. Term used by Campbell in a personal interview.
4. The term 'Afro-Costa Rican of West Indian descent' is being used to make the distinction between those Caribbean blacks who migrated to Costa Rica in the latter part of the nineteenth century, and another group of black persons in Costa Rica, who are referred to as Colonial Blacks. They are distinct from the blacks in Limón as their language is Spanish and their culture is Spanish. They also pre-date the Caribbean blacks in Costa Rica and have fully integrated into the Hispanic culture. They reside mainly in the central plain and there is no interaction between the two groups of blacks in Costa Rica. Afro-Costa Ricans will sometimes be used as a shortened form.

5. 'Afro-Costa Ricans' of West Indian descent were granted citizenship in 1948 after years of being segregated and denied the right to vote or be considered Costa Ricans. See Duncan and Powell (1972, pp. 55-56); see also Meléndez and Duncan (1981).
6. Shirley Campbell, personal interview, 2002.
7. Ibid.
8. One of the objectives of Cuba's Marxist Revolution was to dismantle the hierarchal social structure in which blacks were at the bottom. The official position on race relations in Cuba is that the Revolution has significantly changed the status of blacks in the country. For further reading of issues of race and class in Cuba, see Brock and Cunningham (1991), Moore (1988).
9. This translation is by Donald K. Gordon; see Campbell (1999).
10. Personal Interview, 2002.
11. Ibid.
12. Ibid.

References

Boyce Davies, C. and Savory Fido, E. 1982. *Out of the Kumbla*. New Jersey: Africa World Press.

Brock, L. and Cunningham, O. 1991. 'Race and the Cuban revolution: A Critique of Carlos Moore's "Castro, the Blacks, and Africa"'. *Cuban Studies* 21: 171–85.

Campbell, S. 1988. *Naciendo*. San José, Costa Rica: DPU, UNED.

Campbell, S. 1994. *Rotundamente negra*. Arado, San José, Costa Rica.

Campbell, S. 1999. 'A una abuela cualquiera,' (*Naciendo*). Trans. D. K. Gordon, *Afro-Hispanic Review* 18, no. 2: 37–8.

Christian, B. 1991. 'What do We Think We're Doing Anyway: the State of Black Feminist Criticism(s) or my Version of a Little Bit of History'. In *Changing Our Own Words: Essays on Criticism, Theory, and Writing by Black Women*, ed. C. Wall, 58–74. New Brunswick, NJ: Rutgers University Press.

Duncan, Q. and L. Powell, 1972. *Teoría y práctica del racismo*, San José: Editorial Costa Rica.

Feracho, L. 2005. *Linking the Americas: Race, Hybrid Discourses and the Reformation of Feminine Identity*. Albany, NY: State University of New York Press.

Gordon, D. K. 2003. 'Shirley Campbell's *Rotundamente Negra:* Content and Technique'. In *Daughters of the Disapora*, ed. M. DeCosta-Willis, 435–40. Kingston: Ian Randle Publishers.

Gordon, D. K. 1991. 'Expressions of the Costa-Rican Black Experience: The Short Stories of Dolores Joseph and the Poetry of Shirley Campbell'. *Afro-Hispanic Review* 10: 21–6.

Hampton, J. 1995. 'Portraits of a disaporan people: The Poetry of Shirley Campbell and Rita Dove'. *Afro-Hispanic Review* 14: 33–9.

Hill Collins, P. 2000. *Black Feminist Thought*. New York: Routledge.

Howe, L. S. 1999. 'Nancy Morejón's Womanism'. In *Singular Like a Bird: The Art of Nancy Morejón*, ed. M. DeCosta-Willis, 153–68. Washington DC: Howard University Press.

Huddleston, R. 2004. *English Grammar - An Outline*. Cambridge: Cambridge University Press.

Hudson-Weems, C. 1998. *Africana Womanism: Reclaiming Ourselves*. Troy, MI: Bedford Publishers.

Jackson, R. 1988. *Black Literature and Humanism in Latin America*. Athens, GA: University of Georgia Press.

Jimínez, B. 1995. 'El escritor afro-hispano y el proceso creativo'. *Afro-Hispanic Review* 14, no. 1: 3–9.

Jordan, J. 1981. *Civil Wars*. Boston, MA: Beacon.

Kane, T. S. 1988. *The New Oxford Guide to Writing*. Oxford: Oxford University Press.

Mae, G.H. 1991. 'Speaking in tongues: dialogues, dialects and the black woman writer's literary tradition'. In *Changing Our Own Words: Essays on Criticism, Theory and Writing by Black Women*, ed. C. Wall, 16–37. New Brunswick, NJ: Rutgers University Press.

Martin-Ogunsola, D. 2003. 'Patches of dreams: The Birth of Shirley Campbell's Oeuvre'. In *Daughters of the Diaspora*, ed. M. DeCosta-Willis 424–40. Kingston: Ian Randle Publishers.

Meléndez, C. and Q. Duncan. 1981. *El Negro en Costa Rica*. Editorial Costa Rica, San José.

Moore, C. 1988. *Castro, the Blacks, and Africa*. Center for Afro-American Studies, Los Angeles, CA: University of California.

Mosby, D. 2003. *Place, Language and Identity in Afro-Costa Rican Literature*. Columbia, MO: University of Missouri Press.

Ramsay, P. 2002. 'Entrevista a la Escritora Afro-costarricense Shirley Campbell'. *Afro-Hispanic Review* 22, no. 2: 60–7.

Smith, V. 1991. 'Black feminist theory and the representation of the "Other"'. In *Changing Our Own Words: Essays on Criticism, Theory and Writing by Black Women*, ed. C. Wall, 38–57. New Brunswick, NJ: Rutgers University Press.

Williams, L. V. 1999. 'The revolutionary feminism of Nancy Morejón'. In *Singular Like a Bird: The Art of Nancy Morejón*, ed. M. DeCosta-Willis, 153–68. Washington D.C.: Howard University Press.

CHAPTER 59

THE EARLY USE OF STEAM POWER IN THE JAMAICAN SUGAR INDUSTRY, 1768–1810

Introduction

Galloway in his discussion of the sugar industry argues that, since its inception nearly 1000 years ago, the Jamaican sugar industry has been extremely conservative in its adoption of innovations in the milling and manufacturing of sugar.[1] Tomich accounts for this supposedly technical backwardness in the industry in the '. . . contradiction between slave labour and technological innovations'.[2] Galloway, however, concedes that after 1800, '. . . innovations become a major theme in the history of the industry'.[3] Steam, he notes, was the first innovation of the nineteenth century and inquiries were made by West Indian sugar planters from the very early days of its invention, about its application to power mills on their estates.[4] Watts, contends, however, that despite these early inquiries, steam in a cane estate mill was '. . . never common in the West Indies prior to 1833. Most planters regarded the idea with disfavour.'[5]

This paper assesses Watts' claim by presenting an analysis of the extent of the diffusion of steam power in Jamaica between 1768, when James Watt made his first visit to Boulton's Soho Works near Birmingham, and 1810, when the first Boulton and Watt engine arrived in the island's plantation economy. Through an examination of the early experimentation and uses of steam as a motive force in Jamaica, it is argued that the diffusion of steam power was well under way in the island before the advent of the Watt engine.

The evolution of steam power began in 1698, when Thomas Savery was granted the historic patent for 'Raising water by the impellent force of fire', for a period of 21 years.[6] The solution for the growing power needs in England was, however, not achieved in Savery's machine but rather with the invention of the steam engine in 1712, by Thomas Newcomen, an ironmonger of Dartmouth, in Devon, England.[7] The Newcomen engine was a low-pressure engine which provided power in reciprocating motion, which was ideal for operating pumps.[8] Notwithstanding the benefits of the Newcomen engine it had many problems.[9] James Watt remedied the defects of his predecessors and made the steam engine an instrument of wide application.[10] Like the Newcomen engine, the early Watt engine was a reciprocating low-pressure engine.

During the 1760s there was demand for rotative engines to drive mills, and engine builders started to adapt motion to the Newcomen engine.[11] Watt also followed suit and in 1781 he received a patent for fourteen years for his new invention of a rotative steam engine. Watt's first double-acting steam engine was erected in 1786 at the Albion Mills in England,[12] and it set the firm of Boulton and Watt on the road to fame and fortune. The engine became the standard design for producing rotative power everywhere. Although Watt held his patent, the company of Boulton and Watt did not have a monopoly on steam engine manufacturing. Neither did the company monopolise the steam engine market. Watt's patent did not preclude the manufacturing of Savery and Newcomen type engines.[13] The firms of Bateman and Sherratt of Manchester and Francis Thompson of Ashover, Derbyshire, for example, continued to build these engines in large numbers for both the British and overseas markets.[14]

There was also the pirating of Watt engine designs. Many companies constructed engines on Watt's principles, a noted example being Bateman and Sherratt.[15] In a court battle over infringements, it was revealed that 29 pirated Watt engines were made by this company between 1791 and 1796, one of which was built and shipped from Liverpool to Jamaica, for Lord Penrhyn's sugar estate.[16] Although the court ruled in favour of Boulton and Watt, Bateman and Sherratt continued to have a great deal of engine business and they were still copying Boulton and Watt's engines exactly, leaving everything in readiness only to put on the condenser as soon as Watt's patent had expired in 1800.[17] With the expiry of Watt's patent, the use of the double-acting engine was rapidly extended and competition from rival manufacturers intensified, with these manufacturers selling to both the domestic and foreign markets. By the beginning of the 1800s the diffusion of the Newcomen, Watt and other steam engines was rapid. Steam power was widely adopted not only throughout Britain but also in Europe and America.[18]

Steam Power in Jamaica 1768–1810

During the period between 1760 and 1810, sugar mills in Jamaica were powered either by the natural forces of wind or water, animals, or steam engines. Craskell and Simpson's map of 1763 shows that there were 566 estates in the island in 1763. Of this total, 382, or 67.5 per cent, used animals to turn sugar mills, 150 or 26.5 per cent depended on water-powered mills, and 36 or 6.3 per cent utilised wind power. Ragatz estimated that there were 648 sugar estates in the island in 1768, of which 369, or 56.9 per cent, were cattle mills, 235, or 36.3 per cent, were water powered, and 44, or 6.8 per cent, were wind-operated.[19] He made only passing mention of the use of steam to power mills, arguing that there were experiments in the use of steam power from as early as 1768 but nothing came of these. Robertson's map of Jamaica, which indicates clearly the geographical distribution of sugar mills in Jamaica and the power sources each utilised around 1804, recorded 830 sugar estates. Of this total, 48.1 per cent depended on animal power, 31.6 per cent depended solely on water power, and 9.8 per cent depended on wind mills. Estates utilising a combination of water and cattle accounted for 5.8 per cent; cattle and wind 4.2 per cent, and wind, water and cattle 0.5 per cent. The map does not record the existence of steam engines in the island during this period, which would suggest that none was in operation locally at that time.

The empirical evidence, however, indicates that as soon as the Newcomen engine had acquired rotative motion, experiments were made in Jamaica to adapt it to power sugar cane mills. Contacts were also made with steam engine manufacturers, by some planters residing in England, in an effort to have engines erected on their Jamaican plantations. Most importantly, engines were being erected on estates locally. According to Deerr, the first attempt to apply steam to power sugar cane mills was made in Jamaica.[20] In 1768 John Stewart, otherwise known as Robert Rainey, a millwright, presented a petition to the Jamaican House of Assembly for a patent for his newly invented fire engine to power sugar mills. The petition read thus:

> The petitioner had by great study and application invented a mill of a new construction for grinding sugar canes and the petitioner had great reason to believe [it] will be of infinite service to the island. That the petitioner went to London and had made a compleat mill of a proper size and dimension and arrived in the island a few days ago and brought with him the same praying for the House to take the same into consideration and give him such encouragement as to them seem fit.[21]

A sub-committee of the House, which was appointed to investigate the claim, reported that the complete mill was in the hands of Messrs Read and Chambers to whom it 'stands mortgated for £343 sterling'.[22] A resolution was passed, recommending that the House direct the Receiver General to pay the said Read and Chambers the sum of £343 sterling and that the said John Stewart be at liberty to erect the same where 'he thinks proper . . .'.[23] In 1770, a Committee of the House reporting on Stewart's engine stated that

> . . . John Stewart . . . has put up the same [a fire engine for grinding sugar canes] at Greenwich plantation in the parish of St Andrew and that there is the greatest prospect of it answering for the purpose for which it was intended, as the power of the said fire engine is found to be sufficient for the grinding of canes . . .[24]

It was recommended that a bill be brought to give Stewart the sole right of erecting mills on his design for grinding sugar canes for a certain time. The enabling Act was passed in that same year.[25] Deerr states that Stewart was granted an English patent prior to this Jamaican patent.[26] In promoting his engine, Stewart enumerated the advantages, which in many cases he either overstated or exaggerated, that steam engines had over other sources of power for sugar cane mills, namely, locational flexibility, reliability and dependability, lower initial, operational and maintenance costs, labour-saving and fuel efficiency, and simplicity of operation — hence its compatibility with slave labour. In emphasising the locational flexibility of the steam engine, he noted that

> . . . it may be set in the most convenient spot of the plantation, for water and easy carriage of canes, which must be considerable saving in every plantation, and in some very great.[27]

It was more dependable and could be relied upon during the crucial period of crop time. According to Stewart, it was always ready to work, day and night, right through the crop time without stopping, except for every five or six weeks when the piston was being reclothed, and this took about half an hour, or when the boiler was being cleaned, which operation took about twelve hours including the time the boiler was cooling.[28] It could be easily stopped and therefore, not subjected to accidents.[29] This aspect of reliability and dependability was of extreme importance to the island's sugar planters. They, indeed, could ill afford a mill that was constantly breaking down. The expeditious processing of the cane, once it was cut, was crucial for a successful crop. Steam engines indeed may be reliable but they, like all machines, are subject to malfunctioning, especially in the early period of their installation. In fact, mill engineers had to accompany early engines to see to their maintenance. There was also the problem of spare parts, which in many cases were not manufactured locally and therefore had to be imported from the engine manufacturers overseas. There is no doubt that, whether parts were available locally or imported, there were lengthy waiting periods for these parts, which in turn could adversely affect the production process. In fact, Watt, recognising the problems of breakdowns and the continued need for parts, insisted that spare parts accompany his engines destined for overseas.

The estimated price quoted by Stewart for his engine was £700, a great contrast to the £2,000 he estimated for a wind- and cattle-mill and mules.

> . . . The first cost of a Wind mill, with a Cattle mill, and thirty Mules, that is Twenty-Four constant in work, and Six in reserve . . . at a moderate Computation may be estimated at £2000 sterling or upwards . . . [the steam engine] may not exceed Seven Hundred Pounds. . .[30]

This estimated cost for his engine was comparable to the £640 for Watt's 6 horsepower engines which were sent to Jamaica during the 1800s. It seems hardly likely, however, that at this early stage of the development of the steam engine the price could be so low. His estimate for the wind mill and cattle mill together was double the £1,000 sterling estimated by Bryan Edwards for these two mills in 1793.[31] He was, however, promoting his engine, from which he had hoped to make some monetary gains through sales. Hence it is to be expected that he would be emphasising all the advantages, real or imagined, that his engine had over all other competing sources of power. His showing comparative prices of competing power sources was one measure he was using in advertising his invention. He was of the view that since the engine would require very few repairs and replacement parts, maintenance costs would be low.

> . . . Repairs . . . for the first four or five Years, may not amount to five pounds Yearly and Boylers made from Iron Plates, generally last twelve or fifteen Years . . . But some are made of Copper, which lasts for 20 to 30 years.[32]

This low maintenance cost, according to Stewart, was in contrast to his estimated annual costs of £632.16s for a wind and cattle mill.[33] To emphasise further the economy of his engine, he argued that, with the exception of the brickwork for the boiler, the engine did not require any expensive buildings. A shed to shelter the mill, machinery and boilers, and people, were all that were needed. Stewart asserted that his engine was fuel efficient. According to him, the manner in which he had arranged the boiler in relation to the sugar cane boiling house made the need for additional fuel unnecessary.

> . . . by setting the boiler of the engine close by, or partly on the Gavel of the boiling

house; and one of the clarifiers, (that is, the largest Coppers) . . . next to the Gavel so as the flame from the clarifier may come to the boiler to boil it . . . [34]

This heat, he claimed, was sufficient for the boiler, since it did not require any excessive heat to maintain the boiler pressure. If the heat was excessive, it impaired steam generation, causing the engine to slow down or even stop. Thus the fuel in the boiling house was all that would be required. He strongly recommended wood and cane trash, rather than imported coal as fuel. Thus there were sufficient materials locally that could be used as fuel.[35] This was indeed a practical expedient since it saved the added expenditure of purchasing imported coal. Indeed bagasse and local wood became the chief sources of fuel for engines operating in the island.

In contradiction to the popularly held view that the slaves would not be able to operate the steam engine, Stewart argued that the machinery of the engine was simple and easily understood. Hence there would be no difficulty in training local personnel to man it. He further contended that in England young boys and women were left in charge of steam engines. He, therefore, saw no difficulty in implementing steam engines on plantations worked by slave labour. According to him:

It may be objected that . . . it may not be practicable to make Negroes understand them. . . . But although Fire Engines are very curious and appear misterious to those to whom the principles of them have not been explained, yet there are few Machines more simple and easier understood, or managed . . . . Any man of tolerable capacity (especially if he is a carpenter) may be instructed to manage them, and to set them up to work, by

attending ten to fourteen days. They are frequently attended by boys not more than twelve years old and women of the collieries for several days together.[36]

It should be noted that, given the paucity of whites, and most especially those in the artisan groups, in the Jamaican population during the period of slavery, the chief technicians and artisans in the island and other slave societies of the Caribbean were slaves.[37]

Stewart contended that in its ability to save labour, the steam engine was superior to other power sources. Whereas wind and cattle mills demanded 18 attendants, the steam powered mill required only five, three to work the rollers, one to take out the trash and one to carry the canes.[38] This feature of saving labour, however, was secondary to the other economic gains to be had by using his engine.

An added feature of this engine, according to Stewart, was that it could supply water for the boiler house and distillery, as well as irrigating the cane pieces in times of drought, in addition to its normal task of powering mills.[39] There is, however, nothing novel about this feature, since waterwheels had a similar advantage and were being so utilised on several estates. The island indeed suffered from periods of drought and, depending on their severity, they could have serious effects on the estates' output. Any power source that facilitated irrigation schemes would certainly have been attractive to the local planters.

Stewart argued that he could have erected on any plantation, an engine set in good working order within ten to fifteen days of its arrival in the island from England.[40] This was unrealistic and impractical. To erect the boiler and engine houses, plus digging the well for the water to supply the boiler, and finally to assemble the engine and boiler, were operations that took weeks if not months.

Nowhere has it been shown, in the case of the Watt engines erected in the island, that this operation took less than several months. The difficulties encountered in the establishment of the first Watt engine in the island have been documented fully elsewhere.[41] Stewart had, however, invented a very versatile engine. It could grind sugar canes, grind corn, and raise water for irrigation purposes, for plantation use, and for itself, simultaneously. His method of setting the boiler made it energy-efficient since it used the same fire in the boiling house.

There is no doubt that this steam engine successfully powered a sugar cane mill on a sugar estate in Jamaica for at least a short time and other sugar producing areas in the Caribbean had full knowledge of its existence and apparent success. In a paper read before the Royal Society in 1780, by the Marquis de Cazaud, a planter from Grenada, reference was made to a steam engine having worked eleven years previously in Jamaica.[42] The engine, however, did not pass rapidly into general use. But nonetheless this was a most remarkable and significant achievement in the sugar industry.

Veront Satchell

Notes

Note: *JAJ* as used in the reference notes is the abbreviation for *Journal of the Honourable House of Assembly of Jamaica*.

1. J.H. Galloway, *The Sugar Cane Industry An Historical Geography From its Origin to 1914* (Cambridge, Cambridge University Press, 1989), p. 134.

2. Dale Tomich, *Slavery in the Circuit of Sugar Martinique and the World Economy 1830-1848* (Baltimore, Johns Hopkins: 1990), p. 201. There is much controversy among economic historians as to the extent of technological change that developed in the slave societies of the New World during the era of slavery. The popularly held view is that slavery impeded progress for the simple reason that innovations are incompatible with slavery/slave labour. See, for example, Tomich; Eugene Genovese, *The Political Economy of Slavery: Studies in the Economy and Society of the Slave South* (New York, 1976). The contradictory view of this 'Incompatibility' thesis is that in slave societies innovations were widely implemented and these were integral to economic development recorded in these societies. See Rebecca Scott, *Slave Emancipation in Cuba* (Princeton, 1987); J.R. Ward, *British West Indian Slavery, 1750-1834: The Process of Amelioration* (Oxford: Clarendon Press, 1988).

3. Galloway, op. cit., p. 134; See also Noel Deerr, *The History of Sugar* (London: Chapman and Hall, 1949).

4. Galloway, op. cit., p. 135.

5. David Watts, *The West Indies Patterns of Development, Culture and Environmental Change Since 1491* (Cambridge: Cambridge University Press, 1987), p. 421. Ragatz similarly argues that there was very little or no advance in the technology of sugar production during this period of slavery in the British Caribbean. He claims that the introduction of steam power in the British Caribbean, during this period when its employment in the 'mother country had become common, [did not] make much headway...' This, he argues, was a result of West Indian planter conservatism. According to him, 'the change from animal to steam as a motive force was too great for West Indian conservatism.' Lowell Ragatz, *The Fall of the Planter Class in the British Caribbean 1763-1833* [1928] Reprint (New York: Octagon, 1963).

6. L.T.C. Rolt, *Thomas Newcomen, The Prehistory of the Steam Engine*, (Augustus Kelley, New York, 1964) 35; 2nd ed (Moorland, Harlington, 1977).

7. Ibid., p. 35.

8. Richard Hills, *Power From Steam: A History of the Steam Engine* (Cambridge: Cambridge University Press, 1989), p. 31.

9. Its construction was crude and its machinery cumbrous. It had an insatiable appetite for fuel; hence it was costly to operate. It also had low thermal capacity. Because of these imperfections steam engineers looked to see how they could improve the performance of existing engines. See Von Tunzelmann, *Steam Power and British*

Industrialization to 1860, (Oxford: Clarendon Press, 1978) pp. 16–17.

10. James Renwick, *Treatise on the Steam Engine* (New York: 1836), p. 197.

11. Hills, op. cit., p. 40.

12. Carroll Pursell, *Early Stationary Steam Engines in America: A Study in the Migration of a Technology* (Washington: Smithsonian Press, 1969), p. 14.

13. Hills, op. cit., p. 70.

14. A.E. Musson and E. Robinson, 'Science and Industry in the Late Eighteenth Century' *Economic History Review*, Vol. 13:1 (1960) p. 424.

15. Ibid., pp. 428–429.

16. Ibid., p.433.

17. Ibid., p.437.

18. Eric Robinson, 'The Early Diffusion of Steam Power,' *Journal of Economic History*. Vol. 34: 1 (1974), p. 95.

19. Ragatz, op. cit., p. 61.

20. Noel Deerr and A. Brooks, 'The Early Use of Steam Power in the Cane Sugar Industry' *Transaction of the Newcomen Society*, Vol. 21 (1940/41), p. 12.

21. See Petition of John Stewart, Millwright, *JAJ*, (December 9, 1768).

22. See, *JAJ* (December 16,1768).

23. See 'A Bill for vesting in John Stewart the sole right for erecting Mills for grinding Canes upon his new invented plan.' *JAJ* (December 23, 1768). See also, Deerr and Brooks, 'Steam Power,' p. 550.

24. See, *JAJ* (December 16, 1770).

25. See Private Act entitled 'An Act enabling Robert Rainey, otherwise known as John Stewart, to carry into execution his newly invented mill for grinding sugar canes with the power of a fire engine'. *JAJ* (December 29, 1770).

26. Deerr and Brooks, 'Steam Power,' p. 11.

27. John Stewart, *A Description of a Machine or Invention to Grind Sugar Canes By the Power of a Fire Engine: Such as are used in Raising Water Out of Mines &c.* (1768). p. 9.

28. Ibid.. p. 9.

29. Ibid., p. 6.

30. Ibid., pp. 5, 17.

31. 'Bryan Edwards. .. Jamaican Plantation,' In Michael Craton, James Walvin et al. Eds. *Slavery, Abolition and Emancipation: Black Slaves and the British Empire. A Thematic Documentary* (London: Longmans, 1976), pp. 70–71.

32. Stewart, op. cit., p. 10.

33. Stewart's estimated operating costs of the wind- and cattle-mills:

The labour of ten Negroes	£120	0	0
A white Overseer . . .	£60	0	0
A carpenter and a Smith Extraordinary, to keep the mills in repairs, and their maintenance £60 each . . .	£120	0	0
Corn to feed 24 Mules while working, 2 quarts each twice a day, is 3 bushels per day, suppose for 8 months each year, or 34 weeks, is 612 bushels at 3s. per bushel	£91	16	0
Purchasing mules to keep up the Number, five yearly, at £20 each	£100	0	0
Sail cloth, Ropes and Twine for the Wind mill, computed at £30	0	0	
Iron, nails, planks, timber &c. £ 15	0	0	
Negroes time in bringing cane tops to the pens and watching cattle in the pasture, and other attendance, computed at 4 constant, at £12	£48	0	0

And every Negroes on the Plantation except the boylers and house servants, go out every morning before the sun is up, and pull and bring in grass by the roots, which they carry to feed the cattle in the pens, which prevents their [going] so regular to other work, and going out in the dew so early bare footed, brings fevers on some; and on the whole it may be computed that the labour of four more constant may be lost by this, at £12 each

£ 48	0	0
£632	0	0

Source: Ibid., pp. 14–15.

34. Ibid., pp. 17–23.

35. Ibid., pp. 18, 21, 22.

36. Ibid., p. 25.

37. For a discussion on this topic, see Barry Higman, *Slave Population and Economy in Jamaica 1807—1834* (Cambridge: Cambridge University Press, 1976).

38. Stewart, op. cit., p. 13.

39. Ibid., p. 25.

40. Ibid., p. 17.

41. See Veront Satchell, 'Technology and Productivity Change in the Jamaican Sugar Economy, 1760–1830'. Unpublished PhD Dissertation (UWI, Mona) 1993.

42. Deerr and Brooks, 'Steam Power,' p. 13.

CHAPTER 60

═══════ ◈ ═══════

TRINIDAD'S FREE COLOUREDS IN COMPARATIVE CARIBBEAN PERSPECTIVES

The free coloured population of Trinidad have always possessed grounds for pretension, to which no other coloured colonists could aspire. During the whole period of Spanish administration, they were as impartially treated as the whites.

J.B. Philip: *Free Mulatto*, p. 16

The Two Charters

A very convenient point at which to begin the discussion of the position of the free coloureds in Trinidad is the Cedula of 1783. This Cedula represents Spain's deliberate attempt in the late eighteenth century to develop a plantation economy in Trinidad by relaxing restrictions on access to land, by freeing trade and investment, and by creating a safer climate for capital. For the moment, our attention must be confined to the two clauses which most directly related to the question of the status of the free coloureds. Since the Cedula of 1783 was not abrogated by the English when they captured the island in 1797, its terms were at the centre of the debate in the 1820s on the status of free coloureds. The famous 5th clause reads as follows:

After the first five years' establishment of foreign settlers on the said island, they shall, by obliging themselves to continue therein perpetually, have all the rights and privileges of naturalization granted to them, and to the children they may have brought with them, as well as those that may have been born in the island, in order to be admitted in consequence to the honorary employments of the public, and of the militia, agreeable to the quality and talents of each. [1]

This clause was the bedrock of the case of the free coloureds — that the Spanish government had given them civil equality with the whites. As settlers, they were convinced that they were entitled to the benefits of this clause. The final clause of the Cedula of 1783, though less often quoted, also provided the free coloureds a welcomed shelter. They claimed that it abolished any and all pre-1783 Spanish laws hostile to them. It reads, in part:

And in order that all the articles contained in this regulation should have their full force, we dispense with all the laws and customs which may be contradictory to them; and we command our councils of the Indies, the chancellors and courts of justice thereof, vice-kings, captains and commanders-in-chief, governors and intendants, common justice, the officers of our royal revenues, and our consuls in the ports of France, to keep, comply with, and execute, and cause to be kept, complied with, and execute the regulation inserted in this our royal schedule.[2]

Another document which was vital to the free coloureds' case, and indeed to all the Roman Catholics of the island, was the Capitulation of 1797. This treaty between a defeated Spanish governor and a victorious British general was often regarded as an irrevocable part of the constitution of the island, and even as late as the early 20th century a few persons sought to protect their rights by appealing to it. The clause which was of most importance for the free coloureds was no. XII which reads:

> The free coloured people, who have been acknowledged as such by the laws of Spain, shall be protected in their liberty, persons and property, like other inhabitants, they taking the oath of allegiance and demeaning themselves as becomes good and peaceable subjects of His Britannic Majesty.[3] What could be clearer than this, asked the free coloured leaders? By clutching the 12th clause the free coloureds turned the Capitulation into a sort of victory for themselves, and the term "Capitulant" used to describe those who were present when the English took over the island, instead of a badge of shame, became a mark of pride and privilege. The Cedula of 1783 gave them equal civil rights, and the Capitulation of 1797 confirmed it. Yet the English authorities, as we shall see, placed a wholly different interpretation on these clauses.

Immigration into the Spanish Antilles

There is to date no full-scale study of the free coloureds in Trinidad.[4] This present study is the first in the field. The island falls firmly within the three-tier socio-racial pattern prevailing in the Caribbean. As a Spanish colony for nearly three hundred years, Trinidad shared the fate of Cuba, Santo Domingo, Jamaica and Puerto Rico: neglected and under-populated, perhaps even more so that the larger Spanish islands in the Greater Antilles, Trinidad at the southern end of the Antillean chain of islands possessed some of the pre-conditions for the early birth of a free coloured population. White men were few, white women very rare, and a small number of African women were available. The persistence of Aboriginal Indian communities for longer periods in Trinidad than in other Spanish islands ensured that Indian blood was mixed with those of Europeans and Africans.[5] The small number of white colonists limited the growth of the free coloured population with white fathers.

It cannot be argued that the need to defend the island gave the early free coloureds any advantages in status. Trinidad was more or less defenceless for at least two-and-a-half centuries. It was not avidly sought by rival European nations, nor was it on the route of Spanish fleets to the centres of the Spanish American empire. The level of colonization in Cuba, Santo Domingo and Puerto Rico was higher than in Trinidad in the first two-and-a-half centuries of Spanish rule. Those colonies already had the beginnings of a Spanish creole identity by the middle of the eighteenth century. They were, at this time, too few colonists for anything similar to have happened in Trinidad.

Towards the end of the eighteenth century, Trinidad, like Cuba and Santo Domingo and Puerto Rico, was stimulated economically by new types of policies from the Spanish Crown acting in its own interest and those of the creole landowning and slave-owning class.[6] Basic to this economic stimulation, was an increase in the population through immigration. Some of the immigrants were refugees, white and coloured, sometimes with their slaves, from the rebellious French Antilles. The ports of all the Spanish islands were opened to a freer flow of the African slave trade. However, the three-tier socio-racial structure was filled out by these immigrants in a somewhat different matter. The white population of Cuba and Puerto Rico, especially Cuba, was heavily reinforced; comparatively speaking, white immigration into Trinidad in the 1780s and 1790s was feeble.[7] The capture of the island in 1797 by the British, and its distance from Saint Domingue and Santo Domingo, limited its role as a destination for frightened Spaniards

TABLE 60.1
POPULATION OF TRINIDAD 1813, 1819, 1825

Groups	1813		1819		1825	
White						
Male	1,695		2,047		)	
Female	1,201		1,669		)	
Total	2,896		3,716		3,310	
% of total population		7.6%		9.3%		7.8%
Free Coloureds						
Male	3,774		5,956		)	
Female	4,328		6,529		)	
Total	8,102		12,485		14,983	
% of total population		21.3%		31.2%		35.4%
Slave						
Male	)		)		)	
Female	)		)		)	
Total	25,717		22,854		23,230	
% of total population		67.7%		57.2%		54.9%
Indians						
Male	)		)		)	
Female	)		)		)	
Total	1,265		850		727	
% of total population		3.3%		2.1%		1.7%
Total population	37,980		39,905		42,250	

Sources: C.O. 295/55, p. 366, Return of E. Hodkinson, Commissary of Population

Cecil Goodridge: Land, Labour and Immigration into Trinidad 1783-1833 (unpublished PhD thesis, Cambridge University, 1970), p. 219.

and dispossessed Frenchmen. Because the white population was small, and because Trinidad never went into an era of sugar development in the 1780s and 1790s with the surge and power of Cuba, there were far fewer slaves imported, although Trinidad, like Cuba, had new privileges of free trade in slaves.[8] Trinidad very likely imported more slaves than Puerto Rico in the 1780s and 1790s, although Puerto Rico had a larger white population than Trinidad.[9] The apparent results of these varying patterns of immigration was that a larger proportion of free coloured immigrants entered Trinidad than either Cuba or Puerto Rico. Hence the three-tier structure of Trinidad was mostly reinforced in the middle, the intermediate level, by coloureds. While Cuba and Puerto Rico entered into the early nineteenth century with white majorities, Trinidad continued with a white minority, adding by the 1800s a slave majority, and a strongly represented free-coloured section.[10] Superficially at least, the pattern in Trinidad was a hybrid of the traditional Spanish Caribbean and British Caribbean patterns. Like the British Caribbean, Trinidad in 1797 had a white minority, and a slave majority; like the Spanish Caribbean, especially Puerto Rico, it had a large free-coloured sector. This pattern persisted down to the abolition of slavery (1838), with the free coloureds making significant gains over the white population. Compared to most other Caribbean islands the demographic strength of the free coloured population in Trinidad was outstanding.

TABLE 60.2
COMPARATIVE DEMOGRAPHIC STRENGTH OF FREEDMAN POPULATIONS

Year	Colony	Freedom as % of free population	Freedom as % of non-white population
1825	Barbados	23.6	6.0
1817	Cuba	30.1	33.2
1827	Puerto Rico	38.2	74.5
1817	Curacao	44.6	24.8
1820	Jamaica	48.5	8.8
1826	Martinque	52.0	11.7
1826	St Kitts	57.3	11.3
1830	Surinam	66.0	9.3
1829	Guyana	67.7	8.4
1824	St Lucia	75.4	21.2
1823	Dominica)	)	)
	St Vincent)	75.4	16.0
	Grenadines)	)	)
1825	Trinidad	81.9	39.2
1826	Grenada	82.4	13.7

Sources: E. Williams, *From Columbus to Castro*, pp. 290-1; D. Cohen and J. Greene, *Neither Slave nor Free*, p. 62. 71, 151; B. Marshall, *Social Stratification in the Slave Society of the British Windward Islands*, op. cit, p. 35; E. Cox, *The Shadow of Freedom*, op. cit., p. 59, 61; B. Gaspar, *The Emancipation of the Free Coloureds of St. Lucia 1814-31*, op. cit., p. 3; R. Schomburgk, *A Description of British Guiana*, p. 42; E. Brathwaite, The *Development of Creole Society 1770-1820*, op. cit., p. 152, 168.

Notes: The figures include free blacks except in Surinam and Curaçao. Guyana means Demerara and Essequibo.

Table 60.2 demonstrates the comparative demographic strengths, at a high period of the struggle in the British islands. Only Grenada, which also had a large free coloured population, and Puerto Rico, which was characterised by a notoriously small slave population, could compare favourably with Trinidad.

The Colour Scale

Of the older British West Indian islands, Jamaica is the only one which had a well-established, sophisticated colour scale measuring the distance of persons of mixed ancestry from white persons. It is recognised that these internal gradations were first created in the New World by Spaniards and distilled into a fine art by the French. No researcher has explained how Jamaica came to adopt such a sophisticated colour scale so uncharacteristic of the English in the other British islands. Trinidad which was Spanish for nearly three hundred years received a substantial influx of Frenchmen and free coloureds of French extraction in the last two decades of the eighteenth century. It is not therefore surprising (and one must not forget its vital links with neighbouring Venezuela) that Trinidad had a definite colour scale.

In this respect the island was more like Jamaica and unlike the rest of the British islands.

The main evidence for a detailed colour scale in Trinidad comes from the classification of slaves in the Slave Registry.[11] Our assumption is that the colour scale used for slaves was not peculiar to them, but applied to the free non-white population generally. The colour rating in descending order was something like this:

white
quadroon
mestee
costee
mulatto
cabre
mongrel
sambo
blacks

As usual, the sexual union of a white man and a black woman, African or creole, produced the best known type of coloured person, the mulatto. The majority of coloured slaves were mulattoes,[12] and the term, as elsewhere in the Caribbean, came to be synonymous with the entire group of coloureds. It seems that a cabre woman and a white man could have a mulatto child. A mulatto woman and a white man produced a mestee offspring; and a mestee and a mulatto produced a costee. A mulatto and a black person would usually have a cabre child. Occasionally a black child, rarely a mongrel or a sambo child.[13] A cabre and a black person would usually produce a black child, occasionally a cabre child. A black person and an Amerindian would produce a sambo child or a black child. But a mulatto and a black person could also produce a sambo offspring. A quadroon could result from mating between a mestee and a white person.[14]

Unlike Jamaica, where a law specifically named the cut-off grade above which coloured persons could legally be white,[15] no law has been found in Trinidad regulating the colour scale or assimilating grades to the white population. But there were persons who were so nearly white in appearance as to pass for white.[16] And there were others white enough to be confused sometimes with whites.[17] As elsewhere, the detailed colour scale does not seem to have been employed in everyday life, but chiefly when it was necessary to describe someone with particular accuracy. Thus wills, for instance, might specifically name a cabre or mestee inheritor.[18] As might be expected it was Frenchmen and blacks and free coloureds of French extraction who seemed most adept at distinguishing the different shades of colour. Apparently the term most often used in the street was mulatto, with the adjective 'dark' added when appropriate.[19] The English authorities, especially from the time of Governor Woodford, preferred to speak of coloured persons.

Comparative Disabilities

A review of the literature in English indicates that for the elite free coloureds the most fundamental disabilities were related to their inability to exercise the electoral franchise, and their incapacity to get civil service posts, or to serve in the courts as witnesses, jurors or magistrates. Trinidad did not quite fall into this pattern. It did not have an elected Assembly; nor did it have a jury system; hence free coloureds and whites had a kind of 'negative equality' to use the term of Chief Justice George Smith. The magistrates of the colony in descending order of importance were the governor, three senior judges (often sitting together), the Alcaldes of the Cabildo of Port of Spain, and the Commandants of Quarters. Free coloureds never occupied any of these positions, but they could be witnesses in any civil court, against anybody, in all kinds of action. Since the whites also could not be elected to an Assembly (there being none), the supreme disability of the free coloureds came to be their failure to get jobs in the civil service, and in particular their failure to achieve officer rank in the militia. It was their conviction that they were entitled to these rights from the Cedula of 1783.

The free coloureds of Trinidad had no limit set on the amount of land or slaves they could own; they were not subjected to any special taxes;[20] marriages between whites and coloureds were not legally prohibited, though they were socially disapproved. No sumptuary laws were in force in Trinidad. It is important, however, to mention the confused legal position in the island. It was a point of frequent dispute which or how many Spanish laws were still in force in the island. The British adopted the strategy of leaving Spanish law in place, except where they conflicted with obligatory English law or were specifically abrogated. Additionally, some Spanish laws conflicted confusingly with others, and there was from 1797 a most important disagreement about the interpretation of two documents which were fundamental to the people of the island. Suffice it to say at present that it would have been perfectly possible for some lawyer to produce an ancient Spanish American law, for example on dress, which appeared to apply to a Spanish American province of which Trinidad was a part. When we say there was no Spanish law in Trinidad to cover a case we usually mean that the debate (if there was one) was not conducted as if there was such a law.

In the category of disabilities which we have regarded as humiliating, but not fundamental, Trinidad shared the same sort of grievances as many other colonies in the Caribbean. There were the usual grievances of having to carry lighted lanterns, obey curfews, endure segregation in public places, and refusals to call free coloureds 'Mr.' or 'Madam'. A somewhat unusual disability in Trinidad was the device of asking free coloureds to pay less for the same type of medical treatment as whites.[21] The elite free coloureds, not appreciating the economy, saw the indignity, and feared a lower standard of treatment.

On the whole the free coloureds of Trinidad seemed among the least disadvantaged in the Caribbean. They were discouraged from being professionals, but they were not prohibited lucrative trades and occupations. They could buy, sell or own anything. While other islands to a greater or lesser extent allowed free coloureds to have some or all of these privileges, Trinidad combined them with a scheme of free land grants which lasted from 1783 to 1812. If the Trinidad free coloureds had economic rights equal to the whites, they had in a political sense a negative equality of a sort, since neither they nor the whites had the vote. But of course, in practice, Crown Colony government was conducted by the governor with the aid of an all-white Council, and in this sense the free coloureds were in fact disadvantaged. But the incessant arguments in the colonies with Assemblies about the franchise did not arise in Trinidad, except where the more fundamental question of achieving an elected Assembly arose in the first instance. The need for an Assembly was discussed more often than a franchise.

Another advantage which the free coloureds of Trinidad had, or thought they had, was the strategic position of being able to argue that they had lost, under the English, rights which they possessed under the Spanish. The free coloureds of the French Antilles, especially those of Saint Domingue, were the counterparts in the Caribbean most clearly in a similar position. They could and did argue that they had rights under the Code Noir which they subsequently lost, though without a change of flag. There was a sense though in which most of the free coloureds of the other British islands knew that their position had been eroded by legislation in the eighteenth century. The difference in their position was that they could not point to any Magna Carta like the Code Noir, or the Cedula of 1783. Some accepted this erosion as understandable at the time it was done.[22] The free coloureds in Trinidad, when the British government came to adjudge the question of their rights, did benefit from their restorationist posture.

The response of the Trinidad free coloureds to their disabilities cannot be said to have taken long to mature, because on their own account they were protesting against disabilities introduced by the English; the English administration began in 1797, and by the second decade of the nineteenth century the free coloureds had commenced to organize themselves for resistance. This did not mean that the free coloured population was exempt from internal weakness or devoid of disunity; for one thing, there were those who were oriented to the culture of Spain, others to that of France and still others to that of England,[23] some were Roman Catholics and others Methodists or Anglicans. Then there were divisions between urban free coloureds and elite free coloured planters. It was not really that the free coloureds acted earlier than in other British islands, but that the discrimination came late. In some other Caribbean islands the disabilities were piled on by legislation from the early and mid-eighteenth century. In Trinidad free coloureds claimed that the English immigrants and governors, especially Governor Woodford who arrived in 1813, were the evil ones who overturned the policy of tolerance and equality which characterised the Spanish regime, especially the governorship of Chacon.

Very likely, there were important elite free-coloureds who stayed outside the incipient movement of protest, but there were no reports of splits arising from special concessions to individual élite free coloureds.

Because there was no elected Assembly there was no local authority capable of dividing the élite free coloureds by concessions to individuals, such as happened in Jamaica through the means of private privilege bills. The whites in Trinidad did feel insecure, especially from revolution from the Spanish mainland, and from the local free coloureds. The insecurity did not arise from the proximity of black generals in Haiti, or from slave rebellions or maroon attacks.[24] There was no slave rebellion in the colony, nor clusters of hostile maroons. Free coloureds were probably feared more than the slaves. It was not plausible, therefore, to meet the insecurity by concession to the local free coloureds. An alternative strategy was available to the soldier governors of the island, which was to frighten the free coloureds and troublesome whites by the use of their extensive powers.

The Debate over Status

Between 1800 and 1823 the slaves in the colony apparently were governed by Picton's Slave Code of 1800; in the decade before this, it was Chacon's Code of 1789 which applied.[25] Neither of these codes had clauses applicable to free coloureds as well as to slaves. The famous English ameliorative slave code of 1823 did not confuse slaves with free coloureds. Nor, did generally, the regulations issued by Woodford in his long governorship (1813–1828). It cannot therefore be said that the legal status of the free coloureds in Trinidad, as in some other islands, was complex because slave laws applied to them. The legal ambiguity of the status of the free coloureds in Trinidad arose from differences in the interpretation of the Cedula of 1783 and the Capitulation of 1797. Behind these documents was the potential ambiguity of little known Spanish laws.[26] For instance, if the Cedula of 1783 had

not abrogated all the old disabling laws of the Spanish empire, as the opponents of the free coloureds claimed, then their status was open to great uncertainties.

The main difference therefore between the status of the free coloureds in Trinidad and their counterparts in other British islands was that in Trinidad the first problem was to decide the legal status of the free coloureds and then to redress it; in the other British islands it was more a problem of improving on a legal status which was complex but undisputed. There was therefore in Trinidad a dimension of protest not present in the other Caribbean islands: the interpretation of fundamental laws defining the legal status of free coloureds was itself in question.

Free coloureds in Trinidad were not required to have a white patron, but were still thought of as subordinate children. John Sanderson, an ambitious English lawyer, wrote a polemical book rejecting the claims to civil equality in which he argued that coloureds, as a race derived from Europeans, should be strictly subordinated to them, as children to adults or as women to men.[27] To Woodford, the free coloureds were out of control; they were too numerous, too wealthy and too independent of white society. An essential part of his programme was to create a society of settled ranks in which no free coloured was in a situation of command over a white person. This was one reason why a free coloured could not be given officer status in the militia.

In Trinidad the status of free coloureds in the militia was not just another grievance. The free coloureds claimed to have enjoyed officer status under Chacon. Officer status was the most important position which they actually claimed that they once had. Their role in the militia therefore became a test case for civil equality. It was as if the entire civil service could be penetrated by free coloureds, if indeed it was true that coloured militia officers not only existed but did so on terms of equality with white officers. The élite free coloured leaders as owners of landed property in the country were exactly the sort of persons who would qualify for officer status if coloureds had a right to be officers. The deprivation was therefore most personal: the leaders were talking about posts which they themselves should have. And their white upper class opponents were equally determined on the point of officer status, because they might have to serve under these very coloured militia officers. The power of a militia officer could be used to great effect to wound social enemies.

The supreme leader of the free coloureds, Dr John Baptiste Philip, a medical practitioner whose family were wealthy landowners and slave owners, was humiliated by having to serve in the militia as a private and by being sent into the forested interior to hunt runaway slaves.[28] He had expected to enlist as an officer. It mattered to Philip to have officer status for élite free coloureds, even if in the short run coloureds and whites were not integrated in the militia. For the situation was rather like other places in the Caribbean: there were separate militia companies of whites and free coloureds, and the coloured militia units were officered by whites.

The Stronghold in the Naparimas

The free coloureds of Trinidad had a strong position on the land because of the vital head start in land ownership provided by the free distribution of land to immigrants under the Cedula of 1783. Contemporaries did not portray the free coloureds as a poor community, but as in other Caribbean islands, the majority had little or no property. It is not possible to quantify the extent of free coloureds' land ownership in the entire island, but of the free land distribution between 1783 and 1812 free coloureds received at least five per cent. Subdivision of these lands spread free coloured land ownership over many families. There was, in Trinidad, as in the south of Saint Domingue, a territorial area in which free coloured land ownership was particularly pronounced. This was the Naparimas, the hinterland of San Fernando. In the Naparimas in 1813 there was a total of thirty-eight coloured proprietors with seventeen sugar estates, three coffee estates, one coffee/provision estate and ten provision estates. In this particular area of the island, free coloureds had 35 per cent of the estates and 30.1 per cent of the slaves.[29] In other parts of the island there were scores of free coloured landowners cultivating their own land. A general impression is that land owning among the free coloureds was more widespread in Trinidad after 1783 than in any other British Caribbean island. The situation was somewhat more like that in Puerto Rico where free coloureds' access to the land was widespread. A difference, though, was that in Trinidad legal ownership, not squatter rights, distinguished the position of the coloured land-holders. Because of their strength on the land, the free coloureds in Trinidad were not particularly an urban community, a pattern which distinguished them from many other Caribbean slave societies. In 1811 about 52.9 per cent lived in the countryside; in 1825 the figure was 65.2 per cent.[30]

Free coloureds in Trinidad did not confine themselves to urban occupations. In the towns they did the usual range of jobs, from domestics to skilled artisans, shopkeepers and hucksters. But a class of free coloured small farmers and peasants existed in the countryside; Trinidad, like Puerto Rico, had a coloured peasantry before the abolition of slavery. Since these small farmers could not afford slave labour it must be assumed that they employed members of their families or occasionally coloured or black wage labour. Trinidad had settlements of disbanded soldiers and some of them from the USA, the so-called American refugees, might have been coloureds. On land given by the government, these settlers grew their own food.[31] It has often been said that free coloureds generally spurned field labour on the estates. Regular field work on sugar estates did not have prestige in Trinidad or anywhere else, and this was avoided if possible. There was in Trinidad, however, a category of coloureds who specialised in clearing estate land. These were the persons some of whom moved between Trinidad and Venezuela.

As in the other Caribbean islands, the free coloureds of Trinidad were less prominent as slaveowners than as owners of land or houses. They were also represented as cruel slave masters. It is wise however to apply the same skeptical attitude to this stereotype in Trinidad as Handler did in Barbados. The stereotype of the cruel free-coloured slave-master had less to do with the statistical reality of cruelty and more with the sense of moral outrage which whites, and the slaves themselves, felt in observing punishment being meted out by non-white owners to slaves racially akin to them. It was a privilege to beat slaves and in the literature created by the whites there was more talk of the disabilities of free coloureds as coloureds than of their privileges as free persons.

In Trinidad, land was in plentiful supply and there was no substantial body of poor whites. Poor whites from Venezuela were the objects of the feeble charity of the Cabildo of Port of Spain and not recipients of land. Thus competition for resources and markets between free coloureds and poor whites was minimal. There was no attempt to exclude coloureds from growing export crops. For the most part, what they grew were provisions. There was no pressure to turn the free coloured farmer into an estate worker. Not even Woodford had such a daring objective. Woodford tried to get all social groups to cultivate their land more intensively, and by implication he did not think free coloureds produced as much as they should. The free coloureds were blamed for slovenly agricultural methods and they were never publicly praised as an energetic, enterprising sector of the society. Woodford badgered free coloured landowners. But on the whole the theme of the useless free coloured was not heavily stressed by the authorities.

Trinidad did not experience any massive white immigration which depressed the conditions of the free coloureds. The whites who came in the period of free land distribution came into a society of expanding economic opportunities, not only for themselves but for free coloureds as well. Labour and capital, not land, were the missing elements in commercial agriculture. Because of the supervisory power of the British government, the colony's labour problems could not be solved, either by the clandestine importation of slaves (after 1807) or by the reduction of the landless or unemployed population, as in Puerto Rico in the early nineteenth century, to forced labour.[32]

Resistance without Violence

The free coloureds of Trinidad never resorted to violence to achieve the goal of civil equality. In the 1780s and 1790s when refugees and immigrants, some free coloureds, were entering the island, there was considerable apprehension by the Spanish authorities, especially in 1796, that free coloureds of French extraction might carry the revolutionary ideas of their brothers from the French Antilles into the colony.[33] The British inherited these apprehensions even after the immigration had ceased. There were coloured republicans, but as in many other areas in the world, revolutionary refugees did not carry revolution to the country of exile. Indeed the refugees and immigrants found new economic opportunities to become landowners in Trinidad, and to settle down to become peaceful fathers of families. In Venezuela there was a war of liberation in which coloureds participated as rebels and conservatives. Some of the coloured rebels camped occasionally on the shores of Trinidad, whose neighbouring coastline was strategically part of their battlefield. But Venezuela, not Trinidad, was the object of their subversive attention.

Trinidad did appear to be a colony where free coloured violence could erupt. Of the British islands, the political experience of Grenada between 1763 and 1795 seems most closely to resemble the situation in Trinidad. Grenada had once been French; then the English took it over, and a war of nationalities and cultures began. The free coloureds were also well represented in Grenada.[34] Then came 1795. The abortive Julien Fedon revolt in neighbouring Grenada was not only a bad memory, but an experience of some who were now ex-Grenadians resident in Trinidad, which had a mixed population of Spaniards, Frenchmen and Englishmen, and the different groups of coloureds and slaves oriented to the culture of each of these major European groups. It had absorbed refugees whose antecedents were not always clear. It was near

to revolutionary Venezuela. But on the other hand, it had tough English military governors, and behind them a powerful British military capability. Free coloured violence for civil equality would have been foolhardy in a colony where free coloureds had more privileges than in many other colonies.

Yet the image of the revolutionary free coloureds existed also in Trinidad as in other parts of the Caribbean. Trinidad was not too far from Haiti for the authorities to escape the powerful reverberations of events in that country. As elsewhere in the Caribbean it was remembered that it was the free coloureds of Haiti (Saint Domingue) who by opposing the whites opened the door to slave rebellion and the loss of the colony.[35] No amount of peaceful behaviour could shake the stereotype of the subversive free coloured.

If Trinidad had remained a Spanish colony it might possibly not have had any collective resistance by free coloureds to the civil and political dominance of the whites. With the coming of the English in 1797, anti-free coloured policies were stepped up at the same time that the new controlling metropolitan power began to develop antislavery attitudes and policies. Thus Trinidad's free coloureds felt that need for collective resistance, and also perceived the possibility of success. Not having any local elected Assembly to appeal to, the free-coloured leaders down to 1825 requested relief directly from the British government. This was unlike the British colonies with Assemblies where many years of early appeals to the Assemblies preceded the change of strategy in the 1820s.

In Trinidad, the main organs of government were a governor and a Council. The governor, with or without the Council, could make regulations for the government of the colony, including orders affecting the status of the free coloureds. All the governors, with the exceptions of Col. Fullerton and later Acting Governor Col. Young, were hostile to free coloureds, and there were no friendly voices among the all-white members of the Council. There was therefore no political basis for an appeal for relief to the governor or the Council, for it was these very bodies which had passed the regulations of which the free coloureds complained. In most of the British colonies with Assemblies the free coloureds of the 1820s were complaining against laws made in an earlier period; sometimes as far back as a previous generation. In Trinidad, free coloureds in the 1820s were protesting against regulations made or executive action taken in their own times, certainly since 1797, and especially since 1813. It was constitutionally normal to expect an Assembly to reverse decisions made by a previous Assembly; the balance of forces and views were subject to change in an elected body, and each new Assembly was not bound by the views of its predecessors. But matters were somewhat different with an appointed Council completely dependent on the will of the governor. The views of the governors were that the subordination of the free coloureds was socially necessary for the continuation of the slave society. Consistency of policy was easier in an appointed Council than in an elected Assembly; and consistency in this case worked against the free coloureds.

Because the first appeal was to the British government and not to the local authorities, there was no need to ask for redress in a piecemeal fashion. With the British government there was no need to bargain, to ask for little and expect less, or to accept a new privilege while agreeing to some new disability. The 1823 petition of the free coloureds to the British government was a full exposition of their grievances and a direct request for full civil equality.[36] It was followed

closely by an even fuller revelation of their agonies in the form of a book, *Free Mulatto*, written by the free-coloured leader, Dr John Baptiste Philip.

The absence of an elected Assembly also helped to shape the nature of the collective resistance. There was no need to lobby members of the Council; no opportunity to attempt to shape opinions in the Council by public agitation. All that was necessary was the collection of sufficient names on a petition to impress the metropolitan government, and the ability to win a sympathetic hearing at the Colonial Office or in Parliament by the use of contact men in England or the despatch of special delegates from the colony. It is not that signatures could be obtained without raising the level of consciousness of grievances, but the emphasis was on the appeal to the external authority, not on internal agitation to influence the local authorities. It was not until after 1825, when the British government was half way to a favourable decision, and when the collective resistance moved into a new phase and to the capital, Port of Spain, that the new leaders, chief of whom was the rebel coloured Roman Catholic priest, Francis DeRidder, sought to appeal politically to a local audience of coloureds. This phase of the movement, though the peak of it came ironically after the free coloureds had won the first giant step towards legal equality, gave the authorities more problems than the 1810–25 phase which was dominated by the respectable elite planters. Port-of-Spain was a more volatile community than the Naparima sugar district, more middle and lower class people were involved in the post-1825 period of the movement, and new camouflaged political organisations with a following had sprung up. This was nearer to 'grass roots' political agitation among the free

Blooming with the Pouis

population than the activities of a rural planter committee in the pre-1825 period.

Because the free coloureds asked for full civil equality all at once, the British government responded in like manner with full civil equality. In the drafting of the 1826 Order-in-Council, though, certain problems arose which meant that in the eyes of the free coloureds full civil equality had not been granted to all of them. The adjustments came by 1829 through an unequivocal Order-in-Council. Thus there was a sense in which we can say that it took two attempts to reach the goal of civil equality; the first big step occurring in January 1826, and the final step in 1829; yet the process of getting there was not as fragmented as in the British colonies which had Assemblies. Of course we should remember that one question which occasioned the toughest struggle in British colonies with Assemblies, namely the franchise, was not an issue in Trinidad where the British government resolutely maintained Crown Colony government. The free-coloured leaders supported the status of Crown Colony, but not the policies of the Crown Colony government.[37]

In Trinidad the 'split' in the movement for civil equality was not a confrontation between conservative free coloureds who would be satisfied with less than full civil equality, and radical free coloureds, who would stop at nothing short of it. There were two discreet phases of the same movement: a pre-1825 phase and a post-1825 phase, each of which had a distinct leader, each of which was located in a different area of the colony, and each of which attracted a somewhat different audience. However, some of the junior leaders overlapped both phases of the movement. In the second phase, a schism occurred in the Roman Catholic congregation of Port of Spain, as DeRidder set up his own chapel and attracted a following. In 1811 a serious disagreement had flared up between Church of England free coloureds and Methodist free coloureds, but this did not reflect directly a split on the question of civil rights.[38]

If there were any white liberals among the white elite in Trinidad supportive of the free coloureds' thrust to civil equality we do not know of them.[39] Col. Fullerton, one of the triumvirate of governors in 1803, was opposed to needless oppression of free coloureds. Chief Justice George Smith was so unfriendly to the social pretensions of creole whites in the colony that he looked like a potential ally of the coloureds. But neither Fullerton nor Smith argued that free coloureds should have civil equality with whites. John Lewis, a white English lawyer, was an opponent of Woodford; Lewis once argued the case of the free coloureds as a paid advocate.[40] He did a poor job. Chief Justice George Scotland was the first genuine white liberal in high office, but his administration started after the struggle for civil equality had come to an end. The free coloureds' petitions for equality did not have the support of any whites; nor do we know of any white groups which petitioned on behalf of the free coloureds as was done in Jamaica and St Kitts. In the post-1825 phase of the movement, DeRidder was joined by Abbe Power, a rebel Irish Roman Catholic priest from Grenada. Power was expelled from the island, but later returned and was reconciled to the Church.

Though Fullerton and Young failed the test as white liberals, the free coloureds did recognise that during their administrations a less hostile attitude emanated from the governors themselves. Fullerton tried to act legally and this alone won him the reputation of being a friend of coloureds.[41] Col. Young, commander of the troops who once acted for Woodford during the latter's absence, had a tolerant attitude to coloureds, but not wishing to anger Woodford, did not reverse any of his policies. In the end Fullerton's and Young's reputed friendliness to coloureds was a matter of personal attitude and not favourable legislation. But personal attitude was important to oppressed free coloureds looking for relief. On the whole, Trinidad had no friendly governor who took the lead on behalf of free coloureds.

The Free Blacks

It is not known how many free blacks were in the colony since they were lumped with free coloureds in the official statistics. There is, however, a strong impression that people of mixed racial ancestry were in a sizeable majority.[42] This arises from the large influx of free coloured immigrants in the late eighteenth century at a time when the pre-existing slave population was small. This headstart of the true free coloureds, plus the likelihood of coloured slaves being favoured in manumissions, left them with a solid position in the island. Some free blacks owned houses and lots in Port of Spain and small plots of land in the countryside.[43] They too were entitled to land under the Cedula of 1873. Among the free blacks there is evidence of Mandingos who organized themselves to purchase the freedom of fellow tribesmen, and to continue their religious life. But the free Mandingo community was thinking of returning to Africa rather than of winning civil rights in the colony.[44]

There is no indication that free blacks participated in the struggle of the free coloureds to gain civil equality. In neither of the two phases of the movement were they mentioned as participants. No free black

petition was presented as in Jamaica and Guyana. In the first phase of the movement, élite free coloureds' leaders charged Governor Woodford and his chief agent in the Naparimas, Robert Mitchell, with oppression of the American refugees settled in the Naparimas. Some of these were blacks. They were, however, a special group living near the centre of free coloureds' protest. The other free blacks of the colony, as individuals or as groups, were not mentioned.

In neither of the two phases of the free coloured movement did the leaders refer to the contemporary struggles in other parts of the Caribbean. But this does not mean that they were ignorant of them. The year of the major petition (1823) fell within the period 1822 to 1823 in which most of the other British islands sent in their major petitions to the British government. The free coloureds' leaders in Trinidad did not collaborate with any other colony in choosing a spokesman to represent their case. They chose their own delegates and sent them to London. The passage of refugees from Martinique to Trinidad in 1824, subsequent to serious reprisals on free coloureds there (the Bissette affair), must have provided the opportunity for many persons in Trinidad to become well informed of the situation there.[45] But the conduct of the campaign in Trinidad was in accordance with the general picture in the Caribbean: the free coloureds of each island chose to fight their own battles separately.

The British Government

The British government did not have the opportunity actively to protect the free coloureds of Trinidad against unfriendly regulations between 1797 and 1824. This was because these regulations were not usually sent up to the British government, but were simply implemented by the soldier governors on security grounds. The normal correspondence between governors and the Colonial Office did not contain any discussion of these regulations, nor the regulations themselves, which became known to the Colonial Office only when the free coloureds denounced them. It was therefore in an atmosphere of profound ignorance that the Colonial Office, under the influence of James Stephen Jr., set about, in the 1820s, to discover what the grievances of the free coloureds were.

When the British government became interested in the free coloureds, it did not railroad the local authorities into immediate action. The Judicial Commissioners who visited so many of the British islands had their terms of reference extended specifically to include an investigation of the grievances of the free coloureds in Trinidad. [46] Governor Woodford was given a chance to explain himself. James Stephen Jr. was asked to review the recommendations of the Judicial Commissioners. All of this happened because of the complexity of the free coloureds' claims in Trinidad. Their claims to civil equality were based on a Spanish Cedula which seemed to couple land grants, and a period of residence, with the rights of full citizenship. One question which the metropolitan government had to sort out was whether free coloureds who had not received land grants were entitled under the Cedula to civil equality. [47] These difficulties delayed a decision by the British government. Hence the irony that, in a Crown Colony where the British government had power to act directly, a five-year lag occurred between the presentation of the main petition and the decisive Order-in-Council in 1829.

In view of the reports of the Judicial commissioners and James Stephen Jr., it seems correct to say that in imposing civil equality in 1829 the British government was restoring an old right rather than establishing a new privilege. That is, the British government seemed to have agreed that the Cedula of 1783 did establish civil equality. Of course, in selling the idea of civil equality using Trinidad as a model, the British government sought to get the other islands to legislate free coloureds' equality as a new principle; and in Trinidad itself in subsequent years, the Order-in-Council of 1829 was apparently celebrated as the beginning of a new principle, rather than the restoration of an old right.

Slavery

The slave system of Trinidad after 1783 has unfortunately not yet been fully investigated. [48] In defence of slavery the planters of the colony in the 1820s asserted that slavery was mild and paternal. [49] On the surface, some of the conditions of pre-plantation Spanish colonies — which had, together with Spanish traditions and institutions, disposed the authorities of Spanish colonies to the mild treatment of non-whites, free and enslaved, in the sense of relatively easy access to manumissions and to partial rights of citizenship for those so manumitted — existed in Trinidad. The sugar plantation system was not well developed although it experienced growth in the early nineteenth century. It is known that in 1813 most slave holdings were small, the economy was still not monocultural, and that a significant proportion of the slaves were domestics. This pattern still existed, basically, on the eve of slave emancipation. [50] But the capitalistic drive of the English sugar-planter class, restrained by the scarcity of slaves, was a force in the countryside; and at any rate, in assessing the relative harshness of slave systems, it is well to point out, as Genovese has done, that day-to-day living and working conditions of slaves varied independently from opportunities for religious instruction or access to manumission, or partial recognition of some rights after manumission.[51] The predominance of African-born slaves in a frontier colony where, new estates had to be established by arduous land clearing, contributed to a high rate of mortality. There is also ambivalent evidence that the material conditions of life, such as work, diet and disease, affected unfavourably the physical growth of the slaves.[52] The general shortage of labour tended in the direction of pressure of work on the declining slave population. All this suggests that the slave system was generally positioned towards the harsh end of the scale. While, therefore, the French creole legend of paternal treatment by Frenchmen or French creole masters might apply to some small cocoa estates, it should be realised that sugar production for export demanded hard labour for long hours.[53] There is no evidence of mild day-to-day living and working conditions on sugar plantations.

It is clear from what has been said so far that race relations between whites and free coloureds in Trinidad slave society between 1797 and 1829 was characterised by legal discrimination, but that on the whole this discrimination was not as severe as in some other islands. Nor was there a violent conflict between the two parties such as happened in the French Antilles. By contemporary early nineteenth century Caribbean standards, race relations between whites and free coloureds in Trinidad were less harsh than in many other islands. A tentative conclusion, then, would be that Trinidad experienced a somewhat harsh slavery coupled with relatively less harsh race relations outside slavery between whites and free coloureds.[54] Trinidad was a good place to be manumitted. It is hardly safe, therefore, to attempt to use the status of the free coloureds in Trinidad as an index of the condition of the slave population. In explaining the condition of the free coloureds one could call attention to the relative availability of land and the existence of a moving frontier which interposed distance between competing races; and then there was the supervisory power of the British government, which offered, however limited at first, some protection against the legislation of the local white authorities.

In the first phase of the movement in Trinidad, Dr John Baptiste Philip, the first coloured leader, wrote a book in which he called attention to the anomaly of having a slave-holding public officer as the Protector of Slaves. The élite free-coloured leaders, like free coloureds generally, were owners of slaves, and the Philip family held a large number. The free coloured leaders did not call for the abolition of slavery. Dr Philip himself, though, was in a slightly different position from the rest of his élite supporters. As a medical practitioner, his personal income was not dependent on slave labour. His book leaves the impression that he himself would not have been averse to abolition, if done in an orderly manner and with compensation.

In the second phase of the movement, free coloureds in Port of Spain were dominant; and many of the rank and file did not depend on slave labour. When called upon to assist the whites in defending slavery, many urban free coloureds, by and large, supported the slave emancipation policy of the British government, and began to use the term 'People of African Descent' which might be seen as a sign that they understood that emancipation was on the horizon, and were willing to acknowledge publicly their blood relationship with the blacks.[55] The élite free-coloured planters, however, who were dependent on slave labour on their estates, were generally not supportive of these urban free coloureds, though they did not as a group openly join with the white slave owners. There is thus some evidence that in Trinidad, as in Jamaica, St Kitts and Antigua, some free coloureds, at the eleventh hour, were willing to see the end of slavery. But the threatening, though belated, antislavery posture of Edward Jordan in Jamaica in 1832 did not have a parallel in Trinidad. The people of colour in Trinidad did not have their own newspaper.

In 1842 there was a brief exchange of letters in a newspaper which revealed that the theme of betrayal was not absent from the free-coloured movement for equality. One writer, possibly a person of the same generation as the free-coloured élite of the first phase of the movement, wrote appealing to the youths of the colony to acknowledge Dr. John Baptiste Philip and John Welsh Hobson (one of the leaders) as heroes and patriots;[56] a monument should be erected to their honour. A reply came from another correspondent who charged that these élite leaders selfishly campaigned for their own freedom while neglecting that of the slaves.[57] In the politics of the post-emancipation period it seems that the non-holders of slave property, or those who had possessed only a few slaves, had a moral advantage over those who had owned substantial slave property. It is possibly significant that it was not until the late nineteenth century, when a generation which had not experienced slavery had come to

manhood, that Dr John Baptiste Philip began to get recognition from blacks and coloureds as a fighter for freedom which implicitly was broader than that of free coloureds alone.[58]

Summary

The free coloureds of Trinidad were among the most privileged in the Caribbean, and were better off in land ownership than their counterparts in the other British West Indies, with the possible exception of Jamaica.[59] Their leaders were acutely aware of this superior position in the British West Indies. A distribution of free land between 1783 and 1812 had given them a vital headstart in land ownership, which does not have any parallel in the other British islands. Their demographic strength in the mid-1820s vis-à-vis other sections of the population was also unmatched in the British West Indies except for Grenada. In the struggle for civil equality they had the advantage, unlike their counterparts in other British islands, of being able to argue that they were seeking a restoration of lost rights rather than a bestowal of new privileges. But the struggle for civil equality was complicated by the investigation into the Cedula of 1783, and the lateness of the legal discrimination against free coloureds by the English authorities meant that the protest against it was almost contemporaneous with the imposition of the disabilities themselves. The Crown Colony form of government placed the governor, not a group of planter legislators, (as in the colonies with Assemblies) in the limelight as the enemy. This helped to personalise the struggle.

The absence of an elected Assembly encouraged the free coloureds of Trinidad to appeal directly and immediately to the British government for full civil equality. There was no hope of relief from the local authorities from which white liberals were notably absent. It was only the intervention of the British government which gave the free coloureds a victory which came earlier than in any other island except St Lucia, itself a Crown Colony. But there was a sense in which the free coloureds of Trinidad had received less than their counterparts in most other British islands. Crown Colony government still remained and the subsequent political history of Trinidad in the nineteenth century was to show that the whites were able to use it to protect their political supremacy against the coloureds better than the whites in the colonies with elected Assemblies. Finally, it is prudent to add — since in comparative analysis the temptation is to underplay similarities — that, despite important contrasts, the free coloureds of Trinidad were not in a totally different position from those of other British islands. They too were an intermediate, subordinated group, the victims of racial prejudice and discrimination; neither free nor slave.

Carl Campbell

Notes

1. PP. House of Commons, 1826–27 (428) XXII, Report of the Commissioners of Inquiry into the subject of Land Titles in Trinidad, pp. 191–94.
2. Ibid.
3. G. Carmichael: *The History of the West Indian Islands of Trinidad and Tobago 1498–1900* (Alvin Redman, 1961), pp. 374–5.
4. The most extensive treatment of the free coloureds between 1783 and 1810 can be found in Millette's excellent study of politics of that period. See Millette, *The Genesis of Crown Colony Government. Trinidad 1783-1810.* (Moko Enterprises Ltd., Trinidad 1970). For other works with references to free coloureds in Trinidad, see Eric Williams (ed.) *Documents on British West Indian History* (Port of Spain, 1952); and D. Horowitz: 'Colour Differentiation in American Systems of Slavery', *Journal of Interdisciplinary History*, vol. 3. (Winter 1973).
5. The best treatment of the Aboriginal population under Spanish rule is that of Newson. See. L. Newson: *Aboriginal and Spanish Colonial Trinidad: A Study in Culture Contact* (London: Academic Press, 1976).
6. Carl Campbell: *Credulants and Capitulants* (Port of Spain: Paria Publishing Co.,1992).
7. Millette, *The Genesis of Crown Colony Government*, Table X, Abstract of Population. The white population in 1782 was 126, and in 1797 it was 2,151. The figure given by Newson for 'freemen' (white plus free coloureds) in 1784 is 2,550 which is much higher than Millette's for 1782 (viz. 421). Even if Newson's higher figure is nearer to the truth, and assuming that not more than 30 per cent were whites, the white population would not be more than 850 persons. See Newson, op. cit., p. 186.
8. Millette, *The Genesis of Crown Colony Government*, Table X. The slave population in 1782 was about 310 with an increase to 10,009 by 1797. There is also a huge discrepancy between Millette's figures for the slave population in 1782 and Newson's figure for 1784 (viz. 2,462). The problem arises from the use of different sources: the figures in the Archivo General de Indias being considerably higher than those provided by English investigators such as Capt. Mallet. Newson's

figures indicate that there was a higher level of colonisation in Trinidad before the Cedula of 1783 came into effect. See Newson, *Aboriginal and Spanish Colonial Trinidad*, op. cit., p. 186.

9. There are no reliable figures for the slave trade into Puerto Rico at this time. See Francisco Serrano, *Sugar and Slavery in Puerto Rico. The Plantation Economy of Ponce 1800–50* (University of Wisconsin Press, 1984), pp. 120–4.

10. In 1810 the population pattern was as follows: whites 2,495 (7.9 per cent); coloureds 6,264 (20 per cent); slaves 20,821 (66.6 per cent), Indians 1,683 (5.3 per cent). See Millette, *The Genesis of Crown Colony Government*, Table IX.

11. The entire analysis of the colour scale is based on information in the Slave Registry, T 71/501 and 502. In 1813 coloured slaves (field and domestic) formed 5.9 per cent of the total slave population.

12. About 56.4 per cent of slaves of colour on the estates in 1813 were mulattoes, and about 56.9 per cent of coloured domestic slaves were mulattoes. Together, mulattoes and cabres made up 91 per cent of the coloured slave population. Higman is of the opinion that in Jamaica the Slave Registry overestimated the size of the mulatto section of the slave population. See B. Higman: *Slave Population and Economy of Jamaica 1807–34*. (Cambridge: Cambridge University Press, 1976), p.140.

13. In Spanish times the offspring of a black and an Amerindian was called a 'grifo'. See Newson. op. cit., p. 311. In Jamaica, the coloured slave might be called a 'mongrel' when his classification was uncertain. See Higman: *Slave Population and Economy*, op. cit., p. 140.

14. In Jamaica, the child of a white and 'mustec' would be a mustifino. See Edward Brathwaite, *The Development of Creole Society in Jamaica 1770–1820*. (Clarendon Press, Oxford, 1971), op. cit., p. 167. In Trinidad only one quadroon was recorded, a child of 3 years. The classification 'copper' does not seem to describe the blending of racial types, but rather skin tone of certain persons, including some Mandingos and Ibos. The term 'yellow' also refers to skin tone. See T 71/501, p. 89. Seville Estates: Alex Sommerville; Betway Morgan.

15. Arnold Sio, 'Race and Colour in the Status or the Free Coloureds in the West Indies: Jamaica & Barbados.' *Journal of Belizean Affairs*. There is

however some confusion about the exact cut-off point. See Barry Higman, *Slave Population and Economy in Jamaica, 1807–34.* (Cambridge: Cambridge University Press, 1976), op. cit.ff. 4, p. 298.

16. C.O. 295/63, Woodford to Horton, 4 Aug., 1824, Enclosure; Report of Le Goffe. These coloureds who were nearly white were called 'cafe-au-lait'.

17. In 1803, two white magistrates refused to allow Jose Alvarez, the Deputy Keeper of the Records (of Port of Spain) to act as Keeper on the grounds that he 'might have a portion of mulatto blood in his veins', although he looked like a white man. C.O. 295/10, Fullerton to Hobert, 27 March, 1804.

18. PW., 1822 Will 47/1822, James Innis; also PW., 1827 Will 41/1821. Jean Baptiste Geoffroy.

19. For the effrontry of a certain 'dark mulatto' who dared to allow himself to be seated in the same dining room with white people (1803), see W. Fullerton, A Statement, Letters and Documents respecting the affairs of Trinidad, including a reply to Col. Pieton's Address to the Council of that Island London, 1804), p. 164.

20. A Tax of $16 was placed on free coloureds' balls apparently by Hislop, but was allegedly never collected. C.O. 295/63, Woodford to Bathurst, 3 Sept.,1824, 00.511.

21. J.B. Philip, *Free Mulatto*. (London, 1824), op. cit., pp. 112–5.

22. C.O. 318n6, Humble Petition and Memorial of the coloured inhabitants of Dominica.

23. Millette, *The Genesis of Crown Colony Government*, op. cit., Table Ill. This shows inter alia that the number of coloureds in 1803 who were of English, Spanish or French extraction were, English, 282 (18.8 per cent of coloureds); Spanish, 290 (19.4 per cent of coloureds); French, 922 (61.6 per cent of coloureds).

24. In 1819 there was a report of maroon camps in the forest behind the Naparimas; see J. Philip, *Free Mulatto*, op. cit., p. 149. The absence of studies on slavery in Trinidad makes it difficult to assess the security problem of the planters. Horowitz has faced the same problem; see Horowitz: 'Colour Differentiation in American Slavery', op. cit, p. 520. note 48.

25. For the provisions of the Codes, see E. Williams: *History of the People of Trinidad and Tobago* (London: André Deutsch, 1964), pp. 45–6;

Carmichael: *The History of the West Indian Islands,* op. cit., pp. 379–83.

26. C.O. 318/76, pp. 333–46, Answer of Henry Fuller.

27. J. Sanderson, An Appeal to the Imperial Parliament of the United Kingdom of Great Britain and Ireland (London, 1812), pp. 135–86.

28. J. Philip, *Free Mulatto,* op. cit., pp. 101–2.

29. Calculated from T 71/501,502, and numerous supporting documents.

30. Compiled from C.O. 295/28, p. 9. A General Return of Population, 1811; Also from C.O. 295/62, p. 263. Return of Population, 1824, The towns counted were Port of Spain and St. Joseph. San Fernando, destroyed by fire in 1818 and described in 1824 as a 'wretched borough' was not entered separately as a town in the above censuses. The inclusion of San Fernando would not have greatly altered the balance of residential location. Newson noted that in 1191 the free coloured population was evenly distributed over the island. See Newson, op. cit., pp. 188–90.

31. K.O. Laurence: 'The Settlement of Free Negroes in Trinidad before Emancipation', *Caribbean Quarterly* vol. xix, no. I and 2,1963, pp. 26-52.

32. For a discussion of the Puerto Rican situation, see S. Mintz: 'The Role of Forced Labour in Nineteenth Century Puerto Rico', *Caribbean Historical Review* no. 2, Dec., 1951, pp. 134–41.

33. B. Brereton: *A History of Modern Trinidad 1783–1962* (Port of Spain: Heinemann, 1982), pp. 21–31.

34. For the socio-political configuration of Grenada 1763–95, see Edward Cox, *The Shadow of Freedom: Freedmen in the Slave Societies of Grenada & St Kills 1763-1838.* (PhD Thesis, The Johns Hopkins University, 1917), op. cit., chaps. iv,v.

35. C.O. 29519, Kingston to Sullivan, 11 Jan, 1804.

36. C.O. 295/61, pp. 113-189, Memorial of Philip and Congnet, 19 Nov., 1823.

37. For the free coloureds' attitude to Crown Colony government before emancipation, see C. Campbell: The Opposition to Crown Colony Government in Trinidad before and after Emancipation 1813–46, in B. Higman (ed.), *Trade, Government and Society in Caribbean History. Essays presented to Douglas Hall* (Heinemann Educational Books, Caribbean Ltd., 1983), pp. 53–68.

38. C.O. 295/27, p. 127, Petition of 27 free coloureds; also p. 224, Petition of 23 free coloureds.

39. Millette, *The Genesis of Crown Colony Government,* op. cit., pp. 234–5. An investigation of white colonists' attitude to free blacks also led Brereton to notice the absence of white liberals; see B. Brereton, Changing Racial Attitudes in Trinidad. Slavery and after, in *Some Papers on Social, Political and Economic Adjustment to the Ending of Slavery in the Caribbean* (ACH, Jamaica, 1915) pp. 1–24.

40. C.O. 318116, pp. 347–62, Reply of John Lewis.

41. C.O. 29514, pp. 213–5, Letter of E. Noel to Commissioners, 21 Feb., 1803; also Millette: The Genesis of Crown Colony Government, op. cit., pp. 143–4.

42. A 'guesstimate' by W. Green of the percentage of free blacks in free-coloured populations of the British islands was "at least" 15 per cent (with the exception of Barbados) See. W. Green, *British slave Emancipation* (Clarendon Press, 1976), p. 13.

43. An outstanding black was Jonas Mohammed Bath, a free Mandingo priest. See C. Campbell: 'Jonas Mohammed Bath and the Free Mandingos in Trinidad. The Question of their repatriation to Africa 1831–8' *Journal of African Studies* vol. 2 no. 4, 1975 n6, pp. 467–95. On the question of economic assets of some free blacks, see C. Campbell, 'Black Testatlors. Fragments of the lives of free Africans and free creole blacks in Trinidad' [1783–1877].

44. C. Campbell: 'Jonas Mohammed Bath', op. cit; also C. Campbell: 'Mohammed Sesei of Gambia and Trinidad c. 1788–1833'. *African Studies Association of the West Indies,* Bulletin no. 7, Dec., 1974, pp. 29–38.

45. C.O. 295/62, Woodford to Bathurst, 31 July 1824, no. 562.

46. C.O. 295/63, Woodford to Bathurst, 3 Sept., 1824, no. 571.

47. C.O. 295183, p. 8S, Colonial Office notes. Stephen to Hay (updated).

48. Recent Quantitative studies of the slave population include G. Friedman: 'The Heights of Slaves in Trinidad', *Social Science History* vol. 6.1982, no. 4, pp. 482–515; B. Higman: 'Growth in Afro-Caribbean Slave Population', *American Journal of Physical Anthropology* vol. 50, March 1979, pp. 373-385. A considerable amount of new

information about the slave population of Trinidad has appeared since 1983. See, for example, Ann John: 'The Slave Population of 19th Century Trinidad' (unpublished PhD. thesis, Princeton University 1983); and B. Higman: *Slave Populations of the British Caribbean 1807–1834* (Johns Hopkins Press, 1985). A specific study of slavery in Trinidad remains to be written.

49. Brereton, Changing Racial Attitudes, op. cit. pp. 2–11.

50. Eric Williams: *History of the People of Trinidad and Tobago* (London: André Deutsch, 1964), p. 84.

51. E. Genovese: 'The Treatment of Slaves in Different Countries. Problems in the application of the Comparative Method', in L. Foner and E. Genovese (eds): *Slavery in the New World*, op. cit. pp. 202–10.

52. In 1813 the African born slaves were 56.1 % of the field slaves. See Carl Campbell, The Rise of the Free Coloured Plantocracy in Trinidad 1783–1813. *Boletin de Estudios Latinoamericanos y del Caribe*. No. 29, Dec., (1980), pp. 33–54, Table IV. Also M. Craton: *Sinews of Empire. A Short History of British Slavery* (Anchor Books (974), Campbell: 'The Rise of a Free Coloured Plantocracy', op. cit, p. 268, note 50. Also Barry Higman, 'Growth in Afro-Caribbean Slave Populations.' *American Journal of Physical Anthropology* 50. (1979); Gerald Friedman, The heights of slaves in Trinidad, *Social Science History*. Vol. 6. (19&2), No.4, pp. 482–515; Higman, *Slave Populations of the British Caribbean*, op. cit. pp. 280–92.

53. The non-professional historians of Trinidad have tended to follow the interpretation that slavery was mild, while the professionals have been more skeptical. See J. Mill etc: The Genesis of Crown Colony Government, op. cit., p. 63–5; B. Brereton, *A History of Modern Trinidad 1783–1962* (Port of Spain: Heinemann. 1981), pp. 25–27.

54. For arguments about the absence of any necessary connection between the nature of slavery and the nature of race relations outside it, see H. Hoetink: *Slavery and Race Relations in the Americas. Comparative Notes on their Nature and Nexus* (New York: Harper & Row, 1973), Chap. 1.

55. C.O. 295/95 Grant to Woodford, 26 March, 1832 no. 24, Enclosure, A Petition.

56. Standard 8 Oct., 1842, Letter from 'Dominican'.

57. Standard 24 Oct., 1842, Letter from 'Franciscan'.

58. New Era, 18 Nov., 1872, Report of a Torch Light Procession to the Grave of Dr. Philip.

59. One does not get the impression that the value of the property of the élite free-coloured planters in Trinidad was as great as the top 40 free coloureds of Jamaica. The spread of land ownership among the comparatively smaller free-coloured population of Trinidad might have been in favour of Trinidad. See William Green, *British Slave Emancipation. The Sugar Colonies and the Great Experiment, 1830–65* (Oxford: Clarendon Press, 1976), op. cit., Table 2, p. 15.

CHAPTER 61

LARYNGEAL TUBERCULOSIS: DIAGNOSIS AND PREVENTION OF DISSEMINATION

Laryngeal tuberculosis is the commonest otolaryngological manifestation of tuberculosis. When effective chemotherapy was introduced, the incidence of tuberculosis decreased and laryngeal tuberculosis almost disappeared. Recently, however, there has been a steady rise in the incidence of laryngeal tuberculosis, linked with the increasing incidence of HIV infection. Early detection is necessary to limit the development of severe or fatal sequelae, and to control dissemination. The diagnosis can be difficult, requiring a high index of suspicion; medical treatment with antituberculous drugs gives a rapid, good response.

Introduction

Tuberculosis with its varied presentation and numerous complications is a relatively common disease and a major health problem in developing countries such as Nigeria. Among its many presentations, pulmonary tuberculosis is the commonest. Tuberculosis of the head and neck can involve the cervical lymph nodes, larynx, temporal bone, sinonasal cavity, eye, pharynx, thyroid gland, skin, and skull base. Laryngeal and cutaneous tuberculosis are regarded as two of the most infectious forms of the disease.'[1]

Laryngeal tuberculosis is a frequent complication of pulmonary tuberculosis in developing countries, occurring in up to 27 per cent of previously untreated cases of pulmonary tuberculosis.[2] It is the commonest otolaryngological manifestation of tuberculosis and was the most common disease of the larynx at the beginning of the twentieth century.[3] As the incidence of tuberculosis decreased, due to the introduction and use of effective chemotherapeutic drugs, laryngeal tuberculosis almost disappeared.

The current resurgence of tuberculosis has been of increasing concern to public health. Until the mid-1990s, when the incidence of HIV infection worldwide started to rise, notified tuberculosis cases were decreasing.[4] In patients with more marked immunodeficiency and with CD4 counts of less than 200, the features of tuberculosis are often atypical and there is a higher frequency of extrapulmonary involvement.[5] However, even the highly industrialised world is experiencing a rise in the incidence of laryngeal tuberculosis. An additional factor is sizeable immigration from developing countries.

Atypical mycobacteria are more likely to infect persons with altered host defence mechanisms and are less susceptible to standard antituberculous treatment.[6]

Clinical Features of Laryngeal Tuberculosis

To ensure early diagnosis, it is important for health care providers to recognise the cardinal features of tuberculous laryngitis. Hoarseness is the most frequent complaint. Other symptoms include persistent fever, cough, weight loss and dysphagia or odynophagia out of proportion to the size of the lesion.[7] The laryngoscopic appearances frequently mimic a tumour or chronic nonspecific laryngitis, as the lesion is nodular or exophytic or presents as an area of mucosal ulceration.[3] The most common location of the lesions is the true cords, followed by the epiglottis, false cords, arytenoids, posterior commissure and subglottic area.[8] Only a few cases correspond to the classical descriptions of the disease found in old texts.

Before the advent of chemotherapy, laryngeal tuberculosis was associated with advanced cavitate pulmonary tuberculosis, presenting with more ulcerative and multiple lesions. The disease now presents in a manner similar to chronic non-specific laryngitis or to laryngeal carcinoma. The spread of laryngeal tuberculosis appears to be mainly via lymphatic and haematogenous routes rather than by the direct spread more common previously.[8]

Laryngeal tuberculosis is extremely rare in childhood.[9] The highest incidences of both pulmonary and extra-pulmonary tuberculosis occur in the age ranges 25–35 and 60–70 years.[10] Pulmonary tuberculosis is most often seen in males, whereas the extrapulmonary forms show similar frequencies in males and females.[10]

It has been postulated that the pathogenesis of laryngeal tuberculosis in children differs from that in adults. Primary tuberculous infection of the larynx occurs in children, whereas laryngeal tuberculosis is usually secondary to pulmonary disease in adults.[8]

Diagnosis

It is necessary to detect the disease early to prevent the development of severe or fatal sequelae. This requires a high index of suspicion.[11,12] Histological examination of biopsy material obtained by laryngoscopy is the standard diagnostic procedure.[11] This indicates the difficulties of diagnosis in the general population.

Laryngeal tuberculosis should be considered in the differential diagnosis of patients presenting with chronic hoarseness. It should be suspected when non-specific chronic laryngitis or laryngeal carcinoma runs an unusual clinical course.[13] Indirect laryngoscopy is an essential routine investigation for such patients, particularly when the patient has pulmonary tuberculosis. The laryngoscopic appearances often simulate chronic laryngitis or malignancy.

Although computed tomography (CT) and magnetic resonance imaging (MRI) can accurately demonstrate the sites, pattern and extent of the disease, both modalities have limitations in the evaluation of head and neck tuberculosis.[12] The CT appearances of laryngeal tuberculosis are not specific. The possibility of laryngeal tuberculosis should be raised when bilateral and diffuse laryngeal lesions with or without a focal mass are encountered without destruction of the laryngeal architecture in patients with pulmonary tuberculosis.[12] However, in most developing countries CT and MRI are not readily available, and plain radiographs are of very little value in the evaluation of laryngeal tuberculosis.

Pulmonary tuberculosis should be ruled out before a diagnostic direct laryngoscopy and biopsy are attempted.[2] Proper precautions should be taken to reduce the risk of infection to the surgeon and to other patients who will subsequently use the anaesthetic machine. The anaesthetic circuit may need to be discarded. This is expensive for most hospitals in the developing world, which may rule out direct laryngoscopy in some cases.

Laryngeal tuberculosis is confirmed by the identification of granulomatous inflammation, caseating granulomas and acid-fast bacilli on histopathological examination of biopsied laryngeal tissue.[4] As a result of the difficulties involved in the definitive diagnosis of tuberculous laryngitis, sometimes diagnosis may have to be made on the basis of indirect laryngoscopic, radiological and clinical improvement following antituberculous therapy.[9] Once the diagnosis is established, medical treatment with antituberculous drugs achieves a rapid, good response.

Prevention of Dissemination

Laryngeal tuberculosis is a highly infectious disease; a hazard to both the community and to hospital staff. In general, persons suspected of having laryngeal tuberculosis should be considered infectious if they are coughing or have sputum smears positive for acid-fast bacilli.[14] Outbreaks of tuberculosis should be promptly reported and investigated. All efforts should be made to bring the outbreak under control. Individuals affected, and their contacts, should have sputum smears examined for acid-fast-bacilli and possibly a chest radiograph. Those positive for tuberculosis should be treated immediately, with governmental and/or non-governmental assistance in procuring drugs. This assistance is currently available, but the drugs that patients are usually required to purchase tend to be out of stock in government hospitals.

Physical measures to reduce microbial contamination of the air include the provision of covered sputum cups into which the patients can cough. These should be appropriately disposed of. Isolation rooms should be provided for persons with infectious laryngeal tuberculosis. Three consecutive sputum samples should be negative for acid-fast bacilli before respiratory isolation is discontinued.[15]

Instruments, facilities and utilities that have come in contact with patients with open tuberculosis should be appropriately and effectively sterilised and disinfected. Medical staff working with such patients should use appropriate protective barriers such as a facemask and gloves. The health care facility personnel should be screened regularly for tuberculosis, and appropriate therapy should be instituted when indicated.

Although completely eliminating the risk of transmission of *Mycobacterium tuberculosis* in all health care facilities and the community at large may not be possible, adherence to the above guidelines should reduce the risk.[16]

F. E. Ologe and S. Segun-Busari

Notes

1. J.C. Sherrell, P. Powers, and J.M. Norwood, 'A case of tuberculosis in Memphis', *Am J Med Sci* 320 (2000): 403–5.

2. H. Manni, 'Laryngeal tuberculosis in Tanzania', *J Laryngol Otol* 97 (1983): 565–70.

3. Y. Oestricher, and R. Feinmeser, 'Laryngeal tuberculosis is not such a rare disease', *Harefuah* 140 (2001): 998–1001.

4. M.W.Yencha, R. Linfesty and A.Blackman, 'Laryngeal tuberculosis', *Am J Otolaryngol* 21 (2000): 122–26.

5. G.F. Schecter, 'Mycobacterium tuberculosis infection', in *The AIDS Knowledge Base*, 2nd edn, eds, P.T.Cohen, M.A. Sande and P.A. Volverding, (New York, NY: Little Brown, 1994) 6.5.1–6.

6. I. McDonald, 'Manifestations of systemic disease', in *Otolaryngology: Head and Neck Surgery* eds., C.W. Cummings, et al., 848 (Baltimore, MD: Mosby Year Book, 1998).

7. R.R. Jones, 'Infections and manifestations of systemic disease of the larynx', in C.W. Cummings, et al. (eds), op. cit.

8. A. Soda, H. Rubio, M. Salazar, J. Ganem, D. Berlanga, A. Sachez, 'Tuberculosis of the larynx: clinical aspects in 19 patients', *Laryngoscope* 99 (1989):1147–50.

9. A.W. Johnson, O. A. Mokuolu and O. Ogan, 'Tuberculous laryngitis in a Nigerian child', *Ann Trap Paediatr* 13 (1993): 91–4.

10. F. Galleti, F. Fremi, S. Bucolo, et al., 'Laryngeal tuberculosis: Considerations on the most recent clinical and epidemiological data and presentation of a case report', *Acta Otorhinolaryngol 1taI* 20 (2000):196–201.

11. M. Harney, S. Hone, C. Timen, and M. Donnelly, 'Laryngeal TB: an important diagnosis', *J Laryngol Otol* 114 (2000): 878–80.

12. W. K. Moon, M. H. Han, K.H. Chang, et al., 'CT and MR imaging of head and neck tuberculosis', *Radiographics* 17 (1997): 391–402.

13. B. Richter, M. Fradis, G. Kohler, and G.J. Ridder, 'Epiglottic tuberculosis: differential diagnosis and treatment: case report and review of the literature', *Ann Otol Rhinol Laryngol* 110 (2001):197–201.

14. M.W. Araujo, and S. Andreana, 'Risk and prevention of transmission of infectious diseases in dentistry', *Quintessence* Int 33 (2002): 376–82.

15. E.E. Telzak, et al., 'Factors influencing time to sputum conversion among patients with smear-positive pulmonary tuberculosis', *Clin Infect Dis* 25 (1997): 671–72

16. Y.M. Davis, E. McCray, and P.M. Simone, 'Hospital infection control practices for tuberculosis', *Clin Chest Med* 18 (1997):19–33.

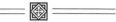

CHAPTER 62

CHRONIC HEART FAILURE

Introduction

Heart failure is characterized by symptoms of breathlessness, fatigue and fluid retention due to symptomatic left ventricular systolic dysfunction. It is a growing public health problem in countries with an ageing population, with patients often being subject to prolonged and repeated hospitalization. In the UK, hospitalization with heart failure as the primary diagnosis represents five per cent of all adult medical hospital admissions, accounting for an estimated 120,000 inpatient episodes each year. Hospital admissions, due to heart failure, increased by 60 per cent from 1980–1991 in a Scottish study. Reducing the number of admissions and re-admissions to hospital is one of the goals of management and is an important outcome measure in the treatment of chronic heart failure.

Ischaemic heart disease and hypertension are the major risk factors for heart failure, and their effective treatment is important in the control of heart failure in the community. Control of symptoms in patients with heart failure requires careful individualization of treatment and the avoidance of drugs known to exacerbate this condition. With increasing ease of cardiac investigation, it is becoming clear that left ventricular systolic dysfunction in the community may be both under-diagnosed and undertreated. The implications are that patients with symptomless disease might benefit from early treatment intervention. This article examines the opportunities for improved pharmaceutical care in patients with chronic heart failure, highlighting the role of the pharmacist in this complex condition.

Public Health Implications of Chronic Heart Failure

In the UK, heart failure affects 0.3–2 per cent of the general population, 3–5 per cent of those over 65 years, and 8–16 per cent of those over 75 years. The annual incidence of new cases is 0.1–0.5 per cent in the general population, and doubles every decade from age 45 years to become greater than 3 per cent among those aged over 74 years (Table 62.1). The annual mortality for chronic stable heart failure is reported to be 10 per cent.

TABLE 62.1:

CLASSIFICATION OF BLOOD PRESSURE FOR ADULTS AGED 18 YEARS AND OLDER

Symptomatic patients
85 people (1.7% of population)
50 persons aged 25-74 years (1.5% of this age group) (38 have IHD and hypertension)
25 persons aged 75-84 years (10% of this age group)
10 or more persons >84 years (10-20% of this age group)
Asymptomatic patients
62 persons aged 25-74 (27 have IHD and hypertension)
50 men aged 25-74 years
12 women aged 25-74 years
New cases diagnosed (n)
15 annually (total)
10 of these > 74 years
GP consultations (n)
60 annually
Hospital admissions (n)
10 annually, affecting 7 patients

Data from McMurray et al., McDonagh et al., Sharpe and Doughty, Mair et al., Morgan et al., McMurray et al., and Fry. GP, general practioner; IHD, ischaemic heart disease

Heart failure is often a consequence of coronary artery disease and may also develop insidiously in elderly patients. In 10 per cent of cases it is associated with atrial fibrillation. Heart failure may also contribute to respiratory symptoms in patients with chronic obstructive pulmonary disease.

The condition is progressive and mortality varies according to its severity and the treatability of any underlying cause. Thromboembolic complications, notably stroke, are associated with heart failure, particularly in patients with atrial fibrillation, in whom the risk may exceed 10 per cent per year, unless the patient is given anticoagulants. Although a specific cause, such as coronary artery disease, longstanding hypertension, valvular heart disease, thyrotoxicosis or severe anaemia, may be present, heart failure often occurs without a single identifiable cause.

In a recent Scottish study of a large sample of adults aged 25–74 years, the prevalence of left ventricular systolic dysfunction was found to be 3 per cent using strict criteria. Half of the patients with dysfunction did not have symptoms. In 2.7 per cent of the asymptomatic men and 0.6 per cent of the asymptomatic women, there was definite evidence of left ventricular systolic dysfunction associated with ischaemic heart disease or with hypertension in the presence of ischaemic heart disease. The true prevalence of left ventricular systolic dysfunction has been estimated from that study using less conservative criteria as being perhaps as high as 7.7 per cent in those aged 25–74 years. There is increasing evidence that some patients with asymptomatic left ventricular dysfunction may be amenable to early treatment, which might delay progression.

In the population at large, recognition of heart failure is complicated by other comorbid conditions that may contribute to a decline in respiratory function or to a patient's reduced mobility. Two studies in GP group practices have confirmed the prevalence of diagnosed heart failure at approximately 1.5 per cent in those aged 70–80 years. In the second of these studies, one third of patients had moderate or severe left ventricular dysfunction.

Heart Failure Symptoms and Disease Markers

The normal heart ejects more than 50 per cent of its contents at each cardiac cycle. In the failing heart, the ejection fraction falls below 45 per cent, in moderate dysfunction it is below 35 per cent, and in severe dysfunction it falls to less than 25 per cent.

Symptoms of heart failure include shortness of breath on exertion (dyspnoea) or on lying (orthopnoea). Pulmonary oedema is a feature of left ventricular failure and is heard on medical examination as crepitations at the base of the lungs. Pulmonary symptoms may worsen at night, giving rise to cough, and mobilization of oedema leads to increased urine production and micturition (including nocturia). Disturbances of sleep because of breathing difficulties (paroxysmal nocturnal dyspnoea) can be distressing; patients may need to prop themselves up using three or more pillows to gain relief from their breathlessness.

A reflex tachycardia and the emergence of a third heart sound give rise to a characteristic 'gallop' rhythm. Reduced blood supply to the periphery makes the hands cold and sweaty, while a compromised supply to the brain and kidney may contribute to confusion and renal failure.

Biventricular failure occurs when the right ventricle also fails. The symptoms include raised venous pressure (seen as a raised jugular venous pressure) and peripheral oedema (often seen as ankle oedema). Congestion in the gastrointestinal tract causes hepatomegaly, abdominal distension and pain.

The physiological disturbances associated with uncontrolled heart failure include haemodynamic and neurohormonal effects. There is reflex sympathetic discharge, rennin secretion and the release of aldosterone and vasopressin, among other neurohormonal effects, contributing to tachycardia, reflex vasoconstriction and fluid retention. The failing heart overfills and is enlarged (cardiomegaly). Disease progression causes structural deterioration of the left ventricle.

Tables 62.2 and 3 show the symptoms of heart failure and the drugs that can worsen the condition. Table 62.4 shows the New York Heart Association classification of the severity of heart failure, based on an assessment of the patient's functional capabilities.

TABLE 62.2
SYMPTOMS OF HEART FAILURE

- Fatigue
- Dyspnoea
- Paroxysmal nocturnal dyspnoea
- Orthopnoea
- Cough (nocturnal)
- Nocturia
- Confusion
- Renal failure
- Abdonimal distension
- Anorexia and nausea

Blooming with the Pouis

TABLE 62.3
DRUGS THAT MAY WORSEN HEART FAILURE

- Non-steroidal anti-inflammatory drugs
- Class 1 anti-arrhythmics
- Class III anti-arrhythmics (except amiodarone)
- Beta-blockers (but may be used to treat heart failure)
- Calcium-channel blockers (verapamil, diltiazem and first-generation dihydropyridines are most problematic)
- Tricyclic antidepressants
- Corticosteroids
- Lithium
- Products containing high sodium (e.g. antacids, effervescent formulations)

TABLE 62.4
NEW YORK HEART ASSOCIATION FUNCTIONAL ASSESSMENT OF HEART FAILURE

Grade	Description	Physical capability
I	Asymptomatic	No symptoms with ordinary physical activity (walking and climbing stairs)
II	Mild	Slight limitation of activity with dyspnoea on moderate to severe exertion (climbing stairs or walking uphill)
III	Moderate	Marked limitation of activity. Less than ordinary activity causes dyspnoea (restricting walking distance and limiting climbing to one flight of stairs)
IV	Severe	Severe disability. Dyspnoea at rest (unable to carry out physical activity without discomfort)

References

Hydson, S. and A. Watson. 'Congestive Cardiac Failure'. In Walker, R. and C. Edwards (eds), *Clinical Pharmacy and Therapeutics*, 2nd edn. London: Churchill Livingstone, 1992; 277-295.

McDonagh, T.A., C.E. Morrison, A. Lawrence et al. Symptomatic and asymptomatic left-ventricular systolic dysfunction in an urban population. *Lancet* 1997; 350: 829-833.

McMurray, J., C. McDonagh, C.E. Morrison, H.J. Dargie. 'Trends in hospitalization for heart failure in Scotland 1980-1900'. *Eur Heart J* 1993; 14: 1158-1162.

Sharpe, N., and R. Doughty. 'Epidemiology of heart failure and ventricular dysfunction'. *Lancet 1998; 352 (Suppl, 1):I 3-7.*

CHAPTER 63

JAMAICAN REGGAE AND THE ARTICULATION OF SOCIAL AND HISTORICAL CONSCIOUSNESS IN MUSCIAL DISCOURSE

It was reported that in Tiananmen Square in 1989 protesters carried a banner that read 'Get up, stand up for your rights', using the Wailers' song to air their discontent.[1] Far from there, in 1990, South Africa's reggae singer Lucky Dube appealed for the unity of Rasta's, Europeans, Indians, and Japanese in his song 'Together as One' (1988), during a concert in Johannesburg. Across the Atlantic, in north east Brazil, the city of Salvador da Bahia has had its own Praca do Reggae since 1998 where reggae fans congregate every week. More recently, in the Caribbean island of Dominica, at a meeting of the United Workers Party in the summer of 2003, a speaker reacted critically to the prime minister's budget speech telling his audience that the one 'who feels it, knows it', thus echoing the Wailers' song of that title. Given the indefinite nature of the term 'forever' and the world events I have encapsulated here, one wonders if 'wherever' would have been a more accurate forecast in the quotation that opens this essay. It is evident then, not only that reggae music is a phenomenon of worldwide appeal and an active item of global popular culture, but that the lyrics of the music are an important source for social consciousness in the wider Caribbean and the world.

Reggae certainly has very profound local roots in Jamaica, but it is a music with an unprecedented global appeal and no longer, as it has been argued, 'a music which could only be created by a Jamaican in Jamaica for Jamaicans.'[2] The impact of this music in popular tastes and cultural practices is unquestionable, either as a commodity marketed through the mass media or as a medium for the diffusion of the ideology and ethos of the Rasta movement. Reggae music has avid listeners in disparate places across world regions, and one could argue that most residents of major world cities surely come across some reggae-related symbol daily and not necessarily because they go into a record shop. Through this music, millions of people around the world have come to know something about Jamaican history and society and have adopted the common wisdom that reggae music has 'conscious lyrics'. Yet, one could still ask, How does reggae music represent Jamaican history and society? What are these lyrics conscious of? And how aware are global listeners of their meaning and sociohistorical significance?

The noted literary and cultural critic Edward Said has written, 'The study of music can be more, and not less, interesting if we situate music as taking place, so to speak, in a social and cultural setting.'[3] Thus, it is the purpose of this article to analyse reggae music in its original Jamaican context looking into the specific ways in which the music relates to the social and cultural history of the country where it emerged. I approach Jamaican popular music in its association with history (and historiography) in a dual perspective. First, reggae is seen as a historical narrative of the events that were taking place as the genre was emerging in the 1960s and 1970s. The lyrics of the music became, as it were, a testimony of the events and transitions of its own time and place. Second, I analyse reggae music as counterhistory, as a way of telling (and rescuing) a story of the Jamaican people 'from below' in the specific sociohistorical context of colonialism and racism, concentrating on the slavery and postemancipation eras. It is my argument that we can consider reggae as a popular representation of the past, one that assumes a counternarrative to colonial and western historical accounts and, in the process, rethinks the country's history as part of its national formation. The essay looks into some of reggae's central elements and foundational characteristics during its early days and development in the 1970s and 1980s, seeking to illuminate our understanding of the reasons for the global fascination with, and appeal of, this music and its culture. In other words, aside from the evident influences of the media, the market, and the music industry, I attempt to seek an explanation to reggae's worldwide popularity in its origins.

The Life and Times of Reggae Music

Music and dance have been central to Afro-Jamaicans since the days of slavery, and reggae music — as all popular Jamaican or Caribbean music — is indeed heir to the way in which slaves used music to 'escape' their sufferings and to enjoy their time out of the labour regime of the plantations. But reggae's more specific roots are to be found in Afro-Jamaican religious musical traditions and in the Afro-North American musical styles and genres that were adapted from the United States of America during the early decades of the twentieth century. Rhythm and blues, and jazz were important for the development of Jamaican popular music, along with Afro-Latin American musical forms such as *rumba*, and the impact of indigenous musical styles like *mento*, *kumina*, revival and *nyabingi*. *Mento* is Jamaican folk music, similar to calypso, where string instruments such as the guitar and the banjo play an important role. *Kumina*, revival, and *nyabinghi*, on the other hand, are all Afro-Jamaican and related to the religious movements or manifestations carrying the same name, all of them characterized by the use of drums. The *nyabinghi* in particular is related to Rastafarian meetings or 'grounations.' This combination of diverse influences responded partly to the high mobility of Jamaican labourers who were exposed to other cultures in the U.S. South and Hispanic America (particularly Panama and Cuba, where the 1920s and 1930s were peak years for the development of Afro-Cuban music). While scholars have debated the degree of influence of each of these different musical traditions, most have acknowledged the presence of each of these ingredients, which are evident to anyone who has listened carefully to early recordings of Jamaican popular music. Indeed, different groups mixed all these influences in their musical productions; jazz-like winds are easily identifiable in the 1960s and coexist with the Afro-Caribbean drumming of songs such as the Folkes Brothers' 'Oh Carolina' (1961) and Toots and the Maytals' 'Bam, Bam' (1966).

The sound systems were another important feature in the development of Jamaican popular music. The electronic ensemble of a record player and one or two speakers emerged around the 1940s and 1950s as mobile infrastructures used to play the music in public to people without ready access to other means of listening to the latest musical recordings. As the sound systems phenomenon grew, the dancehall culture of Jamaica expanded geographically as the owners of the sound systems performed in Kingston and the rural areas, and people organized and gathered for dancing venues. These venues became the local setting for the 'clash' or competition between different sound systems and also one of the most important ways for people to hear new music. While rhythm and blues, and jazz were commonly played by the sound systems, calypso and mento also found their space in the dance halls.[4]

The socio-historical setting for the mixture and cross-fertilization of these musical ingredients was a changing and complex one. After the world economic depression in the 1930s, Jamaica experienced important economic and political transitions. The labour struggles of those years shook the colonial system and cleared the path toward national independence, which was obtained much later, in 1962. Also, the island's population underwent significant mobility in many directions; while migrants were returning from the English-speaking exclaves in Hispanic America, others arrived from their military service in the British West Indies Regiment, and yet others were leaving the country for Britain in search of new opportunities. Also, much of the population was moving from the countryside to the flourishing capital, Kingston. In the early 1940s, the population of the capital increased 80 per cent, and by 1960 the city had 25 per cent of the total population of the island.[5] Most of the rural migrants that searched for a better life as urban workers in the capital ended up on the margins of society, living in the ghettos of Kingston and becoming part of a growing urban proletariat, much of it underemployed or unemployed.

The ghettos had also become the refuge of many Rastas. Rastafari had originated in the 1930s and grew as a religious and social movement during the 1940s and 1950s under the leadership of messianic preachers such as Leonard Howell, Joseph Hibbert, Archival Dunkley, and Robert Hinds. This movement was nourished by the racial Pan African ideas of earlier Jamaicans and adopted Jamaicans such as Robert Love, Alexander Bedward, and Marcus Garvey, as well as religious traditions such as Pentecostalism and Kumina. Its central beliefs became the divinity of the Ethiopian emperor Haile Selassie I (crowned in 1930), the perception of Jamaica as Babylon (a place of captivity and perdition), and the idealization of Africa as Zion or the 'promised land' to which black Jamaicans had to be repatriated. While some leaders of the movement were in the public eye in the early years of its development, Rastafari acquired more visibility in the sixties and seventies. In 1960 the government commissioned three faculty members of the University of the West Indies (M.G. Smith, Roy Augier, and Rex Nettleford) to investigate the movement, its organization and aims, and to write a report that was published that same year as *The*

Rastafari Movement in Kingston, Jamaica. At that time Rastafari's political activism increased (partly through the influence of the Guyanese historian and activist Walter Rodney), and some politicians appropriated their symbols for their political campaigns. Especially during the 1970s, the musical Bandwagon of the People's National Party and the debate between Michael Manley and Edward Seaga around the 'rod of Correction' (a stick said to be a gift from Selassie to Manley) were parts of this symbolism.[6]

The years leading to Jamaica's political independence were also full of social and economic contradictions. While there was significant economic growth based on foreign investment in mining (the bauxite industry), manufacture, and tourism, there was also increasing social inequality. In 1944 constitutional changes relieved the metropolis of some of the administrative political control of the island, and two leading political parties emerged to govern the British colony: the Jamaican Labour Party (JLP) and the People's National party (PNP). Their leaders, Alexander Bustamante and Norman W. Manley respectively, led the country to independence in 1962. The cultural and musical landscape echoed Jamaican sociopolitical transitions as many local composers and performers sought to create — or to accelerate the creation of — a popular music that was originally Jamaican. The result was what came to be known as *ska*, a very danceable genre that combined the influences of rhythm and blues and mento, creating something unlike anything played before in the Jamaican soundscape. This music was highly popular in the early 1960s, and some of its most prominent performers were Byron Lee and the Dragonaires, the Skatelites, Toots Hibbert and the Maytals, and the Wailers. Virtually emerging at the same time as Jamaica gained its independence, *ska* songs such as Derrick Morgan's 'Forward March' (1962) reflected the optimism of the time, encouraging people to have 'fun' and 'dance' because 'we are independent'. Morgan's song also called upon people to have 'joy' and 'praise' both Alexander Bustamante and 'Mr. Manley'.

During the second half of the 1960s, musical tastes changed toward the slower tempo with a style that was named *rocksteady*. In this new musical variant, wind instruments were less present than in *ska*, and the bass had a more prominent role. Also, the lyrics of the music became more explicit about social realities in the country. Both the slower rhythm and the more explicit social content of the music would be present in the style known as reggae, which emerged around 1967 or 1968. Reggae followed the 4/4/ musical time with a downbeat emphasis in 2 and 4 rather than in 1 and 3. The bass acquired yet a more important role than in *ska* and *rocksteady*, by carrying the rhythm (a function usually resting in the drums). Reggae distinguished itself from its predecessors by its strong and critical social commentary, which responded to the social realities of the late 1960s and the repression under JLP leadership. The political tensions were epitomized in the social unrest that erupted when the government did not allow the university lecturer Walter Rodney to re-enter the country.[7] Musically, social tensions were immortalized in the Ethiopian's 'Everything Crash' (1968):

> Look deh now, everything crash!
> Firemen strike, watermen strike
> Telephone company too
> Down to the policeman too!

The song not only referred to the social tensions that had been accumulating for years but also portrayed the inevitable fate in the things to come: 'Every day carry bucket to the well, one day the bottom must drop out!'

During the 1970s reggae became more popular and established itself as the definitive musical trademark for Jamaica, both nationally and internationally. Many of the songs' lyrics responded to social and political circumstances, particularly during the election of 1972 when the leader of the PNP, Michael Manley, capitalized on the use of reggae artists in his political campaign. Delroy Wilson's 'Better Must Come' (1971) became the slogan for the PNP and a cry for change in the conditions of life under JLP government. Indeed, Manley's promise of 'change' and his musical Bandwagon — joined by Wilson, Max Romeo, the Wailers, and other musicians — were of great importance for the victory of the PNP in the 1972 elections. But his move toward 'Democratic Socialism' two years later would serve as a catalyst for one of the most tense and violent political atmospheres in Jamaican history. The politico-ideological shift of the PNP was recorded in music when Max Romeo released his hit 'Socialism Is Love' in 1974.

While some of Manley's socio-economic policies gained him the support of the working classes and marginal groups, others — such as the nationalization of the bauxite industry and the introduction of property taxes – caused discomfort among some of the middle and upper classes that had supported him in 1972. Moreover, Manley's left-oriented rhetoric after 1974 was not exactly what the foreign investors in the country, some of the elites, or the United States of America wanted to hear.[8] Later, the country would enter into a period of 'economic emergency'[9] caused by a combination of the general economic crisis of the decade as well as by the PNP's economic policies and the flight of capital due to the apprehension on the party's political

stance. Bitter political rivalry between the two leading parties and their supporters increased. The political divide was evident in the urban arena, as particular areas developed into garrison constituencies responding to either the JLP or the PNP. In the late 1970s, the United States' Central Intelligence Agency (CIA) was blamed for the crisis and political instability in Jamaica. Most of the events related to those tense years of the mid and late 1970s were reported in the musical narratives of reggae — as happens with many other Caribbean music as calypso and *merengue*.

Marley's 'Rat Race' of 1976 is one of the most representative songs of this period. The song mentioned how the 'political violence fill ya city' and warned: 'Don't involve Rasta in your say, say; Rasta don't work for no CIA.' The lines that followed spoke of 'collective security' and could not have been more pertinent to the time in which the song hit the airwaves; they reflected not only the government's use of police and military forces to confront the political warfare in Kingston but also the recruitment of civilians in policing activities through what was known as the 'Home Guard'.[10] The political state of affairs in the country during the late 1970s is also exposed in 'Tribal War' by Third World in 1977 and echoed in Max Romeo's 'War ina Babylon' (1976): 'War ina Babylon, Tribal War ina Babylon.' In this song, Romeo locates himself as a Rasta living on the outskirts of the city and offers what could easily be a photograph of Kingston's reality in those years: 'I man satta in the mountain top, watching Babylon burning red, red hot'.

The scale of political violence in the late 1970s triggered efforts to accomplish peace among the different sectors. While Manley and Seaga signed a peace agreement in 1976, the people in the ghettos searched for peace in their own way through a truce between the different garrison constituencies in 1978,[11] and that same year reggae musicians performed in the One Love Peace Concert. Some songs from those years referred to the peace efforts in various ways, yet Peter Tosh's 'Equal Rights' (1977) is perhaps the song that better illustrates the process from a critical perspective.

> Everybody is crying out for peace
> I'll say, none is crying out for justice
> 'till men get equal rights and justice

As the 1980 elections approached and the political violence and economic crisis persisted, a number of songs continued to comment on the situation. Released in 1979, 'Armagideon Time' deals with both the social inequalities felt by the popular classes and the economic limitations endured by them.

> A lot of people won't get no supper tonight
> A lot of people going to suffer tonight
> Cause the battle is getting harder
> And this I-ration is Armagideon

The song notes several problems including the lack of 'supper' for 'a lot of people', an issue that was discussed the year before at a summit on world hunger in Jamaica.[12]

As is evident from the limited sample of reggae songs here, most of them were 'in tune' with the society from which they emerged. By stressing this link between music and society, I am trying to highlight how music can be approached as a valuable source that sheds light into a particular time period or as a historical narrative and representation of that specific time. Reggae songs in the 1960s and 1970s provide not only a chronicle of the events and transformations that were taking place in Jamaica, but a particular perception of them written and performed for future generations. Reggae music served also as a popular representation of Jamaican colonial history opening a window to the deeds, events, and figures important for the Afro-Jamaican heritage.

"Do You Remember The Days Of Slavery?": Colonial History in Jamaican Reggae

Due to its association with the Rastafari movement and the Jamaican under-classes, reggae music became representative of the worldview of Afro-Jamaicans. As such, the historical narrative in reggae songs has often portrayed dominant elements of the Rasta philosophy such as the perception of Jamaica as Babylon, Africa as Zion, and Jamaicans as 'Israelites' that have to get back to the 'promised land.' The lyrics of many reggae songs thus came to rescue a history that inevitably linked black Jamaicans with Africa, the place from which their ancestors had been brought as slaves. Therefore, the slavery era and its subsequent history became central themes in reggae's historical discourse.

In reggae, Africa is basically represented as a point of origin for Afro-Jamaicans and as the promised land, where a physical or spiritual return must lead. The demand of Rastafarians for repatriation and their critical position toward Jamaica was framed in the memories of slavery, the slave trade, and the nature of the oppression lived under that system. Jacob Miller's '80,000 Careless Ethiopians' (1974) offers a random figure for those 'careless Ethiopians' who were exiled in 'Babylon' (Jamaica) and need to go back to 'Mount Zion' (Africa): '80,000 careless Ethiopians, shall go down in Babylon.' Bob Marley's cry to 'set the captive free' and for a 'movement of Jah people' to the 'father's land' in the song 'Exodus' (1977) also echoes metaphorically the (continuing) condition of Jamaicans as captives in a world of 'downpression' and 'transgression.' In a constant dialogue between the past and the present, the 'slave' and slavery itself (and, by default, freedom) became images widely used by reggae singers in their compositions. Slavery operated as a metaphor for the discrimination and marginalization of the 1960s and 1970s — a metaphor that was grounded on, or in continuity with, the realities of Jamaica's colonial past.

In 'The Harder They Come' (1972), Jimmy Cliff stated that he 'rather be a free man in my grave, than living as a puppet or a slave', a line that recalls that some slaves committed suicide as a way to 'escape' their bondage.[13] Moreover, in the context of struggle and perseverance of Cliff's song, the line is yet more pertinent if we remember the executions of the slave rebels in the aftermath of the 1831 Baptist War. Most of them remained 'courageous and confident' when they faced death as their punishment for struggling for freedom.[14] Other songs such as Sugar Minnott's 'River Jordon' (1979) advocates for the return to Africa — 'home' — establishing the link of Afro-Jamaican people with the land of their forefathers, a connection that is established through the continuity of the experience of slavery: 'So long we've been down in slavery; where and now we just got to be free, yes we want to be free.' The song goes further to specify harsh realities of slavery: 'So long we've been bound in shackles and chains.'

Marley's 'Slave Driver' (1973) and 'Redemption Song' (1980) also revive the memories of slavery. The latter not only refers to the much needed emancipation from 'mental slavery' but also recalls the very first stage of the ordeal of the slaves by referring to the 'old pirates' who dealt with the slaves by selling them (or 'I') to the merchant ships. In 'Slave Driver', Marley's impersonation notes: 'I remember on the slave ship, how they brutalize our very souls.' He provides a material representation of bondage by stating how, instead of freedom, the slaves remained 'hold to the chain of poverty.' The next step in the slave traffic is remembered by the group Third World in 'Human Marketplace' (1977), a song that opens a window on one of the key experiences of African slaves in their transatlantic voyage.

> Why is this buying and selling still going on?
> In this ... Human Marketplace
> In this ... Human Marketplace

The song repeats the same lines about 'buying and selling' in a 'human marketplace,' recalling the descriptions that students of the slave trade and slavery have provided us about this inhuman process.[15]

Several songs make passing references to such ideas and practices of slavery. But it is Burning Spear, one of the leading starts of roots reggae, who has been most explicit in his denunciation of slavery regarding as 'his task to brush history against the grain,' to appropriate Walter Benjamin's phrase.[16] Spear does this in 'Slavery Days' (1975) by going beyond brief mentions, describing the specifics of slave labour in Jamaica (and the Caribbean, for that matter), and telling the 'half of the story' that needs to be remembered:

> Do you remember the days of slavery?
> (Chorus; repeat in call and response)
> And how they beat us (Chorus)
> And how they worked us so hard (Repeat chorus)
> And how they used us (Repeat chorus)
> 'Till they refuse us (Repeat chorus)

Not only does Spear remind us about the conditions of work in the plantations, but he also speaks about the collective suffering of that experience: 'My brother feels it ... Included my sister too.' The chorus continues: 'Some of us survived/Showed them God we are still alive.' Through 'Survival,' Spear's historical-musical discourse links his narrative of slavery with his personal identification (as a black person) and sense of belonging and lineage with those who experienced slavery. It is in the previous lines that Spear assumes Benjamin's principle, through a critique of a certain view of Jamaican history that cannot (or does not want to) remember the 'days of slavery.' Spear therefore encourages and begs his listeners to try to remember that history — his story.

Jorge L. Giovannetti

Notes

1. 'Marley's Lyrics Find a Place in Student Protest', *Star*, May 18, 1989, Newspaper Clippings Collection, Bob Marley Museum, Kingston, Jamaica.
2. Chang and Chen, *Reggae Routes*, 95.
3. Said, *Musical Elaborations*, xii.
4. On the sound systems, see S. Davis, 'Taking Drums, Sound Systems and Reggae', 33-34, and Stolzoff, *Wake the Town and tell the People*, 41-48.
5. Roberts, *The Population of Jamaica*, 152-54; Clarke, *Kingston, Jamaica*, 78.
6. On reggae and politics, see Giovannetti, *Sonidos de condena*. Walters, *Race, Class and Political Symbols*, offers a more detailed analysis of the uses of reggae and Rasta symbols by Jamaican political parties.
7. R. Lewis, *Walter Rodney: 1968 Revisited*, 7-56; R. Lewis, *Walter Rodney's Intellectual and Political Thought*, especially chaps. 4 and 7.
8. See Manley, Jamaica: *Struggle in the Periphery*, 87-89; Davies and Witter, 'The Development of the Jamaican Economy since Independence';

W. Bell and Baldrich, 'Elites, Economic Ideologies and Democracy in Jamaica', 172-73.
9. 'Economic Emergency', *Jamaica Daily News*, January 20, 1977, 1, 3.
10. García Muñiz, 'Defence Policy and Planning in the Caribbean', 119.
11. 'Vote Today: Leaders Sign Peace Pledge', *Jamaica Daily News*, December 15, 1976, I; 'Peace Comes to West Kingston: TRUCE!', *Jamaica Daily News*, January 11, 1978, I.
12. 'World Battle against Hunger', *Jamaica Daily Times*, June 15, 1978, 6.
13. On suicide among the slaves, more common among male and field slaves, see Patterson, *Sociology of Slavery*, 264-65; Higman, *Slave Population in the British Caribbean, 1807-1834*, 339-47.
14. Turner, *Slaves and Missionaries*, 162.
15. See Tannenbaum, *Slave and Citizen*, 28; Patterson, *Sociology of Slavery*, 150.
16. Benjamin, 'These on the Philosophy of History', 248.

Writing In the Digital Age— The Internet and Research

One of the main reasons students apply for and become members of a university is to be trained as scholars and academics. This means that they are prepared not only for the world of work but also to become academics. One of the main elements involved in being an academic is research. In the undergraduate setting, research is modelled through the research paper, which is a part of almost every course that a student does. Research may be done through primary sources, such as interviews and field trips, and secondary sources, using books, articles, magazines and newspapers, for example. For a number of students, the internet has become the primary means of research.

Potential Uses of the Internet

1. The internet can be used to help you in your pre-writing for idea generation. This can be done by typing your topic or aspects of your topic into your browser and noting the various angles, approaches to your topic. This would help to expose you to the scope of the topic and to decide on the approach you might adopt.
2. Using the internet saves time and allows you to conduct research at times which are convenient to you (even after the libraries have closed).
3. Many texts are freely available online. So you may access e-books, from Shakespeare to Derek Walcott.
4. The internet provides access to scholarly databases, (which would have peer-reviewed articles). The databases would have articles that are accepted as credible. If you are using the internet, be sure to use scholarly databases.
5. The internet allows you to use reputational organizational websites. Sites such as the UN and other dot org (.org) or dot gov (.gov), or dot edu (.edu) sites would generally be acceptable.

Limitations of the Internet

Just about anyone can place information on the world wide web. This is unlike a journal or even the newspaper where there is some screening process before an item is published. What this means is that many persons who write on various topics and are not experts or authorities in the area are able to mount a website and place information on it without any formal screening process. In your academic writing you are expected to use relevant authoritative sources in your essay. If you use poor sources this will undermine your credibility as a writer. This means that you need to assess the websites that you use.

Assessing a Website

(a) Take note of the date the site was last updated.

(b) Evaluate whether the site is affiliated with any reputable organization or institution.

(c) If there is an author, do a search to find out whether he/she is credibile.

(d) Assess the intended audience.

(e) Assess the purpose.

(f) Evaulate whether there is any evidence of authoritative sources being used.

(g) Determine whether the information used is current.

(h) Identify whether the information you have come upon is a blog or a personal page.

Tips for using the Internet

1. If you would like to find information on a subject from a particular country, you might, for example, type in 'alcoholism site: UK' or try placing the words in "quotation marks". This will restrict the information which you receive.

2. Use search engines:
Google
(http://google.com)

Alta Vista
(http:www.altavista.digital. com/cgi-bin/query?pg=aq&what=web)

Northern Light
(http://www.northern light.com/)

Infoseek
(http://www.infoseek.com/)

FastSearch
(http://www.alltheweb.com/)

http://www.lib.berkeley.edu/
TeachingLib Guides/Internet/
ToolsTables.html.
Mamameta search

3. Using the internet to do research can be very time consuming and wasteful. Try to allocate time for your web-search. After the allotted time has passed, turn off the computer or do something else. Do not spend your whole day trying to find information.

4. Refrain from plagiarizing. The internet allows for cutting and pasting of information but doing so is plagiarizing and this is an acute academic offense. You have plagiarized if you:
    (a) cut and paste information and attempt to pass this off as your own work
    (b) paraphrase without citing the source of the information
    (c) use a direct quote — a line or two from a source — without acknowledging the source.

5. Access your university's online catalogue to conduct your preliminary research. This will allow you to become familiar with what is available at your campus library and would mean that you will be able to go to the library armed with necessary information, thus reducing the time spent searching.

Documentation and Citation

One of the most important functions of any institution of learning, particularly a university, is the dissemination of knowledge and information. This is essential not only for purposes of teaching and learning, but also for providing a theoretical basis on which further research may be carried out, from which important links can be made, which will in turn enhance our knowledge and understanding of issues in a particular area. For this reason, it is imperative that **all** sources used in academic writing, be accurately and consistently cited and documented, employing the documentation style appropriate for each discipline.

The documentation styles which are considered appropriate to various disciplines are:

APA — American Psychological Association (Social Sciences)
Chicago Style (History, some Social Science disciplines, for example, economics)
CSE – Council of Science Editors (Biology, Zoology, Anatomy, etc.)
MLA – Modern Language Association (most disciplines within the Humanities)

Guidelines for each of the above mentioned styles are available in their respective manuals. It is your responsibility as academic writers to ensure that all sources used in your essays, articles and reports adhere to the prescribed documentation and citation style of your discipline. Additionally, since style manuals are modified from time to time, you need to ensure that the style manual you are consulting is the most recent and updated edition.

Janice Cools